LEWIS SPERRY CHAFER

SYSTEMATIC THEOLOGY

Volume Seven

DOCTRINAL SUMMARIZATION

by

LEWIS SPERRY CHAFER
D.D., LITT.D., TH.D.

Late President and Professor of Systematic Theology
Dallas Theological Seminary

kregel PUBLICATIONS

Grand Rapids, MI 49501

Systematic Theology (eight volumes in four), by Lewis Sperry Chafer, © 1993 by Kregel Publications, a division of Kregel, Inc., P.O. Box 2607, Grand Rapids, Michigan 49501, by special permission of Dallas Theological Seminary. All rights reserved.

Cover Design: Alan G. Hartman

Library of Congress Cataloging-in-Publication Data

Chafer, Lewis Sperry, 1871-1952.
  [Systematic Theology]
  Chafer systematic theology / by Lewis Sperry Chafer.
    p.   cm.
  Originally published: Systematic theology. Dallas, TX.: Dallas Seminary Press, 1947-1948.
  Includes bibliographical references and indexes.
  Contents: v. 1   Prolegomena, Bibliology, Theology Proper, Angelology, Anthropology and Harmatiology
             v. 2   Soteriology, Ecclesiology and Eschatology
             v. 3   Christology and Pneumatology
             v. 4   Doctrinal summarization, Biographical sketch and indexes
  1. Theology, Doctrinal. I. Title. II. Title: Systematic theology
BT75.C28   1993   230'.044—dc20   92-34956
                                                    CIP

ISBN 0-8254-2340-6 (deluxe hardback)

      1 2 3 4 5 Printing/Year 97 96 95 94 93

LIST OF DOCTRINES

DOCTRINAL SUMMARIZATION

iv   LIST OF DOCTRINES

DOCTRINAL SUMMARIZATION

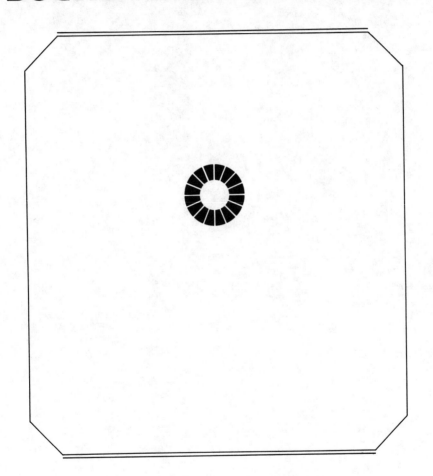

ABIDING

The word μένω, which is translated *abide,* is used about 120 times in the New Testament. Other English terms used to translate this word are equally significant—'remain, dwell, continue, tarry, endure' (Matt. 10:11; Luke 19:5; Acts 9:43; 27:31; 1 Cor. 13:13; 2 Tim. 2:13). The Apostle John employs this verb sixty-four times and in his writings the Authorized Version translators have rendered the word *abide* twenty-one times. The meaning of this Greek term is thus clearly indicated as that which remains, dwells, continues, tarries, or endures; it is what abides in the position in which it is placed. In reference to spiritual reality the word *abide* indicates a constancy in relation to Christ. It is also true that Christ referred to His own abiding in the believer (cf. John 15:5), which relationship could never fail since it depends only on His faithfulness. There is little basis, consequently, for the sentiment expressed in certain hymns wherein Christ is petitioned to abide with the believer.

The general meaning of the word *abide* lends itself to at least two ideas—one which suggests a continuing in union with Christ and another which suggests a continuing in communion with Christ. The most revealing passage is John 15:1–17, where the believer is enjoined to abide in Christ as a branch abides in the vine. This passage will not support the notion that to abide in Christ means to remain in *union* with Him; when this superficial rendering is accepted, only false doctrine ensues. On the other hand, it is clear that the word of exhortation directs the believer to remain in *communion* with Christ as He remained in communion with His Father. As the sap flows from the vine into the branch that remains in contact, so the spiritual vitality flows from Christ to the believer who abides. Communion depends upon agreement and agreement requires complete subjection of one to his superior: thus it is imperative that the commandments of the one shall be kept by the other. Christ said that by keeping His Father's commandments He abode in His love. There was, of course, no attempt on Christ's part to preserve a union with His Father. That had been unbroken and unbreakable from all eternity; but, on the human side, He did maintain communion by doing the Father's will.

3

Three verses in this context (John 15:1–17) set forth the doctrinal significance of abiding in Christ, namely,

John 15:2. "Every branch in me that beareth not fruit he taketh away: and every branch that beareth fruit, he purgeth it, that it may bring forth more fruit."

Having asserted that He is the True Vine and that His Father is the Husbandman and, later, that the saved ones are the branches, Christ declares that a *branch in Him*—which terminology connotes the most vital and immutable union that could ever exist—may fail to bear fruit. It is at this point that the meaning of the word *abide* as used in this context is determined. The branch is not in Christ because it bears fruit; but being in Christ, the branch may or may not bear fruit. Thus it is demonstrated that abiding in Christ is not a matter of maintaining union with Christ, but of maintaining communion with Him. When communion with Christ is preserved on the part of one in Christ, the sap of spiritual vitality is imparted which results in fruit being borne. This verse declares plainly that there are those in Christ, by so much therefore saved and safe forever, who at a given time are not bearing fruit. Respecting such, God reserves the right to remove them from their place in this world (cf. 1 Cor. 11:30; 1 John 5:16), directly to heaven's glory. It should not be supposed that any ever go to heaven because they are fruitful, because they keep the commandments of Christ, or because they abide in Christ. Entrance into heaven depends only on union with Christ. A branch in Him will go to heaven without being fruitful, though unfruitfulness must be accounted for in the loss of rewards before Christ's judgment seat in heaven. Branches in Christ which are fruitful are not said to be saved or kept saved thereby, but are "purged" or pruned that they may bear more fruit.

John 15:6. "If a man abide not in me, he is cast forth as a branch, and is withered; and men gather them, and cast them into the fire, and they are burned."

This verse—most depended upon by those who contend that the believer's salvation is not secure—must be approached, as this whole theme of abiding requires, on the basis of the outworking of divine power in the one who is saved. Those believers who do not abide in communion with Christ, though saved, are powerless with respect to testimony and all service. Being broken off from communion, they are withered in spiritual power. The judgment which falls immediately upon them is not from God, however, but from men (cf. 2 Sam. 12:14). It is what James refers to when he states that justification is by works

(James 2:14–26). Justification must be on the ground of works in the sphere of the believer's relation to men; for they judge only by that which they observe. Before God justification is by faith, but the world knows nothing of such a faith. It is, indeed, most demanding to require that the one who professes to be a child of God should adorn the doctrine which he follows. The Christian is admonished, nevertheless, to walk circumspectly before those who are without. By a reasonable manifestation of the divine life in the believer, the world may come to "know" and "believe" regarding Christ (cf. John 13:34–35; 17:21–23). To the children of the kingdom Christ said that the world, seeing their good works, would glorify the Father in heaven for this reason (Matt. 5:16). As used in this passage, the figure which likens the judgments which men impose to "gathering" and "burning" of withered branches is exceedingly strong and must be interpreted in the light of existing facts. Men do not gather and burn their fellow men in a literal sense; but they do enter into very drastic judgment of the one who professes to be saved and yet does not manifest the ideals which belong to that life. This warning of Christ's to believers respecting the merciless attitude of the world is timely and important. It is probably the only instance in which Christ introduces this theme when contemplating the Christian in his relation to the *cosmos* world. The unrelenting attitude of the world towards the believer is indicated by the words of Christ following verses 1–17: "If the world hate you, ye know that it hated me before it hated you. If ye were of the world, the world would love his own: but because ye are not of the world, but I have chosen you out of the world, therefore the world hateth you" (John 15:18–19).

John 15:10. "If ye keep my commandments, ye shall abide in my love; even as I have kept my Father's commandments, and abide in his love."

This particular verse, referred to above, determines what is actually required of the believer to the end that he may abide in communion with Christ. The issue is stated simply: "If ye keep my commandments." Keeping the commandments of Christ is easily recognized as the ground of fruit-bearing communion with Christ; it is in no sense the ground of union with Christ, which is gained by faith alone. By keeping His perfect will, communion is sustained, which communion opens the way for the divine inflow of vital power by which fruit will be borne. No reference is made by Christ in this connection to the commandments of Moses. The phrase *my commandments* is not employed by Christ until He reaches the upper room and is an anticipation of the present heavenly relationship to Christ true of all who believe. Christ cites His own relation to the Father as an illustration—"even as I have kept my Father's commandments, and abide in his love." He kept His Father's commandments, not to create or preserve union with the Father but to preserve communion with the Father.

The results of abiding are both negative and positive. On the negative side Christ said, "Without me [apart from me, or separated from life-giving communion] ye can do nothing" (John 15:5). On the positive side four effects are listed which flow from the abiding life: the purge which is pruning (vs. 2), prayer effectual (vs. 7), joy celestial (vs. 11), and fruit which is perpetual (vs. 16).

In conclusion, it may be restated that the context is addressed to those who are saved and does not concern their salvation nor its endurance; but it does concern a life-receiving contact or fellowship with Christ—an abiding in His love which results in the outflow of fruit to the glory of God, the experience of celestial joy, and immeasurable efficacy in prayer.

ADAM

God sees but two representative men and all humanity is comprehended either in one or the other. He sees the first Adam with a race fallen and lost in him, and He sees the Last Adam with a new creation redeemed and exalted in Him. Vital distinctions are observable between these two headships. The truth revealed respecting Adam may be divided into that found in the Old Testament and that found in the New Testament.

1. ACCORDING TO THE OLD TESTAMENT. The Old Testament contribution to this doctrine from which important facts and features may be drawn is almost wholly historical. Adam appears as one directly created by God and as the progenitor of the human race. Record is made of his estate as created, of his relationship to God, of his temptation, and of his fall. He is thus presented as a living person and endowed with the same capacities as all other men who appear in the Sacred Text. Not only does Genesis record Adam's origin and estate, but all subse-

quent Scripture builds its teaching on the reality and truthfulness of the Genesis account. In this the Bible is consistent with itself. Having declared the origin of the race after the manner set forth in Genesis, it treats those records as true. There is no shadow of suspicion that any other theory relative to man's origin exists. Thus he who rejects the Genesis account rejects the whole Bible in so far as it bears upon the origin, development, history, redemption, and destiny of the race. In the doctrinal scheme of the Bible Adam and Christ are so interwoven and interdependent that it must be concluded that if the Genesis account respecting Adam be erroneous—on the theory he was a character who never existed—the record respecting Christ is subject to question also.

It is evident that Adam was created a full-grown man with the capacity which belongs to maturity. He is said to have given names to all creatures as they passed before him. He walked and talked with God, and of him God could say that His creation was very good. There would be little meaning to Adam's temptation and fall as the head of the race if, as has been asserted, he was immature in his mind and character.

2. ACCORDING TO THE NEW TESTAMENT. The New Testament teaching regarding Adam and Christ is one of type and antitype; but in every respect save one—namely, that each is the head of a creation of beings —the typology is one of contrast. Two primary passages are to be considered and also other secondary passages.

a. ROMANS 5:12–21. Observing but two representative men, God sees likewise just two works—one of disobedience and one of obedience— and two results—one of death and one of life. The race is thus divided into two main classifications: those in Adam, lost and undone, and those in Christ, saved and secure forever. This most important passage bearing upon the relation between Adam and Christ—theological to the last degree—draws out the distinctions which exist between Adam and Christ.

As he was warned of God, Adam died both spiritually (which took place at once) and physically (which occurred eventually) as a result of his first sin, and the race that was included with him shared in the same twofold judgment of death. Resulting from Adam's first sin are two lines of effects reaching down alike to every member of Adam's race. One is the sin nature, which results in spiritual death and is transmitted *mediately* from parent to child; the other is imputed sin with its penalty of physical death, which is transmitted *immediately* from Adam to each individual member of his race. A person dies physically not because

Adam alone sinned, not because of personal sins, and not because of the sin nature; he dies because of his own share—in the seminal sense—in the original sin which drew out the judgment of death. Because its natural head in creation, Adam is seen as representative of the entire race. In that headship position he contained the race and his lapse, or sin, is imputed with its penalty of physical death to his posterity as an *actual* imputation; because of what is antecedently their own sin, then, physical death as a judgment falls on all alike, even on those, such as infants, who have not sinned—as Adam did—willfully (Rom. 5:14). This divine principle of reckoning heavy responsibility to an unborn posterity is seen again in Hebrews 7:9–10 where Levi, the great grand-son of Abraham, is declared to have paid tithes to Melchizedek, being yet in the loins of his great grandfather Abraham (cf. Gen. 14:20). Romans 5:12 declares that all his race sinned in Adam and when Adam sinned. No other interpretation than that will carry through the remaining verses of this context.

b. 1 CORINTHIANS 15:22. This Scripture reads: "For as in Adam all die, even so in Christ shall all be made alive." Such is the Authorized Version reading of this important declaration. There is no difficulty regarding the first clause, that "in Adam all die"; but as for the rest of the verse, the same numerical all—πάντες—who suffer the death penalty are not necessarily in Christ, though all—πάντες—will be made alive: for, as Christ said, "the hour is coming, in the which all that are in the graves shall hear his voice, and shall come forth" (John 5:28–29). It is more fully in accordance with the context which follows (1 Cor. 15:23–24) if the passage is understood to mean that all men die because of Adam and all men—the same numerical all—will be raised by or because of Christ. For the context continues by saying that every man will be raised in his own classification; every man will be raised—that disclosure precludes a restriction of the context to those only who are in Christ by position. Such a limited type of resurrection, nevertheless, is later declared by the words "they that are Christ's at his coming" (vs. 23). The subject in view is clearly universal death through Adam and universal resurrection through Christ. Romans 5:18 presents a similar case with a twofold use of πάντες.

c. SECONDARY PASSAGES. In 1 Corinthians 15:45 it is asserted that, in contrast again, Adam was made a life-receiving soul while Christ is a life-giving Spirit. In like manner (vs. 47), Adam was "of the earth, earthy"; the Second Man is none other than the Lord from heaven. Though the believer has borne the image of the earthy, he is appointed to bear the image of the heavenly. He will be "conformed to the image" of Christ (Rom. 8:29). Again in 1 Timothy 2:13–14 it is said that Adam, quite in contrast to Eve, was not deceived in his transgression. Adam sinned knowingly and willfully. In Romans 5:14 reference is made to those who, because of immaturity and incompetency, have not sinned after "the similitude of Adam's transgression" (that is, knowingly and willfully). Thus also in Jude 1:14 Enoch is declared to be the "seventh from Adam," as throughout the entire Bible Adam is recognized for a living man, the beginning of the human race. In the genealogy of Christ given by Luke Christ is traced back to Adam who, it is averred, *was the son of God* (Luke 3:38). Christ Himself upholds the Genesis record respecting Adam and Eve (cf. Matt. 19:4–6; Mark 10:6–8).

ADOPTION

1. THE USUAL MEANING. The Bible recognizes the usual meaning of the word *adoption*, which is the placing of one rightfully outside blood ties into the position of a legal child (not, a natural child) in the family. Though not known at first among Jews, adoption was practiced by the Egyptians. Exodus 2:10 records the adoption of Moses by Pharaoh's daughter (cf. 1 Kings 11:20). The adoption of Esther (cf. Esther 2:7, 15) demonstrates that the custom was practiced by Jews in Babylon. Greece and Rome were evidently included among those who followed this custom. The Apostle Paul, indeed, uses this term only when writing to Gentiles. He writes to such about the national placing of Israel above other peoples—"To whom pertaineth the adoption" (Rom. 9:4–5)—as an adoption, but this instance bears closely upon the spiritual, New Testament use of the word. However, it is evident from Exodus 4:22; Deuteronomy 32:6; Isaiah 64:8; Jeremiah 31:9; and Hosea 11:1 that Israel, though called the son of Jehovah, is a son only by virtue of decree or sovereign placing and not by virtue of natural or spiritual ties in their relation to Jehovah as a child.

2. THE NEW TESTAMENT MEANING. The spiritual use of the word *adoption* signifies the placing of a newborn child—in point of maturity

—into the position of privilege and responsibility attached to an adult son. Here an important distinction appears between two Greek words, namely, τεκνίον—used to denote little children who are under the authority of parents, tutors, and governors (cf. John 13:33)—and υἱός —used to denote an adult son. Christ accordingly spoke of Himself as *Son of man*, and by employing the latter meant that He is One of full maturity. Perplexity may arise over why a born, and thus a natural, child should be adopted at all; for adoption, as usually conceived, could add nothing to rights which are gained by natural birth. It is thus, however, that the true spiritual meaning of *adoption* appears. The naturally born child is by adoption advanced positionally to his majority and given at once the standing of an adult son. Since spiritual adoption occurs at the time one is saved and thus becomes a child of God, there is no childhood period recognized in the Christian's experience. The one reference in 1 Corinthians 3:1 to "babes in Christ" sustains no relation to an immaturity which is due to brief experience with the Christian life; it is a reference to limitations which belong to an unspiritual or carnal state. The believer who is carnal may have been saved for many years.

In its distinctive significance, spiritual adoption means that the one thus placed has at once all the privilege—which is that of independence from tutors and governors—and liberty of a full-grown man. The Christian is enjoined to "stand fast" in the liberty wherewith Christ has made him free and not to be "entangled again with the yoke of bondage," which is evidently a reference to the legal or merit system (Gal. 5:1). Spiritual adoption also imposes the responsibilities belonging to full maturity. This is clear from the fact that, whatever God addresses to any believer, He addresses to all who believe. No portions of the hortatory Scriptures intended for Christians are restricted to beginners in the Christian life. The same holy walk and exercise of gifts is expected from all the children of God alike. Since the Christian life is to be lived in the power of the indwelling Holy Spirit, this requirement is reasonable; for the enabling power of the Spirit is as available for one as for another. Practically, long years of experience in the Christian life will doubtless tend to skilled adaptation to that new manner of life; but those years add no more resource than is given by the Spirit from the beginning to those who are saved. The whole field of Christian responsibility is by so much related to this doctrine of adoption.

Adoption assumes a practical meaning as set forth in the Galatian and Roman Epistles. In the former it becomes a deliverance from slavery, from guardians, and from nonage; in the latter it signifies a deliverance from the flesh (cf. Rom. 8:14–17). All of this is directly due to the new, complete responsibility which full maturity imposes and to the divine plan that the believer's life is to be lived from the start in the power of the Holy Spirit.

The final placing as exalted mature sons awaits the redemption of the body, which will occur at the return of Christ (Rom. 8:23). This, too, is related to the "glorious liberty of the children [not, little children] of God" (Rom. 8:21).

Dr. C. I. Scofield presents this same definition of adoption in the notes of the *Scofield Reference Bible:* "Adoption (*huiothesia,* 'placing as a son') is not so much a word of *relationship* as of *position*. The believer's relation to God as a child results from the new birth (John 1:12, 13), whereas adoption is the act of God whereby one already a child is, through redemption from the law, placed in the position of an adult son (Gal. 4:1–5). The indwelling Spirit gives the realization of this in the believer's present experience (Gal. 4:6); but the full manifestation of the believer's sonship awaits the resurrection, change, and translation of the saints, which is called 'the redemption of the body' (Rom. 8:23; 1 Thes. 4:14–17; Eph. 1:14; 1 John 3:2)" (p. 1250).

ADVOCACY

In its usual or general meaning an advocate is one who undertakes in the cause of another person. The original word used in the New Testament is παράκλητος and its translation as in John 14:16, 26; 15:26; 16:7—*comforter*—is unsatisfactory. It doubtless is the work of the Holy Spirit to lend comfort unto those to whom He ministers, but His work as Advocate in their behalf is much more extended, including all the work of the Spirit in and through the believer. In its Biblical or spiritual meaning, advocacy represents divine enablement and assistance. Two Persons of the Godhead are recognized as Advocates.

1. CHRIST. In His earthly ministry of three years Christ was Advocate for His own in the world, and before He left the world He promised another Advocate to continue this service. By the use of the word *an-*

other, Christ implies that His own ministry has been that of an advocate (John 14:16).

As a legal representative in the court of heaven Christ now functions
as the Christian's Advocate or defense (1 John 2:1), but never does He
assume the work of prosecution. That charges are preferred in heaven
against the believer and before the Father on the throne is certified in
Revelation 12:10, which reads, "For the accuser of our brethren is cast
down, which accused them before our God day and night." The
heavenly Advocate's ministry is twofold, namely, advocacy and intercession. In the latter service He is concerned with the Christian's weakness, ignorance, and immaturity, while in the former service He undertakes even on behalf of the Christian that has sinned. The declaration
is: "If any [Christian] man sin, we have an advocate with the Father,
Jesus Christ the righteous" (1 John 2:1). In the first chapter of 1 John
the effect of the believer's sin upon himself is set forth; but the second
chapter opens with a contemplation of the far more serious problem of
the effect of the Christian's sin upon God. When recognizing this problem of evil, the Arminian assumes that there is no specific cure through
Christ's advocacy for the Christian's sin and that the saved one who has
sinned must be dismissed from his saved estate because of the sin. Such,
indeed, would be necessary were it not for the present advocacy of
Christ in which He pleads the value of His death for that very sin which
is in question. As Advocate in heaven, Christ pleads the fact that He
bore this sin. The righteous ground of His death for sin secures the believer's release—so far as divine condemnation is concerned. God accepts always the death of His Son as the basis of His release of those
who have sinned. The advocacy of Christ in heaven respecting the believer's sin is so complete and perfect that by it He wins a title which
He gains nowhere else, namely, *Jesus Christ the righteous.*

The present advocacy of Christ in heaven is self-appointed. It is included in His work as Savior. It is wrought for every believer at all
times without regard to the believer's own understanding of it or any
supposed cooperation with it. It is not therefore a subject of petition;
it is rather a subject of praise and thanksgiving.

2. THE HOLY SPIRIT. When about to leave the world Christ promised
another advocate (John 14:16), and thus pointed to the Holy Spirit
with clear instructions respecting the work which the Spirit would
undertake. The advocacy of the Spirit is also one of intercession and
direct aiding. Reference is made to His intercession in Romans 8:26–
27. It is declared that "he maketh intercession for the saints according

to the will of God." In His enabling ministry the Spirit empowers unto every good work and overcomes every foe. So great are the provisions for the child of God in this present age!

The Spirit is not a mere substitute for, or a successor to, Christ; He has His own incomparable ministry which is peculiar and specific. He is the all-sufficient One who has been sent into the world by both the Father and the Son.

3. THREE GENERAL USES OF THE WORD *Advocate*. From the foregoing it will be seen that there are three general meanings to the word *advocate*—a legal advocate, which Christ is now in heaven; an intercessor, which Christ and the Holy Spirit now are; and a general helper, which Christ was while on earth and which the Holy Spirit is throughout this age.

AGE
(See DISPENSATIONS)

ANGELS

According to Colossians 1:16, creation included "things" invisible as well as things visible and angels are among the things that are invisible. They comprise a vast company of spirit beings concerning whom the Scriptures bear abundant testimony, but whose existence and ministrations have been strangely neglected in works on theology. Angels are mentioned about 108 times in the Old Testament. From the Greek word for angels, ἄγγελος, is derived the term used in English. In any case, the word means simply *messenger* and in rare instances is used thus of men (cf. Luke 7:24; James 2:25; Rev. 1:20). Christ used the term when referring to departed human spirits (Matt. 18:10; cf. Acts 12:15). The position angels hold by creation is above men (Ps. 8:4–5; Heb. 2:6–7; 2 Pet. 2:11). The record of the origin of the angels by creation is given in Psalm 148:2–5 and in Colossians 1:16.

The angels are classified as follows: (1) The Angel of Jehovah, which terminology refers to the preincarnate appearing of the Son of God and therefore is not rightly classified as reference to an angel; yet the term is used of Him. His appearings in this form are recorded as ten theophanies. As the Revealer of God and the One whom Jehovah sends, He is a veritable Messenger (Ex. 23:20; cf. 32:34; 33:2). (2) Gabriel, meaning "the mighty one" (Dan. 8:16; 9:21; Luke 1:19, 26-38). (3) Michael, the archangel, a name meaning "Who is like God?" and he is head of the armies of heaven (1 Thess. 4:16; Jude 1:9; Rev. 12:7), and Israel's prince (Dan. 10:21; 12:1). (4) Cherubim, the defenders of God's holiness (Gen. 3:22-24; Ex. 25:17-22; Isa. 37:16; Ezek. 1:5; 28:14). (5) Seraphim (Isa. 6:2). (6) Principalities and powers—sometimes used of good and sometimes of evil angels (Rom. 8:38; Eph. 1:21; 3:10; 6:12; Col. 1:16; cf. 2:10, 15; Titus 3:1; 1 Pet. 3:22; Luke 21: 26). (7) "The elect angels" (1 Tim. 5:21). (8) Angels known by their ministries—angel of the waters (Rev. 16:5), angel of the abyss (Rev. 9:1), angel with power over fire (Rev. 14:18), seven angels with trumpets (Rev. 8:2), "the watchers" (Dan. 4:13, 17, 23). (9) Satan and the demons, and (10) Jeremiel or Uriel, Raphael, etc., mentioned only in the Apocryphal writings.

The general facts regarding the angels are: (1) They are legion (Ps. 68:17; Dan. 7:10; Matt. 26:53; Heb. 12:22; Rev. 5:11); they form the hosts of heaven (Luke 2:13. Note the R.V. term, *Jehovah of hosts*). Numerically, angels neither increase nor decrease. (2) Whether they have any kind of bodies cannot be determined. They appear as men when so required (Matt. 28:3; Rev. 15:6; 18:1). They are said to fly (Isa. 6:2; Ezek. 1:6; Dan. 9:21; Rev. 4:8; 14:6). (3) Their abode is evidently in heaven; but reference is thus made to the second heaven, the stellar spaces (Matt. 24:29). Christ passed through the angelic sphere going to and coming from earth (Eph. 1:21; Heb. 2:7; 4:14). (4) The ministries of the angels are varied and are all described in the Sacred Text (Ps. 34:7; 91:11; 103:20; 104:4; Dan. 4:13, 17, 23; 6:22; Matt. 4:11; Luke 16:22; Acts 5:19; 8:26; 10:3; 12:7; 27:23; 1 Cor. 11:10; Col. 2:18; Rev. 22:8-9). (5) The vast empires of angels are doubtless occupied with many enterprises and the execution of their governments. They do behold the things of earth (Luke 12:8-9; 15:10; 1 Cor. 11:10; 1 Tim. 3:16; Rev. 14:10). (6) Their presence is recorded at creation (Job 38:7), at the giving of the law (Acts 7:53; Gal. 3:19; Heb. 2:2; cf. Rev. 22:16), at the birth of Christ (Luke 2:13), at the scene of His temptation (Matt. 4:11; cf. Luke 22:43), at the resurrection (Matt. 28:2), at the ascension (Acts 1:10), and just so they will be at the second coming (Matt. 13:37–39; 24:31; 25:31; 2 Thess. 1:7).

Angels are generally classified as unfallen or holy angels (Mark 8:38) and fallen (Matt. 25:41). There will yet be war in heaven between the two classes of angels (Rev. 12:7–10). The fallen angels are either free (cf. the demons) or bound (2 Pet. 2:4; Jude 1:6).

ANTHROPOLOGY

Like Angelology, Anthropology is a major division of Systematic Theology and has had its due treatment in an earlier portion of this work (Vol. II). As a review of some salient features of the subject, certain truths may be restated.

1. As a Modern Science in secular education Anthropology is treated wholly apart from Biblical revelation, having in view only man's development and achievements. Whatever is said respecting man's origin is from an evolutionary point of view and nothing is included relative to spiritual values or man's destiny. Biblical Anthropology enters a much wider field, then, and contemplates important considerations.

2. The Origin of Man, according to the stand taken by intrabiblical Anthropology, is accepted as declared in Genesis and as incorporated in all subsequent Scriptures, namely, that man is a direct creation of God. To deny the Genesis account is not only a denial of that portion of God's revelation, but becomes a fostering and sustaining of unbelief respecting every word God has spoken.

3. Man Made in the Image and Likeness of God. This is the unqualified declaration of the Bible. It therefore follows that God may be known somewhat with regard to the character of His Being by that which man is, apart from that in man which the fall has engendered. The comparisons thus drawn must be restricted to spiritual, rather than supposed physical, divine characteristics.

4. The Material Part of Man was a direct creation from existing substances.

5. The Immaterial Part of Man was breathed into him as the very breath of God and thus he became a living soul.

6. The Fall of Man was accomplished through the design and influence of Satan. The sin which caused the fall of man was not only suggested by Satan, but was the identical form of it which Satan had himself followed and by which he fell from that high estate into which he was placed by creation, namely, acting independently of God through disobedience and thus repudiating all divine right and authority over himself (cf. Gen. 3:5; Isa. 14:12–14).

7. The Fall and Its Penalty are visited upon the whole human family. That penalty to which spiritual death is due is transmitted *mediately* from parent to child, while the penalty of physical death is imputed *immediately* from Adam to each individual member of his race, the divine reckoning being that each member of the race was seminally in Adam when the first man sinned and therefore each member shared in that sin. This reckoning of Adam's sin to his race is a *real* imputation, rather than a *judicial* imputation. This divine principle of reckoning is clearly indicated in Hebrews 7:9–10, where Levi, who as a priest was supported by the tithes of the people, did, nevertheless, pay tithes when Abraham paid tithes to Melchizedek since he was as a great grandson in the loins of father Abraham.

8. God Has Moved in the direction of a cure for man's lost estate. The terms upon which this cure may be received are as definite as any can be. He who in the beginning disobeyed God and sinned is called upon to obey the gospel of God's grace. In the present age the salvation which God offers is unto a place in the highest glory and in no way to be compared with that estate of innocence from which Adam fell.

ANTICHRIST

If the doctrine of antichrist is built on etymology of the word, the field is going to be broad indeed, for all that is opposite to Christ is antichrist. Thus, as John says, "Even now are there many antichrists" in the world (1 John 2:18)—and this reference includes the spirit of antichrist (1 John 4:3)—alluding to any who in spirit or in person is opposed to Christ.

On the other hand, if the doctrine is limited to a future person, there is occasion for some discussion about who that person is and the Scriptures bearing upon him. If the person predicted is identified by his ambitious assumption to be Christ, he is rightly called *antichrist* and is easily represented by the first beast of Revelation (13:1-10). If he is identified as the one who declares himself to be God, as in Ezekiel 28:1-10, he is at once likened to the man of sin of whom Paul writes in 2 Thessalonians 2:3-10. Likewise, Daniel sees a little horn or king who conquers other kings and assumes a place of authority over the other kingdoms.

Though the titles differ, the beast of Revelation 13:1-10, the man of sin of 2 Thessalonians 2, the little horn of Daniel 7, and the wicked prince of Daniel 9 seem to be no other than the one who will federate kingdoms, but will be destroyed at the coming of Christ. His way evidently is being prepared by those who, according to the Spirit, teach antichristian doctrine, denying the fact of the incarnation of the Logos. Probably these are even now preparing for the coming of the person of antichrist. Christ referred to one who would come in his own name (John 5:43) whom the Jews would receive. His nationality is believed to be Jewish since Ezekiel predicts of him that he shall "die the deaths of the uncircumcised" (Ezek. 28:10). A true child of God is justified in observing the direction of events which take place in the fulfillment of prophecy.

APOSTASY

Two words of quite different meaning are often confused, namely, *apostasy* and *heresy*. The former describes one who has first embraced some creed or doctrine and afterwards turned from it. Apostasy is well described as "a total departure from one's faith or religion; abandonment of creed and renunciation of religious obligations" (*Standard Dictionary*, 1913 edition). On the other hand, heresy refers to a belief which is held in variance with standards or accepted features of doctrine. The term *heretic* does not imply having embraced doctrine from which one has finally departed. That which is branded as heretical may have been an unaltered conviction or contention. The history of the church in its treatment of heretics is deplorable. Of this history the same Standard

Dictionary records: "Heresy was formerly a crime in most European countries, and as such punishable by law. It consisted generally of a refusal to accept a prescribed article of faith, altho the canon law enumerates 82 different varieties. Punishment for heresy was common in medieval times on the part of all dominant religious sects and was practised by the first colonists in America. The writ *'de heretico comburendo,'* by which heretics could be burnt, was passed originally against the Lollards in 1401, and was repealed under Charles II., 29 Car. c. 9, in England, and several toleration acts have since stopped civil punishment for heresy. Ecclesiastical penalties are still enforced against heretical members both in the Protestant and Catholic churches."

Nothing could be more beside the point than persecution based upon the supposition that credence respecting doctrine is something subject to the control of the individual's will. An enlightened mind may change the attitude of some heretic, but nothing else could avail. This fact reaches far into the field of practical effort, in behalf of the saved that they may be more spiritual, and of the unsaved that they may come to a saving knowledge of Christ. Teachers of doctrine and evangelists would do well to analyze their methods and appeals that these may be brought into conformity with the unalterable fact respecting the ability or inability of the human mind. That every truth of Scripture is a revelation from God means more than the fact that God has caused it to be written as Scripture; it reaches on to the individual, to whom it must come as a personal discovery to the mind by the power of the Holy Spirit. It must be a profound intuition respecting a given truth, to which the unaided mind—because of inherent limitations—could not attain. As for the progress which saved people may make in the knowledge of God's truth, it would be well to give attention to two major passages— John 16:12-15 and 1 Corinthians 2:9—3:3.

The experience of apostasy is to the human mind one of God's great mysteries. Why, indeed, should evil ever be found in His universe, which universe was in the beginning as free from evil as its maker? Scripture without hesitation records various apostasies. These are:

1. THAT OF THE ANGELS. Of the fallen angels it is said that they "kept not their first estate" (Jude 1:6), and of Satan it is said that "he abode not in the truth" (John 8:44) and that "iniquity was found in" him (Isa. 14:13-14; Ezek. 28:15). For the apostasy of the angels there is no remedy; on the contrary, it is predicted in words which cannot be revoked that all fallen angels are to spend eternity in the lake of fire

(Matt. 25:41), which is God's answer to the apostasy of the angels.

2. THAT OF ADAM. Of this aspect of truth much has been written earlier; but it should be observed that Adam became an apostate by his one sin and that as he fell he could and did propagate only after his fallen nature. The first to be born into the world by natural birth proved a murderer.

3. THAT OF ISRAEL. Apostasy with some degree of restoration was the constant experience of the nation Israel, all of which was predicted, which prediction but discloses the fact that sin is never a surprise to God. He can always foresee it, as He does. Israel is now in her last apostasy. There will never be another after she is restored from the present estate of separation from covenant blessings (cf. Deut. 28:15–68; 30:1–8; Isa. 1:5–6; 5:5–7).

4. THAT OF CHRISTENDOM. The Church of Rome represents the extent of apostasy to which men can go regardless of the fact that it was quite pure and scriptural in its beginning. The final "falling away" is predicted for the days of tribulation (2 Thess. 2:3) and the period of the "last days" of the Church on earth is marked by apostasy (cf. 1 Tim. 4:1–3; 2 Tim. 3:1–5).

Some have declared that there is no hope for an apostate. Such a declaration overlooks the power and grace of God. Some apostates, such as are named in the New Testament and have lived in all generations, will never be restored; but this is not saying that they could not have been restored. A heretic who has held heretical ideas from the beginning of his mature life may be instructed and so led into the truth. Those in error are always subject to correction in love. So unbelief may be overcome by a revelation of the truth.

ASCENSION

So much that is vital within the field of typology is involved in this specific feature of Christology that there is occasion for an individual doctrinal consideration of its character. While it may be true that during the forty days of His postresurrection ministry Christ moved back and forth freely between earth and heaven, it is of doctrinal importance and within the bounds of that which is written to recognize two ascensions—one directly following the resurrection and the other when He visibly departed on the clouds at the end of the forty days. Though no Scripture directly describes the first ascension, it is implied in the record of what Christ said to Mary in the early morning at the tomb, "Touch me not; for I am not yet ascended to my Father: but go to my brethren, and say unto them, I ascend unto my Father, and your Father; and to my God, and your God" (John 20:17). That He ascended on this same day subsequent to the resurrection is evident, for He said unto His disciples at evening of that day, "Behold my hands and my feet, that it is I myself: handle me, and see" (Luke 24:39).

In this first ascension which followed directly upon His resurrection, two important types were fulfilled. It would not have been reasonable for this twofold fulfillment to have been delayed until the end of the forty days on earth—especially as one of the types, that of the "wave sheaf," represents Christ in resurrection. Of all the sheaves of grain on the hills of Palestine but one from each homestead was waved ceremonially before Jehovah, and that on the day following the Sabbath (cf. Lev. 23:11) and as a representation of all the sheaves of the harvest. Thus Christ when He ascended from the tomb appeared as an earnest of the mighty harvest of souls whom He had redeemed, who came with Him out of the tomb and who share His resurrection life and glory. He was thus the "firstfruits of them that slept," a representation of that resurrection of believers that is yet to be (cf. 1 Cor. 15:20–23).

The other type which Christ fulfilled in connection with His first ascension was that of the high priest presenting the blood in the holy of holies on the Day of Atonement. Thus Christ the true High Priest presented His own blood and the acceptance of that sacrifice for sinners answers every need of the sinner forever. The importance of the presentation in heaven of the emblem of His finished work in redemption, reconciliation, and propitiation cannot be estimated nor should it be slighted.

At His second ascension, which occurred at the end of His postresurrection ministry of forty days, Christ was seen returning on the clouds of heaven. He then undertook His present session at the Father's right hand, and with it the far-reaching ministries which continue throughout this age and which provide all security for those who are saved. It was then that He became "Head over all things to the church" (Eph. 1:21–22), the Bestower of gifts (Eph. 4:7–11). He took up the twofold, priestly ministries of intercession (Rom. 8:34; Heb 7:25) and advocacy (Rom. 8:34; Heb. 9:24; 1 John 2:1).

ASSURANCE

In the general signification of the doctrine, assurance is a confidence that right relations exist between one's self and God. In this respect it is not to be confused with the doctrine of eternal security. The latter is a fact due to God's faithfulness whether realized by the believer or not, while the former is that which one *believes* to be true respecting himself at a given time. Assurance may rest upon personal righteousness, which assurance was in the past age a recognition of one's own righteous character; but in the present age it is a recognition of that righteousness of God which is imputed to all who believe. Isaiah declares, "And the work of righteousness shall be peace; and the effect of righteousness quietness and assurance for ever" (Isa. 32:17). Thus also the Apostle writes of the confidence which is engendered by understanding (Col. 2:2), and they who understand God's provisions and who have entered intelligently into them have just this. Likewise in Hebrews 6:11 there is reference to "the full assurance of hope," and in 10:22 to "full assurance of faith." Although it may be concluded that assurance is altogether experimental, resting as it does on a true faith, a true hope, a true understanding, and an imputed righteousness, such feeling may lead one to say without any presumption, "I know that I am saved," or, as the Apostle testified of himself: "I know whom I have believed, and am persuaded that he is able to keep that which I have committed unto him against that day" (2 Tim. 1:12). So far as the Scripture cited above is concerned, assurance rests not only on the Word of God but as well upon Christian experience. These two grounds of confidence—that of experience and that based on the Word of Truth—should be considered specifically.

1. BASED ON CHRISTIAN EXPERIENCE. The inward witness of the Holy Spirit is a definite Christian experience. The Apostle Paul states: "The Spirit itself [R.V., himself] beareth witness with our spirit, that we are the children of God" (Rom. 8:16), and the Apostle John declares, "If we receive the witness of men, the witness of God is greater: for this is the witness of God which he hath testified of his Son. He that believeth on the Son of God hath the witness in himself: he that believeth not God hath made him a liar; because he believeth not the record that

God gave of his Son" (1 John 5:9–10). In Hebrews 10:2 it is asserted that those "once purged" should have had no more conscience of sins. That is to say, the removal of all condemnation (cf. Rom. 8:1) should create a corresponding experience. In 1 John 3:10 a real experimental distinction between the "children of God" and the "children of the devil" is manifested. The difference is exhibited in the matter of lawless sinning. The context, which begins with verse 4, has altogether to do with lawless sinning, that is, sinning with no consciousness of its seriousness. The Christian lives with a grieved or an ungrieved Holy Spirit inside, and he cannot sin without an inner distress (cf. Ps. 32:3–5). 1 John 3:9–10—"Whosoever is born of God doth not commit sin; for his seed remaineth in him: and he cannot sin, because he is born of God. In this the children of God are manifest, and the children of the devil: whosoever doeth not righteousness is not of God, neither he that loveth not his brother"—does not teach that Christians do not sin (cf. 1 John 1:8, 10); it rather teaches that the believer being indwelt by the Spirit of God cannot sin lawlessly. It is also to be observed that the presence of this living Christ in the heart through the advent of the Spirit should cause a suitable experience, if the believer's relations to God are spiritual rather than carnal. Again, the Apostle writes in respect to the indwelling Christ: "Examine yourselves, whether ye be in the faith; prove your own selves. Know ye not your own selves, how that Jesus Christ is in you, except ye be reprobates?" (2 Cor. 13:5). It is inconceivable that Christ should dwell in the heart without some corresponding experience. Therefore the Apostle directs that self-examination be undertaken on the one issue of the indwelling Christ. Certain results from that indwelling are normal.

a. THE FATHERHOOD OF GOD A REALITY. It is one thing to know about the triune God and quite another thing to *know* God. Knowledge of God as Father is achieved in the human heart by the work of the Son, Christ Jesus. He said, "All things are delivered unto me of my Father: and no man knoweth the Son, but the Father; neither knoweth any man the Father, save the Son, and he to whomsoever the Son will reveal him. Come unto me, all ye that labour and are heavy laden, and I will give you rest" (Matt. 11:27–28). The rest which is thus promised to the soul is that which results when God is known as Father. This knowledge is secured to all who believe in Christ as Savior.

b. A REALITY IN PRAYER. Doubtless unsaved persons attempt to pray, though without the ground of access to God which Christ is; but the individual who comes really to know God finds a new experience in prayer. It is incredible that He who lived by prayer when here on the earth should not impel the one in whom He lives to the exercise of the potentialities of prayer.

c. THE WORD OF GOD DESIRED. Similarly, if Christ indwells, there must be a new interest created in the heart for the Word of God on the part of the one who is saved. The new spiritual life which came by the second birth, like physical life, must be fed and thus the Word of God becomes the "sincere milk" to some and "strong meat" to others; so all who are saved do have a normal desire for the Truth of God. If there is no appetite for spiritual food, there is some serious reason.

d. A NEW PASSION FOR THE SALVATION OF MEN. If Christ who died that lost men might be saved has come to live in a human heart, there must be of necessity and normally a new passion for lost souls created in that heart. Divine love, it will be remembered, is the first-named section of the manifold fruit of the Spirit.

e. A NEW SENSE OF KINSHIP. And, finally, to be born of God is to enter the family and household of God. It is because of the truth that saved ones are actually sons of God that Christ is pleased to call them *brethren* (Rom. 8:29). This relationship is so genuine that there must be, of necessity, a corresponding sense of kinship arising in the heart. The Apostle John, therefore, presents this searching test of reality: "We know that we have passed from death unto life, because we love the brethren. He that loveth not his brother abideth in death" (1 John 3:14).

In all the lines of evidence relative to personal salvation to be based on Christian experience one qualifying feature must be considered, namely, that it is possible to be saved and at the same time to be living a carnal life, and when in the carnal state no believer's experience can be normal. The evidence cited above, then, since it is drawn from Christian experience, applies only to those who are adjusted to the mind and will of God. The conclusion to be reached in this aspect of the present theme is not that carnal believers are unsaved, but rather that Christian experience, depending as it does upon that which is wrought in the heart by the Holy Spirit, will not be normal when the Spirit's work in the heart is hindered by carnality. Thus for a very great proportion of believers the evidence of assurance based on Christian experience is without validity because of carnality.

2. BASED ON THE WORD OF GOD. Since that which God covenants and promises cannot fail, evidence respecting one's salvation which is based upon the Word of God proves absolute. In 1 John 5:13 it is

written: "These things have I written unto you that believe on the name of the Son of God; that ye may know that ye have eternal life, and that ye may believe on the name of the Son of God." Thus has God revealed it is the divine purpose that everyone who believes to the saving of his soul may *know* that he is saved, not in this instance through uncertain Christian experience but on the ground of that which is written in Scripture. Though the truth stated in the above passage no doubt applies to all the promises of God unto those who are saved, the Apostle evidently is referring to that which he has just stated (vs. 12), namely, "He that hath the Son hath life." It becomes, then, a matter of self-knowledge whether one has had a recognized transaction with the Son of God regarding one's salvation. When such a transaction occurred may not be known, but the saved one must recognize that he depends only on Christ as his Savior. He may say with the Apostle (2 Tim. 1:12), "I know whom I have believed." The Lord has said, "Him that cometh to me I will in no wise cast out" (John 6:37). To those who have thus come to Christ for His salvation there can be no other conclusion, if Christ's word is honored, than that they have been received and saved. The Word of God thus becomes a title deed to eternal life, and it should be treated as an article of surety, for God cannot fail in any word He has spoken.

a. DOUBTING ONE'S OWN COMMITTAL. Multitudes are in no way certain that they ever have had a personal transaction with Christ regarding their own salvation. Obviously the cure for any uncertainty about one's acceptance of Christ is to receive Christ *now,* reckoning that no self-merit or religious works are of value but that Christ alone can save.

b. DOUBTING THE FAITHFULNESS OF GOD. Others who lack assurance of their own salvation do so because they, though having come to Christ in faith, are not sure that He has kept His word and received them. This state of mind is usually caused by looking for a change in one's feelings rather than looking alone to the faithfulness of Christ. Feelings and experiences have their place, but, as before stated, the crowning evidence of personal salvation—which is unchanged by all these—is the truthfulness of God. What He has said He will do, and it is not pious or commendable to distrust personal salvation after having definitely cast one's self upon Christ.

ATONEMENT

Complexity arises in some minds respecting the use of the word *atonement* and this is due to certain facts.

1. IN THE OLD TESTAMENT. So far as the English translation is concerned, the use of the term *atonement*—excepting the mistranslation of Romans 5:11—is restricted to the Old Testament. Though there it is a translation of two Hebrew words, but one of them, *kāphar*, is generally in view and it is used about seventy times. Its meaning is 'to cover.' This, the distinct and limited meaning of the Hebrew word, should not be invested with New Testament ideas, which contemplate a finished or completed work. Under the Old Testament provision the one who had sinned was himself fully forgiven and released, but the ground upon which it could be wrought was itself only typical and not actual. God forgave and restored where sin was only *covered* by animal sacrifices, but the true basis upon which forgiveness could ever be granted was the intention on God's part to take up the sin later that He had forgiven and deal with it righteously and effectively through the sacrificial death of His Son on the cross. That efficacious death was typified in the required animal sacrifice. According to Romans 3:25 —"Whom God hath set forth to be a propitiation through faith in his blood, to declare his righteousness for the remission of sins that are past, through the forbearance of God"—the fact that Christ bore the sins which were committed before, which sins had already been forgiven on the typical ground that they were covered, ranks as one of the major accomplishments of His death. It is as though unnumbered promissory notes had been handed to Christ for Him to pay. If the notes are paid as promised, God is thereby proved to have been righteous in the forgiving of sin with no other demands having been made upon the sinner than that an offering be brought which, regardless of how much it was understood by that sinner, was in God's sight an anticipation and recognition of His final meeting of every holy demand against sin by the efficacious blood of Christ. In other words, God pretermitted or passed over the sins, not judging them finally at the time they were forgiven. Such a course, it is obvious, would be a very unrighteous dealing if those sins were not in due time to be brought into

judgment. All sins of the Mosaic age were thus shown to have been "covered" but not "taken away." In contrast to this temporary expedient, all sin which God forgives has been and is now "taken away." In two New Testament passages that vital contrast appears. It is written: "For it is not possible that the blood of bulls and of goats should take away sins. . . . And every priest standeth daily ministering and offering oftentimes the same sacrifices, which can never take away sins: but this man, after he had offered one sacrifice for sins for ever, sat down on the right hand of God; from henceforth expecting till his enemies be made his footstool. For by one offering he hath perfected for ever them that are sanctified" (Heb. 10:4, 11–14). Added to this is the direct statement of John 1:29, "Behold the Lamb of God, which taketh away the sin of the world." This great declaration from John was a doctrinal innovation of immeasurable proportions. The same contrast between the divine dealings with sin in the past dispensation and in the present dispensation is indicated again at Acts 17:30.

2. In the New Testament. Though appearing once by an unfortunate translation in the New Testament (cf. Rom. 5:11), the word *atonement* is not really found in the New Testament. It is as though the Holy Spirit in jealousy for the truth is not allowing room for such an error respecting the divine plan of dealing with sin in the present age. The etymological meaning of *atonement* is 'at-one-ment'; those once estranged are brought into agreement. The New Testament word for this great truth is *reconciliation*. There would be no doctrinal error committed should *at-one-ment* be substituted for *reconciliation*, but the careful student must be much influenced by the fact that 'atonement' as such is confined to the old order and is not used by the Spirit respecting any feature of the new order in Christianity.

3. In Theology. By common usage and yet with little reason, modern theologians have seized upon the word *atonement* as a term to represent all that Christ did on the cross. In earlier portions of this work (Vol. III) upwards of fourteen stupendous achievements by Christ in His death have been indicated. These reach beyond all present time into other ages and past human situations into angelic spheres. It is not possible that the limitless outreach of Christ's death should be represented in any single one or a dozen words; and from the fact that the term in question does not belong to the New Testament vocabulary and from the fact that it is employed in the Old Testament to represent one idea wholly foreign to and superseded in the New Testament, no word related to Christ's death is more inapt as a reference to that which

He really wrought for men of the present age. As the extent of Christ's death is understood, so, correspondingly, the use of the term *atonement* will cease.

This discussion may be summarized by quoting from an extended article on the theme to be found in the *International Standard Bible Encyclopaedia:*

> In the English New Testament the word "atonement" is found only at Romans 5:11 and the American Revised Version changes this to "reconciliation." While in strict etymology this word need signify only the active or conscious exercise of unity of life or harmony of relations, the causative idea probably belongs to the original use of the term, as it certainly is present in all current Christian use of the term. As employed in Christian theology, both practical and technical, the term includes with more or less distinctness: (*a*) the fact of union with God, and this always looked upon as (*b*) a broken union to be restored or an ideal union to be realized, (*c*) the procuring cause of atonement, variously defined, (*d*) the crucial act wherein the union is effected, the work of God and the response of the soul in which the union becomes actual. Inasmuch as the reconciliation between man and God is always conceived of as effected through Jesus Christ (2 Cor. 5:18–21) the expression, "the Atonement of Christ," is one of the most frequent in Christian theology. Questions and controversies have turned mainly on the procuring cause of atonement, (*c*) above, and at this point have arisen the various "theories of the Atonement" (I, 321, 1915 edition).

AUTHORITY

Though recognizing God as supreme, the general theme of *authority* may be extended from that point on almost without end. All the material is subject to a twofold division, namely, (1) authority which is external to man, and (2) that which is internal.

1. EXTERNAL. This conception includes the authority of God, of the separate Persons of the Godhead, of angels, of human governments, of the apostles, of the Bible, and of the church. The subject matter includes every situation wherein one or more intelligences determine the actions of others. Comment bearing upon each of these several divisions is in order.

a. THE TRIUNE GOD. By right of creation—the most absolute of all prerogatives—comes the ground of divine authority. To be the Originator, the Designer, and the Executor of all that exists becomes at once the basis for transcendent, peerless, and incomparable authority. Whatever lesser authorities there may be, it must be predicated of them that they are only relative and such as are allowed by the One who is supreme. The fact and extent of other authorities than that of God should not be contemplated apart from recognition of the over-all authority of God. Authority in the hands of those who are unworthy of it is most dangerous, and so it is cause for great thanksgiving that God is what He is; His is perfect trustworthiness, perfect wisdom, perfect purpose, infinite power, and infinite love.

b. THE FATHER. In the present relationship which exists within the Godhead, the Father is revealed as granting authority to the Son and directing the Holy Spirit. It is to the Father that Christ ever turned in prayer and expectation, and the believer is directed to pray to the Father (John 16:23) with the same recognition of His supreme authority and power.

c. THE SON. Though Christ could say, "All power [R.V., authority] is given unto me in heaven and in earth" (Matt. 28:18; cf. 1 Cor. 15:25–28), He does, nevertheless, acknowledge that the power is granted Him by the Father. He said accordingly, "For as the Father hath life in himself; so hath he given to the Son to have life in himself; and hath given him authority to execute judgment also, because he is the Son of man" (John 5:26–27). Much indeed is implied when He claimed "all authority" and "judgment." These are the prerogatives of God. There is no intimation here that in His adorable Person the Son is inferior to the Father. In the outworking of creation and redemption, however, it has pleased the Persons of the Godhead to be related to each other as They are. Christ in consequence did His mighty works through the power and authority of the Holy Spirit. All such representation of the Son is better understood when it is remembered that Christ was living in the human sphere and adapting Himself to that limitation. Respecting Christ's authority, note Matthew 7:29; 9:6, 8; 21:23–27; Mark 1:22, 27; 11:28–29, 33; John 5:27.

d. THE HOLY SPIRIT. The Holy Spirit is sent forth by both the Father and the Son, which fact indicates that He receives authority from those who send Him; He indeed exercises great authority in the world. He it is who restrains evil, who convicts the world, and who guides and empowers the believer (cf. Acts 13:2).

e. THE ANGELS. When angelic creation is described as in Colossians 1:16, there is mention of "thrones, dominions, principalities," and "powers." By these terms reference is made to the authority which the angels exercise within their own order and sphere. It is true, as in the case of Satan, that some authority is granted them in their appointed relations with men (cf. Luke 4:6; 12:5; 22:53; Acts 26:18; Eph. 2:2; Col. 1:13; Rev. 6:8; 9:3, 10, 19; 13:4-5, 7, 12; 20:6).

f. THE CIVIL RULERS. The Word of God not only requires subjection to earthly authority, but declares that rulers are appointed of God. Such, indeed, is the supreme authority of God over all else as to control even government (cf. Prov. 24:21; Rom. 13:1-7; 1 Pet. 2:13-17).

g. THE APOSTLES. Very special authority was extended to the apostles and for this the Apostle Paul contended throughout his ministry; not for self-advancement, of course, but that his God-given right might be exercised in full according to the plan and will of God (Luke 9:1; 2 Cor. 10:8).

h. THE BIBLE. Reflecting the supreme authority of God as actually His revealed will, the Word of Truth is to be obeyed by all who come under His divine rule.

i. THE CHURCH. This kind of rule may be perverted, as in the case of Rome, but the Word of God directs that subjection be rendered by all within the church to those who are set over them in authority. The practical outworking of ecclesiastical authority has been the cause of endless strife throughout the history of the church.

2. INTERNAL. Without perhaps the same degree of definiteness, there is to be recognized the authority which arises through spiritual and moral appeal, through conscience, through customs, and through sentiment. All this and more like it may so dominate the mind and heart as to become a motivating influence.

BABYLON

The Old Testament traces the origin, history, and destiny of the ancient capital city of Shinar (Gen. 10:10; 14:1). It is not within the scope of this outline study to trace the history and development of the ancient city itself. *The International Standard Bible Encyclopaedia* presents this history quite fully and from the Biblical viewpoint. The name *Babylon* means 'confusion,' and is linked with disorder from the day of the confounding of human language as recorded in Genesis onward to the final destruction of great Babylon as recorded in Revelation. Of the theory that the ancient city will yet be rebuilt for it to be destroyed in fulfillment of prediction, little can be said in its favor. On the contrary, such a fruition directly contradicts the Scriptures (cf. Isa. 13:19–22; Jer. 51:61–64); however, confusion or babel continues until order is restored in the earth by Christ when He comes again. No more accurate or complete statement with respect to the local and larger meaning of Babylon has been found than that prepared by Dr. C. I. Scofield in the notes of his *Reference Bible* under Isaiah 13, verses 1 and 19:

> The *city*, Babylon, is not in view here, as the immediate context shows. It is important to note the significance of the name when used symbolically. "Babylon" is the Greek form: invariably in the O. T. Hebrew the word is simply Babel, the meaning of which is *confusion*, and in this sense the word is used symbolically. (1) In the prophets, when the actual city is not meant, the reference is to the "confusion" into which the whole social order of the world has fallen under Gentile world-domination. . . . Isa. 13:4 gives the divine view of the welter of warring Gentile powers. The *divine* order is given in Isa. 11. Israel in her own land, the centre of the divine government of the world and channel of the divine blessing; and the Gentiles blessed in association with Israel. Anything else is, politically, mere "Babel." (2) In Rev. 14:8–11; 16:19 the Gentile world-system is in view in connection with Armageddon (Rev. 16:14; 19:21), while in Rev. 17 the reference is to apostate Christianity, destroyed by the nations (Rev. 17:16) headed up under the Beast (Dan. 7:8; Rev. 19:20) and false prophet. In Isaiah the political Babylon is in view, literally as to the then existing city, and symbolically as to the times of the Gentiles. In the Revelation both the symbolical-political and symbolical-religious Babylon are in view, for there both are alike under the tyranny of the Beast. Religious Babylon is destroyed by political Babylon (Rev. 17:16); political Babylon by the appearing of the Lord (Rev. 19:19–21). That Babylon the *city* is not to be rebuilt is clear from Isa. 13:19–22; Jer. 51:24–26, 62–64. By political Babylon is meant the Gentile world-system. . . . It may be added that, in Scripture symbolism, Egypt stands for the world as such; Babylon for the world of corrupt power and corrupted religion; Nineveh for the pride, the haughty glory of the world.
>
> Verses 12–16 look forward to the apocalyptic judgments (Rev. 6–13). Verses 17–22 have a near and far view. They predict the destruction of the literal Babylon then existing; with the further statement that, once destroyed, Babylon should never be rebuilt (cf. Jer. 51:61–64). All of this has been literally fulfilled. But the place of this prediction in a great prophetic strain which looks forward to the destruction of both politico-Babylon and ecclesio-Babylon in the time of the Beast shows that the destruction of the actual Babylon typifies the greater destruction yet to come upon the mystical Babylons (pp. 724–25).

The end of symbolical Babylon or confusion is described in Revelation under three aspects—the ecclesiastical, commercial, and political.

Chapter 17 records the final destruction of ecclesiasticism. This destruction is of the great system known as Rome. The identification is so exact that the Church of Rome does recognize it to some extent. She incorporates all the mysteries of ancient Babylon with those of her own forming. Being centered in the city of Rome, she sits upon seven hills (Rev. 17:9), she reaches her agelong ambition to rule the kings of the earth (Rev. 17:18), she was in the day that John wrote the center of world trade (Rev. 18:3, 11–13), she is the corrupter of nations (Rev. 17:2; 18:3; 19:2), and the persecutor of saints (Rev. 17:6). Following the removal of the true Church from the earth, this apostate church will gather into her fold all that remains of a professing Christendom (Protestantism) and will be permitted to realize her unholy ambition to rule over the earth, riding the scarlet-colored beast. From this place of authority she is cast down and destroyed by political Babylon as headed up by the beast. That apostate church is by inspiration termed "THE MOTHER OF HARLOTS." In chapter 18 commercialism with its confusion is brought to destruction. It falls under the hand of God in a judgment which the kings execute as God wills (cf. Rev. 17:17, 20). The destruction of commercialism as recorded by John is in three parts—(a) the fact of the destruction (Rev. 18:1–8), (b) the human viewpoint thereof (vss. 9–19), and (c) the angelic viewpoint (vss. 20–24). A world system which is built on greed and desire for riches can have no understanding of a future state of society wherein that element will be wholly lacking. For the sake of gain nations have gone into devastating wars and destroyed the lives of their young men and wasted their resources. A world undominated by greed is in prospect but beyond human imagination. Finally, the whole structure of human government, Gentile authority in its last form under the rule of the beast and all that belongs to this vast political structure, gives way under the mighty crushing power of the returning King of kings (Rev. 19:11–21). Thus the way is cleared for "the God of heaven" to "set up a kingdom which shall never be destroyed" (Dan. 2:44–45; cf. Ps. 2:7–9; Isa. 63:1–6; 2 Thess. 2:8–12).

Confusion must reign in every part of human existence on the earth when the divine order and arrangement is disturbed, which arrangement provides for Israel, the center of all earthly realities, to be inside her land in blessing under Messiah's rule with the nations sharing in that benediction. Such is the glorious future predicted, but it cannot be realized apart from the destruction of every form of babel that now infests the earth.

BAPTISM, REAL

Early writers on the general theme of baptism distinguished between *real* baptism, which is wrought by the Holy Spirit, and *ritual* baptism, which is administered with water. These terms well serve to distinguish between the two forms of baptism which are so clearly identified in the New Testament. Great significance should be attached to the fact that the same term, βαπτίζω, is used in defining each of these baptisms, and it follows that any definition of this great New Testament word, if it is to be true, must be as applicable to the one form of baptism as to the other. The root word, βάπτω, which is used but three times by the New Testament—cf. Luke 16:24; John 13:26; Revelation 19:13—occurs in the first two passages with its primary meaning, which is *to dip*, while the use of the word in the third passage—Revelation 19:13—illustrates its secondary meaning, which is *to dye* or *stain* (cf. Isa. 63:1–6). This evolution of the word from its primary meaning to a secondary meaning is reasonable. That which is dyed or stained by dipping—βάπτω —persists as βάπτω when dyed or stained by any other method. In like manner, the word βαπτίζω in its primary import means *to immerse* or *submerge;* but in its secondary meaning, which is a development from the primary import, it refers to an influence which one thing may exercise over another, or as Dr. J. W. Dale defines it "to bring into complete subjection to an influence or to imbue with virtues." As an immersion serves to bring the thing immersed under the influence of the element into which it is submerged, so in the evolution of the present word a thing becomes baptized by another when even without physical intusposition or envelopment one thing exercises a positive influence over another. Apart from the recognition of this distinction, little understanding of many uses for this word will be gained. A complete baptism is recognized in the New Testament, for example, when without an intusposition or physical envelopment an individual is baptized into the remission of sin, into repentance, into the name of the Father, the Son, and the Holy Ghost, baptized by drinking the cup of suffering, or as Israel was baptized into Moses by the cloud and the sea, or when one is brought under the power of the Holy Spirit, or when by the Spirit all believers are baptized into Christ's Body. The term *secondary* as related to the latter sense or use of βαπτίζω does not imply inferiority; it is secondary only so far as one meaning is derived from the other. The secondary import of this word is employed in all passages which refer to real (the Spirit's) baptism and the relative importance of this baptism over every other is immeasurable. No less an authority than Dr. J. W. Dale, who with great scholarship and sincerity spent much of his lifetime in preparing four large volumes on the subject of baptism, has asserted that in his opinion βαπτίζω is used only in its secondary meaning in the New Testament.

Baleful neglect of the doctrine of the Spirit's baptism is reflected in lexicons and theological works on baptism. Definitions are given and statements made which seem not to recognize the special use of βαπτίζω in relation to the Holy Spirit or the Body of Christ. Men may differ, as they have, over the meaning of this word in ritual baptism, but there is no room for a difference of opinion over the use of the word or its meaning and implications when employed to indicate that baptism which the Holy Spirit accomplishes. Some writers, indeed, have assumed to discuss this word without reference to its use in relation to real baptism.

Much has been written earlier in this work (Vol. VI more especially) on real baptism or that baptism which the Holy Spirit accomplishes, and it has been pointed out that, according to the definition assigned the secondary meaning of this word, the gift of the Spirit by Christ is a baptism (cf. Matt. 3:11; Mark 1:8; Luke 3:16; John 1:33; Acts 1:4-5), and since the Holy Spirit is received by every believer at the moment he is saved, he is thus baptized by the Spirit, having been brought under the influence of the Spirit. However, as true as this interpretation is, it should be distinguished from the erroneous teaching which contends that the Spirit is received as a second work of grace, which teaching confounds the Spirit's filling—that which is unto an empowered life—with the Spirit's baptism into Christ's Body, that which is unto position and standing before God.

What is termed *the baptism by the Spirit*—not, *in* or *unto the Spirit* —is His mighty undertaking by which He joins the individual believer to Christ's Body and thus to Christ Himself as the Head of the Body. Because of this great achievement on the part of the Spirit, the believer is from that moment in Christ and is thus brought under the influence of His Headship. No influence could be more transforming, more purifying relative to position, or more vital in its outworking than that engendered by a removal from the fallen headship of Adam into the exalted Headship of Christ. No other transformation is comparable to this. Though there is no physical intusposition when one is brought under the influence which the gift of the Spirit provides and though there is no physical intusposition when one is brought by the Spirit into the Headship of the resurrected Christ, the New Testament designates these influences as baptisms and sets them forth as vital and real above all other baptisms. Especially is union to Christ seen to be distinctive in point of far-reaching transformations. It is thus properly designated the real baptism. This vast theme has its due consideration under Pneumatology (Vol. VI).

BAPTISM, RITUAL

In approaching the theme of ritual baptism it is recognized that over this subject the most bitter divisions have been allowed to arise in the church—divisions and exclusions for which it is difficult to account in the light of two facts: (1) the great majority of those who are given to separations confess that there is no saving value in the ordinance and (2) all who look into it with freedom from prejudice recognize that fruitful, spiritual Christians are to be found on each side of the controversy. In a work on Systematic Theology which purports to be faithful in declaring all aspects of Biblical doctrine, the consideration of ritual baptism cannot be eliminated, though to do so would be easier and to avoid countering good men would in itself be desirable. If the history of the controversy as it has been waged in the past few generations is a fair basis on which to estimate the present and the future, an extended work on theology itself—in spite of the way it reaches into all such vast fields of inexhaustible themes—may, like friendships, Christian unity, and fellowship, be discredited and shunned for no other reason than that this one ordinance is presented in a way which is contrary to the views which another holds. In such a matter as the mode of ritual baptism and what it represents, agreement with all good men is impossible when some of them are on each side of the controversy. It is reasonable, however, that those who are quite free to publish their own views should accord the same liberty to those who disagree. Securing converts to an idea certainly is not intended in the discussion to follow. That which is sincerely believed on each side of the controversy is to be stated as nearly as can be done apart from personal prejudice. The value to the student of such a declaration may not be questioned, for, regardless of his own convictions and however they were formed, he should know precisely what others believe who hold different views, else how can he be assured that he is justified in the position he defends? A man is on weak ground when he speaks vehemently and dogmatically respecting his own belief and yet does not know or understand what, in exact terms, his opponent believes. That an individual after many years of investigation should come to the point of personal convictions on such a divisive theme as this needs no apology.

This unhappy discussion has usually centered upon the question of the mode by which ritual baptism should be administered. The immersionist (this designation though inaccurate, as will be demonstrated later, is used here by way of accommodation) is one who demands an intusposition of the whole body in water. The affusionist is one who sprinkles or pours the baptismal water. With regard to proportion in membership, the former class of Christians may claim perhaps one-third and the latter two-thirds of the Protestant Church. However, the issue is not one of the mode of expressing an idea or teaching; it concerns the actual idea to be expressed. In the case of the immersionist, the object believed to lie back of the ordinance is to enact the believer's codeath, coburial, and coresurrection with Christ, and with that in view the mode he employs is to him appropriate. In the case of the affusionist, the object lying behind the ordinance is to represent the coming of the Holy Spirit into the believer's life with all the varied values of that Presence. With this in view, the mode he employs is to him appropriate. The immersionist rejects all forms of affusion simply because it does not express his understanding of the meaning of the ordinance. In like manner, the affusionist rejects the mode the immersionist employs simply because it does not express his understanding of the meaning in the ordinance. The disagreement, when centered on the mode without reference to the meaning, has been carried on in aimless and hopeless fashion. Less assertive human determination of mode and more humble and gracious consideration of the meaning in ritual baptism is greatly to be desired.

The instructed affusionist recognizes much significance in the facts that the greatest operations of the Holy Spirit are in the New Testament termed baptisms—the same word being used as is employed when referring to ritual baptism—and that the Apostle writes of "one baptism" (Eph. 4:5), not, one mode of baptism. By the affusionist this reference to "one baptism" is explained on the grounds that ritual baptism is but the outward sign or symbol of an inward reality, which reality is wrought by the Holy Spirit, and that the real and the ritual baptisms thus combine to form *one baptism* as substance and corresponding shadow (cf. 1 Cor. 12:13; Gal. 3:27). The affusionist also believes that, as there is one unquestioned ordinance—the Lord's Supper—which represents the death of Christ, it is reasonable to expect that there would be, not a second ordinance representing that death, but an ordinance representing the work of the Holy Spirit.

When ritual baptism is deemed to be a cleansing from defilement (cf. Acts 22:16), the immersionist contends that, in so far as baptism is a cleansing, water symbolizes the cleansing blood of Christ and that the water when applied must cover the entire body. On the other hand, the affusionist, believing that it is the blood of Christ which cleanseth from all sin and that His blood must be applied by the Holy Spirit, understands ritual baptism to be related thus to the work of the Holy Spirit. The affusionist observes that all ceremonial cleansings prescribed in the Old Testament were accomplished by sprinkling, pouring, or laving, but not by intusposition.

The immersionist relates ritual baptism to Christ's death, burial, and resurrection and on the ground of the fact that the believer is said to have been baptized into Christ's death, burial, and resurrection according to Romans 6:1–10 and Colossians 2:11–13. It is believed by the immersionist that, on the strength of these passages, the candidate for ritual baptism should enact the death, burial, and resurrection of Christ as a recognition of the relation which these hold to salvation, forgiveness, and justification, whereas the affusionist believes that these Scriptures cited above are related only to the ground of sanctification, concerning which no ordinance has been prescribed. The affusionist, if instructed in the truth at all, believes that the codeath, coburial, and coresurrection referred to in these two passages have only to do with the judgment of the sin nature, that no instruction is given to enact what Christ has done but rather the believer is enjoined to "reckon" that to be achieved which Christ has wrought and to be encouraged to believe that deliverance from the power of sin is thus made possible, the Holy Spirit being free so to act for children of God.

The claim of the affusionist is that, though immersion may have been practiced from early times, it was not until the last three or four hundred years that ritual baptism was given any meaning other than as related to the Holy Spirit's work in the believer. On the basis of this, it is believed that through a misinterpretation of both Romans 6:1–10 and Colossians 2:11–13 ritual baptism came to be considered by those practicing immersion to be an independent, unrelated, and sufficient baptism in itself, thus proposing so to speak two distinct baptisms. Affusionists, it may be said, are often misunderstood because they do not stress the mode of ritual baptism. They believe that ritual baptism does not consist in the *way* it is done, but in the *thing* that is done.

So, also, those among immersionists who practice trine immersion require that the candidate be dipped face down (since Christ bowed His head in death) three times—once in the name of the Father, once in the name of the Son, and once in the name of the Holy Ghost. The majority of immersionists reject trine immersion as having no direct warrant in the New Testament and because they see in it an enacting three times of that which Christ did but once.

Since it is true that the meaning of ritual baptism is expressed to some degree by the mode of its administration, it is important to note that which may be intimated in the Scriptures respecting the mode. The vast majority of adherents to the church assume that the mode practiced by their denomination and to which they have been accustomed from childhood is the right and only mode. Some, however, upon reading the Authorized Version translation, which reflects the personal convictions of some of its translators, believe that the mode is there indicated in the text and this without an understanding of what the original declares. Though beyond the field of investigation on the part of those who consider only the text in English, the truth here, as in every doctrinal issue, is determined by the original. In this connection it is of interest to note that, while in every generation of recent history there have been scholarly men who believed in and practiced immersion, there have been, as pointed out by Dr. A. T. Robertson, the Greek scholar of the Southern Baptist Church, but eighteen worthy New Testament lexicographers and every one of these, being clergymen, practiced affusion in their ministry. Dr. Robertson also declares that no immersionist has ever written a New Testament lexicon; but he fails to give a reason why these eighteen men, though in their lexicons they give *immersion* as the primary meaning of βαπτίζω, practiced affusion as he asserts they did. In seeking the answer, rather than to assume that these good men were untrue to their convictions, it would be well to look more carefully at the Greek text which they interpret and to give scope, as these men evidently did, to the more vital, secondary meaning of the word βαπτίζω. This line of investigation should consider (1) the meaning of the word, (2) the Scriptures involved, (3) the prepositions employed, and (4) the baptism incidents recorded.

1. THE MEANING OF THE WORD. Continuing the discussion, as begun above under real baptism, respecting the primary and secondary meanings of the two words βάπτω and βαπτίζω, it is now to be emphasized that the secondary meaning of βαπτίζω obtains in all instances where there is a baptism apart from a physical intusposition or envelopment. To illustrate this, Christ termed His anticipated sufferings a baptism (Matt. 20:22-23). This could not refer to the ritual baptism by John which was then long accomplished, nor to a baptism with the Spirit in which He as Son could have no part. This passage means nothing unless suffering is itself a true baptism. Hence the affusionist in his credence believes that even ritual baptism, which to him represents the work of the Holy Spirit, calls for no physical envelopment.

Again, the same technical distinction in meaning obtains between the two Greek words βάπτω and βαπτίζω in their primary sense as is seen between *dip* and *immerse,* which are the English equivalents. A dipping involves two actions—*putting in* and *taking out,* whereas to immerse involves but one action—*putting in,* and in the case of the baptism into Christ with its limitless advantages (cf. 1 Cor. 12:13; Gal. 3:27) to be taken out is the one thing not desired. In the light of this it is clear that to say, as has commonly been said, that "βαπτίζω means *to dip* and only *to dip* throughout all Greek literature" is erroneous and misleading when the word does not mean *to dip* in any Greek literature. All of this indicates the inaccuracy in use of the word *immersion* to represent a ritual baptism by dipping. In this same connection, it is both suggestive and instructive to consider the use of βαπτίζω in the Septuagint, a Greek translation of the Old Testament thought to have been made by seventy scholarly men about two hundred years before Christ. The accepted meaning of this word is disclosed there. It will be found that βαπτίζω translates five Hebrew words—*to affright* (once), *to come* (once), *to pierce* (once), *to dye* (three times), and *to cleanse* (sixteen times). Some of these actions could not include an intusposition and none of them require it. Truth, then, must be established by more than bald, dogmatic, erroneous human assertions. The affusionist claims it cannot be proved that the mode of ritual baptism is indicated in the meaning of the word βαπτίζω.

2. THE SCRIPTURES INVOLVED. Three passages develop the doctrinal significance of Christ's death, burial, and resurrection as one achievement on His part and as a substitution for others, namely, Romans 6:1-10; 1 Corinthians 15:3-4; and Colossians 2:11-13. 1 Corinthians 15:3-4 clearly declares Christ's death, burial, and resurrection as a substitute for sinners that they may be saved; it is unto forgiveness and justification for them. However, in the other passages— Romans 6:1-10 and Colossians 2:11-13—Christ's death, burial, and resurrection are referred to (in Colossians His death is termed a circumcision) as a judgment of the old nature. Not apprehending the stupendous importance and meaning of Christ's death for the believer's sin nature and not realizing that this achievement by Christ calls for no re-enacting by an ordinance, some, being impressed with the meaningful words in these Scriptures (baptism, burial, and resurrection), have concluded that the mode of ritual baptism is indicated by these two passages. Over against this the affusionist, if aware of the truth at all, contends that these Scriptures, like 1 Corinthians 15:3-4, teach that which Christ has done—a thing to believe—and not a thing to be done. Cocrucifixion, codeath, coburial, and coresurrection, being wrought and accomplished for the believer, become a baptism, a dominating influence over the believer which is as immeasurable in its extent and value as infinity itself. Considering further the Scripture involved, it may be observed that much has been made of the statement in John 3:23 which reads, "And John also was baptizing in Ænon near to Salim, because there was much water there: and they came, and were baptized." When the arresting words *much water* are properly understood as *many springs*—such as would be required for the physical needs of the throngs of people and their beasts—the passage contributes nothing toward a modal ideal for ritual baptism. Ænon is likely to be identified as a sloping hillside with springs of water, but no body of water available.

Thus, again, the affusionist contends that it cannot be proved from the important Scriptures involved that ritual baptism is appointed to be given by immersion.

3. THE PREPOSITIONS EMPLOYED. The usual impression regarding the mode of ritual baptism which one might gain who reads only the English text of the New Testament is molded more by the prepositions that are used in the English text than by any other factor in the case. Four prepositions come up at once for consideration. The point to be developed which concerns all of serious mind is that the particular

translation of these prepositions as found in the English text is not the only meaning which the same English text assigns to these words in other like instances. All familiar with the Greek text recognize that a great latitude of meaning is given to prepositions, and that usually the correct sense will be determined by the more or less obvious meaning belonging to the text in which the word is found. It should hardly be needful to state that because a certain translation appears in the English text it is not necessarily the best rendering. The prepositions to be considered are:

a. 'Eν, which has 36 possible meanings and which in Matthew 3:6 has been translated '*in* Jordan' is also translated in the English Bible by the words *at, on,* or *with* 330 times, could be so translated in the text cited. The sense is somewhat changed when it is translated 'at Jordan' rather than 'in Jordan.'

b. 'Aπό has 20 English meanings, and is used thus in Matthew 3:16: "And Jesus, when he was baptized, went up straightway out of the water." This preposition, here translated *out of,* is translated by the word *from* 374 times in the New Testament and could properly be so translated in Matthew 3:16, in which case the declaration would be that Jesus went up straightway *from* the water.

c. Eἰς has 26 meanings in English and is used in Acts 8:38 for the declaration that "they went down both *into* the water, both Philip and the eunuch; and he baptized him." This preposition is translated in the New Testament 538 times by the word *unto* and could as accurately be so rendered here. It will be observed that going unto or into the water did not constitute the baptism, for Philip also went in with the eunuch.

d. 'Eκ has 24 English meanings and is translated in Acts 8:39 thus, "And when they were come up *out of* the water . . ." This same word is translated *from* 168 times in the New Testament and could as correctly have been so translated here. Thus it would read that Philip and the eunuch went down unto the water and came up from the water.

Though the immersionist depends much on the way these prepositions are translated in order to establish the mode of ritual baptism, the affusionist contends that the mode of baptism cannot be determined by the prepositions used.

4. THE INCIDENTS RECORDED. First in this kind of list would be the baptism of Christ, which event has had an extended treatment as a division of Christology (Vol. V) and need not be restated here. It is often declared by those who practice immersion that the believer is to "follow Christ in baptism" assuming that Christ was baptized by im-

mersion; but, whatever the mode employed, the believer may follow Christ in moral issues only—not in His official acts—and His baptism, being altogether unique and wholly unrelated to any feature of the Christian ritual, is official and therefore never presented in the New Testament as an example. Christ was baptized at the hands of John but not by John's baptism as such, which was unto repentance and the remission of sins. Similarly, what is termed *John's baptism,* since it was not accepted by the Apostle Paul—he rebaptized twelve men who had submitted to John's baptism (cf. Acts 19:1-7)—does not constitute Christian baptism. It is pointed out by the affusionist that the baptism of all three thousand converts of Pentecost by immersion is an impossibility owing to the unpreparedness of the vast throng and of those who officiated, and owing also to the lack of adequate facilities for such a stupendous undertaking. But the case of the three thousand being baptized could easily be a reference to the Spirit's baptism. So, also, it is noted by the affusionists that the Apostle Paul stood up where he was upon the arrival of Ananias (Acts 9:18) and was baptized. The case of Philip baptizing the eunuch, as has been indicated, is much varied by the interpretation given the prepositions that are used.

The affusionist claims that no mode of ritual baptism is directly taught in the New Testament, but that as sprinkling, pouring, and laving were prescribed in the Old Testament for consecration and cleansing and as the Jews of Christ's day were accustomed only to such modes, it is most probable that these modes were brought forward into the new order. Had there been a change from the Old Testament requirement to a new mode for the church, it ought to have been indicated clearly. It may be concluded, then, that the mode of ritual baptism is not determined either by the meaning of the word $\beta a\pi\tau i\zeta\omega$ or the Scriptures involved, the prepositions or the incidents recorded. Had these obvious facts been recognized, much of the present useless contention and separation might have been avoided.

PEDOBAPTISM. Any consideration of the general theme of ritual baptism is not complete unless some attention is given to pedo or infant baptism. Here again there is difference of opinion and practice, but the same demarcation which divides over mode of baptism is not found at this point. Though the great majority of affusionists practice pedobaptism, some practice it and have infants baptized by dipping in water. The pedobaptism problem is not so much one of mode, then, as of baptizing infants at all. Those who reject infant baptism do so with emphasis upon the idea that ritual baptism must be restricted to believers, therefore it could not apply to children. The same company declare that they find no warrant in the New Testament for the practice. On the other hand, the very large proportion of the professing church do baptize infants and for various reasons. (1) By some who practice pedobaptism it is assumed that there is saving merit in ritual baptism, which feature of the doctrine is rejected by the great majority of Protestants administering infant baptism. (2) It is believed by a large percentage that there is some connection between the rite of circumcision as required for the Jewish child according to the Old Testament and the baptism of children according to the New Testament. In the attempt to establish and magnify its one-covenant idea, Covenant Theology has contended for this supposed relationship between the two dispensations. Israelites, however, were not partakers of their covenants on the ground of circumcision; they were born into covenant relationship to God. Therefore, it is not demonstrated that children by baptism become "children of the covenant." To be consistent, those who baptize infants because of an assumed covenant relationship should baptize only male children and only on the eighth day. (3) Others believe that since the household was included in five out of seven baptisms mentioned in the Acts infants were included. Those opposing pedobaptism claim it cannot be demonstrated that there were infants or small children in these particular households. But such as defend pedobaptism believe that it is highly probable some children were included and that the term *household* is not intended to represent childless homes, but the normal family with its children. (4) Instructed parents in presenting children for baptism magnify the household promises set forth in the New Testament (cf. 1 Cor. 7:12–14), believing that the promises for blessing, though not for salvation, extend to the families of God's children. It is contended that it is the right of Christian parents to assert their faith respecting the future salvation of their child by the baptism of that child. The energy with which pedobaptism is rejected often all but implies that the one who so resists holds perhaps unconsciously that ritual baptism is a saving ordinance. Whatever may or may not have been included in the records set forth in Acts, household baptism was enjoined and practiced.

In concluding this discussion of ritual baptism it may be stated that all who claim the right of private judgment in the matter of the mode of their baptism should accord the same right to others. There should be latitude enough in any assembly of believers for these variations. The sin—if such there be—of administering this ordinance in an unscriptural way could never compare with the greater sin of exclusion, separation, and the breaking of the outward manifestations of the unity of the Spirit. That believers remain in the unbroken bonds of fellowship and affection is, according to the New Testament, far more important than is the mode of ritual baptism. The world is to be impressed with the love of Christians one for the other (cf. John 13:34–35; 17:21–23). It is needless to point out that separations and contentions over a mode of baptism have little value in the eyes of the unsaved.

BIBLIOLOGY

Having been considered at length in Volume I of this work, this, the first major division of Systematic Theology, need be given no more than a brief restatement here. Nothing could be more fundamental in the sphere of human knowledge than that God has caused His own Word to be written in a form which man can comprehend and has preserved that Word through the ages of human history for the benefit of all men. The extent of the field of knowledge thus added to man's own restricted observation is beyond human computation. Since this vast unfolding of added truth has come to men and has been their possession for more than three millenniums and has all been incorporated into that which man now understands, it becomes no more than a speculation to talk of what man could have known had he been left to himself or to ponder what, in its far-reaching effect, has been revealed to him through the ages. Man began under the direct tutelage of God in the Garden of Eden and has ever been indebted to God for many and varied revelations. Shutting God out of all consideration and thus ignoring the source of practically all that they know, unbelieving men are filled with vainglory over what is assumed to be the attainments of man. Some facts are discovered about the stars and their systematic arrangement, yet with little or no disposition to recognize the One who created the stars and who upholds all things. Thus in astronomy, as in other branches of science, the inability of fallen man to see beyond the reach of his own limited powers is evident. No sense of appreciation seems to exist that he has been given an eye to see or an arm to achieve. All of this is exceedingly unnatural, as likewise is the rejection of God's revelation, and speaks of a fallen humanity under the domination of the great enemy of God. On the other hand, to the mind that by saving grace has been rescued from the insanity of sin and is enlightened by the Spirit of God, the Bible becomes what it actually is, the very Word of God to man which imparts treasures of knowledge as marvelous as the realms of light from whence they proceed. No declaration is more revealing nor could there be a more accurate analysis of the mass of unregenerate humanity in its attitude toward the Scriptures than that which affirms: "But the natural man receiveth not the things of the Spirit of God: for they are foolishness unto him: neither can he know them, because they are spiritually discerned" (1 Cor. 2:14). And how the sphere of human limitations is unveiled by Christ when He said: "Except a man be born again, he cannot see the kingdom of God" (John 3:3)! So, also, it is declared, "Through faith we understand" (Heb. 11:3).

As science creates nothing but rather seeks to discover the character of the realities which God has caused to exist, so the theologian strives to comprehend, analyze, and systematize that which God has revealed. The theologian creates nothing; his sphere of endeavor, strictly speaking, is not even that of demonstrating that the materials he handles are real or trustworthy. If by him the Word of God is held in doubt, he is by so much disqualified even to enter the theologian's field of investigation. Accepting all that the Bible claims for itself, however, the theologian is concerned with the Bible's message.

Evidence that the Bible is God's Word written appears in a form both *external* and *internal*. That which is external lies in the field of the Bible's unique history, its essential character, and its effects. That which is internal relates to its own claims for itself, which claims are fully sustained.

Various major divisions of the structure of the Bible and consideration of its doctrinal message have already been presented and enlarged upon throughout this work. The more vital facts respecting the character of the Bible are:

1. A REVELATION FROM GOD. By this declaration it is asserted that the Bible presents material and facts which could not otherwise be known by man. To become aware of these truths and to list them may well occupy the student for a lifetime. Though there are many subjects presented in the Bible about which men would naturally have some information apart from revelation, it is clear that in the greater spheres

of truth he is wholly restricted to that which God has disclosed, and the true value of what he might know naturally is completely qualified when seen in its relation to that which is revealed.

2. INSPIRED BY GOD, which means that all Scripture proceeds from God as if His very breath (cf. 2 Tim. 3:16). Portions of the truth revealed may have some recognition by men apart from revelation. Its declaration in the Sacred Text of God's utterance, nevertheless, is said by God in God's own way, and therefore is correct to infinity. Such a statement refers only to the original writings and not to translations of Scripture, though doubtless God has exercised competent direction and protection over translations; certainly there is no direct statement from God that translations would be made without error. Concerning the original text, it is said that holy men "spake as they were moved" (or borne along) by the Holy Spirit (2 Pet. 1:21).

3. UNDERSTOOD ONLY BY DIVINE ILLUMINATION. Even things of Scripture otherwise commonplace are known in their true value only by the illuminating of the Spirit. Three human attitudes toward the Bible are declared in 1 Corinthians 2:14—3:1. The unsaved or "natural man" cannot "receive" revealed truth, the spiritual man "discerneth all things," and the carnal Christian can receive only the milk and not the meat of the Word of God. Christ promised that the Holy Spirit would guide into all truth (John 16:13–15), and the Apostle states that the Spirit is given to the believer that he may know the things of God (1 Cor. 2:12).

4. MUST BE RIGHTLY INTERPRETED. The whole field of hermeneutics, which is a theological discipline in itself, is introduced here. Doubtless the key to the understanding of the Bible is the recognition of the specific purpose of God in each of the succeeding ages of human history. Dispensational distinctions have always engendered true expository preaching, while Covenant Theology has tended toward a closing and slighting of the Word of God.

5. A LIFE-IMPARTING MESSAGE. The Word of God is active and dynamic. Isaiah declares that it will "accomplish" that which God purposes for it to do (Isa. 55:11), Jeremiah likens the Word of God to fire and to a hammer that breaketh in pieces the rock (Jer. 23:29), and in Hebrews 4:12 it is said to be "quick and powerful"—that is, living and active. Happy is he who through knowledge of the Scriptures is able to wield this living power.

6. ITS CANONICITY DETERMINED BY GOD, that is, the choice from all existing literature of the books that were to form the two Testaments

was under the care of God. Having caused certain documents to be written with a view to their place in the Sacred Volume, it is certain that He would cause them to take the place which He had assigned them. It is true that men acted in the forming of the canon, including in it such books as had the evident imprint of God upon them; but still God was guiding them in the selection, just as He guided the men who wrote the text itself.

7. SPEAKS WITH THE AUTHORITY OF GOD. The primary character of the Bible is such as to lend it authority. It speaks as the voice of Him who created all things and to whom all things belong. To those who believe the Bible and heed its precepts it becomes an unerring lamp unto the feet and a light unto the path (Ps. 119:105). The Word of God fails not.

BLASPHEMY

No sin of man is more obviously a repudiation of God and insult to His holy Person than that of blasphemy, which sin in its usual form consists of taking a name of Deity upon the lips in an empty, idle, and trifling manner. There is such a sin as that of addressing God Himself with blasphemy. In his coming day the beast, or man of sin, will assault God and His name (Rev. 13:6), and thus in the hour of God's judgments upon men they will blaspheme God and curse His name (Rev. 16:9, 11, 21). However, blasphemy in general is not addressed to God and consists in a more or less irreverent use of His name in oaths and curses addressed to other people or things. Over against this may be cited the formal reverence on the part of Israel when for centuries they, with more or less real consideration, refused to pronounce the name of Jehovah, considering that particular name too sacred for human utterance.

1. THE OLD TESTAMENT DOCTRINE. This doctrine is set forth in the following Scriptures: Exodus 20:7; Leviticus 24:10–16; 1 Kings 21:10–23; 2 Kings 19:6, 22; Isaiah 37:6, 23; 65:7. The punishment for blasphemy, like that related to every other of the Ten Commandments, was stoning unto death. It is asserted that David's sin caused the enemies of Jehovah to blaspheme (cf. 2 Sam. 12:14).

2. THE NEW TESTAMENT DOCTRINE. A much wider range for the

possibilities of evil through blasphemy is presented in the New Testament. A fivefold division may be suggested.

a. BLASPHEMY BY JEWS AGAINST CHRIST, which took place according to Acts 13:45 and 18:6: "But when the Jews saw the multitudes, they were filled with envy, and spake against those things which were spoken by Paul, contradicting and blaspheming"; "And when they opposed themselves, and blasphemed, he shook his raiment, and said unto them, Your blood be upon your own heads; I am clean: from henceforth I will go unto the Gentiles." In the light of the penalty by stoning which they risked, it is evident that the hatred for, and resistance of, the truth on the part of the Jews toward Christ was as violent as it could be. The precise form of their blasphemy is not revealed. Probably it was a direct cursing of Christ, whom the Apostle proclaimed as God manifest in the flesh.

b. BLASPHEMY AGAINST IDOLS. In Acts 19:37 intimation is given that it was somewhat common for men unsympathetic to an idol to blaspheme that venerated object.

c. BLASPHEMY AGAINST THE PERSON OF GOD. This is most serious by its very nature. Reference is not to the taking of the name of God in vain; it is rather blasphemy directly addressed to God and against Himself. The passages, already cited above, were Revelation 13:6 and 16:9, 11, 21.

d. CHRIST ACCUSED OF BLASPHEMY. It was claimed by the Jews in their unbelief toward Christ that He blasphemed when saying He had power on earth to forgive sins and when He actually did forgive sin. They said, "Why doth this man thus speak blasphemies? who can forgive sins but God only?" (Mark 2:7; cf. Matt. 9:3; Luke 5:21).

e. BLASPHEMY IN RELATION TO THE HOLY SPIRIT. This special form of attack has been termed *the unpardonable sin*. That blasphemy against the Holy Spirit in a certain form of it was said by Christ to be something unpardonable is certain. After the Jews had ascribed to Satan the works which Christ wrought by the Holy Spirit, it is written that Christ said to them, "Wherefore I say unto you, All manner of sin and blasphemy shall be forgiven unto men: but the blasphemy against the Holy Ghost shall not be forgiven unto men. And whosoever speaketh a word against the Son of man, it shall be forgiven him: but whosoever speaketh against the Holy Ghost, it shall not be forgiven him, neither in this world, neither in the world to come" (Matt. 12:31–32); "Verily I say unto you, All sins shall be forgiven unto the sons of men, and blasphemies wherewith soever they shall blaspheme: but he that shall blaspheme against the Holy Ghost hath never forgiveness, but is in danger of eternal damnation: because they said, He hath an unclean spirit" (Mark 3:28–30). For want of attention to all that is involved in these and other related Scriptures, there has been a most injurious application on the part of preachers, especially evangelists, of these very Scriptures to the present age. First, it should be noted that this sin against the Holy Spirit consisted in asserting that Christ's works, which were wrought by the Holy Spirit, were accomplished on the contrary by Satan. Such a setting could not be found now since Christ is not in the world as He was then, nor is He undertaking in the same way to do works by the Holy Spirit. It is therefore impossible for this particular sin to be committed today. To say that attributing works that men may be doing in the power of the Spirit to Satan is the same offense is to go utterly beyond what is written. The possibility of this particular sin being committed ceased with Christ's removal from the earth. But even more emphatically it is to be declared that the so-called unpardonable sin cannot be present where there is a "whosoever will" gospel being preached, else reservations must be made to the effect that a "whosoever will" gospel must except those who have committed an unpardonable sin. Every invitation and promise related to the salvation of lost men would have to carry those same restrictions if there were an unpardonable sin. The promises and invitations would then be addressed to those only who have not so sinned. That no such condition is ever imposed in any grace relationship of the present need not be argued. In attempting to project an unpardonable sin into this age, men have seized upon almost any serious evil as the unpardonable sin, but always without Biblical support. Often Hebrews 6:4–9; 10:26–29; and 1 John 5:16 have been referred to as added Scripture bearing upon supposedly unpardonable sin. These passages, however, though deeply serious in their import, bear no relation to an unpardonable sin. When considering the subject of blasphemy against the Holy Spirit, it may well be noted that, quite beyond human explanation, men do not swear in the name of the Third Person. From this fact it may be concluded that there is now and ever has been a peculiar sanctity belonging to the Holy Spirit. His very name and title implies this.

3. BLASPHEMY IN GENERAL. Such taking of the name of God in vain as is prohibited by Exodus 20:7 consists in using a name of Deity with an oath whether consciously or carelessly done. Usually the thoughts of the one thus profaning the name are not directed to God in any sense at all.

BLINDNESS

In general, the truth respecting blindness is set forth by the Scriptures with reference to that which is physical, that which is judicial, and that which is spiritual. The theme is extensive and vital. These three aspects of blindness though somewhat related should be considered separately.

1. PHYSICAL. At a time when physical blindness due to disease met with no control, to be blind physically was a very common experience and, no doubt, that Christ in His day healed so many who were blind is to be explained by the fact that physical blindness and its healing are symbolical of both judicial and spiritual blindness and their healing. The cure of physical blindness was itself an amazing reality; there could be no doubt respecting its actual achievement by Christ. But ever to be kept in mind is the truth that He who wrought such wonders in healing the physically blind by so much proved regarding Himself how He is able to heal other forms of blindness as well. It was the testimony of one whom He healed, "Whereas I was blind, now I see" (John 9:25). Growing out of this incident, a lengthy discussion between Christ and the Pharisees ensued. The healing of the blind man resulted in his own salvation, for later he said, "Lord, I believe." It is in this context that Christ connected the physical disability with Israel's judicial blindness. For a moment at least, too, the Pharisees seemed to realize the possibility of their being blind themselves. This passage reads: "And Jesus said, For judgment I am come into this world, that they which see not might see; and that they which see might be made blind. And some of the Pharisees which were with him heard these words, and said unto him, Are we blind also? Jesus said unto them, If ye were blind, ye should have no sin: but now ye say, We see; therefore your sin remaineth" (John 9:39–41). Here it is made clear that physical blindness and its cure symbolizes judicial blindness and its healing. Even blind Pharisees were able to see this relationship.

2. JUDICIAL. Only the Jews are concerned in this phase of the doctrine of blindness, and a difficult problem arises when it is remembered that this failure of sight comes upon them as a judgment from God. Racial responsibility is in view, otherwise no accounting can be made

for the fact that later generations must suffer for the sins of their fathers. Such a situation would be more difficult to understand were it not for Jehovah's revealed purpose to bring that people eventually into everlasting blessing. The principle of racial sin and suffering as well as racial righteousness and blessing is announced in the second commandment, which declares: "I the LORD thy God am a jealous God, visiting the iniquity of the fathers upon the children unto the third and fourth generation of them that hate me; and shewing mercy unto thousands of them that love me, and keep my commandments" (Ex. 20:5–6). The Jews of this dispensation are suffering, in part, for the sins of their fathers many centuries ago. Still, their sin in its national character will eventually be remembered no more. This hope is declared in the Scripture with great assurance. It is written, "Thus saith the LORD, which giveth the sun for a light by day, and the ordinances of the moon and of the stars for a light by night, which divideth the sea when the waves thereof roar; The LORD of hosts is his name: if those ordinances depart from before me, saith the LORD, then the seed of Israel also shall cease from being a nation before me for ever. Thus saith the LORD; If heaven above can be measured, and the foundations of the earth searched out beneath, I will also cast off all the seed of Israel for all that they have done, saith the LORD" (Jer. 31:35–37). Isaiah predicted blindness as due to fall upon Israel when he wrote the message, "And he said, Go, and tell this people, Hear ye indeed, but understand not; and see ye indeed, but perceive not. Make the heart of this people fat, and make their ears heavy, and shut their eyes; lest they see with their eyes, and hear with their ears, and understand with their heart, and convert, and be healed" (Isa. 6:9–10). This prediction assumes vital importance when it is observed that various New Testament passages quote it and as related to the present unforeseen age. Isaiah went on to say that a remnant of Israel which he described as a "tenth" (Isa. 6:13) will be enlightened. This same blindness the Apostle declares to be "in part" (Rom. 11:25), thus allowing again for the remnant of Israel who are to be saved in this age. Christ Himself takes up the Isaiah prediction as recorded in Matthew 13:14–15: "And in them is fulfilled the prophecy of Esaias, which saith, By hearing ye shall hear, and shall not understand; and seeing ye shall see, and shall not perceive: for this people's heart is waxed gross, and their ears are dull of hearing, and their eyes they have closed; lest at any time they should see with their eyes and hear with their ears, and should understand with their heart, and should be converted, and I should heal them" (cf. Mark 4:12; Luke

8:10; Acts 28:26–27). The rejection of Christ, indeed, was wholly within the counsels of God. When the Jews failed to believe, the Apostle John states, "But though he had done so many miracles before them, yet they believed not on him: that the saying of Esaias the prophet might be fulfilled, which he spake, Lord, who hath believed our report? and to whom hath the arm of the Lord been revealed? Therefore they could not believe, because that Esaias said again, He hath blinded their eyes, and hardened their heart; that they should not see with their eyes, nor understand with their heart, and be converted, and I should heal them. These things said Esaias, when he saw his glory, and spake of him" (John 12:37–41). The natural branches had to be broken off for a time, to the end that a Gentile day of grace and the outcalling of the Church might be realized (cf. Rom. 11:17–27). Likewise the Apostle states that a veil is lying over the hearts of Israel in the present age. He declares, "But their minds were blinded: for until this day remaineth the same vail untaken away in the reading of the old testament; which vail is done away in Christ. But even unto this day, when Moses is read, the vail is upon their heart. Nevertheless when it shall turn to the Lord, the vail shall be taken away" (2 Cor. 3:14–16). As difficult as the problem may be in itself, the Scriptures assert that for their own national sins Israel is nationally blinded, but not all of them and only for the period of the outcalling of the Church. Of this angle it is written, "For I would not, brethren, that ye should be ignorant of this mystery, lest ye should be wise in your own conceits; that blindness in part is happened to Israel, until the fulness of the Gentiles be come in. And so all Israel shall be saved: as it is written, There shall come out of Sion the Deliverer, and shall turn away ungodliness from Jacob: for this is my covenant unto them, when I shall take away their sins" (Rom. 11:25–27).

3. SPIRITUAL. The theme of spiritual blindness falls into two general divisions, namely, that of the unsaved and that of the carnal Christian.

a. Following directly upon the reference to a judicial blindness of Israel as declared in 2 Corinthians 3:14–16, is the disclosure regarding Satan's veiling of the minds of the unsaved relative to the gospel by which they may be saved. It is written, "But if our gospel be hid, it is hid to them that are lost: in whom the god of this world hath blinded the minds of them which believe not, lest the light of the glorious gospel of Christ, who is the image of God, should shine unto them" (2 Cor. 4:3–4). Added to this important statement are other Scriptures which set forth truth regarding the fact that the unsaved are under the mighty power of Satan (cf. John 8:44; Eph. 2:1–2; Col. 1:13; 1 John 5:19). Any effort which reaches the unsaved, if it is to deliver them, must be sufficient to lift this veil which Satan has imposed (cf. John 16:7–11).

b. The carnal Christian's blindness and limitation when attempting to understand the Scriptures are described in 1 Corinthians 3:1: "And I, brethren, could not speak unto you as unto spiritual, but as unto carnal, even as unto babes in Christ." The cure, as has been seen, for the blindness of the unsaved is the enlightenment which comes through salvation, while the cure for the blindness of the carnal believer is a more complete yielding to the indwelling Spirit.

BLOOD

In spite of the fact that circulation of the blood as the current through which all vitality moves and waste is eliminated was not established by science until 1615 A.D., the body's blood has in all human history been recognized, though it involved mystery, as the container of life and the symbol of relationships. The shedding of blood has always been accompanied by some degree of fear and daring. Bloodshed spells the taking of life. None who consider the Scriptures can doubt the truth that God relates blood to the life. Early in Genesis (9:4–6) He declared: "But flesh with the life thereof, which is the blood thereof, shall ye not eat. And surely your blood of your lives will I require; at the hand of every beast will I require it, and at the hand of man; at the hand of every man's brother will I require the life of man. Whoso sheddeth man's blood, by man shall his blood be shed: for in the image of God made he man." Blood had to be eliminated from Jewish foods, nor could it be mingled with sacrifice other than in shedding it. The direct statement of Leviticus 17:11 gives a clear and final declaration from God, "For the life of the flesh is in the blood: and I have given it to you upon the altar to make an atonement for your souls: for it is the blood that maketh an atonement for the soul." The Biblical doctrine accordingly is subject to a threefold division—(1) sacrificial blood, (2) cleansing blood, and (3) blood as the seal of a covenant.

1. SACRIFICIAL. The all-inclusive declaration on this point which

sums up the Old Testament order and the New avers that "without shedding of blood is no remission" (Heb. 9:22). It is *shed* blood which has always been required for deliverance, and thus it was in the type and the antitype, Christ in His crucifixion. The mystery of all that enters into the required blood sacrifice for sin cannot be traced through to its end. It traverses more of unknown realms than it does this realm. The truth of God's requiring a blood sacrifice as the righteous ground for the remission of sin was established beyond all dispute in Old Testament times. Though the many offerings sustained no efficacy in themselves to take away sin, they did speak of the immutable necessity of a ransom or redemption by blood as a cure for sin. To challenge this fact is not only to overlook the teaching set forth in the types and the New Testament's direct explanation of Christ's death, but it is to assume that the human valuation of sin may be equivalent to the divine evaluation. What authority, indeed, has a mortal—a mere creature—to arrogate to himself the right to sit in judgment upon God and declare unnecessary the principle which God has established and to which He at infinite cost unto Himself has conformed in all ages? The glorious message is, indeed, that efficacious blood has been shed and that men are invited to receive the value of it, that Christ's blood was shed as a sacrifice which God Himself provided to meet His demands against sin, and that this way of dealing with sin, from Abel's lamb to the day of Christ's death, is the only interpretation which fully and rightly construes all that the Bible presents on this its central theme of salvation.

2. CLEANSING. At least two major New Testament passages proclaim the cleansing power of Christ's blood, and these so relate His work of purification to the Old Testament types that they serve both as a revelation respecting the present efficacy of Christ's blood and as clear interpretations of the types, with regard to their meaning and value. The passages are:

Hebrews 9:13-14. "For if the blood of bulls and of goats, and the ashes of an heifer sprinkling the unclean, sanctifieth to the purifying of the flesh: how much more shall the blood of Christ, who through the eternal Spirit offered himself without spot to God, purge your conscience from dead works to serve the living God?" As the typical signification served for a ground upon which the unclean might be purified, so, and "much more," the blood of Christ purges the conscience (in removing the sense of guilt by the divine witness in the heart that a perfect forgiveness has been accomplished).

Hebrews 9:22–23. "And almost all things are by the law purged with blood; and without shedding of blood is no remission. It was therefore necessary that the patterns of things in the heavens should be purified with these; but the heavenly things themselves with better sacrifices than these." In this instance the purging is of things which were ceremonially, or in conformity to the law, being cleansed by the sacrificial blood of beasts. So the blood of Christ as a much better sacrifice serves to purify heavenly things. What such a purification involves and what it accomplished is again within the higher sphere of reality where human knowledge is lacking and where conjecture is useless. "It is not possible," the same writer states in similar vein, "that the blood of bulls and of goats should take away sins" (Heb. 10:4); nevertheless, the sacrifice which Christ has completed perfects forever them that in their salvation are set apart unto God (Heb. 10:14).

Likewise two passages out of very many in the New Testament may be cited which present the doctrine of cleansing through the blood of Christ.

Revelation 7:14. "And he said to me, These are they which came out of great tribulation, and have washed their robes, and made them white in the blood of the Lamb." While the reference is to tribulation saints, as the passage declares, the truth—equally applicable to all who are saved in this age—is the same in any case; believers are purified perfectly by the cleansing blood of the Lamb.

1 John 1:7. ". . . the blood of Jesus Christ his Son cleanseth us from all sin." In this Scripture the constant cleansing of the believer is in view—that cleansing which is conditioned upon walking "in the light, as he is in the light," which walk means ever the immediate confession of every known sin. In Numbers 19:1–22 this perpetual cleansing, as the antitype, finds its type.

3. SEAL OF THE COVENANT. An interesting and illuminating volume was written by Dr. Henry Clay Trumbull on *The Blood Covenant* in which he traces the history of blood covenants among the various peoples of the earth, but of far greater value is the plain declaration that there is now in force a covenant made in Christ's blood (Matt. 26:26–29; Mark 14:24; Luke 22:20; 1 Cor. 11:25). God's purposes and His provisions are established in righteousness with surety through the redemption consummated by the shed blood of Christ.

BLOOD AND WATER. H. L. E. Luering, writing in the *International Standard Bible Encyclopaedia*, presents the following which bears on the meaning of John 19:34:

The physiological aspect of this incident of the crucifixion has been first discussed by Gruner (*Commentatio de morte Jesu Christi vera*, Halle, 1805), who has shown that the blood released by the spear-thrust of the soldier must have been extravasated before the opening of the side took place, for only so could it have been poured forth in the described manner. While a number of commentators have opposed this view as a fanciful explanation, and have preferred to give the statement of the evangelist a symbolical meaning in the sense of the doctrines of baptism and eucharist (so Baur, Strauss, Reuss and others), some modern physiologists are convinced that in this passage a wonderful phenomenon is reported to us, which, inexplicable to the sacred historian, contains for us an almost certain clue to the real cause of the Saviour's death. Dr. Stroud (*On the Physiological Cause of the Death of Christ*, London, 1847) basing his remarks on numerous postmortems, pronounced the opinion that here we had a proof of the death of Christ being due not to the effects of crucifixion but to "laceration or rupture of the heart" as a consequence of supreme mental agony and sorrow. It is well attested that usually the suffering on the cross was very prolonged. It often lasted two or three days, when death would supervene from exhaustion. There were no physical reasons why Christ should not have lived very much longer on the cross than He did. On the other hand, death caused by laceration of the heart in consequence of great mental suffering would be almost instantaneous. In such a case the phrase "of a broken heart," becomes literally true. The life blood flowing through the aperture or laceration into the pericardium or caul of the heart, being extravasated, soon coagulates into the red clot (blood) and the limpid serum (water). This accumulation in the heart-sac was released by the spear-thrust of the soldier (which here takes providentially the place of a postmortem without which it would have been impossible to determine the real cause of death), and from the gaping wound there flow the two component parts of blood distinctly visible" (I, 489, 1915 edition).

BODY

The general Biblical truth regarding the body yields to a threefold division, namely, (1) the human organism, (2) Christ's physical organism, and (3) Christ's mystical Body.

1. THE HUMAN ORGANISM. In the New Testament a marked distinction must be made between σῶμα and σάρξ. The former is generally used to indicate physical flesh, while the latter is broader in its import, referring at times to the physical body (cf. Heb. 5:7) and at other times incorporating that which is immaterial and ethical into its mean-

ing, with specific reference to the fallen nature of man. The great Apostle wrote, "I know that in me (that is, in my flesh,) dwelleth no good thing" and in the same context also: "sin [the nature] that dwelleth in me," "sin which is in my members," and "Who shall deliver me from the body of this death?" (Rom. 7:15–25). These declarations demonstrate the truth that the Apostle included in the word *flesh* all which constitutes the unregenerate man. The present body is unredeemed as yet even though redemption has been applied to the soul and spirit. This essential truth respecting the believer's body—that it remains unredeemed—is declared in Romans 8:23, where the saved one is said to be waiting for the redemption of his body, which redemption will occur when Christ returns. As for the future of the believer's body, it is said to become, when redeemed and changed, like Christ's glorious body (Phil. 3:21), and to be conformed to His body instantly at the rapture (cf. 1 Cor. 15:42–44, 51–52). Since the human body is the medium of expression for the immaterial part of man, the flesh is also conceived as being the expression of the "old man," or sin which is in the members of the body. In this connection the Apostle refers to "the body of sin" (Rom. 6:6). In like manner, he compares the flesh with its sin nature to a body of death (Rom. 7:24), or a dead body which he must carry with him wherever he goes. This, again, is the same "body of the sins of the flesh" which Christ judged when He died unto the believer's sin nature (Rom. 8:3; Gal. 5:24; Col. 2:11). Distinguishing between the body and the spiritual life within it that God bestows on faith, the Apostle suggests that the life from Him is a "treasure" which is held in an earthen vessel (2 Cor. 4:7). This body which in its present living state is mortal—subject to death—will, if death does not ensue, put on immortality; and should death ensue, the body which because of death puts on corruption will at the resurrection of saved ones put on incorruption. The body which is to be the believer's forever in glory is adapted to the spirit of man, while that same body in its present estate is adapted to the soul of man (1 Cor. 15:44–46); and whether the Christian goes by death and resurrection and so through corruption into incorruption or by translation into immortality being instantly changed from mortal to immortal, the end is a standardized reality. It will be a body like Christ's glorious body (Phil. 3:21). There is as much promise for the future of the believer's body as there is for the future of his soul and spirit.

It seems evident to some from 2 Corinthians 5:1–8 that an intermediate body is prepared in heaven for believers who by death are separated from the present organism, which organism will see corruption until the resurrection. The intermediate body would be occupied until Christ comes and the present body is reclaimed in all its resurrection glory. The body referred to in 2 Corinthians 5:1–8 is said to be "our house which is from heaven," one that in character belongs to the sphere of eternal things and serves to avoid even a moment of disembodiment for the believer.

2. CHRIST'S PHYSICAL ORGANISM. That which is essential to a true humanity and required if an all-sufficient, bloodshedding sacrifice were to be made, namely, a human body, was acquired by Christ through His physical birth. For that body He gave thanks when about to come into the world, and all in view of the failure of animal sacrifices to deal finally with the problem of sin (Heb. 10:4–7). It is significant that a record has thus been made of Christ's valuation of His physical body and that His primary thought was for this to be made an all-satisfying sacrifice. With reference to His kingship and so likewise to a rejected King's death He said, "For this cause came I into the world" (John 18:37). In vain do artists attempt their imaginary portraits of Christ in His humiliation. That appearance has gone forever (cf. 2 Cor. 5:16). Thus, also, Christ's human body served as a veil to hide His essential glory. Only once did His glory penetrate that veil (2 Pet. 1:16–18). It is probable that His glory was still somewhat veiled during the forty-day postresurrection ministry and until His final ascension. John, who saw Christ in every situation when He was here on earth, even as Christ appeared after resurrection, fell at His feet as one dead when he saw Christ in glory (Rev. 1:17). In that body in which He lived and died He arose, and in that same body He is being glorified. Thus glorified, He will in that same body come again.

3. CHRIST'S MYSTICAL BODY. The figure most employed to represent the relationship which obtains between Christ and the Church is that of the human body with its many members and its head. The immeasurable reality given the believer as he comes into his new position in Christ by the Spirit's baptism is illustrated by the idea of joining a member to some human body; and, as the functions of the members in such a body differ, so the service of believers varies according to the will of the living Head. Vital union to Christ is the glorious truth which the figure sets forth. No such relationship obtained in the Old Testament order, nor will it appear in the coming kingdom.

BREAD

As the staff of life, the most universal and the most complete article of human food, bread at once becomes the symbol of God's supply for human needs. Thus, and by such a line of reasoning, bread has been considered a sacred element, and is especially so regarded by the Egyptians. In the Jewish economy bread sustained a typical significance while to the Christian it is symbolic. These general divisions of the subject may well be observed more specifically.

1. THE STAFF OF LIFE. Bread is the term used by the Bible to indicate physical nourishment in general. As early in human history as Genesis 3:19 it is recorded that God said to Adam, "In the sweat of thy face shalt thou eat bread." The word *bread* occurs twenty-five times in Genesis and over a hundred times in the Pentateuch. Manna was termed bread—that which God rained from heaven for Israel (Ex. 16:4). For the most part, it would seem that bread was, in olden times, often the only item of food. Because of these facts nothing could serve better than bread as a symbol of God's care.

2. THE TYPICAL SIGNIFICANCE. In this feature of the doctrine the more important particular is the wave loaves, which during the Feast of Pentecost were waved before Jehovah (cf. Lev. 23:17–20). The anti-type is the Church as seen by God ever since she began to be on the Day of Pentecost. The feast which immediately preceded Pentecost in Israel's calendar was that of First-Fruits, which anticipated Christ in resurrection. He became indeed the First-Fruits of them that slept (1 Cor. 15:20). It is deeply impressive and suggestive respecting God's perfect order that the Feast of Pentecost was measured off to occur just fifty days after the Feast of First-Fruits. This careful measurement is indicated by the words in Acts 2:1, "And when the day of Pentecost was fully come." On this succession of feasts and the meaning of the wave loaves, Dr. C. I. Scofield writes in his notes bearing upon Leviticus 23:16–17: "The feast of Pentecost, vs. 15–22. The anti-type is the descent of the Holy Spirit to form the church. For this reason leaven is present, because there is evil in the church (Matt. 13:33; Acts 5:1, 10; 15:1). Observe, it is now *loaves;* not a sheaf of separate growths loosely bound together, but a real union of particles making one homogeneous *body.* The descent of the Holy Spirit at Pentecost

united the separate disciples into one organism (1 Cor. 10:16, 17; 12: 12, 13, 20). The wave-loaves were offered fifty days after the wave-sheaf. This is precisely the period between the resurrection of Christ and the formation of the church at Pentecost by the baptism of the Holy Spirit (Acts 2:1-4; 1 Cor. 12:12, 13). . . . . With the wave-sheaf no leaven was offered, for there was no evil in Christ; but the wave-loaves, typifying the church, are 'baken with leaven,' for in the church there is still evil" (*Scofield Reference Bible*, pp. 156–57).

3. THE SYMBOLIC MEANING. Having declared Himself to be the Bread which came down from heaven (cf. John 6:41), and having asserted that His flesh must be eaten and His blood must be drunk, and that the eating and drinking is needful if eternal life were to be received (John 6:48–58), Christ points out: "The words that I speak unto you, they are spirit, and they are life" (John 6:63). Apart from the explanation on Christ's part that He is referring to spiritual rather than physical realities, there is little left to do other than to join the many who then said, "This is an hard saying; who can hear it?" (John 6:60). However, in the context Christ has as definitely declared that this same gift of eternal life is conditioned with respect to its reception upon believing on Him (John 6:47), and, again, "This is the work of God, that ye believe on him whom he hath sent" (John 6:29). Likewise, "Him that cometh to me I will in no wise cast out" (John 6:37). It therefore follows that the demand for His flesh to be eaten and His blood to be drunk is an intensified and realistic figure pointing to the most actual reception of Christ as Savior. This figure of speech or intensification of truth becomes at once a correction of the error so prevalent, namely, that to believe upon Christ means no more than an acknowledgment of the historical fact of Christ including the worthy purpose of His life and death. That such credence is insufficient must ever be urged. It is only as there is Spirit-wrought vision and understanding and as the individual becomes committed to Him as a living Savior that saving faith can be exercised. There comes to be a repose in saving faith; for it is one thing to believe that Christ represents all He claimed to be, but quite another thing to depend upon Him with complete abandonment for a personal salvation. One thus committed to Christ can say with Peter, "Lord, to whom shall we go? thou hast the words of eternal life" (John 6:68). Such a testimony becomes clear evidence of the kind of confidence which rests in Christ alone. As food and drink are taken into one's very being and assimilated, in like manner Christ must be received and assimilated.

It is not accounted strange, therefore, when Christ chooses bread for the symbol of His flesh as if something to be eaten and wine—"the blood of grapes"—for the symbol of His blood. It is in Jacob's prophecy of Judah and his future with its foreshadowing of Christ that this remarkable passage respecting "the blood of grapes" occurs. The passage reads: "Binding his foal unto the vine, and his ass's colt unto the choice vine; he washed his garments in wine, and his clothes in the blood of grapes" (Gen. 49:11). Equally significant is the incident that occurred when Melchizedek met Abraham and "brought forth bread and wine" (Gen. 14:18)—symbols certainly of a completed redemption. What this meant to Abraham is not wholly revealed; however of Abraham Jesus Christ said, "Abraham rejoiced to see my day: and he saw it, and was glad" (John 8:56). Just how much and specifically what Christ included in the words "my day" remains unknown. It is likely, however, in view of the fact of Abraham's being the sole example of the outworking of grace as this has been set forth in the New Testament, that Abraham, as one "born out of due time," saw the finished work of Christ and was saved in the same measure in which all are saved who now enter into the value of His finished work. The reception of the elements, bread and wine, not only speaks of redemption but also of a constant appropriation of Christ as the branch draws upon the vine. The breaking of bread furthermore is a testimony directly to Christ respecting this vital dependence upon Him.

BRIDE

At least seven figures with their varied contributions to the truth are needed to set forth the relation which Christ sustains to the Church—the saved ones of this dispensation. He is the Vine and they are the branches; He is the Shepherd and they are the sheep; He is the Chief Cornerstone and they are the stones in the building; He is the High Priest and they are a kingdom of priests; He is the Last Adam, the Head of a new order of beings, and they are that New Creation; He is the Head of the Body and they are the members in particular; He is the Bridegroom and they are the Bride. Under Ecclesiology (Vol. IV) these distinctions have been developed at length. Latent in all these illustrations will be discovered the intimation regarding the whole immeasurable field of relationship which exists between Christ and the Church. Of the first six of this series of figures, it may be pointed out that they represent the present affiliation between Christ and the Church, whereas the seventh—that of the Bridegroom and the Bride—represents that between Christ and the Church which is wholly future. The great company of believers—some on earth and vastly more in heaven—are now the espoused of Christ. But they, like the Lord Himself, await the day of marriage union. That union, it is revealed, occurs in heaven after Christ has come again to receive them unto Himself. The Scriptures which describe the marriage of the Lamb and the wedding supper in heaven declare, "Let us be glad and rejoice, and give honour to him: for the marriage of the Lamb is come, and his wife hath made herself ready. And to her was granted that she should be arrayed in fine linen, clean and white: for the fine linen is the righteousness of saints. And he saith unto me, Write, Blessed are they which are called unto the marriage supper of the Lamb. And he saith unto me, These are the true sayings of God" (Rev. 19:7-9). The wedding "supper" which is celebrated in connection with the marriage in heaven should be distinguished from the marriage "feast" (cf. Matt. 25:10, R.V.), which is celebrated on earth when the King returns with His Bride and begins His beneficent reign. The time and circumstances under which the marriage feast is to be observed are set forth in Matthew 25:1-13. In this context virgins are seen going forth to meet the Bridegroom *and the Bride* (cf. Matt. 25:1 in D and other ancient authorities for the text). The fact that the Bride accompanies the King on His return to earth is taught in various Scriptures—notably Revelation 19:11-16, which portion presents not only the last description of Christ's return to the earth but also the only description of His advent to be given in this final, prophetic book. The order of events in this context is to be observed, whereby the wedding supper and the marriage in heaven immediately precede the return of Christ to the earth with His Bride. Luke 12:35-37 presents a description of the same appeal and warning to Israel in the light of the King's return that is found in Matthew 25:1-13. It reads: "Let your loins be girded about, and your lights burning; and ye yourselves like unto men that wait for their lord, when he will return from the wedding; that when he cometh and knocketh, they may open unto him immediately. Blessed are those servants, whom the lord when he cometh shall find watching: verily I say unto you, that he shall gird himself, and make them to sit down to meat, and will come forth and serve them." Israel alone is addressed and respecting the return of her Messiah with power and great glory. It is that event for which the Jews will be taught to watch after the Church is removed from the earth. The Lord states that when they see these things begin to come to pass they may know that He is near, even at the doors.

Truth respecting the Bride is consummated to some extent in the prophetic picture of Christ's coming kingdom on earth as that is presented in Psalm 45:8-15. In this picture the King appears with the queen upon His right hand in gold of Ophir. She is addressed as *daughter* and as *the king's daughter*. The virgins who attend her are not the queen but are brought to her with joy and gladness. Of them it is said "they shall enter into the king's palace." Thus the virgins of Matthew 25:1-13 are identified in their relation to the bride. Why should not Israel pay tribute of honor to the queen, the bride of their King? The virgins are the queen's companions and those among them who are ready to enter with her into the "ivory palaces" (vs. 8), which is the King's palace (vs. 15).

No small error has been proposed when it is claimed that Israel is the bride of Christ. It is true that Israel is represented as the apostate and repudiated wife of Jehovah yet to be restored. This, however, is far removed from the "chaste virgin" (cf. 2 Cor. 11:2) which the Church is, still unmarried to Christ. It is Israel that will be reigned over in the coming kingdom. But it is the promise to the Bride that she shall reign with Christ. Such a promise could not be addressed to those over whom Christ will reign. Dr. C. I. Scofield presents the following note under Hosea 2:2: "That Israel is the wife of Jehovah (see vs. 16-23), now disowned but yet to be restored, is the clear teaching of the passages. This relationship is not to be confounded with that of the Church to Christ (John 3:29, *refs.*). In the mystery of the Divine tri-unity both are true. The New Testament speaks of the Church as a virgin espoused to one husband (2 Cor. 11: 1, 2); which could never be said of an adulterous wife, restored in grace. Israel is, then, to be the restored and forgiven wife of Jehovah, the Church the virgin wife of the Lamb (John 3:29; Rev. 19:6-8); Israel Jehovah's earthly wife (Hos. 2:23); the Church the Lamb's heavenly bride (Rev. 19:7)" (*Scofield Reference Bible*, p. 922).

The types of the Old Testament foreshadow many important aspects of truth regarding the Bride. It may be said in respect of the Truth that whenever a man is a type of Christ his wife will be a type of the

Church, notable cases being Adam and Eve, Isaac and Rebekah, Joseph and Asenath, Moses and Zipporah, Boaz and Ruth, David and Abigail, Solomon and his true love of the Canticles.

No human imagination can measure the change that will be wrought by the power of God in those who comprise the Bride of the Lamb. He, the infinite One, will be ravished with the adorable loveliness of His Bride, and so for all eternity. She will have been perfected to this immeasurable and infinite degree.

BURIED

Special significance is rightfully attached to the fact that as often as three times, when relating the saving events through which Christ passed, the Scriptures include His burial. It is written: "For I delivered unto you first of all that which I also received, how that Christ died for our sins according to the scriptures; and that he was buried, and that he rose again the third day according to the scriptures" (1 Cor. 15:3–4); "How shall we that are dead to sin, live any longer therein? Know ye not, that so many of us as were baptized into Jesus Christ were baptized into his death? Therefore we are buried with him by baptism into death: that like as Christ was raised up from the dead by the glory of the Father, even so we also should walk in newness of life" (Rom. 6:2–4); "In whom also ye are circumcised with the circumcision made without hands, in putting off the body of the sins of the flesh by the circumcision of Christ: buried with him in baptism, wherein also ye are risen with him through the faith of the operation of God, who hath raised him from the dead" (Col. 2:11–12). Speaking of these three passages it may be indicated that the first refers to Christ's death, burial, and resurrection as a ground for the salvation of the lost. This Scripture is the recognized declaration of that which enters into the gospel of God's saving grace. The two remaining passages refer to Christ's death as judgment on the sin nature of those who are saved—that aspect of His death which provides freedom for the Holy Spirit to control the sin nature as that for which Christ has paid the penalty. It is the ground of the believer's experimental sanctification, which aspect of sanctification is made possible by and is wholly dependent on what Christ has accomplished. The death of Christ is referred to in Colossians 2:11–12 as His circumcision which was a substitution for others, whereas the other passage—Romans 6:2–4—adds crucifixion to that which Christ wrought as substitute for others. Thus the judgments against the believer's sin nature which demanded crucifixion, death, and burial with Christ to the end that he might share in His resurrection life fell upon Christ as substitute. Christ suffered these judgments on behalf of others.

The truth now under contemplation is that Christ's burial has been listed as an important factor in each of these three passages cited above, and as having doctrinal meaning. Regardless of disclosure, too little emphasis has been given this subject by theologians. In the matter of His bearing the sins of the unsaved, the burial of Christ is foreshadowed by the "scapegoat." This type is full and clear. Two goats were required on the Day of Atonement to represent typically that which Christ wrought. One goat was slain and its blood was sprinkled as a purification and cleansing. To the second goat was transmitted the sins of the people and that goat was led away into the wilderness to be seen no more. In His death for the unsaved, accordingly, Christ provided His blood which is efficacious for the cleansing and the judgment of sin, but also He *took away* sin (cf. John 1:29; Heb. 9:26; 10:4, 9, 11). That final disposition of sin is accomplished in His burial. He went into the tomb a sin offering sacrificed unto death. He came out completely unrelated to the burden of sin. Such is the doctrinal significance of the words, "and . . . was buried." There could be no tracing of the disposition of sin achieved in the tomb as there never was tracing of the further life and existence of the scapegoat after it was released in the wilderness. In that burial which was an aspect of Christ's undertaking in behalf of the believer's sin nature, too, there is also evidently a disposition of those judgments which duly fell upon Him. Into this, again, none can enter with clear understanding. Its immeasurable reality is known only to God.

It should be observed that the Apostle employs at times a technical word in place of the more common word, *to bury*. He declares that the believer's body is *sown* when placed in the grave (cf. 1 Cor. 15:42–44). A thing may be buried to dispose of it or to the end that it may be forgotten, but that which is sown is done with the expectation that something will come up where the seed was placed. The believer's body must be raised, and will at length be raised at the coming of Christ (cf. 1 Thess. 4:13–18).

CALLING

In its primary doctrinal meaning the word *call* suggests an invitation from God to men. This meaning is extended to form a ground upon which the ones invited are designated *the called ones*. The efficacious call of God is equivalent to His sovereign choice. Since there are two elect companies now in the world—Israel and the Church—these are alike seen as called of God. However, Israel's call is national while the call of those who comprise the Church is individual. The certainty of Israel's call is declared in the words, "For the gifts and calling of God are without repentance" (Rom. 11:29). Thus Israel's blessing, which reaches into eternity to come, is guaranteed. The word *call* is closely related in meaning to the word *draw*. Christ said, "No man can come to me, except the Father which hath sent me draw him: and I will raise him up at the last day" (John 6:44). The declaration which this passage advances is decisive. Not only is it asserted that none can come to God apart from this drawing, but that all thus drawn will certainly respond, for Christ said "I will raise him up at the last day." The words *draw* and *call* indicate the divine method of choice, though the latter may be used with specific reference to the estate of those thus blessed. They therefore are *the called ones*. At this point it may be observed that the name *believer* is in contrast to the term *the called ones*. The former indicates a human responsibility, while the latter indicates a divine responsibility.

As there is a drawing which is general through the preaching of the gospel, so there is a general call. Christ said once: "And I, if I be lifted up from the earth, will draw all men unto me" (John 12:32). Likewise, as there is a divine drawing which is not resisted (cf. John 6:44), so there is a calling by the Spirit which is not resisted and rightly styled *an efficacious call*. It is wholly within the bounds of this type of call that believers are termed *the called ones*. They are thus differentiated from the mass who, though subject to a general call and drawing, are not efficaciously called. A truth to be observed is that God indicates and separates His elect ones who comprise the Church not by any general effort, such as the death of Christ for the whole world or the proclamation of the gospel through which that death is presented as a ground of salvation to those who are lost, but He selects them rather by a potent influence upon each elect person, which influence assures the reception of Christ as Savior. So definite and certain proves the call that it is equivalent to the realization of divine election itself. The Apostle accordingly writes of an "effectual working" of God's power which determined his ministry (Eph. 3:7). It is an upward or high calling (Phil. 3:14); it is a heavenly calling (Heb. 3:1). It demands a holy walk (Eph. 4:1, R.V.; 2 Thess. 1:11); it engenders hope (Eph. 4:4); and by outward demonstration the believer is appointed to certify, to give proof of, his calling by the life he lives (2 Pet. 1:10).

There is a peculiar use of the word *calling* when by it reference is made to the estate of those who are called and at the time they are called. To this the Apostle testifies when he writes: "But as God hath distributed to every man, as the Lord hath called every one, so let him walk. And so ordain I in all churches. Is any man called being circumcised? let him not become uncircumcised. Is any called in uncircumcision? let him not be circumcised. Circumcision is nothing, and uncircumcision is nothing, but the keeping of the commandments of God. Let every man abide in the same calling wherein he was called. Art thou called being a servant? care not for it: but if thou mayest be made free, use it rather. For he that is called in the Lord, being a servant, is the Lord's freeman: likewise also he that is called, being free, is Christ's servant. Ye are bought with a price; be not ye the servants of men. Brethren, let every man, wherein he is called, therein abide with God" (1 Cor. 7:17–24).

The divine and efficacious call is one of the five mighty workings of God in behalf of each elect person under grace. Having referred to them as "the called according to his purpose," the Apostle goes from Romans 8:28 onward to declare that those whom God foreknew, He predestinated; those whom He predestinated, He called; those whom He called, He justified; and those whom He justified, He glorified (Rom. 8:29–30). In this connection, the word *foreknow* does not mean a mere prescience or knowledge of that which is to be; it here indicates the active exercise of eternal love for the individuals comprising the company who are the elect of God in this age. For these He also predetermined their destiny. Observe the functioning of predestination. It includes precisely the same company numerically and to the last individual whom He calls with an efficacious calling; and it is the same elect company who, without loss of even one, He both justifies and glorifies. In this sequence of five divine achievements, four represent the sovereign action of God. It is *calling* alone which incorporates some human responsibility in its outworking, and yet without the slightest infringement upon that infinite certainty that all who are called will be both justified and glorified. A call suggests some cooperation in the form of a human response to the call. In this respect, the divine call is wholly different from the other four sovereign undertakings—foreknowledge, predestination, justification, and glorification—which admit of no human action or responsibility whatever. The question at once arises whether, when one link in this chain is restricted up to the point that it depends at all upon human concurrence, the whole vast undertaking described by these five words is not jeopardized relative to its certainty of fruition. Should God coerce the individual's will the essential character of a call would be wholly obliterated, and the action of the human choice which is so evident in the Biblical declaration of the way of salvation be invalidated. Thus the question becomes one of whether God is able so to persuade, to induce, to prevail upon the human understanding and will respecting the choice of Christ as Savior and all that the choice secures that the called one will, without a possible exception, respond by exercise of saving faith in Christ—even the faith itself being imparted (cf. Eph. 2:8). The assurance is that God can and does so influence men by the enlightenment which the Spirit accomplishes that they, with a certainty that permits of no possibility that even one should fail to respond to the divine call, will every one be justified and redeemed in answer to personal and saving faith in Christ. This is what constitutes an efficacious call. Of great importance in this whole program of salvation is the fact that, when the called one is enlightened and persuaded by the Spirit rather than being coerced, his own will acts in unhindered and unimpaired volition. It has remained true that "whosoever will may come." However, in the counsels of God, which counsels may properly be disclosed alone to those who are saved but which constitute no message to the unsaved, it remains also true that no human will acts in the acceptance of Christ by faith who has not been brought to understand what Satan-blinded minds never do understand, namely, that all divine grace is their portion and infinite blessing theirs in Christ Jesus for the receiving on the basis of faith.

Calling, then, is that choice on the part of God of an individual through an efficacious working in the mind and heart by the Holy Spirit, to the end that the will of the one who is called may be moved by its own vision and determination in the exercise of saving faith. By so much two great necessities are preserved and equally satisfied, namely, only those are called whom God has predetermined to be justified and glorified, and those who are thus called elect from their own hearts and enlightened minds to receive Christ as Savior.

CARNALITY

Together with two other doctrines—that of the *natural man* and that of the *spiritual man*—the doctrine of the *carnal man* completes the threefold division of the human family in their relation to, or attitude toward, the Word of God. The designations in the original text are: ψυχικός, which indicates the unchanged, unregenerate man; πνευματικός, which designates the spiritual man or one who is characterized by the presence and manifest power of the Holy Spirit; and σαρκικός, which denotes the carnal or fleshly believer (cf. 1 Cor. 2: 14—3:4).

Carnality is caused not by the unspiritual things which one may do, but fundamentally by a lack of yieldedness to the mind and will of God. The carnal Christian does unspiritual things because he is carnal or fleshly. The passage which directly declares who are fleshly and why is found in 1 Corinthians 3:1-4: "And I, brethren, could not speak unto you as unto spiritual, but as unto carnal, even as unto babes in Christ. I have fed you with milk, and not with meat: for hitherto ye were not able to bear it, neither yet now are ye able. For ye are yet carnal: for whereas there is among you envying, and strife, and divisions, are ye not carnal, and walk as men? For while one saith, I am of Paul; and another, I am of Apollos; are ye not carnal?" In this context it is revealed that the carnal person is a true believer and therefore saved. Such are addressed as *brethren*—a salutation which never includes unregenerate persons, and they are said to be *babes in Christ*. While, because of carnality, they are termed *babes in Christ,* nothing could give greater assurance of their security for time and eternity than the fact that they are "in Christ." This revealing passage not only indicates the limitations of the carnal believer but reveals the state of affairs which, in the case of the Corinthians, came about because of their carnality. Being unyielded to God, they could not receive the "strong meat" of the Word of God; they could only receive the "milk." By so much their spiritual limitations are revealed. Their carnality was manifest in the divisions among them, with the tendency to follow human leaders. Such conduct signified a violent disregard for the unity of the Spirit—the one Body of believers—which unity the Apostle declares must be kept (Eph. 4:3). Since this sin of sectarian divisions is first on the list of evils for which the Apostle condemns the Corinthian believers—there is even mention of it before he points out their immoralities—its exceeding sinfulness in the sight of God becomes plain; yet like divisions are evident whenever sectarianism and denominational loyalty are stressed above the doctrine of the one Body of believers.

The term *carnal* is a translation of the word σαρκικός, which term means that one is influenced by the σάρξ—not a reference now to the physical body, but to the fallen nature which every believer retains as long as he is in his unredeemed body. The flesh is ever opposed to the Spirit of God (Gal. 5:17) and is never removed in this life, but may be held in subjection by the Spirit when and as the believer is depending in yieldedness upon Him. The Apostle testifies that "in me (that is, in my flesh,) dwelleth no good thing" (Rom. 7:18), and that when exercising his own strength he experienced nothing but failure in his conflict with the flesh. It was by the power of the Spirit of life in Christ Jesus that he became free from the power of sin and death—that spiritual death which manifests itself through the flesh (Rom. 8:2). He also forgets not to indicate that his victory by the Spirit depends, on the divine side, upon that aspect of Christ's death in which He brought the sin nature into judgment (Rom. 8:3). The result is such that the believer may experience all the will of God wrought in and through him—but this will never be wrought *by* him (Rom. 8:4). The Christian's responsibility is to "walk after the Spirit." This does not suggest living after some code or rule of life, but rather a subjection to the guidance and purpose of the Spirit who indwells him. When thus yielded, it becomes the Spirit's task to "work in" the believer "both to will and to do" of God's good pleasure (Phil. 2:13).

Though much is disclosed by the Apostle respecting carnality and the flesh, his more important teaching on the subject is found in 1 Corinthians 3:1–4, already considered, Galatians 5:16–21, and Romans, chapters 7 and 8. Having declared in Romans 8:4 that the believer's responsibility is to walk by means of the Spirit, the Apostle writes freely of the distinction between being in the flesh, which is the estate of the unregenerate person, and having the flesh within, which is the condition that characterizes all who are saved. Those believers who are dominated by the flesh respond to the flesh and those that are dominated by the Spirit respond to the Spirit (Rom. 8:5). In any case the carnal or fleshly mind functions in the realm of spiritual death and the spiritual mind in the realm of life and peace (Rom. 8:6). The reason for the carnal mind facing in the way of spiritual death is that it means enmity against God, not being subject to God's will, nor can it be (Rom. 8:7; cf. Gal. 5:17). The unsaved, being in the flesh, cannot please God (Rom. 8:8). However, the believer is not in the flesh as his estate though the flesh is in him. If someone is regenerated he will bear evidence of the presence of the indwelling Holy Spirit (Rom. 8:9). Too much emphasis can hardly be given to the fact that the Christian may function in his life within either the realm of spiritual death—separation from God—or the realm of things related to the Holy Spirit, He who is the Originator and Director of the spiritual life. Therefore, the Apostle declares: "For if ye live after the flesh, ye shall die [or, be in the realm of spiritual death—separation from God]: but if ye through [by means of, or, depending on] the Spirit do mortify [reckon to be dead in Christ's death] the deeds of the body, ye shall live [i.e., in the realm of the spiritual life]" (Rom. 8:13-14). Carnality means, then, a manifestation of the flesh which in turn is a demonstration of that which belongs to spiritual death. There is no implication in this extended declaration respecting the flesh and carnality that the believer may turn about or become unsaved. This presentation by the Apostle, however, is wholly within the sphere of the believer's walk as that which may be energized either by the flesh or by the Spirit. The Christian is saved and safe in Christ, yet in his manner of life he may prove σαρκικός or πνευματικός.

CHASTISEMENT

Chastisement and scourging—here to be distinguished from the larger theme of suffering—because the Father's correction of His own offspring (Heb. 12:6) are in character far removed from condemnation. It is written that "there is therefore now no condemnation to them which are in Christ Jesus" (Rom. 8:1) and "he that believeth on him is not condemned" (John 3:18), and of such as believe it is also said that he "cometh not into judgment" (John 5:24, R.V.). One who stands in the imputed merit of Christ, as every saved person does, could not come into condemnation; nevertheless, for sin in which a Christian willfully persists there may be chastisement from the Father, who is Himself a perfect disciplinarian. The course ever to be followed by a child of God who has sinned and when he sins is outlined in 1 Corinthians 11:31–32, which reads: "For if we would judge ourselves, we should not be judged. But when we are judged, we are chastened of the Lord, that we should not be condemned with the world." This order is clear. First, the believer who has sinned may and should make full confession to God, which confession is self-judgment and is an expression outwardly of an inward repentance of heart. If self-judgment is achieved, that divine forgiveness which restores the believer to fellowship with God is granted and right relations to God are restored again. On the other hand, if the believer, having sinned, refuses to confess it in genuine repentance or goes on justifying his sin, he must in God's time and way be brought under the correction of the Father. This judgment or correction by the Father assumes the form of chastisement and to the end that the child of God need not be condemned with the world.

The whole theme of suffering—a theme yet to be considered—extends far beyond but still includes the doctrine of the believer's chastisement. It embraces that which Christ suffered from the Father in which none may share, that which Christ suffered from men in which believers may share, that which the believer suffers as a chastisement from God the Father in which Christ does not share, that which believers suffer from men in which Christ does also share, and that which constitutes Christ's burden for a lost world in which Christians may share.

Chastisement, or discipline as such, may be contemplated under four general divisions, namely:

1. PREVENTATIVE. Only one example of preventative chastisement has been recorded in the Sacred Text, but such could easily be the experience of any child of God should circumstances demand. Having been caught up into the third heaven, the Apostle Paul was enjoined that he should not tell here on the earth what he had seen and heard, and accordingly, lest he should so transgress, a thorn was given him in the flesh. Though thrice he besought the Lord for its removal, the situation (2 Cor. 12:7–9) was not relieved. This became a preventative chastisement.

2. CORRECTIVE. Chastisement which is corrective in motive has been outlined at the beginning of this discussion. It is the Father's correction of His erring child. Both chastisement and scourging are indicated in Hebrews 12:6: "For whom the Lord loveth he chasteneth, and scourgeth every son whom he receiveth." The universality of both chastisement and scourging may be explained on the ground of the Father's unwillingness to allow any exceptions among those who deserve to be disciplined. It is certain that the Father does not chasten or scourge believers whether they so require or not. Such an interpretation not only contradicts 1 Corinthians 11:31, which declares that "if we would judge ourselves, we should not be judged," but must needs disrupt the whole purpose of chastisement. A difference is evidently to be found between chastisement and scourging. The former is that manner of correction which might be repeated; the latter represents the conquering of the human will which, once achieved, needs hardly to be done again. No anarchy or rebellion can be tolerated in the Father's household. The surrender of one's life to God is both reasonable and required (Rom. 12:1–2). Yielding to God may be accomplished easily if all resistance is avoided, or be made difficult and painful when a long conflict is maintained.

3. ENLARGING. The object of chastisement is said to be "unto holiness." So, also, the "fruit of righteousness" becomes the portion of those who are exercised thereby. Christ's word recorded in John 15:2 indicates how discipline may be applied from God to the end that the believer may be more fruitful. He declares of God: "Every branch that beareth fruit, he purgeth it, that it may bring forth more fruit." This does not suggest the correction of willful evil; it is all done that more fruit may be borne to the glory of God. It is designed so that a good man may become a better man.

4. VINDICATIVE. Again, but one illustration is found in the Bible of this specific form of chastisement. To Job it was given to demonstrate against the challenge of Satan that he loved God apart from all personal benefits or advantages which He had bestowed. No evil had been recorded against Job till then. In truth, Jehovah three times describes Job as "a perfect and an upright man, one that feareth God, and escheweth evil" (Job 1:1, 8; 2:3). But Satan in converse with Jehovah declared that Job served Jehovah only for selfish motives and that Jehovah was not really loved for His own worthiness. Though Job knew nothing of the issue which had arisen in heaven over him, he nevertheless vindicated Jehovah in three successive tests. The first was

in the loss of property and family. His reply under this test was worded: "Naked came I out of my mother's womb, and naked shall I return thither: the LORD gave, and the LORD hath taken away; blessed be the name of the LORD. In all this Job sinned not, nor charged God foolishly" (1:21–22). The second test involved the loss of health and wifely comfort. At this point he said: "What? shall we receive good at the hand of God, and shall we not receive evil? In all this did not Job sin with his lips" (2:10). Similarly Job stood the third test involving faith when, as recorded, he asserted concerning God: "Though he slay me, yet will I trust in him" (13:15).

CHRISTIAN

As a title which belongs to those who are saved, though itself now more employed than any other, *Christian* appears in the Sacred Text but three times: "And the disciples were called Christians first in Antioch" (Acts 11:26); "Then Agrippa said unto Paul, Almost thou persuadest me to be a Christian" (Acts 26:28); "If any man suffer as a Christian, let him not be ashamed" (I Pet. 4:16). The term *Christian* is evidently a Gentile designation for believers, since the word *Christ* upon which this title was constructed suggests recognition of the anointed Messiah and no unbelieving Jew was prepared to acknowledge the Messianic claims of Christ. This acknowledgment, indeed, became the very crux of the problem of a Jew's relation to the new faith. It is significant that Saul of Tarsus, when saved, "straightway . . . preached Christ in the synagogues, that he is the Son of God" (Acts 9:20). Messianism was ever the theme of those who preached to the Jews that Jesus is the Christ. All might be able to identify the person who had been known as *Jesus of Nazareth,* but it was the determining test that He be acknowledged as the Christ or the Messiah, and thus the Son of God. The Jews spoke of believers as *Nazarenes.* This had no complimentary implication. Very early in the days of Christ's ministry on earth, however, Nathaniel voiced the accepted idea when he inquired, "Can there any good thing come out of Nazareth?" Also, the orator Tertullus when arguing before Felix thought it well to condemn Paul as "a ringleader of the sect of the Nazarenes" (Acts 24:5). It will thus be observed that believers did not assign the name *Christian* to themselves, though Peter employed it in reference to that which had become a recognized practice (1 Pet. 4:16). It seems probable that this custom of designating believers was not the expression of a conviction that Jesus is the Messiah; it was rather based upon Christ's familiar name as a religious leader. The designations *brethren,* used about 200 times in the New Testament, *saints,* used about 60 times, *disciples* (beginning with its appearance in the Acts) used about 30 times, and *believers* meaning those who believe, used about 80 times, thus hold a preference according to the Acts and Epistles of the New Testament.

Beyond the problem of what may be an appropriate title is the fact itself of being identified one way or another. What, according to the New Testament and thus upon the authority of God, makes one a believer or Christian? Answers to this question are varied, sometimes falling so low that the title *Christian* is assigned to one who merely holds citizenship in a so-called Christian country. Over against this, the reality which the saved one represents reaches out beyond all human comprehension. Under Soteriology (Vol. III) thirty-three simultaneous and instantaneous divine undertakings and transformations which together constitute the salvation of a soul have been named. All of these are wrought at the moment saving faith in Christ is exercised. Three of these great realities alone may be cited here, namely:

1. A NEW PURIFICATION. That divine forgiveness which has been achieved as a part of salvation is complete and extends to all sins—past, present, and future—so far as condemnation is concerned. Romans 8:1 therefore declares: "There is therefore now no condemnation to them which are in Christ Jesus." It still remains true that the believer's sin may, as seen elsewhere, lead to chastisement. Forgiveness nevertheless is unto purification and wrought through the blood of Christ. It proves so complete that not one shadow or stain will be seen upon the saved one—even by the eyes of infinite holiness—throughout eternity. Divine forgiveness is not based on the leniency of God, but rather on the fact that the condemning power of every sin has spent itself upon the divinely provided Substitute. God's forgiveness is a legal recognition of the truth that Another has borne the judgment for the one who is forgiven. The purification is thus as complete and perfect as the ground upon which it is wrought.

2. A NEW CREATION. An actual and wholly legitimate sonship relation to God is divinely engendered when a soul has been saved. The one who is saved becomes the offspring of God. He becomes therefore

an *heir of God* and a *joint heir* with Christ. The Apostle John testifies of Christ that to "as many as received him, to them gave he" sonship standing (John 1:12)—not a mere option or choice in the direction of regeneration, for He causes them to become in the most absolute sense the sons of God. As such they are fitted and destined to take the honored place in the Father's family and household in heaven. God is now "bringing many sons unto glory" (Heb. 2:10).

3. A NEW STANDING. Because of the perfect identity and union of the believer with Christ which is wrought by the Holy Spirit, it may be said of the one saved that he has been "made . . . accepted" (Eph. 1:6). This standing is not a fiction or fancy, but such that by it the believer becomes at once not only clothed in the righteousness of God, but himself the very righteousness of God. This immeasurable reality depends wholly on the one fact that the child of God being blessed is in Christ. Such a limitless position before God is made legally possible through the sweet savor aspect of Christ's death when as Substitute He "offered himself without spot to God" (Heb. 9:14), thus releasing all that He is in Himself to be the portion of those whom He saves. This provision through His death is actualized and sealed unto eternal reality by a vital union with Christ.

A Christian, then, is not one who does certain things for God, but instead one for whom God has done certain things; he is not so much one who conforms to a certain manner of life as he is one who has received the gift of eternal life; he is not one who depends upon a hopelessly imperfect state, but rather one who has reached a perfect standing before God as being in Christ.

CHRISTIANITY

That body of truth which is now known as *Christianity* was identified by the early church as *The Faith* and *This Way* (Acts 9:2). According to Acts 6:7 a great company of the priests were "obedient to the faith," and Jude (1:3) contended for the faith once-for-all delivered. Not until Ignatius of Antioch (d. 107?) was the term *Christianity* introduced. It, like the word *Christian,* has come into general use today as a representation of that which the apostles revealed in the New Testament, and was itself brought into existence by virtue of Christ's death, resurrection, and present ministry in heaven, as well as by the advent of the Holy Spirit into the world. Of all the religious systems which have been fostered in the world, but two have the distinction of being designed, originated, and (eventually, though not as yet) consummated according to the specific purpose of God. These are Judaism and Christianity. Though Covenant Theology, with its extended doctrinal influence, has either confused or ignored the distinctions which obtain between the two divinely fostered systems, a recognition of the difference between them is the essential foundation of any beginning or progress in the right understanding of the Scriptures. To demonstrate the truthfulness of this statement, it should be added that, while both of these systems incorporate instructions for daily life here on earth, it can be ascertained by reason of evidence which any unprejudiced person may trace that Judaism is a system belonging to one nation—Israel, that it is earthly in its scope, purpose, and the destiny which it provides, while Christianity is heavenly in its scope, purpose, and the destiny which it provides. It will be seen, as well, though including much that is common to both that they are alike the outworking of opposite principles, and that they are not and could not be in force at the same time. Judaism alone was in action from the call of Abraham to the death and resurrection of Christ and will again be the outworking of the divine purpose in the earth after the Church has been removed, but Christianity is the only divine objective in the present age, which age is bounded by the two advents of Christ. Too often it is assumed that Judaism has been terminated or merged into Christianity. A favorite expression of this notion is to the effect that Judaism was the bud and Christianity the blossom. Over against this misconception is the truth that both Judaism and Christianity run their prescribed courses unimpaired and unconfused from their beginnings into eternity to come. By far the larger portion of Bible prophecy concerns Israel with their land, that is, the nation, the Davidic throne, the Messiah-King, and His kingdom. This and much more together form the eschatology of Judaism. Here it can be seen again that it is exceedingly inaccurate to speak of Systematic Theology as Christian Theology, since the former incorporates vast ranges of truth which are wholly foreign in their primary application to that which belongs to Christianity. Because much theological teaching is confused in these fields of truth, it is essential that particular emphasis be added here.

Though it was given to the Apostle Paul to formulate and record the realities which together constitute Christianity, he did not himself make its initial announcement. Christ in the Upper Room Discourse (John 13:1—17:26) declared the new and vital features of Christianity. This occurred at the very end of His earthly ministry and was set forth as an anticipation of that which was about to be inaugurated. The earthly ministry of Christ was restricted, in the main, to Israel and carried on wholly within the scope of their covenants of promise. In the Upper Room Discourse are found the important factors of relationship to the Father, to the Son, and to the Holy Spirit which are peculiar to Christianity. However, as divinely planned, the great Apostle was raised up to receive and formulate the new system, based as it is on the death and resurrection of Christ and the values gained at Pentecost.

At this point certain terms with reference to their shades of meaning may well be introduced:

1. NEW TESTAMENT THEOLOGY, which embraces that which is distinctively Christian in the New Testament. New chapters are added to Judaism in connection with the unfolding of that which constitutes Christianity.

2. PAULINE THEOLOGY, which is doctrine restricted to the writings of Paul but which nevertheless unfolds much regarding Judaism, especially in its contrasts with Christianity (cf. the larger portion of the Epistle to the Hebrews).

3. MY GOSPEL (Rom. 2:16), which designation is used by the Apostle when referring to all the revelation that was given him, namely, the gospel of saving grace revealed to him in Arabia (cf. Gal. 1:11–12) and also the revelation respecting the Church as the one Body of Christ composed, as it is, of believing Jews and Gentiles. To all this should be added the range of truth which sets forth the Christian's peculiar responsibility in daily life, with the new and incomparable provisions for holy living through the power of the indwelling Holy Spirit. The Apostle's designation, "my gospel," is equivalent to Christianity when a direct, constructive, and unrelated (to Judaism, etc.) consideration of Christianity is in view.

As a summarization, it may be restated that Christianity incorporates the gospel of divine grace which is based on the death and resurrection of Christ, the fact of the one Body with all its relationships and destiny, and the new and vital way of life through the Holy Spirit's enablement.

CHRISTOLOGY

Recognizing that an entire volume of this work has been assigned to Christology (Vol. V), the subject may be again approached in what is intended to be a highly condensed review. The theme (has been and) is well divided into the seven positions in which Christ has been set forth by the Bible, namely:

1. THE PREINCARNATE SON OF GOD. The fact of His preincarnate existence is established not only by direct statements of Scripture but by every implication. Some of these lines of proof are:

a. CHRIST IS GOD. It follows that if Christ is God then He has existed from all eternity. Evidence that He is God may be seen in His titles— Logos, Only Begotten, Express Image, First Begotten, Elohim, and Jehovah; in His divine attributes—eternity (Mic. 5:2), immutability (Heb. 1:11–12; 13:8), omnipotence (1 Cor. 15:28; Phil. 3:21), omniscience, and omnipresence; in His mighty works—creation, preservation, forgiveness of sin, raising the dead, and execution of all judgment.

b. CHRIST IS CREATOR. In this regard the Scriptures are explicit (Rom. 11:36; Col. 1:15–19; Heb. 1:2–12). If He is Creator, He has existed before creation.

c. CHRIST IS NAMED AS ONE EQUAL TO OTHERS IN THE TRINITY. In all references to the Persons of the Godhead, Christ the Son shares equally. In all purposes of God, as far as revealed, He assumes those parts which only God can assume. He is thus before all things.

d. THE MESSIAH OF THE OLD TESTAMENT IS GOD. Since Christ is the Messiah of the Old Testament, He is necessarily God and from all eternity.

e. THE ANGEL OF JEHOVAH IS CHRIST. This is clearly proved in earlier pages of the present theological work and is unfailing evidence of Christ's pre-existence, indeed.

f. THE DIRECT BIBLICAL ASSERTIONS IMPLY THE PRE-EXISTENCE OF CHRIST. Such assertions are numerous and conclusive.

g. THE DIRECT TESTIMONY OF SCRIPTURE IS THAT CHRIST HAS EXISTED FOREVER (e.g., John 1:1–2; Phil. 2:5–11; Heb. 1:1–3).

2. THE INCARNATE SON OF GOD. The theme respecting the incarnate Christ occupies about two-fifths of the New Testament. The general

outline of this aspect of Christology may be stated under seven divisions:

a. OLD TESTAMENT ANTICIPATIONS. These are both typical and prophetic in character.

b. BIRTH AND CHILDHOOD. Very much that is fundamental in doctrine is properly based on the birth of Christ. Here is to be introduced His various sonships—the title Son of God suggesting the divine; Son of man, the racial; Son of Mary, the human; Son of David, the Messianic and Jewish; Son of Abraham, the redemptive. Here also will be unfolded the entire theme of His hypostatic union of two natures; the mediatorial aspect of Christ's Person and His death; His earthly ministry to Israel as Messiah, Immanuel, and King; His ministry to the Gentiles as Savior, Judge, and Ruler; His ministry to the Church as Head, Lord, and Bridegroom. Here too is learned the twofold object of His earthly ministry, first to Israel respecting her covenanted kingdom and later to Jews and Gentiles respecting the Church which is His Body. Again, yet more of major import is brought forward, namely, Christ's three offices—that of Prophet, which incorporates all His teaching ministry; of Priest, which incorporates the sacrifice of Himself for the world; and of King, which incorporates the whole Davidic covenant together with the predictions and their fulfillment in His future reign.

c. BAPTISM. The baptism of Christ was a major event in His earthly life and of far-reaching significance since by it He was consecrated to the office of Priest, which office, like that of King, endures forever.

d. TEMPTATION. Judging from the extended description given this crisis, the temptation is possessed evidently of great importance. It became the crucial attack of Satan against the humanity of Christ, the issue being whether or not He would abide in His Father's perfect will. That He would was assured by His very nature as God and was determined from all eternity; yet the test was allowed so that finite minds might be satisfied about the impeccability of the Savior.

e. TRANSFIGURATION. The transfiguration, it is declared, was a setting forth of the power and coming of Christ in His kingdom (Matt. 16:28; Mark 9:1; Luke 9:27), that is, the event pictures the glory of the coming kingdom. When transfigured, Christ was about to turn from the kingdom ministry which had engaged John, the disciples, and Himself over to the new heavenly purpose concerned with a people qualified for glory through His death and resurrection. It was therefore essential that the kingdom not only be promised but displayed, that its future certainty might not be lost from view with the crushing disappointment which His death as a rejected king engendered.

f. TEACHING. Probably no clearer evidence respecting the scope and purpose of Christ's first advent can be discovered than is indicated in His teaching, especially that of the major discourses. His ministry to Israel and to the Church are therein distinguished completely—to those not blinded by theological prejudice.

g. MIGHTY WORKS. When Christ said, "If I had not done among them the works which none other man did, they had not had sin: but now have they both seen and hated both me and my Father" (John 15:24), He disclosed to some extent the reason why He wrought miracles. His mighty works attested His claim to be the Messiah and so His rejection was without excuse because of that evidence.

3. THE EFFICACIOUS SUFFERINGS, DEATH, AND BURIAL OF THE SON OF GOD. Considering these three events separately:

a. HIS SUFFERINGS. The evidence presented in John 19:28 intimates that the actual bearing of the judgments of sin fell upon Christ in the hours of His suffering which terminated in death. It was just before He said "It is finished" that John declares of Him, "Jesus knowing that all things were now accomplished, that the scripture might be fulfilled, saith, I thirst." What was actually experienced by Christ in those six hours upon the cross cannot be known in this world by any man; yet the value of it is received by those who believe.

b. HIS DEATH. It was required of any efficacious sacrifice that it should be delivered unto death and the shedding of blood. The death of Christ is the antitype of every typical sacrifice and determined the nature of that particular type. Typical sacrificial deaths through bloodshedding were such as God required because of the truth that Christ would thus be sacrificed. The range of Biblical testimony respecting Christ's death may be examined in seven divisions, namely: (1) types, (2) prophecies, (3) historical declarations of the Synoptic Gospels, (4) declarations of the Apostle John in his Gospel, Epistles, and Revelation, (5) declarations of the Apostle Paul, (6) of the Apostle Peter, and (7) of the Letter to the Hebrews.

If it be inquired, as constantly it is, Who put Christ to death? it may be pointed out that He was offered by the Father (Ps. 22:15; John 3:16; Rom. 3:25), of His own free will (John 10:17; Heb. 7:27; 9:14; 10:12), by the Spirit (Heb. 9:14), and by men—Herod, Pilate, the Gentiles, and Israel (Acts 2:23; 4:27). To this may be added that part in His death which was contributed by Satan (cf. Gen. 3:15).

The death of Christ achieved a vast array of objectives. At least fourteen of these are indicated in this work under Soteriology (Vol. III).

c. HIS BURIAL. As the scapegoat type anticipated, Christ carried away the burden of sin into oblivion. He went into the grave a sin-bearer and He came out the Lord of glory.

4. THE RESURRECTION OF THE SON OF GOD. Again, the Old Testament witness to that which concerns Christ is seen in types and prophecies. In the New Testament this theme is declared (1) by the predictions of Christ and (2) by the historical fact that He rose from the dead —an event more fully proved than perhaps any other of history. Christ was raised by the Father (Ps. 16:10; Acts 2:27, 31–32; Rom. 6:4; Eph. 1:19–20), by the Son Himself (John 2:19; 10:17–18), and by the Spirit (1 Pet. 3:18).

In disclosing the factors which enter into Christianity, the Apostle to whom this revelation was given places the resurrection of Christ in a central and all-important position. The death of Christ provides, but the resurrection constructs. Through Christ's death demerit is cancelled and the merit of Christ is made available, but by the resurrection of Christ the new Headship over a perfected New Creation is established forever. The importance of His resurrection may be seen from the following facts which in turn declare the reasons for the rising. Christ arose (a) because of what He is (Acts 2:24). That is, it is impossible that He the Son of God should be held in the place of death. (b) He arose because of who He is (Rom. 1:3–4). The resurrection served to prove His position as "Son of God with power, according to the spirit of holiness." (c) He arose to be Head over all things to the Church (Eph. 1:22–23). (d) He arose to bestow resurrection life upon all who believe (John 12:24). (e) He arose to be the source of resurrection power in the lives of His own who are in the world (Matt. 28:18; Rom. 6:4; Eph. 1:19–20). (f) He arose because His work which provided the ground for justification was completed (Rom. 4:25). (g) He arose as the pattern or first-fruits of all who are saved (1 Cor. 15:20–23; Phil. 3:20–21; 1 Tim. 6:16). (h) He arose to sit on David's throne and thus to fulfill all covenant promises to Israel (Acts 2:30).

In the sight and estimation of God, the resurrection of Christ is of sufficient import to be celebrated once every week and so the first day of the week on which it is celebrated supplants, in the present age, the Sabbath of the old order.

5. THE ASCENSION AND SESSION OF THE SON OF GOD. a. HIS ASCENSION. The departure of Christ for heaven has been already considered

under the doctrine of ascension in this volume. It is mentioned again here only to complete the structure of doctrine belonging to Christology. Two ascensions have been indicated—one immediately after the resurrection when the return of Christ into heaven as First-Fruits and as Priest presenting His blood occurred. The second ascension was that of final departure from the earth when He took up His present ministry in heaven.

b. HIS SESSION. The whole of Christ's present ministry in heaven has been practically ignored by theologians and especially by Arminians, to whom this ministry is repulsive since it guarantees the eternal security of all who are saved. Seven aspects of His present ministry are to be recognized, namely: (1) exercise of universal authority. He said of Himself, "All power is given unto me in heaven and in earth" (Matt. 28:18); (2) Headship over all things to the Church (Eph. 1:22–23); (3) bestowment and direction of the exercise of gifts (Rom. 12:3–8; 1 Cor. 12:4–31; Eph. 4:7–11); (4) intercession, in which ministry Christ contemplates the weakness and immaturity of His own who are in the world (Ps. 23:1; Rom. 8:34; Heb. 7:25); (5) advocacy, by which ministry He appears in defense of His own before the Father's throne when they sin (Rom. 8:34; Heb. 9:24; 1 John 2:1); (6) building of the place He has gone to prepare (John 14:1–3); and (7) "expecting" or waiting until the moment when by the Father's decree the kingdoms of this world shall become the kingdom of the Messiah—not by human agencies but by the resistless, crushing power of the returning King (Heb. 10:13).

6. THE SECOND COMING AND KINGDOM OF THE SON OF GOD. a. THE SECOND COMING. The stupendous event of the second advent of Christ with all its world-transforming results is to be distinguished from His coming into the air to gather the Church to Himself both by resurrection and translation. His second advent concerns the Jews, the Gentiles, and angelic hosts including Satan and his angels, and is related to the Church only as she is seen returning with Him and reigning with Him.

b. THE KINGDOM. Though the long-promised, earthly, Davidic kingdom of Christ was offered to Israel at His first advent, it was forthwith rejected and postponed in the counsels of God until He comes again. One of the basic theological misconceptions is the attempt to relate Christ's kingdom on earth simply to His first advent. Since no earthly kingdom came into view even then, it is claimed by theologians that His kingdom must be spiritual and that all expectation based on covenants and promises of the Old Testament was misunderstood by the apostles and prophets in so far as that may have been construed literally. Nevertheless, according to every word of Scripture, a scope which extends to the greatest of all prophetic expectations, Messiah will come again and will do literally what it has been predicted He will do for the kingdom.

7. THE CONCLUSION OF MEDIATION AND THE ETERNAL REIGN OF THE SON OF GOD. Following the conclusion of the millennial kingdom, which is itself the last form of Christ's mediation, certain immeasurable events occur with all their transforming results, namely: (a) Satan is released from the abyss (Rev. 20:3); (b) armies are formed and a revolt against God occurs again (Rev. 20:7-9); (c) the passing of the old heaven and the old earth (Rev. 20:11); (d) the great white throne judgment (Rev. 20:12-15); (e) the creation of the new heaven and the new earth (2 Pet. 3:10-14; Rev. 21:1); (f) the descent of the bridal city out of heaven (Rev. 3:12; 21:2, 9-10); (g) the actual surrender of mediation, but not of the Davidic throne. From the reading of 1 Corinthians 15:25-28 translated according to the Authorized Version, a belief has been engendered that Christ surrenders His reign at the end of the kingdom age. Having declared that Christ receives the kingdom and its authority from the Father (1 Cor. 15:27), however, the passage really goes on to say that, after the mediatorial reign of a thousand years, Christ will go on reigning forever by the same authority of the Father. It is the testimony of the Davidic covenant that He shall reign on David's throne forever and ever (2 Sam. 7:16; Ps. 89:20-37; Isa. 9:6-7; Luke 1:31-33; Rev. 11:15).

CHURCH
(See ECCLESIOLOGY)

CLEANSING

The possibility of the believer's cleansing from spiritual defilement and in a manner wholly satisfying to God is comforting and assuring beyond measure. Since sin is the experience of all in this world, a provision whereby defilement may be cleansed is of surpassing import to all.

The doctrine of divine cleansing of human defilement is subject to a threefold division, namely:

1. IN THE OLD TESTAMENT. Various cleansings were prescribed and provided in the Old Testament order, but none of them was in itself efficacious. These were accepted of God for what they typified and hence, as far as the divine achievement in cleansing is concerned, all was complete; but still the ground upon which the cleansing had been wrought was an anticipation of that which Christ would do regarding that defilement when He went to the cross. The ground of cleansing could only be accounted perfect in that the anticipated death of Christ was as certain in the reckoning of God as it is at this time, since the death has been historically achieved. Water was usually the typical cleansing agent, applied by sprinkling or bathing, and in the case of the solution formed with ashes of the red heifer had to be mixed with the symbol of sacrifice. Though typical cleansing was extensive in the Old Testament, it was no more so nor more vitally imperative than the cleansing which the New Testament provides.

2. OF THE UNSAVED. A once-for-all cleansing is a part of the saving grace of God toward the lost when they believe unto salvation. The efficacy of Christ's sacrifice provides, as divinely applied in the reckoning of God, a washing in the blood of the Lamb (Rev. 7:14). That this does not indicate a literal, physical washing is obvious; nevertheless, the results with all their supreme value are the same.

3. OF THE BELIEVER. Sin is always sin and defilement always defilement whether related to the saved or to the unsaved, and as such can be cleansed in no other way than by the blood of Christ. For the child of God, such cleansing is set forth in 1 John 1:7, 9, which Scripture declares: "But if we walk in the light, as he is in the light, we have fellowship one with another, and the blood of Jesus Christ his Son cleanseth us from all sin. . . . If we confess our sins, he is faithful and just to forgive us our sins, and to cleanse us from all unrighteousness." In verse 7 the assurance is given that as the believer walks in the light, which means a constant and full adjustment to all the revealed will of God for him, the blood of Christ goes on cleansing him from all sin. The same condition, stated in other words, is present in verse 9, when it is said that "if we [Christians, only] confess our sins"—that is, make the required adjustments—God is both faithful and just (faithful to His

promise and purpose, and just in what He does for the believer in view of the fact that Christ has borne the sin) to forgive and to cleanse from all unrighteousness. Nothing could be more effective or advantageous for the believer than that he maintain unbroken fellowship with the Father and with the Son (1 John 1:3, 7). Union with Christ is established forever by the exercise of saving faith, but communion with the Father and the Son may be, and too often is, broken. This, however, may be restored by confession when the sin is forgiven and its stain washed away. Such cleansing was typified by the sprinkling with water in which was mixed the ashes of a red heifer (Num. 19:2–9).

COMMANDMENTS

The term *commandments* is found in and represents an integral part of both the Mosaic and Christian systems, but with widely different significance. In fact, the variance between the two systems is clearly represented by these different uses of the word. Of the three major classifications of humanity commandments are addressed in the Scriptures to the Jew and the Christian, but not to the Gentile, or for that matter anyone unsaved—either Jew or Gentile—in this age, the reason being that divine commandments serve only to direct the daily life of those who are in right relation to God. For the Jew in the old order this affiliation was wrought by a physical birth which brought him into covenant relation to God, and for the Christian this is achieved by a spiritual birth which brings him into sonship relation to God. Of the Gentiles, however, it must be said: "That at that time ye were without Christ, being aliens from the commonwealth of Israel, and strangers from the covenants of promise, having no hope, and without God in the world" (Eph. 2:12), and as for a lost estate there is now "no difference" even between Jew and Gentile (Rom. 3:9; 10:12). It follows, then, that no commandments are now addressed to Jews. In the present age the first issue between God and an unsaved person—Jew or Gentile—is not one of correction or direction of daily life, but of personal salvation through faith in Christ. Therefore, directions for daily life are not addressed to the unsaved in this age.

1. IN THE OLD TESTAMENT. The divine counsels for Israel which came by Moses and which remained in effect until the death and resurrection of Christ fall into three major divisions, namely, the commandments (Ex. 20:1–17) which directed Israel's moral actions, the judgments (Ex. 21:1—24:11) which governed Israel's social activities, and the statutes or ordinances (Ex. 24:12—31:18) which guided Israel's religious activities. These three forms of divine requirement were interrelated and interdependent; one could not function fully apart from the other two. The modern notion that the Mosaic commandments are still in force, but that the judgments and ordinances have been abolished, can be entertained only when inattention exists respecting the form and nature of the Mosaic commandments. Great grace from God to the Jews of old is observable in the fact that apart from any merit of their own they were by sovereign election—each one of them—born physically into covenant relationship with God. Similarly, great grace was upon them which, when they sinned, provided restoration into right relations with God through blood sacrifice. Such restoration was granted to every Israelite. The whole nation was restored to a right relationship with God on the Day of Atonement. There was, however, always a remnant of all those in the nation who manifested a particular renewal or spiritual reality. Some of these are listed in the eleventh chapter of Hebrews, and many more are recorded throughout the Old Testament and in the early portions of the New Testament.

Upon examination (Num. 15:32–36), it will be discovered that the penalty of death was divinely imposed for the breaking of the ten commandments. Concerning this severity in the penalty for infraction of the Mosaic Law, it is written: "He that despised Moses' law died without mercy under two or three witnesses" (Heb. 10:28). That the Mosaic system is not now in force is evident from the fact that not all its conditions are applicable. The Sabbath enjoined by the Mosaic Law is superseded for the present age by the Lord's Day, and the promise of long life upon the promised land which God had bestowed has no relation to the Church. To her there was no land given, for she is definitely said to be a people who are "strangers and pilgrims." In like manner, a long life here contradicts the truth that the Christian is waiting for the return of Christ to receive him into glory (1 Thess. 1:9–10). The commandments of Moses are declared directly by the Scriptures to be abolished and done away for the present age (cf. John 1:17; Rom. 6:14; 7:1, 3–4; 2 Cor. 3:6–11; Gal. 3:23–25). 2 Corinthians 3:7 determines the fact that it is the Ten Commandments of Moses as well as the judgments and ordinances which were done away. If it be feared that the disannulling of the commandments of Moses as such involves the loss of their great principles of righteousness, it may be observed that every truth contained in the Mosaic system of morals—excepting that related to the Sabbath day—has been restated under grace, but is there adapted to grace and not to law. The first of the Ten Commandments of Moses appears nearly fifty times in and adapted to the new relationships under grace. The commandments of Moses partake of the nature of elementary instructions adapted to minors who are "under tutors and governors," but to those who were in such relation to God by covenant nevertheless as to be according to His will and purpose for them. This relationship which the nation Israel sustained to Jehovah should not be confused with the high and holy relationship which Christians now sustain toward God by reason of being in Christ. It is because of the fact that Israel was in covenant relation to God that the manner of life set forth in the Mosaic system could be addressed to them. Observing to do all that Moses required did not bring them into the Jewish covenants; they were enjoined to keep the law because God in grace, apart from all merit of their own, had placed them in covenant relation to Himself. Students who recognize and teach these most fundamental facts are sometimes accused by Covenant theologians of holding that people of the old order were saved and constituted what they were by keeping the Law of Moses, all of which is a misconception. The godly Jew was subject to blessing for his faithfulness in that which Jehovah required of him. But the Mosaic Law only holds the distinction of being Jehovah's rule of life for His people in the age that is past. These are the commandments which they "brake" (Jer. 31:32) and which are yet to be incorporated into (Deut. 30:8), although as a covenant to be superseded by, the new covenant which has still to come (Jer. 31:31–34; Heb. 8:8–13).

2. FROM CHRIST. The second use of the word *commandments*, when reference is made by it to a system or to principles governing human action, occurs when it signifies the commandments of Christ. When setting forth the principles which are to obtain in the coming kingdom age (Matt. 5:1—7:29), Christ drew certain contrasts between that which enters into the Mosaic system and that which will obtain in the kingdom (Matt. 5:17–48). The oft-repeated formula is, "Ye have heard that it was said [by Moses] . . . but I say unto you." In none of these contrasts, however, did Christ use the term *my commandments*. This designation was not used until He came to the upper room the night

before He was crucified, at which time He introduced the body of truth especially belonging to the Church in the present age of grace. There is nothing accidental here. This phrase on the lips of Christ designates, and by it He distinguishes, the range of truth which belongs to the present age. Thus at the end of His ministry on earth and after the forty days of instruction following His resurrection, He directed His disciples to teach all things that He had commanded them (Matt. 28:20), but did not include the Mosaic system. It is to be noted that Christ's first injunction was "a new commandment" (John 13:34), and that love is enjoined here as the evidence required to indicate that marvelous unity which all believers form (cf. John 17:21–23)—a unity wrought by the Holy Spirit and to be kept or manifested by love one for another. No such unity ever existed before. That which is included under the words "my commandments" was taken up and expanded by the Apostle Paul in his epistles. References to Christ's commandments are many—John 13:34–35; 14:15, 21; 15:10; 1 John 2:3; 3:22–24; 4:21; 5:2–3; 2 John 1:4–5. Cf. Matthew 28:20; Luke 24:46–48; Acts 1:3; 1 Corinthians 14:37; Galatians 6:2; 1 Thessalonians 4:2.

CONFESSION

Confession is an outward expression of an inward conviction. It assumes three distinct forms in the Bible.

1. OF CHRIST. The individual's confession of Christ is to be seen in two particulars:

a. AS SAVIOR. Of this particular confession of Christ the Scriptures declare: "That if thou shalt confess with thy mouth the Lord Jesus, and shalt believe in thine heart that God hath raised him from the dead, thou shalt be saved. For with the heart man believeth unto righteousness; and with the mouth confession is made unto salvation" (Rom. 10:9–10); "Hereby know ye the Spirit of God: Every spirit that confesseth that Jesus Christ is come in the flesh is of God: and every spirit that confesseth not that Jesus Christ is come in the flesh is not of God: and this is that spirit of antichrist, whereof ye have heard that it should come; and even now already is it in the world. . . . Whosoever shall confess that Jesus is the Son of God, God dwelleth in him, and he in God" (1 John 4:2-3, 15); "For many deceivers are entered into the world, who confess not that Jesus Christ is come in the flesh. This is a deceiver and an antichrist" (2 John 1:7). Too often these texts—especially Romans 10:9-10—have been thought to refer to a confession of Christ which an individual might make in public. Earnest men have taken this Scripture to mean that an individual must make a public confession of Christ as a prerequisite to salvation, little recognizing the fact that the majority of those who are believers were saved under circumstances in which no public confession of Christ was possible. The confession here enjoined is directed to God and not to men. It is the response of the heart to God by which acceptance of Christ as Savior is sealed. When confronted with Jehovah's promise respecting a son, Abraham believed—literally, amened—God (Gen. 15:6). Thus every soul born of God turns to Him with a heartfelt acknowledgment of Christ as Savior. It is the response of the soul and spirit saying in the innermost being, "Abba, Father." It should also be noted that, since in upwards of 150 New Testament passages salvation has been conditioned upon faith or believing alone, it cannot be true that any other requirement is laid upon the unsaved for salvation, else these many and central passages are incomplete and to that extent misleading. All who hear the call of God do respond in their hearts to that call, if they are saved at all.

b. IN THE KINGDOM. According to Matthew 10:32-33, Christ's confession of His own in the future kingdom will depend upon their confession of Him on earth. This will evidently be a most vital consideration in the kingdom age. The passage declares: "Whosoever therefore shall confess me before men, him will I confess also before my Father which is in heaven. But whosoever shall deny me before men, him will I also deny before my Father which is in heaven."

2. OF SIN. The second aspect of this doctrine divides, likewise, into two main divisions, which are:

a. THE OLD TESTAMENT REQUIREMENT. Since any covenant person or persons may be restored to the experimental blessings of their relation to God by confession—though in no instance is an unconditional covenant itself or the position before God which it secures in danger of being sacrificed—the people of Israel were thus restored, and this provision became a vital feature of Old Testament doctrine (cf. Lev. 5:5; 16:21; 26:40; Num. 5:7; 1 Kings 8:33, 35; 2 Chron. 6:24, 26; 30:22; Ezra 10:11; Neh. 1:6; Ps. 32:5; 51:1-19; Prov. 28:13; Dan. 9:4).

As with the case of the Christian in the present age and as stated above, the covenant position and standing of Israel could not be lost, but fellowship with God if lost because of sin could be restored by confession. Two specific instances of individual confession within the old order should be observed with attention. David's notable sin, even if involving immeasurable evil and the sacrifice of his personal blessings, did not destroy his salvation, for he said, "Restore unto me the joy of thy salvation." He also recognized that his sin, though an injury to many, was primarily against God. This he indicated with the words: "Against thee, thee only, have I sinned, and done this evil in thy sight" (Ps. 51:4). Likewise the prodigal of Luke 15:11–21, who also belonged to the old order, did not sacrifice his sonship by reason of sin, but was restored to communion with his father through confession, in which confession he said, "Father, I have sinned against heaven, and in thy sight, and am no more worthy to be called thy son" (Luke 15:21). It is to be observed how both of these confessions recognize that sin is primarily against God. Since there is here as elsewhere a progress of doctrine, the general theme of confession will be more clearly presented in connection with relationships which obtain on this side of the death of Christ.

b. THE NEW TESTAMENT REQUIREMENT. Confession, being the outward expression of an inward conviction, is closely related to repentance. The problem before the believer who has sinned is not restoration to the saved estate, which estate depends wholly upon the immutable Person and merit of Christ and therefore continues what it is so long as the basis abides upon which it rests; it becomes rather a matter of fellowship with the Father and with the Son. Two cannot walk together except they be agreed and God cannot have communion with evil; however, when the sinning Christian turns to God in full acknowledgment of the sin, accepting God's estimation of it, agreement is established again and restoration to fellowship is at once experienced. On the divine side, there is both cleansing and forgiveness required and also provided, and these are wrought in the faithfulness of God to His promise and purpose, and in justice since Christ has borne the sin in question (1 John 1:9). Naturally, such provisions are intended only for those who are actually sons of God and thus enter into a union with God which cannot be broken. Confession should always be unto God and to no one else unless, perchance, some other person has been injured by the sin. It should be recognized also that true confession is a complete admission of the evil wrought. Asking God to forgive is wholly beside the issue. He has said that He will forgive and cleanse the saved one who *confesses* his sin. This promise should be taken exactly as given, and faith should reckon that when sincere confession has been made the promise is kept, regardless of emotions respecting the sin which may continue. Two important passages bear on the Christian's confession of sin: "For if we would judge ourselves, we should not be judged. But when we are judged, we are chastened of the Lord, that we should not be condemned with the world" (1 Cor. 11:31–32); "But if we walk in the light, as he is in the light, we have fellowship one with another, and the blood of Jesus Christ his Son cleanseth us from all sin. . . . If we confess our sins, he is faithful and just to forgive us our sins, and to cleanse us from all unrighteousness" (1 John 1:7, 9; cf. James 5:16).

3. OF MEN. As noted above, it is a major feature of the future kingdom relationships that Christ will confess before the Father and the angels those who confess Him before men. The passage reads, "Whosoever therefore shall confess me before men, him will I confess also before my Father which is in heaven. But whosoever shall deny me before men, him will I also deny before my Father which is in heaven" (Matt. 10:32–33). This Scripture is wholly within the kingdom revelation and therefore could not apply to the Christian in the present age. A similar feature for the Church is seen, however, in Revelation 3:5.

CONSCIENCE

As a native faculty of every human being, conscience is most difficult of understanding and has too often been wholly neglected in works on Anthropology and psychology. When Immanuel Kant presented what has come to be the time-honored threefold division of the immaterial part of man as intellect, sensibility, and will, he failed to include conscience, vital feature of human existence though it is. The subject at best is shrouded in mystery. Personality seems to express its full scope and inclusiveness when it wills and executes its purpose guided by the intellect and the sensibilities; nevertheless, over and above this manifestation of personality, conscience sits in judgment whether the action be good or bad. The assumption of conscience as not having part in that which otherwise engages the entire being and yet being intuitively aware of each action to the extent of rendering judgment upon the deed suggests the peculiar and elusive character of this faculty. A wide range of opinion exists respecting the conscience. At the one extreme lies the contention that conscience is an acquired attitude of mind, a mere habit formed by the discipline of early training, which training accentuated the values of good and evil. The acid test of this opinion is somewhat brought to light by uncivilized people who have had no moral ideals held before them. Since conscience is capable of being weakened and seared, it could be expected that, whatever may have been its native strength in the early childhood of heathen peoples, it would be all but destroyed as one's years advance. At the other extreme lies a conviction that conscience is the voice of God speaking directly in the human soul. A test for this theory to pass would be the evident fact that conscience is capable of being weakened and wholly defeated—tendencies which are not easily associated with the actual voice of God. The Bible assumes the presence of conscience in man as a native factor of his being and predicates such limitations of it as to make it a fallible human characteristic. Though subject to weakening through abuse, conscience is presented in the Scriptures as a monitor over human actions. It seems to be something inborn and universal rather than an acquired faculty, and to be a voice of human origin rather than the voice of God. When an induction is made of all Scripture bearing on the conscience, the dependable facts representing this human competency will be revealed. The word occurs thirty times in the New Testament.

The following general divisions of the subject are suggested: (1) The conscience acts judicially, accusing or excusing (Rom. 2:15). (2) The conscience acts punitively, inflicting remorse and self-punishment. (3) The conscience anticipates future judgments and then acts by way of prediction. (4) The conscience acts socially in judging others (Rom. 14: 4; 1 Cor. 8:13).

The truth respecting the human conscience is even more complex in the case of a believer. Being indwelt by the Holy Spirit and therefore subject to the mind and voice of the Spirit, the question may be raised whether a Christian really lives at all by the restricted impressions which an unaided conscience engenders. The Holy Spirit becomes the new Monitor, and the child of God either grieves or does not grieve the Holy Spirit. It is therefore written: "And grieve not the holy Spirit of God, whereby ye are sealed unto the day of redemption" (Eph. 4:30). It is possible that the Holy Spirit works in and through the human

conscience when registering His reactions to the believer's thought and
conduct. The Apostle thus testified of himself, "My conscience also
bearing me witness in the Holy Ghost" (Rom. 9:1).

CONVERSION

Conversion, which appears forty times in the original (ἐπιστρέφω),
means no more than a turning about, and calls for a twofold treatment,
namely:

1. PHYSICAL IMPLICATIONS. In this the first use of the terminology
convert or *conversion* the meaning to be conveyed is no more than the
turning about of a physical body. At various times it is declared of
Christ that He "turned" or "turned about" (cf. Matt. 16:23, στρέφω),
which intimates simply that He turned His body about. He was thus
"converted." Christ warned the disciples against casting pearls before
swine lest the swine turn and rend them, or "be converted" and rend
them (cf. Matt. 7:6, στρέφω).

2. SPIRITUAL IMPLICATIONS. As a moral or spiritual act also, the
individual may turn about. The Apostle writes: "For they themselves
shew of us what manner of entering in we had unto you, and how ye
turned to God from idols to serve the living and true God; and to wait
for his Son from heaven, whom he raised from the dead, even Jesus,
which delivered us from the wrath to come" (1 Thess. 1:9–10). However, being only the human action of mind and will, conversion in the
moral or spiritual sense is not equivalent to salvation, which in all
its mighty transformations is ever and only a work of God for the
individual who exercises saving faith in Christ. This the second and
more important aspect of the term *conversion* may indicate no more
than reformation. It is the foremost counterfeit of true salvation. When
doing the work of an evangelist, it is possible to secure conversions
which are self-wrought, moral changes quite apart from genuine salvation with its forgiveness, new birth, and imputed righteousness. The
student would do well to avoid the use of the word *conversion* when
salvation is in view. Men are not saved except they be spiritually converted. They will then turn from all other confidences respecting their
salvation to Christ alone (cf. 1 Thess. 1:9). Israel too might be said to

turn about (cf. Ps. 19:7; Isa. 6:10; Matt. 13:15; 18:3; Mark 4:12; Luke 22:32; John 12:40; Acts 3:19; 15:3; 28:27; James 5:19).

CONVICTION

The original Greek word ἐλέγχω which may be translated either *convict* or *convince*—used seventeen times in the New Testament—represents in general the process whereby one is caused to reach certain conclusions or impressions in his mind. Too often it is assumed that this approach is through the emotions and that conviction consists in a spiritual depression and sorrow for sin. It is rather to be observed that the emotion which may arise in the heart is itself due to conviction, a convinced state of mind, and is not the convinced state of mind itself. Under a misapprehension it is supposed that sufficient sorrow for sin will soften the heart of God to the end that He may forgive, or that the sorrow for sin will result in a complete abandonment of its practice. In neither of these suppositions is the truth to be found. God's attitude toward the individual's sin has been thoroughly changed and this because of the fact that Christ has borne his sin. Through the death of Christ for sin, God is now propitious. There remains no occasion for Him to be appeased or propitiated either by human tears or sorrow. Likewise, to reach a point in conviction where some reforms are secured is far removed from the salvation of the individual. If through the enlightenment which conviction imparts, however, the individual is led to be cast completely upon God for His saving grace, the desired result of a spiritual transformation will be gained.

With this more specific meaning of *conviction* in mind, attention may be given to the central passage bearing on this theme, namely, John 16:7-11, which reads, "Nevertheless I tell you the truth; It is expedient for you that I go away: for if I go not away, the Comforter will not come unto you; but if I depart, I will send him unto you. And when he is come, he will reprove the world of sin, and of righteousness, and of judgment: of sin, because they believe not on me; of righteousness, because I go to my Father, and ye see me no more; of judgment, because the prince of this world is judged." This threefold ministry of the Spirit to the unsaved by which they are enlightened or convicted, which enlightenment evidently overcomes the blindness which Satan has imposed respecting the gospel, is most essential if any intelligent acceptance of Christ is to be achieved. This satanic blindness is described by the Apostle, "But if our gospel be hid, it is hid to them that are lost: in whom the god of this world hath blinded the minds of them which believe not, lest the light of the glorious gospel of Christ, who is the image of God, should shine unto them" (2 Cor. 4:3–4). None other than the Holy Spirit can lift this veil. The Spirit does so by causing the individual to comprehend three cardinal, indivisible truths. They are cardinal since they comprise the very structure of the gospel of God's grace. They are indivisible since no portion of them is ever wrought apart from the whole. As the three themes are being taken up separately, it is of great importance to recognize that these subjects are mentioned in the text as constituting the substance of the Spirit's unfolding or revelation to the unsaved. The same complete unveiling of these truths is as definitely required in each unregenerate person as the universality of their blindness requires. Of itself and apart from Satan's blinding, the gospel is not difficult to understand and looks most attractive to those unto whom it comes through the enlightenment of the Spirit. Apart from an understanding of the gospel and the Spirit-wrought willingness to receive it, none are saved. Hebrews 6:4–9 implies that much enlightenment may come to the unsaved which they have power to resist and that, so long as they continue to resist the grace of God, the only hope for their salvation is by themselves set aside. The passage, however, does not teach that Christians may be lost. Verse 9 determines the fact that the unsaved are referred to in that which was said in verses 4–8. Returning now to the central passage:

1. OF SIN. Reference here is to the one sin that "they believe not on me." Too often it is assumed that it is the Spirit's work to make people conscious of and sorry for their sins; rather, He reveals to the unsaved simply the one sin of rejecting Christ. This emphasis of the Spirit is reasonable in the light of the truth that Christ has borne all sin in His death. There remains but the one issue—that of believing or receiving what Christ has done and Himself as the glorified Savior.

2. OF RIGHTEOUSNESS. Thus, again, the Spirit unveils what it is impossible for the unenlightened, unregenerate person to comprehend, namely, that in the invisible Christ now at the right hand of God has been provided every merit and quality which one could ever need for time or eternity. Though the unsaved cannot enter deeply into the com-

plex doctrine of imputed righteousness, it is essential that they know how salvation depends on their turning from all confidence in self or any other hope and on placing expectation wholly and only in Christ. This certainly proves an important feature of the Spirit's work if an intelligent acceptance of Christ as personal Savior is ever to be secured.

3. OF JUDGMENT. In the use of the word *judgment* at this point allusion is made to the cross of Christ by which Satan, "the prince of this world," was judged (cf. Col. 2:14–15). The entire fact has to do with Satan's hold upon humanity on the ground that they are unlike God through sin. By bearing the sin of the world efficaciously (John 1:29), the Son of God wrought a judgment against Satan which should be acknowledged as the greatest of all judgments. The unsaved are expected to recognize that they, like criminals, have been apprehended, brought into judgment, found guilty, and led out to be executed, only to have Another, by His own choice, intervene and suffer execution in the sinner's stead. Thus it comes to pass that the sinner is placed as a judged criminal beyond his own execution. Certainly this is not a thing to be undertaken by the sinner, then, but is something to *believe*.

When the whole field of truth which the Spirit reveals to the unsaved, by whatever agency He may elect, is revealed, it becomes evident that the issue before the unsaved as God presents it is one of believing what has now been accomplished by Christ and of resting with confidence in the Saviorhood of Christ. It is plain that he who attempts to preach the divine message should do so with all this truth in mind. In other words, the gospel which the Holy Spirit can indite is what has been set forth by the three phrases: "of sin, of righteousness, and of judgment."

COVENANTS

Since the days of Johannes Cocceius (1603–1669) who, more than any other, introduced a one-covenant-of-grace idea, many theologians have promoted the notion that God is undertaking but one objective throughout human history. Scripture must be ignored or greatly misinterpreted to the end that such idealism may be advanced. The one-covenant idea could not avoid being a means with which to close the

Scriptures from human understanding. It does not necessarily follow —as some contend—that because there is but one righteous ground upon which God can deal graciously with sinners, namely, by the blood of Christ shed for them, there must be but one covenant relationship between God and man. That God has earthly as well as heavenly purposes and in addition transforming blessings adapted to each group and the sphere to which they belong will be seen by any unprejudiced student of the Sacred Text. In relation to His earthly people, Israel, and their blessings God has made various covenants. Some of these are conditional and some unconditional, which terms suggest that in some covenants God has them to depend upon human faithfulness, while in others He merely declares what He will do wholly apart from the question of human worthiness or faithfulness.

Without much Scripture upon which to base it, Covenant theologians have supposed the existence of a covenant between the Persons of the Godhead in relation to the part each would assume in the whole divine program of the ages, especially in redemption. The most that can be said for this contention is that it is reasonable; yet, all the same, difficulties are engendered. For this assumes that there was a beginning in the plan and purpose of God and that separate Persons of the Godhead sustained individual interests.

God has nevertheless entered into nine covenants with man on the earth. With these nine agreements all Scripture is related. Attention therefore to their provisions will be most essential. It is true that the earlier relationships between God and man included here are not termed covenants, but still they partake of the nature of covenants. The first three covenants—Edenic, Adamic, and Noahic—defined human life at its beginning. The Edenic Covenant conditioned unfallen man's life in Eden and is in seven parts. The Adamic Covenant governed fallen man in his estate outside of Eden and falls into seven parts. The Noahic Covenant provided for man after the flood and is likewise in seven parts. These along with all the remaining covenants have a more complete treatment earlier, under Bibliology (Vol. I). The fourth covenant in order is the Abrahamic, which also falls into seven divisions—(1) "I will make of thee a great nation," (2) "And I will bless thee," (3) "And make thy name great," (4) "And thou shalt be a blessing," (5) "And I will bless them that bless thee," (6) "And curse him that curseth thee," (7) "And in thee shall all families of the earth be blessed" (Gen. 12: 1–3).

In the fifth covenant, which has been named the Mosaic (Ex. 19:5), is a covenant made with Israel as a nation alone and that in the conditional manner. An unconditional covenant cannot be broken by man since it places no dependence upon him. A conditional covenant may be disrupted, and the Mosaic Covenant indeed, which is more familiarly known as the law, was broken. God declares so much in Jeremiah 31: 32 (cf. Heb. 8:9). This covenant had governed Israel's conduct as a redeemed people. It was given to them, however, not as a means of redemption or attainment unto a covenant relation to God, but because they were in right relation to God as a redeemed nation under God's covenant with that people descended from Abraham. It should take no effort to recognize that the Mosaic Covenant was never addressed to Christians; yet certain divisions of the professing church have failed to see why the saints of God of the present age cannot be under the law (John 1:17; Rom. 6:14; 7:4, 6; 2 Cor. 3:6–13; Gal. 3:23–25).

The sixth covenant, which is the Palestinian (cf. Deut. 30:1–10), presents the conditions upon which Israel entered their promised land. It, too, is expressed in seven parts, which are clearly set forth in the one passage bearing upon it. The land will be for them an everlasting possession and to it they will yet return, for Jehovah's covenants with Israel cannot be broken. The seventh covenant is the Davidic, which was made with David (cf. 2 Sam. 7:14–15) and comes in five parts. David's posterity fails not; his throne is established forever; a kingdom or sphere of rule continues forever; and Jehovah reserved the right to chasten David's sons, but the covenant cannot be broken. It is unconditional (cf. 2 Sam. 7:12–16; Ps. 89:1–37). David therefore must never lack for a son to sit upon his throne (Jer. 33:17); and as the eternal Son of God, who in His humanity is a son of David, will sit on that throne forever (Luke 1:31–33), there has not lacked one in all generations before Christ was born of David's line, or since, to sit upon the throne (cf. Ps. 2:6–9; Matt. 25:31). The eighth covenant is with Israel and conditions their life in the kingdom (cf. Jer. 31:31–34). It replaces and yet includes the Mosaic commandments (cf. Deut. 30:8), though in heightened form. It, too, is unconditional and falls into four parts.

There remains to be recognized a heavenly covenant for the heavenly people, which is also styled like the preceding one for Israel a "new covenant." It is made in the blood of Christ (cf. Mark 14:24) and continues in effect throughout this age, whereas the new covenant made with Israel happens to be future in its application. To suppose that these two covenants—one for Israel and one for the Church—are the same is to assume that there is a latitude of common interest between God's purpose for Israel and His purpose for the Church. Israel's covenant, however, is new only because it replaces the Mosaic, but the Church's covenant is new because it introduces that which is God's mysterious and unrelated purpose. Israel's new covenant rests specifically on the sovereign "I will" of Jehovah, while the new covenant for the Church is made in Christ's blood. Everything that Israel will yet have, to supply another contrast, is the present possession of the Church—and infinitely more.

CREATION
(See EVOLUTION)

The power of reason which belongs in some degree to every rational human being asserts itself by inquiring about the origin of all things. Consciousness of self and of all surrounding one identifies realities which engender the twofold conviction that, regardless of the remoteness of the time, what appears must have had a beginning and—since all creation is so marvelously designed and arranged—that there must have been a mind of infinite competency and omnipotent power to create or cause all things to exist. Merely to drive the idea of origin back into oblivion, as the evolutionist does, serves only to confuse the mind and enlarge the sphere of uncertainties; for the central problem will remain—the problem of a first cause is no nearer solution. Regardless of a supposed process of development, the germ out of which it might be claimed that creation with its unnumbered supernatural features has developed in accord with natural or accidental methods, there is still call for explanation of the astounding necessity that said germ enfolded the universe in itself. There arise, therefore, but two basic ideas respecting origin: (1) that of natural development and (2) that of divine creation. Lying in between these two wholly irreconcilable propositions are various shades of theistic evolution—an attempt on the part of men to account for the undeveloped form of life and matter with which the universe is supposed to have begun by ascribing them both to Deity. The crass unbelief and rejection of God and His Word which in reality characterizes every form of evolution is mitigated not at all by such excursions into the realms of fiction as the theistic evolutionist takes to bring God into the picture, for he not only rejects the divine revelation in its literal form but minimizes in every respect the divine elements that may have become incorporated into his scheme of interpretation. The general doctrine of creation may, then, be divided into (1) that which accepts the divine revelation and (2) that which rejects the revelation.

1. ACCEPTING REVELATION. The creation of a universe out of nothing is an achievement so beyond the range of human understanding that it can be received as truth only through a sufficient confidence in, and recognition of, the One who creates. It is written, "Through faith we understand that the worlds were framed by the word of God, so that things which are seen were not made of things which do appear" (Heb. 11:3). Faith is the basic requirement; but to the unregenerate man Almighty God is not sufficiently real to serve as a cause for anything. The Apostle declares, "But the natural man receiveth not the things of the Spirit of God: for they are foolishness unto him: neither can he know them, because they are spiritually discerned" (1 Cor. 2:14). Therefore, to say to the unsaved man that God has done, is doing, or will do anything provides no satisfactory explanation for the manner in which it is done. Without a sufficient recognition of God, which only regenerate persons can possess, the unregenerate are shut up to natural forces when attempting to discover the origin of life and matter. Godless scientists boast, of course, that they accept nothing which is not demonstrated by proved facts; but when approaching the problem of origins they either advance the most unproved, grotesque, and absurd speculations or else withdraw into the awkward silence to which reasonable men flee when they realize that they do not know. Science may assert that the Christian does not know how creation was accomplished, and that is true to the extent that he does not know God's method; but he does know God as his Creator. The Christian's satisfaction respecting the origin of things is not due to mere unenlightened, fantastic credulity; rather, he has found One who can do all He says that He has done or ever will do, and thus ends his quest for a sufficient Cause.

It should be noted at this point again that the unsaved cannot recognize God. They are equally incapable of understanding the ground of faith upon which the enlightened, regenerate person stands. Argument avails nothing. The two schools of thought on the subject are not only widely separated in viewpoint, but remain hopelessly apart until the unregenerate come to know God. The divine-creation revelation does not contend, as falsely charged, that nothing has produced nothing.

This assertion made by the spiritually unenlightened only demonstrates anew their inability to recognize God. To them He, by reason of being nothing in their concept, could produce nothing. On the other hand, to say that God the infinite One produced something out of nothing may defy human comprehension, but it does not exhaust the resources of infinity. The revelation regarding divine creation, incidentally, is not restricted to the early chapters of Genesis, at the beginning of Scripture. The entire Bible is constructed on the divine-creation truth. The Sacred Text not only asserts divine creation at its beginning, but upholds it and proceeds on its sure foundation in every succeeding step where there is unfolding of truth.

2. DISREGARDING REVELATION. Exceedingly damaging indictments must be brought against every form of evolutionary belief. It contradicts what God says. The effect of this sin is far-reaching. So far as can be done by man, it dismisses God from His universe. By divine arrangement, God's character and immediate presence is the norm as well as reason for every moral standard in the universe. A man who does not recognize God is, apart from feeble social ideals which reflect some knowledge of God, a law unto himself; the moral wreckage in the world of education is thus directly traceable to "scientific" theories embraced by educational leaders who repudiate God. There is but one cure for the utter failure of the race, and that is for the individual to be born spiritually from above, to come thus to know God, to know His power, His character, and His faithfulness.

CREEDS

Primarily the knowledge of Bible doctrine is an individual attainment. In this field great works on theology have been produced, accordingly; but for general unification men have formulated creeds and upon these they choose to find a common agreement. Creeds are closely related in their character to works on Systematic Theology. Both alike, however, and for the same reason, are rejected by modern religious leaders. Since the New Testament sets forth so much more doctrine than the Old Testament, creeds are usually based on New Testament revelation. Doubtless, Deuteronomy 6:4 is the most theological passage in the Old Testament. Creeds have special value as reflectors of the theology of their times. None are inspired, of course, and none infallible. Vast ranges of essential truth have been advanced by expositors and theologians indeed since the great majority of creeds were formed. A grave danger exists of failing to recognize the larger field of truth whenever or wherever these creeds are adopted and defended as a sufficient expression of that which the Word of God presents. Similarly, personal subscription to some creed may be a means by which one may be classified as orthodox, and yet that one may be destitute of a firsthand study of the Scriptures. Any such device which allows men to pass as trained ministers but which tends to make arduous and continuous study of the Sacred Text nonessential should be exposed and faithfully avoided. At the present time, many greatly restricted doctrinal statements are being drawn by the ever increasing number of independent forms of Christian work which, being unrelated to other bodies of believers and having no doctrinal standards consequently upon which to rest, must thereby declare their belief to the public.

The major creeds of the past fall into two general groups: (1) those formulated before the Reformation and (2) those formulated after the era of the Reformation.

1. Prereformation Creeds. a. the apostle's creed, sometimes called the *Roman Creed,* is best known and more generally used than others. Being highly condensed, it is suited to public recitation. As with all creeds, the aim of the writers was to declare what they believed to be cardinal truth; but this creed, like all others, is characterized by that which has been omitted as well as by that which has been presented. Few people, however, are ever aware of that which is omitted in creeds or theological writings.

b. the nicene creed, or creed of 318—so-named because of the number of bishops who collaborated in its formation—was adopted at Nice, A.D. 325, and was reaffirmed at Constantinople in 381. Its primary aim was to contradict Arianism, in its own defense of Trinitarianism.

c. the athanasian creed was the statement of Athanasius, bishop of Alexandria, the chief combatant of Arius.

2. Postreformation Creeds. a. the schwabach articles, dated 1529.

b. the augsburg confession, 1530.

c. the schmalkald articles, 1537.

d. the formula of concord, 1577.

e. CONSENSUS GENEVENSIS, 1551, with its twenty-six articles.

f. THE HEIDELBERG CATECHISM, 1562.

g. THE CANONS OF THE SYNOD OF DORT, 1618–1619.

h. THE THIRTY-NINE ARTICLES of the Church of England, 1563.

i. THE WESTMINSTER CONFESSION OF FAITH, formed by Reformed church leaders, 1648.

CRITICISM

According to its broad usage the word *criticism* indicates more than an unsympathetic attack upon what is written in the Scriptures; it reaches out to incorporate analysis and evidence in general, and proves as advantageous in establishing that which is true as it does in detecting error where human error exists. Carelessness obtains in the use of terms which classify criticism. The student is enjoined to give heed to suitable definitions and to conform to the distinctions set forth.

Dr. James Orr has written illuminatingly on this theme in the *International Standard Bible Encyclopaedia*. The following is a quotation from his statement:

So much has been said and written in recent years on "Criticism" that it is desirable that the reader should have an exact idea of what criticism is, of the methods it employs, and of the results it reaches, or believes itself to have reached, in its application to Scripture. Such a survey will show the legitimacy and indispensableness of a truly scientific criticism, at the same time that it warns against the hasty acceptance of speculative and hypothetical constructions. Criticism is more than a description of phenomena; it implies a process of sifting, testing, proving, sometimes with the result of establishing, often with that of modifying or reversing, traditional opinions. Criticism goes wrong when used recklessly, or under the influence of some dominant theory or prepossession. A chief cause of error in its application to the record of a supernatural revelation is the assumption that nothing supernatural can happen. This is the vitiating element in much of the newer criticism, both of the Old Testament and of the New Testament.

Criticism of Scripture ("Biblical criticism") is usually divided into what is called "lower or textual criticism" and "higher criticism"—the latter a phrase round which many misleading associations gather. "Lower criticism" deals strictly with the *text* of Scripture, endeavoring to ascertain what the real text of each book was as it came from the hands of its author; "higher criticism" concerns itself with the resultant problems of age, authorship, sources, simple or composite character, historical worth, relation to period of origin, etc. The former—"textual criticism"—has a well-defined field in which it is possible to apply exact canons of judgment: the latter—"higher criticism"—while invaluable as an aid in the domain of Biblical introduction (date, authorship, genuineness, contents, destination, etc.), manifestly tends to widen out illimitably into regions where exact science cannot follow it, where, often, the critic's imagination is his only law.

It was only gradually that these two branches of criticism became differentiated. "Textual criticism" for long took the lead, in association with a sober form of Biblical "introduction." The relations now tend to be reversed. "Higher criticism," having largely absorbed "introduction" into itself, extends its operations into the textual field, endeavoring to get behind the text of the existing sources, and to show how this "grew" from simpler beginnings to what it now is. Here, also, there is wide opening for arbitrariness. It would be wrong, however, to deny the legitimate place of "higher criticism," or belittle the great services it is capable of rendering, because of the abuses to which it is frequently liable.—II, 749

To be added to this consideration is the terminology *destructive criticism*, which refers to the effort made by unsympathetic men who aim at a breaking down of the testimony of the Sacred Text. Too often all Biblical "criticism" is thought to be of this type, destructive rather than constructive. It may, however, be either one or the other.

CROSS

In its more important use in the New Testament, the term *cross* refers to the framework of wood upon which Christ was crucified. It becomes at once not only a symbol of His death by crucifixion but a synonym of the words *sacrifice, suffering,* and *death*. The unique manner in which the inanimate timber on which Christ was crucified is linked with the very Person of the One slain there is to be seen in Galatians 6:14, where the terminology *cross* becomes, through use of the words "by whom," identified with that which Christ became in His death. The passage reads, "God forbid that I should glory, save in the cross of our Lord Jesus Christ, by whom the world is crucified unto me, and I unto the world."

In its doctrinal significance, the word *cross* is subject to a twofold usage, namely, (1) that which relates to Christ's sufferings and death and (2) that which relates to the believer's suffering and sacrifice.

1. CHRIST'S SUFFERINGS AND DEATH. One passage may be cited under this heading, namely, 1 Corinthians 1:18, which reads: "For the preaching of the cross is to them that perish foolishness; but unto us which are saved it is the power of God." Here the whole value of Christ's sufferings and death is in view. To the unsaved, apart from the enlightenment of the Spirit, the message of redemption is "foolishness." Thus the Apostle declares in 1 Corinthians 2:14 also, "But the natural man receiveth not the things of the Spirit of God: for they are foolishness unto him: neither can he know them, because they are spiritually discerned." Likewise he states, "But we preach Christ crucified, unto the Jews a stumblingblock, and unto the Greeks foolishness; but unto them which are called, both Jews and Greeks, Christ the power of God, and the wisdom of God" (1 Cor. 1:23–24). In this revealing body of Scripture the attitude of the unsaved, here termed *foolishness,* is not to be considered an intimation that they are making light of the cross by ridicule; it is rather that the best explanation of Christ's death which they are able to conceive falls so far below the truth that it proves to be foolishness, that is, it would have been folly for Christ to die if actuated only by the objectives these unregenerate people assign to His death. The historic fact of Christ's death, unique event as that was (the only holy man that ever walked on earth was forsaken of God and crucified as a malefactor), does require an explanation on the part of every thoughtful person. To claim, as some have done, that Christ's death was to the end that divine sympathy might be shown for those who are lost fails of the truth completely. Though He might display the sympathy of God, in so doing there would be no relief provided the one for whom Christ suffered either in respect to the cause of his woe or to the woe itself. To declare that Christ's death is of value to the extent that it reveals the evil character of sin and with the intent that sinners might turn from sin, once that is exposed, is to miss the essential truth again; for if all people could be persuaded to abandon sinful practices and even were they enabled to sin no more, there would still not be one person saved by such an achievement. Efforts to reform the lost apart from regeneration—the true objective in Christ's death—are well termed the folly of the ages. To suppose that Christ died as a martyr, the unwilling victim of a mob, and that to die for one's convictions must be glorious is likewise to be misled about the real meaning of His death. For Christ

was not an unwilling victim, for He said of Himself that He laid down His life that He might take it again (John 10:17). In the second place the death of a hero, no matter how glorious, provides no reconciliation between God and man respecting sin. There is but one answer to the question of why Christ died. This has been stated in the Old Testament thus, "But he was wounded for our transgressions, he was bruised for our iniquities: the chastisement of our peace was upon him; and with his stripes we are healed. All we like sheep have gone astray; we have turned every one to his own way; and the LORD hath laid on him the iniquity of us all" (Isa. 53:5-6), and in the New Testament by the words, "Behold the Lamb of God, which taketh away the sin of the world" (John 1:29). To each individual the death of Christ should mean what it did to the great Apostle when he said: "The Son of God, . . . loved me, and gave himself for me" (Gal. 2:20).

2. THE BELIEVER'S SUFFERING AND SACRIFICE. Here all thought of making satisfaction for sin, as in the death of Christ, is excluded. It is only as the cross of Christ represents His personal sacrifice and suffering that it becomes, too, the symbol of the believer's sacrifice and suffering. The denial of self that the life may be lived for God is in view. Christ said, "If any man will come after me, let him deny himself, and take up his cross, and follow me" (Matt. 16:24). A true definition of the believer's cross-bearing has been given in 2 Corinthians 4:10-11, where it is said: "Always bearing about in the body the dying of the Lord Jesus, that the life also of Jesus might be made manifest in our body. For we which live are always delivered unto death for Jesus' sake, that the life also of Jesus might be made manifest in our mortal flesh." By self-adjustment to the will of God, being ready even for a martyr's death, the attitude of Christ Himself was reproduced in the Apostle who was ministering to the Corinthian believers (cf. Rom. 9:1-3; 12:1-2; Phil. 2:5-8; 3:7-9; Heb. 10:4-7).

DARKNESS

The fact that darkness means an absence of light is used by the Scriptures to illustrate truth in five different aspects. No physical reality is more impressive—unless it be life and death—than the phenomenon of darkness and light. The various uses of the term *darkness* in the Bible are connected with:

1. OPPOSITION TO THE CHARACTER OF GOD. Writing of the holiness of God, the Apostle John has said, "And in him is no darkness at all" (1 John 1:5). Similarly, James has said, "With whom is no variableness, neither shadow of [cast by, R.V.] turning" (James 1:17). Light thus becomes a vivid illustration of the transparent purity of God. His glory is radiant with Shekinah light. Some of Christ's intrinsic glory was manifested in His transfiguration. Perfect holiness can be indicated only by celestial light.

2. MORAL ESTATE OF THE UNSAVED WORLD. When Christ came into the world, it was said of Him that He appeared as Light which shineth in a dark place, and yet the darkness comprehended it not (John 1:5). The perfect Light which God is cannot be comprehended by the darkness of this world. Darkness first came into this world when sin entered. Its reality is faithfully described by God in His Word, but men do not heed or understand the divine testimony. They "loved darkness rather than light" (John 3:19). In the beginning there was light enough, but men turned from the light. The Apostle states: "Because that, when they knew God, they glorified him not as God, neither were thankful; but became vain in their imaginations, and their foolish heart was darkened" (Rom. 1:21). The experience of the blind man is symbolical, "Whereas I was blind, now I see" (John 9:25). To the lost world about Him Christ declared, "This is your hour, and the power of darkness" (Luke 22:53). When one is saved he is translated out of the power of darkness into the kingdom of the Son of God's love (Col. 1:13). Truth is itself as light and the lack of it as darkness. Of the believer it is recorded that he has been "called out of darkness into his marvellous light" (1 Pet. 2:5).

3. THE CARNAL CHRISTIAN. Having declared that "God is light," the Apostle John asserts further: "If we say that we have fellowship with him, and walk in darkness, we lie, and do not the truth" (1 John 1:6). Fellowship or communion depends upon agreement, and where sin is practiced and defended by a believer there can be no perfect fellowship with God. To walk in the light is to be subject to the light, that is to say, when God reveals to one whatever in the life runs contrary to the Light which God is, there should be adjustments to that new revelation. To walk in the light is not to be sinlessly perfect; it is to be adjusted to all that God discloses unto the heart concerning His will for

one's individual life. For one to say as a pretense or supposition that he is walking in the light when evil has been tolerated, is to assert that which is not and could not be true. If, however, the believer walks in the light of God by being adjusted to His will, fellowship with God is maintained without effort and the stain of all sin is removed by the blood of Christ, for this blessed provision goes on cleansing (1 John 1:5-7). The darkness in which the believer may walk must be distinguished from the darkness of the lost estate; his darkness is due to carnality, and its limitations are seen in the fact that his sin has not disturbed personal union with God, but only his communion with Him. There are various drastic costs which the believer pays when he walks in darkness; loss of fellowship with God is one of them.

4. THE TRIBULATION. It is specifically revealed that when Christ returns to the earth He will come to a universal condition of "gross darkness" which shall cover the people (Isa. 60:2). The tribulation period which is ended by Christ's advent with power and great glory will be a time "of darkness and of gloominess" (Joel 2:2). According to all major references concerned with it, the tribulation is the hour of supreme darkness and distress over all the world.

5. FINAL ESTATE OF THE LOST. There is a place called "outer darkness" (Matt. 25:30) which becomes the last and unending abode of those who go there. That such a place has existed from the time of the fall of the angels is evident since some of the angels are in "chains of darkness" due to that early departure from God, awaiting a day of judgment (2 Pet. 2:4). They are not merely in physical darkness, but a place and condition utterly void of that Light which God is.

DAYS

A considerable number of specific days is mentioned in the Bible and these are for the most part themes of prophecy. All of them may well be considered separately.

1. CREATION. Genesis clearly declares that there were six successive days in which God created the heavens and the earth of today. The best of scholars have disagreed on whether these are literal twenty-four hour

periods or vast periods of time. From the standpoint of the ability of God, there is no question to be raised since He must be able to create all things in the briefest time. A literal twenty-four hour period seems to be implied when each is measured by words like, "And the evening and the morning were the first day," etc. On the other hand, it is reflected in nature that much time has passed since the forming of material things, and the Bible does use the word *day* symbolically when referring to a period of time. The coming kingdom of a thousand years is styled *The Day of the Jehovah.* Any point of time throughout the present age is known as *the day of salvation.* Peter declares: "But, beloved, be not ignorant of this one thing, that one day is with the Lord as a thousand years, and a thousand years as one day" (2 Pet. 3:8). So, also, Christ represented the present age as the hour that was coming "and now is" (cf. John 5:25–28).

2. SABBATH. It pleased God, after six creative days having Himself rested on the seventh, to require of Israel as an integral part of their law that they cease from labor and activity on each seventh day. Other extra sabbaths were sometimes added and each seventh year was to be a sabbatic period when it would be required that the land rest throughout the year. The seventh-day Sabbath, being a feature of the Mosaic system, continued as long as the Mosaic law was in force. According to Hosea 2:11, a time should eventually come when Sabbath observance would cease and when God's judgments would fall upon Israel. The same Sabbath will, however, be resumed in the tribulation and likewise in the kingdom that is to follow. It is not accidental that the Sabbath has been mentioned in connection with the tribulation in Matthew 24:20.

3. LORD'S DAY. "The first day of the week" (cf. Matt. 28:1; John 20:1) is called in this age of the Church the Lord's day, and on the ground of the fact that on this day Christ arose from the tomb and became Head over the New Creation of God. Such observance of the New Creation day was anticipated in Psalm 118:22–24 (cf. Acts 4:10–11). The Authorized Version declares that John "was in the Spirit on the Lord's day" (Rev. 1:10), but this is not necessarily a reference to the first day of the week. The original text reads literally, *Lordish day,* or "day which is characterized by Lord." It can mean, therefore, either Lord's day or Day of the Lord. Since John's vision as set forth in all of Revelation was of the extended period designated as the Day of the Lord, it seems evident that it must be this day of which John speaks. The Lord's day is only designed for the Church and so it ceases when that body of people is removed from the earth. With its cessation Israel

is restored to her place of earthly favor and her Sabbath re-established.

4. DAY OF THE LORD. The greatest expectation of the Old Testament was that of the Day of the Lord, yet it had not come when the Old Testament record closed and it has not come to the present time. It is still future (cf. 1 Thess. 5:1-2). It is related to Christ's second advent and not to His first advent. This period extends from Christ's coming "as a thief in the night" (Matt. 24:43; Luke 12:39-40; 1 Thess. 5:2; 2 Pet. 3:10; Rev. 16:15) to the passing of the heavens and the earth that now are and the melting of the elements with fervent heat. It seems highly significant that, in the same context and under the same theme in which those outmost boundaries of the Day of the Lord are given (2 Pet. 3:8-12), it is declared that one day with the Lord is as a thousand years and a thousand years as one day. It is essential that every student make a complete induction of all in the Bible which pertains to the Day of the Lord and thus gain for himself firsthand knowledge of all that has been divinely determined for this extended period. It may then be seen that this day includes the judgments of God upon the nations and upon Israel and that these judgments occur at Christ's return. It includes both Christ's return and the kingdom of a thousand years which follows. It extends indeed to the final dissolution with which the kingdom ends (2 Pet. 3:8-13; Rev. 20:1-15).

5. DAY OF CHRIST. By this term—so far as it relates to the earth—reference is made to a distinctive moment of time in which the dead in Christ will be raised and living saints will be translated, which moment is rightly extended into other scenes where vast changes are to be wrought that are the portion of the saints in glory. The Apostle John as seer or forerunner traces these glories for the Church in heaven and as well the agonies on the earth which belong to the tribulation and occur at the same time. The Day of Christ is the termination of the Church's pilgrim journey on the earth (cf. 1 Cor. 1:8; 5:5; 2 Cor. 1:14; 5:10; Phil. 1:6, 10; 2:16), and includes the event when saints are judged before the judgment seat of Christ (2 Cor. 5:10) and the marriage of the Lamb (Rev. 19:7-8). A notable correction in the Authorized Version is called for in 2 Thessalonians 2:2 where the term *Day of Christ* occurs, for *the Day of the Lord* is referred to in the original Greek according to textual criticism (see R.V.). Nothing is predicted as having to take place before the Day of Christ, but, as in the 2 Thessalonians context, there are stupendous events which must precede the Day of the Lord.

6. LAST DAY. Since it is the time in which Christ will raise those who

are saved (cf. John 6:40, 44, 54), the terminology *the last day* is evidently a reference to the last day of the Church on earth and must therefore be a major feature of the Day of Christ.

7. LAST DAYS FOR ISRAEL. One passage out of many will serve to declare the distinctive character of Israel's last days on earth—the days of her kingdom glory: "And it shall come to pass in the last days, that the mountain of the LORD's house shall be established in the top of the mountains, and shall be exalted above the hills; and all nations shall flow unto it. And many people shall go and say, Come ye, and let us go up to the mountain of the LORD, to the house of the God of Jacob; and he will teach us of his ways, and we will walk in his paths: for out of Zion shall go forth the law, and the word of the LORD from Jerusalem. And he shall judge among the nations, and shall rebuke many people: and they shall beat their swords into plowshares, and their spears into pruninghooks: nation shall not lift up sword against nation, neither shall they learn war any more. O house of Jacob, come ye, and let us walk in the light of the LORD" (Isa. 2:2–5).

8. LAST DAYS FOR THE CHURCH. A very unusual amount of New Testament Scripture, including all second Epistles excepting 2 Corinthians as well as other New Testament portions, bears on this important period. In contrast to Israel's last days, the last days for the Church are evil in character. One passage, again, may be quoted: "This know also, that in the last days perilous times shall come. For men shall be lovers of their own selves, covetous, boasters, proud, blasphemers, disobedient to parents, unthankful, unholy, without natural affection, trucebreakers, false accusers, incontinent, fierce, despisers of those that are good, traitors, heady, highminded, lovers of pleasures more than lovers of God; having a form of godliness, but denying the power thereof: from such turn away" (2 Tim. 3:1–5; cf. 1 Tim. 4:1–5; James 5:3; 2 Pet. 3:3; 1 John 4:17). An exceptional use of this term is to be found in Hebrews 1:2 wherein the church age is seen to be part of the "last days" in God's dealing with men.

9. DAY OF JUDGMENT. By the phrases, "Day of Judgment or Judgment Day," reference is evidently made to the final trial of the wicked who are raised to stand before the great white throne following the kingdom age and preceding the eternal state (Rev. 20:5, 11–15). Additional Scriptures to be considered are Matthew 10:15; John 12:48; 2 Peter 2:9; 3:7; Jude 1:6.

10. MAN'S DAY. This theme, obscured at times by translators, is referred to but once in the New Testament, namely, 1 Corinthians 4:3,

which reads, "But with me it is a very small thing that I should be judged of you, or of man's judgment: yea, I judge not mine own self." In this passage the phrase *man's judgment* is really a reference to human opinion current in this age, which might properly (and literally) be translated *man's day*.

11. DAY OF SALVATION. The Apostle declares that *now* is the day of salvation (2 Cor. 6:2), and is thereby referring to any moment within the church age as a time when Christ may be received as Savior. His statement is based on Old Testament prophecy.

12. DAY OF GOD. The one reference to the Day of God (2 Pet. 3:12) is evidently an identification of the eternity yet future when the new heavens and the new earth will have been created.

DEATH

Being, as it is, a penalty for sin, death in its varied forms is foreign to the original creation as it came from the hand of God. Being a penalty, such portion of it as may be removed will be dismissed forever; other portions of it, being eternal, cannot be removed. The entire theme may be divided into three aspects of death—the physical, the spiritual, and "the second." Physical death is separation of soul and spirit from the body, spiritual death is the separation of soul and spirit from God, and second death is the final and permanent form of spiritual death if the individual has not been saved from that. To Adam God had said as a threatened penalty for the sin of disobedience, *Dying thou shalt die* (Gen. 2:17, Hebrew). This judgment, which later fell upon Adam, would have included all the forms of death, even second death— had he not been saved from it by divine grace. As God had warned, Adam died spiritually the day that he partook of the forbidden fruit, and thus became subject to the second death. On that day, also, he began to die physically, and, though many hundreds of years may have intervened, he finally perished physically.

While this is true of Adam personally, it must be observed that Adam's position as a natural head of the race was such that the whole human family are directly affected by his sin, and thus "death passed upon all men" (Rom. 5:12). The initial, single sin of Adam is the cause, or occasion, for the penalty of death in all its forms falling universally upon all the members of the human race. The fact that death in its varied forms descends upon the race calls for a separate consideration of the relation each form of death sustains to mankind as originating in Adam's one initial sin.

1. PHYSICAL. That great feature of human experience—physical death—is described in respect to its cause in Romans 5:12–14: "Wherefore, as by one man sin entered into the world, and death by sin; and so death passed upon all men, for that all have sinned: (for until the law sin was in the world: but sin is not imputed when there is no law. Nevertheless death reigned from Adam to Moses, even over them that had not sinned after the similitude of Adam's transgression, who is the figure of him that was to come." In this passage it will be seen that sin did not originate with Adam in Eden, but as a tragic thing which had already become the occasion for the fall of Satan and many angels it found entrance into the world through the one man, Adam, and from Adam to the race in his loins. In the instance of physical death all men partake of the penalty, because of the fact that in the divine reckoning all men shared as participants in Adam's first sin by being, as they were, represented in his natural headship. The phrase, *for that all have sinned,* has too often been supposed to refer to the personal sins of all men within their lifetime. In the passage quoted above, however, it may be seen that the Apostle makes special effort to resist the idea that this form of death is due to personal sins. Physical death, he points out, is not due to the breaking of the law, for men died before the law was given; nor is it due to willful disobedience such as characterized Adam's sin, since those—infants and unaccountable persons—die who do not sin willfully as Adam did. It only remains, therefore, that physical death is due to participation in Adam's sin. The truth respecting seminal headship being so little understood, it is not easily considered or accepted by uninstructed minds. As a limitless forest of oak trees may be embraced in one acorn, so a race was contained in Adam. The Biblical principle which proceeds on the basis that unborn generations do act in their fathers, or share in that responsibility which their fathers bear, is declared in Hebrews 7:9–10. Here Levi, who lived by tithes being paid to him and who was a great grandson of Abraham, paid tithes, although being then only in the loins of his great grandfather, Abraham. The passage reads: "And as I may so say, Levi also, who receiveth tithes, payed tithes in Abraham. For he was yet

in the loins of his father, when Melchisedec met him." So far as Scripture reveals, there can be but one cause of physical death; it is due to the individual's personal participation in Adam's one initial sin. The participation was universal, hence the penalty—physical death— is universal. It is physical death which will later be destroyed (cf. 1 Cor. 15:26; Rev. 21:4). This "the last enemy" will be cancelled by a reversing of it; that is, all that have died will be raised to die no more (cf. John 5:25–28; 1 Cor. 15:22). The divine cure for physical death is resurrection.

2. SPIRITUAL. Though spiritual death began with the same initial sin of Adam, it becomes effective on humanity in a different manner than does physical death. The first sin of Adam caused him to be transformed downward into a different kind of being from that which God had created. He, furthermore, could propagate only after his kind, and thus the race was born in spiritual death received by heredity from the first man, Adam. Each person of the race is born spiritually dead— separated from God—and receives that fallen kind of nature directly from one's parents. Thus spiritual death comes *mediately* through an unbroken line of posterity. Over against this, physical death is received from Adam *immediately,* as each person dies in body because of his own personal share in Adam's first sin. The cure for spiritual death is regeneration or the passing from inward death unto life.

3. SECOND. As there is no cessation of consciousness in either physical or spiritual perishing, there can evidently be no cessation of consciousness in the second death. It rather is the eternal perpetuation of spiritual death—unending separation of soul and spirit from God. The Apostle John writes of the second death and asserts that it is linked with "the lake of fire." The meaning seems to be that those who enter the second death also enter "the lake of fire" (Rev. 20:12–15). A most important feature of this depressing doctrine is the teaching of Revelation 20:6 which states: "Blessed and holy is he that hath part in the first resurrection: on such the second death hath no power, but they shall be priests of God and of Christ, and shall reign with him a thousand years."

On the general theme of this second death Dr. C. I. Scofield makes the following comment: " 'The second death' and the 'lake of fire' are identical terms (Rev. 20:14) and are used of the eternal state of the wicked. It is 'second' relatively to the preceding physical death of the wicked in unbelief and rejection of God; their eternal state is one of eternal 'death' (i.e. separation from God) in sins (John 8:21, 24). That the second death is not annihilation is shown by a comparison of Rev. 19:20 with Rev. 20:10. After one thousand years in the lake of fire the Beast and False Prophet are still there, undestroyed. The words 'forever and forever' ('to the ages of the ages') are used in Heb. 1:8 for the duration of the throne of God, eternal in the sense of unending" (*Scofield Reference Bible*, pp. 1351–52).

The death of Christ becomes an exception to all aspects of human death. While He died physically, it was not, as with others, a penalty for a share that He ever had in Adam's sin; for with that He, being unfallen in His humanity, had had no part. In respect to spiritual death, there is no clear declaration of how far Christ entered that realm. He of course did say, "My God, my God, why hast thou forsaken me?" (Matt. 27:46). Where God is silent the devout mind should hesitate to intrude.

DEITY
(See GOD)

DEMONOLOGY

In considering demons and the service which they render Satan, it is important to distinguish between demon possession or control and demon influence. In the one case the body is entered and a dominating control gained, while in the other case a warfare from without is carried on by suggestion, temptation, and influence. Investigation of the Scriptures in regard to demon possession reveals:

First, that this host is made up of bodiless spirits only. The following Scriptures verify such a statement: "When the unclean spirit is gone out of a man, he walketh through dry places, seeking rest, and findeth none. Then he saith, I will return into my house from whence I came out; and when he is come, he findeth it empty, swept, and garnished.

Then goeth he, and taketh with himself seven other spirits more wicked than himself, and they enter in and dwell there: and the last state of that man is worse than the first" (Matt. 12:43–45); "And all the devils besought him, saying, Send us into the swine, that we may enter into them" (Mark 5:12).

Second, that they are, moreover, not only seeking to enter the bodies of either mortals or beasts, for their power seems to be in some measure dependent upon such embodiment, but they are constantly seen to be embodied thus, according to the New Testament. A few of these passages are given here:

"When the even was come, they brought unto him many that were possessed with devils: and he cast out the spirits with his word, and healed all that were sick" (Matt. 8:16); "As they went out, behold, they brought to him a dumb man possessed with a devil. And when the devil was cast out, the dumb spake" (Matt. 9:32–33); "And they came over unto the other side of the sea, into the country of the Gadarenes. And when he was come out of the ship, immediately there met him out of the tombs a man with an unclean spirit, who had his dwelling among the tombs; and no man could bind him, no, not with chains: because that he had been often bound with fetters and chains, and the chains had been plucked asunder by him, and the fetters broken in pieces: neither could any man tame him. And always, night and day, he was in the mountains, and in the tombs, crying, and cutting himself with stones. But when he saw Jesus afar off, he ran and worshipped him, and cried with a loud voice, and said, What have I to do with thee, Jesus, thou Son of the most high God? I adjure thee by God, that thou torment me not. For he said unto him, Come out of the man, thou unclean spirit. And he asked him, What is thy name? And he answered, saying, My name is Legion: for we are many. And he besought him much that he would not send them away out of the country. Now there was there nigh unto the mountains a great herd of swine feeding. And all the devils besought him, saying, Send us into the swine, that we may enter into them. And forthwith Jesus gave them leave. And the unclean spirits went out, and entered into the swine: and the herd ran violently down a steep place into the sea, (they were about two thousand;) and were choked in the sea" (Mark 5:1–13); "And the people with one accord gave heed unto those things which Philip spake, hearing and seeing the miracles which he did. For unclean spirits, crying with loud voice, came out of many that were possessed with them: and many taken with palsies, and that were lame, were healed" (Acts 8:6–7); "And it came to pass, as we went to prayer, a certain damsel possessed with a spirit of divination met us, which brought her masters much gain by soothsaying" (Acts 16:16).

Third, that they are wicked, unclean, and vicious. Many passages might be quoted in proof of this observation:

"And when he was come to the other side into the country of the Gergesenes, there met him two possessed with devils, coming out of the tombs, exceeding fierce, so that no man might pass by that way" (Matt. 8:28); "And when he had called unto him his twelve disciples, he gave them power against unclean spirits, to cast them out, and to heal all manner of sickness and all manner of disease" (Matt. 10:1); "There met him out of the tombs a man with an unclean spirit, who had his dwelling among the tombs; and no man could bind him, no, not with chains: because that he had been often bound with fetters and chains, and the chains had been plucked asunder by him, and the fetters broken in pieces: neither could any man tame him. And always, night and day, he was in the mountains, and in the tombs, crying, and cutting himself with stones" (Mark 5:2-5); "And they brought him unto him: and when he saw him, straightway the spirit tare him; and he fell on the ground, and wallowed foaming" (Mark 9:20). It might be added that there seem to be degrees of wickedness represented by these spirits, for it is stated in Matthew 12:43-45 that the demon, returning to his house, "taketh with himself seven other spirits more wicked than himself."

The question is often raised whether demon possession obtains at the present time. Although the Biblical records of such control are almost wholly limited to the three years of the public ministry of Jesus, it is incredible that demon possession did not exist before that time or has not existed since. In this connection it should be remembered that these beings are not only intelligent themselves, but directly governed and ordered by Satan, whose wisdom and cunning have been so clearly set forth in the Scriptures. It is reasonable to conclude that they, like their monarch, are adapting the manner of their activity to the enlightenment of the age and locality attacked. It seems evident that they are not now less inclined than before to enter and dominate a body. Demon possession in the present time is probably often unsuspected because of the generally unrecognized fact that such spirits are capable of inspiring a moral and exemplary life as well as of appearing as the dominating spirit of a spiritist medium or as the power behind the grosser manifestations that are recorded by missionaries concerning conditions which they observe in heathen lands. These demons, too, like their king, can appear either as "angels of light" or "roaring lions" when by the former impersonation they may more perfectly further the stupendous undertakings of Satan in his warfare against the work of God. Demon influence, like the activity of Satan, is prompted by two motives: one to hinder the purpose of God for humanity and one to extend the authority of Satan himself. They, therefore, at the command of their king, willingly cooperate in all his God-dishonoring undertakings. Their influence is exercised both to mislead the unsaved and to wage an unceasing battle against the believer (Eph. 6:12). Their motive is suggested in what has been revealed by their knowledge of the authority and Deity of Christ, and as well by what they know of their eternal doom. The following passages are important in this connection: "And, behold, they cried out, saying, What have we to do with thee, Jesus, thou Son of God? art thou come hither to torment us before the time?" (Matt. 8:29); "And there was in their synagogue a man with an unclean spirit; and he cried out, saying, Let us alone; what have we to do with thee, thou Jesus of Nazareth? art thou come to destroy us? I know thee who thou art, the Holy One of God. And Jesus rebuked him, saying, Hold thy peace, and come out of him" (Mark 1:23–25); "And the evil spirit answered and said, Jesus I know, and Paul I know; but who are ye?" (Acts 19: 15); "Thou believest that there is one God; thou doest well: the devils also believe, and tremble" (James 2:19).

Satan, though proposing to supersede the Almighty, is not omnipotent; but still his power and the extent of his activity are immeasurably increased by the cooperation of a host of demons. Satan is not omniscient, yet his knowledge is greatly extended by the combined wisdom and observation of many sympathetic subjects. Satan is not omnipresent, but he is able to keep up an unceasing activity in every locality by the loyal obedience of the satanic host.

DEPRAVITY

Depravity is a theological rather than Biblical word, which distinction indicates that the term, though not found in the Sacred Text, by so much like the words *Deity* and *Trinity,* represents a truth that is clearly taught in the Scriptures. This doctrine, furthermore, is misunderstood and often resented because of the fact that the Scripture has not been heeded or because the term *depravity* actually refers to that which God sees when He looks at fallen man and not to what man sees when he looks at himself or his fellow men. These two grounds of misunderstanding unite in one general declaration when it is stated that depravity is what God declares that He sees, and precisely what He sees, when He looks at fallen man. The student would therefore do well to give unprejudiced and exhaustive consideration to all that is recorded in the Bible on this theme. Theologians employ also the phrase *total depravity,* which does not mean that there is nothing good in any unregenerate person as seen by himself or by other people; it means that there is nothing in fallen man which God can find pleasure in or accept.

The picture looks dark, and would be much darker still were it not for the divinely provided remedy which announces full and free salvation. This picture of mankind does not stand alone. A large portion of the angels "kept not their first estate," and for them no hope is offered whatever; they are unrevokably doomed to the lake of fire prepared for them (Matt. 25:41). Likewise, the Gentiles who lived between Adam and Christ are described in Ephesians 2:12 as doomed souls: "That at that time ye were without Christ, being aliens from the commonwealth of Israel, and strangers from the covenants of promise, having no hope, and without God in the world." The estate of man after the fall and before the flood is declared in Genesis 6:5: "And GOD saw that the wickedness of man was great in the earth, and that every imagination of the thoughts of his heart was only evil continually." David testified of himself, "Behold, I was shapen in iniquity; and in sin did my mother conceive me" (Ps. 51:5; cf. Job 14:4; Ps. 58:3). Similarly, three major passages may be cited from the New Testament which cover all men of this and other ages, namely:

"There is none righteous, no, not one: there is none that understandeth, there is none that seeketh after God. They are all gone out of the way, they are together become unprofitable; there is none that doeth good, no, not one. Their throat is an open sepulchre; with their tongues they have used deceit; the poison of asps is under their lips: whose mouth is full of cursing and bitterness: their feet are swift to shed blood: destruction and misery are in their ways: and the way of peace have they not known: there is no fear of God before their eyes" (Rom. 3:10–18); "Now the works of the flesh are manifest, which are these; Adultery, fornication, uncleanness, lasciviousness, idolatry, witchcraft, hatred, variance, emulations, wrath, strife, seditions, heresies, envyings, murders, drunkenness, revellings, and such like: of the which I tell you before, as I have also told you in time past, that they which do such things shall not inherit the kingdom of God" (Gal. 5:19–21); "And you hath he quickened, who were dead in trespasses and sins: wherein in time past ye walked according to the course of this world, according to the prince of the power of the air, the spirit that now worketh in the children of disobedience: among whom also we all had our conversation in times past in the lusts of our flesh, fulfilling the desires of the flesh and of the mind; and were by nature the children of wrath, even as others" (Eph. 2:1–3; cf. John 3:6; Rom. 5:12).

Distinction should be made between depravity as such, which is universal throughout all human history from Adam's fall onward, and the estate today of men "under sin," which estate is the result of a divine mandate declared to the end that God's grace may have its perfect exercise and manifestation (John 3:18; Rom. 3:9; 11:32; Gal. 3:22), and is evidently a condition which obtains only in the present age of grace when it can be said that there exists no difference between Jew and Gentile.

DISCIPLES

In this doctrine concerned with disciples, as in all other instances, the student would do well to employ Bible terms precisely as they are employed by the Scriptures. The word *disciple* means no more than a pupil, a learner, or a follower, and is not equivalent to the terminology *believer* or *Christian*. Observe that when Paul came to Ephesus, according to Acts 19:1, he found "certain disciples," but these proved to be only disciples of John the Baptist and not Christians at all. They had no knowledge of the Holy Spirit (cf. Rom. 8:9), and so, learning of Christ, they were rebaptized by the Apostle in the name of Jesus Christ.

While this term *disciple* is used interchangeably at times with the title *apostle* when referring to the twelve whom Christ chose to be with Him, the terms are not to be considered equivalent. An apostle is a hand-picked, qualified witness. None, therefore, became apostles who were not directly chosen of God, and it was required for membership with the Twelve that they have had association with Christ on earth. Strange assumption derived no doubt from Rome obtains on the part of those who claim for themselves an unbroken apostolic succession from the first apostles on. This claim must rest on something outside the Word of God, when no provision is made therein for continuation of the apostolic office, nor has it even been intimated as a possibility. It is pure assumption to claim that some ordination imposed by men constitutes one in line with the apostles of old. If such an order existed, it would be well for it to depend on apostolic success rather than on a supposed apostolic succession.

All believers are disciples in the sense that they are being taught of God through the indwelling Spirit and whatever instrumentality the Spirit may employ. The important fact is that the truth of Scripture reaches the believer's understanding and heart as a revelation from God (cf. John 16:12-15; 1 Cor. 2:9-12). The term *disciple* implies no more of a relation to God than that of learner. One revelation may come by means of the Spirit even to the unsaved, and that the way of salvation being revealed through the gospel. None other than those called of God, however, receive the gospel.

DISPENSATIONS

Two words often used as synonyms when treating dispensationalism are nevertheless quite different in their specific meaning. These should be considered separately.

1. AGE (αἰών). This term, which is translated *world* thirty-one times in the Authorized Version of the New Testament, means a block or period of time. It hardly need be said that there is no observable relation between the English noun *world* and a period of time. By reason of this confusion in terms, the whole revelation respecting successive ages was soon lost to view because of the translation. A clear illustration of how the translators worked is set forth in Hebrews 1:1-2, which in the popular Authorized Version reads: "God, who at sundry times and in divers manners spake in time past unto the fathers by the prophets, hath in these last days spoken unto us by his Son, whom he hath appointed heir of all things, by whom also he made the worlds." Here the translation *worlds* has come from αἰών and by this term it is here declared that Christ arranged or programmed the successive ages of time. The disclosure is not the same as in verse 10 of the same chapter which states that Christ created all material things. No estimate could ever be made of the misunderstandings which have followed this error in translation. The same is true of the thirty-one instances where the rendering *world* is used in place of *age*. A notable passage on this point is Matthew 13:38-40: "The field is the world; the good seed are the children of the kingdom; but the tares are the children of the wicked one; the enemy that sowed them is the devil; the harvest is the end of the world; and the reapers are the angels. As therefore the tares are gathered and burned in the fire; so shall it be in the end of this world"

(cf. Matt. 13:49; 24:3; 28:20; Mark 4:19; 10:30; Rom. 12:2; 1 Cor. 2:6; 2 Cor. 4:4; Gal. 1:4; Eph. 2:2; 2 Tim. 4:10; Heb. 11:3). Here in the first instance the field is said to be the *cosmos* world, while in the second and third instances the harvest is the consummation of the age, and not the end of the material world as the Authorized Version translation implies. In another notable passage—Matthew 24:3—reference is not made to the present age, but to the Jewish age which has yet seven years to run after this one has been completed. The disciples knew little of this present unforeseen age at the time that Christ was speaking. The sign of the end for the Jewish age, however, is declared in Matthew 24:15 and in answer to the question respecting this age as seen in verse 3. The evil one referred to by Christ as the sign is described in 2 Thessalonians 2:3–10 and there it has been said that he will not appear until the removal of the Church. The Mosaic age, which extended from the giving of the law to the law's end in the death of Christ, was interrupted by the intercalary age known as "the times of the Gentiles," which intercalation period began with the captivities and ends with the glorious reappearing of Christ. Accounting for a portion of this Gentile era God did measure out 490 years relative to Israel, which time along with "Gentile times" was nevertheless broken into by the present unforeseen intercalary age of the Church. The final tribulation period is measured in time by definitely predicted years for Israel, while the character of that period is delineated by the feet and toes of the colossal image which record the end of Gentile times.

2. Dispensation. Translated from the word οἰκονομία, meaning primarily *stewardship,* a dispensation is a specific, divine economy, a commitment from God to man of a responsibility to discharge that which God has appointed him. The Apostle declares of himself: "For this cause I Paul, the prisoner of Jesus Christ for you Gentiles, if ye have heard of the dispensation of the grace of God which is given me to you-ward" (Eph. 3:1–2). A stewardship was committed to the Apostle for him to receive, formulate, and proclaim the sacred secret respecting the hitherto unrevealed fact and provisions of saving grace as they are demonstrated in the Church. In uncounted instances Covenant Theology is disturbed by the recognition of dispensational distinctions; even the new manifestation of divine grace becomes one of those disturbing features of truth. If there be, as Covenant theologians contend, but one covenant of grace and that covenant operating uniformly in every age, to what, indeed, must the Apostle be referring when he asserts that a dispensation respecting a hitherto unrevealed economy

of divine grace is committed unto him? Regardless of an unproved and unscriptural notion which may be embraced by a great number of men who have done no more than to receive without investigation what is taught in their schools, in the present age God is making a distinct and peculiar demonstration of His grace through the Church, which is Christ's Body. "Unto me, who am less than the least of all saints, is this grace given, that I should preach among the Gentiles the unsearchable riches of Christ; and to make all men see what is the fellowship of the mystery, which from the beginning of the world hath been hid in God, who created all things by Jesus Christ: to the intent that now unto the principalities and powers in heavenly places might be known by the church the manifold wisdom of God" (Eph. 3:8–10). Thus it comes about by means of this company of redeemed Jews and Gentiles (Eph. 3:6), which company has not existed as such in any other age, that the mystery or sacred secret, hidden from past ages, is made known and that revelation reaches to angelic hosts. Because past, present, and future ages (cf. Eph. 1:10; 3:1–6) are so clearly defined in the Scriptures, Covenant theologians acknowledge different ages or time-periods, but then they treat them as merely different ways of administering one and the same divine purpose. Regardless of every feature known to earlier ages, it will be seen that the Word of God builds all its doctrinal structure on an age past, a present age, and a future age. To deny these varied divisions, however, gathered as they are about the different revealed purposes of God, is to cease to be influenced duly by the precise Scripture which God has spoken.

DISPERSIONS OF ISRAEL

In the light of her unchangeable covenants, one of which is possession of the land of promise (cf. Deut. 30:1–8), it is essential that Israel's dispossessions of the land be recognized. These dispossessions, then, involve regatherings also. There was clear prediction of three dispersions and three regatherings. Three dispersions have occurred as predicted, and two regatherings. Israel is now scattered in her third and final dispersion, awaiting more or less consciously the last regathering. One of the most common impressions respecting Israel is that they always have been and always will be scattered among the nations, as they are at this time. Attention to the Word of God will correct such a misleading error. It should be observed that, unless Israel remains a separate people under the specific purpose and covenant of God, and in no way related to, or any part of, the Church, there would be no meaning to Israel's dispersions or regatherings. The three dispersions and regatherings may well be considered separately. As an introduction to this consideration, it may be observed that, since in the Scripture Israel is the key to all earthly prospects and blessings, nothing will ever be normal in the earth when this nation is out of her land. All peace and tranquility for the earth await the final placing of Israel on their own promised land.

1. DISPERSION INTO EGYPT. The history of Israel in Egyptian bondage, the manner of their going thither, and the miracle of their deliverance are all known to readers of the Bible, but it is not so generally known that the Egyptian bondage was predicted centuries before. When a deep sleep fell upon Abraham and Jehovah ratified His unconditional covenant with him respecting the everlasting title to the land, God said to him: "Know of a surety that thy seed shall be a stranger in a land that is not their's, and shall serve them; and they shall afflict them four hundred years; and also that nation, whom they shall serve, will I judge: and afterward shall they come out with great substance. And thou shalt go to thy fathers in peace; thou shalt be buried in a good old age. But in the fourth generation they shall come hither again: for the iniquity of the Amorites is not yet full" (Gen. 15:13-16). The return of the nation to the land under the leadership of Moses and Joshua marks the end of the first dispersion. It began, continued, and ended as Jehovah predicted it would to Abraham.

2. THE CAPTIVITIES. Because of their sins, both the northern and southern kingdoms were allowed to go into bondage. The bondage ended seventy years after the southern kingdom was taken captive, but still not all that were taken abroad returned. The important fact is that a representation of the whole nation was reassembled in the land. A period of captivity for the southern kingdom was predicted by Jeremiah. He wrote: "And this whole land shall be a desolation, and an astonishment; and these nations shall serve the king of Babylon seventy years. And it shall come to pass, when seventy years are accomplished, that I will punish the king of Babylon, and that nation, saith the LORD, for their iniquity, and the land of the Chaldeans, and will make it perpetual desolations" (Jer. 25:11-12). Daniel learned from this specific passage when the time of bondage would be fulfilled. Of this experience Daniel

records: "In the first year of Darius the son of Ahasuerus, of the seed of the Medes, which was made king over the realm of the Chaldeans; in the first year of his reign I Daniel understood by books the number of the years, whereof the word of the LORD came to Jeremiah the prophet, that he would accomplish seventy years in the desolations of Jerusalem" (Dan. 9:1–2).

3. PRESENT DISPERSION. The present dispersion exceeds the other two in point of duration and in the manner in which Israel is now scattered among all the nations of the earth. Beginning with the destruction of Jerusalem in the year 70 A.D., the final scattering continues to the present hour and is a major characteristic of the present age, which characteristic must continue until the Church be removed from the world. It is then that Israel will at once come under renewed blessing and guidance of Jehovah and return to her own land. However, the return is accompanied also by other mighty events, all of which are unprecedented and directly or indirectly related to Israel's restoration. In this aspect of prophetic truth very much Scripture is involved.

The final return to their land is one of the major themes of Old Testament prophecy concerning the Jew. Concerning the present captivity Moses wrote:

And ye shall be left few in number, whereas ye were as the stars of heaven for multitude; because thou wouldest not obey the voice of the LORD thy God. And it shall come to pass, that as the LORD rejoiced over you to do you good, and to multiply you; so the LORD will rejoice over you to destroy you, and to bring you to nought; and ye shall be plucked from off the land whither thou goest to possess it. And the LORD shall scatter thee among all people, from the one end of the earth even unto the other; and there thou shalt serve other gods, which neither thou nor thy fathers have known, even wood and stone. And among these nations shalt thou find no ease, neither shall the sole of thy foot have rest: but the LORD shall give thee there a trembling heart, and failing of eyes, and sorrow of mind: and thy life shall hang in doubt before thee; and thou shalt fear day and night, and shalt have none assurance of thy life: in the morning thou shalt say, Would God it were even! and at even thou shalt say, Would God it were morning! for the fear of thine heart wherewith thou shalt fear, and for the sight of thine eyes which thou shalt see. And the LORD shall bring thee into Egypt again with ships, by the way whereof I spake unto thee, Thou shalt see it no more again: and there ye shall be sold unto your enemies for bondmen and bondwomen, and no man shall buy you.— Deut. 28:62–68

That which was to serve to accomplish this dispersion is described at length: "Remember, I beseech thee, the word that thou commandedst thy servant Moses, saying, If ye transgress, I will scatter you abroad among the nations" (Neh. 1:8); "I will scatter them also among the heathen, whom neither they nor their fathers have known: and I will send a sword after them, till I have consumed them" (Jer. 9:16); "Because my people have forgotten me, they have burned incense to vanity, and they have caused them to stumble in their ways from the ancient paths, to walk in paths, in a way not cast up; to make their land desolate, and a perpetual hissing; every one that passeth thereby shall be astonished, and wag his head. I will scatter them as with an east wind before the enemy: I will shew them the back, and not the face, in the day of their calamity" (Jer. 18:15–17); "And I will scatter toward every wind all that are about him to help him, and all his bands; and I will draw out the sword after them. And they shall know that I am the LORD, when I shall scatter them among the nations, and disperse them in the countries" (Ezek. 12:14–15); "I lifted up mine hand unto them also in the wilderness, that I would scatter them among the heathen, and disperse them through the countries" (Ezek. 20:23); "And I will scatter thee among the heathen, and disperse thee in the countries, and will consume thy filthiness out of thee" (Ezek. 22:15). James must therefore address his Epistle "to the twelve tribes which are scattered abroad." That Israel will yet return to her land and experience great national blessing is one of the Bible's most positive predictions—a forecast which yields to no fanciful notions for its interpretation. It must either be accepted in its literal form or ignored completely. Too often the latter is done. Men of course must ignore these Scriptures who deny any real distinction between Israel and the Church, for, as before declared, dispersion and regathering is utterly foreign to the Church. Upwards of fifty assertive passages declare that Israel will be regathered into their own land from this the third and final dispersion. Two of these passages may be cited:

"And it shall come to pass, when all these things are come upon thee, the blessing and the curse, which I have set before thee, and thou shalt call them to mind among all the nations, whither the LORD thy God hath driven thee, and shalt return unto the LORD thy God, and shall obey his voice according to all that I command thee this day, thou and thy children, with all thine heart, and with all thy soul; that then the LORD thy God will turn thy captivity, and have compassion upon thee, and will return and gather thee from all the nations, whither the LORD thy God hath scattered thee" (Deut. 30:1–3); "And say unto them, Thus saith the Lord GOD; Behold, I will take the children of Israel from among the heathen, whither they be gone, and will gather them on every side, and bring them into their own land: and I will make them one nation in the land upon the mountains of Israel; and one king shall be king to them all: and they shall be no more two nations, neither shall they be divided into two kingdoms any more at all: neither shall they defile themselves any more with their idols, nor with their detestable things, nor with any of their transgressions: but I will save them out of all their dwellingplaces, wherein they have sinned, and will cleanse them: so shall they be my people, and I will be their God. And David my servant shall be king over them; and they all shall have one shepherd: they shall also walk in my judgments, and observe my statutes, and do them. And they shall dwell in the land that I have given unto Jacob my servant, wherein your fathers have dwelt; and they shall dwell therein, even they, and their children, and their children's children for ever: and my servant David shall be their prince for ever. Moreover I will make a covenant of peace with them; it shall be an everlasting covenant with them: and I will place them, and multiply them, and will set my sanctuary in the midst of them for evermore. My tabernacle also shall be with them: yea, I will be their God, and they shall be my people. And the heathen shall know that I the LORD do sanctify Israel, when my sanctuary shall be in the midst of them for evermore" (Ezek. 37:21–28).

ECCLESIOLOGY

The term ἐκκλησία, translated *church* or *assembly*, means a called-out company. Its counterpart in the Old Testament is the congregation; but Israel's congregation was never the true Church of the New Testament. Israel constituted nevertheless an assembly in the wilderness (Acts 7:38) as did the mob of Ephesus in the theater likewise (Acts 19:32, 41). The deeper spiritual use of the word *church* refers to a company of saved people who are by their salvation called out from the world into living, organic union with Christ to form His mystical Body over which He is the Head. That outward form of church which is a mere assembly of people must be restricted to those of one generation, indeed of one locality, and may include the unsaved as well as the saved. Over against this, the Church which is Christ's Body and Bride is composed of people of all generations since the Church began to be, is not confined to one locality, and includes only those who are actually saved. The spiritual meaning is thus seen to be far removed from mere recognition of a building which may be called a church, a congregation however organized, or any form of sectarian constituency.

The Pauline doctrine of the true or spiritual Church is second only in importance to the doctrine of salvation by grace. That salvation of which he wrote leads to and provides the supernatural material out of which the true Church is being formed. The two taken together constitute what the Apostle termed "my gospel." Both of the doctrines which composed his gospel were a revelation to the Apostle directly from God (Gal. 1:11–12; Eph. 3:1–6). Each revelation concerned hitherto unannounced and, up to the Day of Pentecost, nonexisting conceptions. Exception to this general statement may be found in the doctrinal patterns set forth by certain Old Testament types which foreshadow phases of truth belonging to the Church alone, and as well by the first twelve chapters of John's Gospel in which Christ is held up as a Savior of the lost, though in anticipation of that qualification as Savior which was afterwards gained through His actual death and resurrection. That the true Church was only an anticipation during the earthly ministry of Christ may be demonstrated in various ways. Christ Himself declared it to be yet future (Matt. 16:18), a crucified and risen Savior had not yet become the Object of saving faith (Gal. 3:23–25), and no one could believe in or preach the present grace-salvation at a time when he did not believe that Christ would die or be raised from the dead (Luke 18:31–34). There could be no Church until it was purchased with His precious blood (Eph. 5:25–27), until He arose to give it resurrection life (Col. 3:1–3), until He ascended to be the Head over all things to the Church (Eph. 1:20–23), or until the Spirit came on Pentecost through whom the Church might be formed into one Body and through whom the Church might be co-ordinated by His indwelling presence.

God has four classes of intelligent creatures in His universe—angels, Gentiles, Jews, and Christians—and there is more difference to be observed between Christians and either Jews or Gentiles than between angels and Jews or Gentiles. Should this statement seem extreme, it must be because the true and exalted character of the Christian is not comprehended. No angel is a son of God by actual generating birth from above, nor is any angel made to stand before God in the $\pi\lambda\acute{\eta}\rho\omega\mu\alpha$ —i.e., fullness—of Christ (John 1:16), which fullness is the $\pi\lambda\acute{\eta}\rho\omega\mu\alpha$ of the Godhead bodily (Col. 2:9–10).

Human history on earth has extended at least six thousand years. This long time may be divided into three periods of approximately two thousand years each: from Adam to Abraham two thousand years, with but one stock or kind of people in the world; from Abraham to Christ another two thousand years, with two kinds of people in the world— Gentiles and Jews, and from Christ's first advent to the present and indeed to His second advent, with three kinds of people in the world —Gentiles, Jews, and Christians.

No Scripture is addressed to angels and very little to Gentiles. About three-fourths of the Bible concerns Israel directly and about one-fourth concerns the Church. Failure to discern between Judaism and Christianity, as the case is with many theologians, proves misleading and wholly without excuse. No attitude of men toward God's truth is more revelatory respecting their habitual neglect of a personal, unprejudiced study of the Bible than the implications and suppositions which some advance concerning God's purpose in the world. That He has been doing but one thing and following but one purpose on earth is a far-reaching error.

There is abundant Scripture to indicate that the present divine purpose must be the outcalling of the Church from both Gentiles and Jews.

Seven figures are employed in the New Testament to set forth the relation which exists between Christ and the Church. All seven are needed to the end that the whole revelation respecting this relationship may be disclosed. In connection with each figure and as its parallel there is a similar truth to be observed regarding Israel. (1) Christ is the Shepherd and Christians are the sheep. Israel, too, was the flock of God and the sheep of His pasture. This language brings out Christ's shepherd care and the helplessness of His sheep. (2) Christ is the Vine and believers of today are the branches. Israel was Jehovah's vineyard. This comparison speaks of Christ's strength and life being imparted, without which nothing could be done to enhance His glory. (3) Christ is the chief Cornerstone and Christians are the building. Israel had a temple, but the Church is a living temple for the habitation of God through the Spirit. Here the figure conveys the thought of interdependence and indwelling. (4) Christ is the High Priest and New Testament believers are a kingdom of priests. Israel had a priesthood; the Church in its entirety is a priesthood. This figurative speech introduces truth respecting worship and service. (5) Christ is the Head of the Church which is the Body. Israel was a commonwealth, an organized nation; the Church is an organism very much alive by reason of partaking of one life and being related to its living Head. This comparison speaks of vital relationship and of gifts for service. (6) Christ is the Head of a New Creation and Christians are with Him in that Creation as its vital members. Israel was of the old creation and attached to the earth; the Church is of the New Creation and related to heaven. This figure dwells upon the believer's marvels of position and standing, since he is in Christ. (7) Christ is the Bridegroom and the Church is the Bride. Israel was the repudiated (yet to be restored) wife of Jehovah; the Church is the espoused virgin Bride of Christ. This relationship for

Christians, foreseen in various types, is all of another sphere and future. It sets forth the glory of Christ in which the Church as His Bride will share above. What marvelous things are wrought in this company of believers that they should become suitable as a bride for the Second Person of the Godhead and such a one as will ravish His heart throughout all eternity!

Pauline Ecclesiology is divided into three major divisions of doctrine: (1) the Church which is Christ's Body, His Bride, His fullness (John 1:16; Col. 2:9–10), and He is made full in them (Eph. 1:22–23); (2) the local church, which is an assembly composed of those who in any locality profess to be followers of Christ; and (3) the high calling for a daily life in conformity with the position which the believer sustains, being in Christ. Along with this is the doctrine of the empowering, indwelling Spirit by whom alone the high calling can be realized. It is evident from the Bible that God had a rule of life for Israel which was the Law of Moses, and that He will yet have a legal requirement for them in the future kingdom. It is equally evident that He has indicated the manner of life which belongs to the Christian, and that it rests not on a merit basis, but calls for a life to be lived on the exalted standards of heaven itself. Let no student imagine that he has progressed far in sound doctrine if he does not comprehend the consistent teaching of the New Testament which declares that the Christian is not under the Law of Moses or any other form of obligation which has for aim the securing of merit.

It is never taught in the Scriptures that Israel as a nation will appear in heaven, though this destiny is open at present to individual believers from among the Jews. The destiny of the nation is earthly, extending on forever into the new earth which is yet to be. The destiny of the Church is heavenly. As His Bride and Body, the Church will be with the Bridegroom and Head wherever He goes.

ELDERS

Since elders (or bishops) are the divinely ordered rulers in the local, visible church, the general doctrine of the local church as regards its government may rightfully be introduced under this heading. The term *elder* is common to both Testaments and in general contemplates those of maturity and authority. No mere novice was to be made an elder (cf. 1 Tim. 3:6). The first reference to elders in the Old Testament seems to take recognition of their advanced years. Old men by reason of their experience are naturally valued for counsel (cf. 1 Kings 12:8; Ezek. 7:26). Later in Biblical history the designation *elder* gained the added idea of authority.

The word *elder* has three meanings in the New Testament. (1) A reference to age or maturity (cf. Luke 15:25; 1 Tim. 5:2). (2) A continuation of the Old Testament office of elders over Israel (cf. Matt. 16:21; 26:47, 57; Acts 4:5, 23). (3) A name for one officer of the local church to whom is assigned authority especially in the direction of spiritual matters pertaining to the church which he serves. It is now generally recognized that the title *elder* (πρεσβύτερος) relates to the same person as does the title *bishop* (ἐπίσκοπος). It seems probable that the word *elder* is recognition of the person chosen to bear the name, while the word *bishop* is descriptive of the office or position which that person occupies. The term *elder* contemplates what the man is in himself, then, while the term *bishop* contemplates what he has been appointed to do.

Among modern churches there are three general forms of government. (1) There are those who employ the word *episcopal* for their manner of government, which indicates leadership more or less absolute in the hands of men known as bishops. (2) There is a congregational form of organization which theoretically brings every matter to the whole membership for decision. (3) There lies, between these two extremes, a representative form of government in which the membership or congregation by its vote commits governmental responsibility to selected men—elders and deacons. To the elder is given in general the care over spiritual things and to the deacon the care over temporal things. This form of church management, after which the United States government with its Senate and House of Representatives was patterned, remains fundamentally a congregational government since these officers serve at the appointment of that local body. Elders or deacons are not supposed to be rulers who impose their will upon the congregation, as is too often the case. They are elected by the congregation rather as a committee might be and upon them is imposed the responsibilities which are assigned to governing men. The churches which have been organized under this representative form of administration should never lose sight of the fact that they are, first and last, congregational in their type of government. This truth is not lessened because of the commitment of responsibility to representative elders and deacons. Such men should discharge all of that, but no more than that, which is committed unto them. These chosen officers should seek to know what is the wish of the whole membership and to enact that alone. Never should they impose any personal convictions upon the congregation contrary to the mind of the membership. For mere convenience some elders are classed as *teaching elders,* who are the clergy, and others as *ruling elders,* who are the church officers. Here the terminology *ruling elder* implies no more than that he rules as the membership's representative. Elders may be elected to rule for their lifetime or for a restricted period. The latter has more in its favor.

ELECTION

Having recognized the sovereign right of God over His creation and having assigned to Him a rational purpose in all His plan, the truth contained in the doctrine of election follows in natural sequence as the necessary function of one who is divine. When there arises unbelief and resistance in the human mind against the tenet of divine election, it is engendered only because this larger conception of divine necessity has not been considered. It is hard, indeed, for men who have adopted the idea that they are independent of God and therefore in no way related to Him—the view of all who are unsaved—to receive any truth relative to the sovereign rights of a Creator over His creatures.

The principle underlying divine election seems to be evident in all God's creation, but is not resented usually when it operates outside the limited field of a destiny for human beings. A principle of selection is everywhere to be seen, which principle cannot be attributed to mere accident, chance, or blind fate. That any man is born at all when he might have been forever nonexistent must be an act of selection on the part of divine sovereignty. That a man is born in one age of privilege rather than another of less privilege can be no matter of mere chance. That one has been born of godly parents rather than in pagan darkness is a divine determination. That one inherits wealth, culture, or position in place of painful limitations, that one has mental gifts and competency must not be a human arrangement; yet these very conditions, being wrought of God, all partake of the nature of divine selection. The great covenants of God are divine promises of selective benefits to favored groups of people. This again is of the nature of divine election. Record is made of "elect angels" (1 Tim. 5:21). Such, indeed, would be God's right to do with His creatures as He may choose. It is both true and reasonable that God has not caused anything or any being to exist without having a worthy purpose to realize through that creation. That some of His creation serve one purpose and some another is itself a matter of divine choice. Human resentment arises only when it is indicated that some are more favored than others respecting destiny. Were God thought to be an ungoverned tyrant, it could be allowed that He might do as He pleases with His own, whether this prove right or wrong; but when it has been disclosed that He is infinitely righteous and holy and that He is actuated by infinite love, difficulty will arise in the natural mind over how God can have elect people for whom He achieves more than He does for others or how some can be blessed while others are not.

There is no doubt whatever about the Bible teaching that God has chosen an elect people; but the contemplation of all that is involved in this truth reaches out into realms of existence that can be known only to God, far removed as they are from the human sphere of understanding. Being thus limited, it ill becomes the earth dweller to sit in judgment on God respecting divine election. God's essential character has been disclosed and He can be trusted where men cannot possibly understand. He is infinitely wise, infinitely holy, and infinitely just and good. When exercising His sovereign right in election, He does not transgress His character or deny Himself. Since He does elect some for special glories and destinies and since He proves infinitely right in all He does, it follows that His eternal elective purpose must be as righteous as He is righteous.

There are two major elections of God.

1. ISRAEL. Throughout the Olivet Discourse Christ refers to Israel as *the elect*. The most casual contemplation of this discourse (Matt. 24: 1—25:46) will disclose the truth that only Israel is in view as the elect of God. Similarly, a revealing Scripture from Paul (Romans 9:1—10: 4) sets forth the truth respecting Israel's election. Too often this portion of Scripture has been applied to believers today who comprise the Church. The salient facts in the case which make it impossible, however, are that in Israel's election there is a national objective and that an individual Jew, though belonging to the elect nation, did not have any

personal election assured him. God is thus sovereign in His dealings with Israel. He disregards the enmity and hatred of the nations as they resent the fact of Israel's election. The election is made a public matter, indeed, for Jehovah selects, preserves, and defends this one people out of all the nations of the earth. They are His "chosen people" above all the nations and chosen specifically for His glory. In relation to Israel's election, then, God acts in sovereign authority. All other nations must eventually take a subordinate place. During Israel's kingdom on earth, accordingly, the nation or peoples that will not serve Israel shall perish (Isa. 14:1–2; 60:12). No true interpretation of the Old Testament is possible if the fact of Israel's national, sacred, eternal election be rejected.

2. The Church. As certainly as Israel's election has been public and national, so certainly the Church's election is private—hence for them alone to appreciate—and individual. So wide a difference must obtain between the issues involved in a public, national election and a private, individual election that little in common exists between them. Respecting the private character of the individual's election, it may be indicated that there is no more dangerous or injurious practice in the application of God's Word than that of displaying the truth of personal election before the unsaved. It neither belongs to them nor does it allude to them. Its presentation to them can only create resentment, as it does, and blind their minds respecting the one and only truth which God now addresses to them, namely, personal salvation by grace alone through Christ Jesus. The message to the unsaved, regardless of the deep theological issues which are latent in it, is simply, "Whosoever will may come." When any do come and are saved, they may then glory in the revelation that their lives were chosen in Him from before the foundation of the world (Eph. 1:4). Every preacher of God's Word should be awake to this immeasurable danger of introducing the theme of personal, individual election before unregenerate persons.

In this age of grace there is an election which includes all who are saved. This company constitutes the Church, the Body and Bride of Christ, and together with the resurrected Christ constitutes the New Creation with all its purpose and destiny in heaven. The New Testament gives abundant testimony to the fact of the divine purpose and character of this heavenly people. It also discloses that each member of this select company is chosen personally and individually by God before all ages of time. In the New Testament the same term *the elect* is used both for Israel (Matt. 24:22) and the Church (Rom. 8:33).

When addressing the Father in His great High Priestly prayer (John 17) and when thus referring to the believers in this age of the Church, Christ employed but one cognomen which He used seven times. The title which Christ used exclusively when speaking to the Father of believers is most significant. It must be the supreme title in the vocabulary used in conversation between the Father and the Son. The designation—"those whom thou hast given me"—itself asserts the most absolute elective purpose on the part of the Father and the Son. Human imagination would not have gone far astray if it should picture a situation in eternity past when the Father presented individual believers separately unto the Son, each representing a particular import and value not approached by another. Like a chest of jewels, collected one by one and wholly diverse, these love-gifts may have appeared before the eyes of the Son of God. Should one be missing, He, the Son, would be rendered inexpressibly poor by so much. Immeasurable and unknowable riches of grace then are in the wonderful words: *those whom thou hast given me.*

That all humanity has not been included in this election is most certain. It includes only those particular ones given to Christ. According to Psalm 2:7-9 the Father will yet give to the Son the nations for His subduing judgments to rest upon them, that they may be His possession; but this has no relation to a bestowal of individuals in eternity past. Theirs is of a truth unto a sublime exaltation in glory.

Romans 8:28. In this passage reference is made to ones called "according to his purpose." In the context which follows the most absolute doctrine of predestination, preservation, and presentation for this elect, or called, people has been set forth. Not all humanity are called; but those who have been called are justified and glorified.

Ephesians 1:4. Of each believer it is said that he was chosen in Christ before the foundation of the world and for the heavenly purpose that he may be in glory before Him. Thus, again, it becomes clear that not all of humanity are chosen. Christ declared: "No man can come to me, except the Father which hath sent me draw him" (John 6:44), implying a selection. There nevertheless is also a universal call or drawing (cf. John 12:32), but that is far removed from the personal drawing of the elect whom the Father hath given to the Son.

3. SUPPOSED PARTIALITY. To contend as some have that God, to be impartial, must bestow His greatest riches of blessing upon all alike is to sit in judgment upon the Creator, which judgment ill becomes the creature, to deny God's sovereign right to order His creation as He will,

and to deprive God of the freedom to introduce variety into His universe. Must every creature be an archangel? Has not God as much right to display His measureless variety in matters pertaining to man's relation toward Him as in matters connected with man's relation to his fellow man on earth? This is an issue quite apart from the vexing problem of sin. However, it must be recognized also that sin has been permitted to enter the universe with its ruin of a part of the angels and with the total ruin of the human race. All of this, indeed, was in the eternal counsels of God, for He determined before the foundation of the world that His efficacious Lamb would be slain (Rev. 13:8). As a starting point, then, for a right understanding and evaluation of problems related to divine election, it is essential to receive the Biblical testimony that all men are ruined spiritually, being born into a fallen race. The gathering out of an elect company to appear in heaven perfected forever involves not only redemption, which answers the claims of God's holiness, but dealing with the willful rejection of God, which rejection is as universal as the fall because a fruit of that fall. God alone could provide such a redemption, and there can be no salvation apart from that redemption. It is equally true that God alone can deal with the human will in this regard.

4. Human Will. In the first instance, it is well to observe that God did not create the human will as an instrument to defeat Himself; it was created rather as a means by which He might realize His own worthy purposes. Though as Sovereign He could do so, God does not coerce the human will; He rather works within the individual both to will and to do of His good pleasure (cf. Phil. 2:13). An efficacious call to salvation, then, is a call which none ever finally resists (cf. Rom. 8:30). Everyone whom God predestinates He calls, and everyone whom He calls He justifies and glorifies. There could not be failure in one instance among the millions who are called. The vision which He creates in the heart and the limitless persuasion He exercises induce a favorable reaction on the part of all thus called, which reaction is rendered infinitely certain. The important truth to be observed in all of this is that, though divine persuasion be limitless, it still remains persuasion, and so when a decision is secured for Christ in the individual he exercises his own will apart from even a shadow of constraint. The divine invitation still is true that "whosoever will may come." However, it also is true that none will ever come apart from this divine call, and that the call is extended only to His elect. What God's righteous relation is to those whom He does not call is another doctrine quite removed from the teaching of election.

5. PRACTICAL OUTWORKINGS. As in the great covenants God has made, so in every outworking of His will the principle of divine selection is exhibited. The following classifications will demonstrate this:

a. FIVE ELECTIVE DECREES. Theologians may be classed according to the order in which they place the five elective decrees of God. The following tabulation of these decrees is in an order which may be defended from the Scriptures:

(1) Decree to create.
(2) Decree to permit the fall.
(3) Decree to elect some to salvation.
(4) Decree to provide a Savior.
(5) Decree to save the elect.

As an illustration of the importance of this order, it may be seen that to place the decree to elect some to be saved before the decree to create would place God in the position of creating a portion of humanity with a view to their being reprobated forever. A complete treatment of the five elective decrees has been undertaken in Volume III devoted to Soteriology.

b. FIVE POINTS OF CALVINISM. Because of the Calvinistic attitude toward divine election, its generally recognized five points are here named:

(1) Total inability of the fallen man.
(2) Unconditional election.
(3) A limited redemption.
(4) Efficacious divine grace.
(5) The perseverance of the saints.

c. FIVE POINTS OF ARMINIANISM:

(1) Conditional election according to God's foreknowledge of supposed human worthiness.
(2) A universal redemption, but only those who believe to be saved.
(3) Salvation by grace through faith. (Because of a supposed enabling grace divinely bestowed upon all at birth, all may cooperate in their salvation if they will to do so.)
(4) Grace not irresistible.
(5) Falling from grace possible.

d. FIVE POINTS OF JUDAISM. As an outworking of God's elective purpose for Israel, five points of Judaism may be indicated:

(1) An everlasting nation.
(2) An everlasting possession of their land.
(3) An everlasting throne.

(4) An everlasting king.
(5) An everlasting kingdom.

ESCHATOLOGY

The doctrine of things to come is extensive indeed. It may be safe to estimate that as much lies ahead yet to be experienced as has transpired in the past. Biblical prophecy is virtually history prewritten. Apparently God delights to disclose that which He will do. To do so is an achievement which humanity can neither approach nor understand. In this competency God demonstrates the truth that He is superior to all others. The advantage to the human family of being informed respecting the future when ability to discern it for themselves has been denied them is exceedingly great; yet to the vast majority of people, including even Christians, God's revealed disclosures respecting the future are as though they had never been written. Those who habitually neglect the study of prophecy must of necessity go uninformed about the meaning of the past, the present, and the future. What God chooses to do is a sublime unity in itself. When the consummation of that unity is not envisaged, there can be no ground left for a right appreciation of the direction, value, and meaning of either the past or the present. God has not provided men with the material set forth by His predictions in vain. He expects that what He has said shall be welcomed just as all other portions of the Bible are received, and furthermore He has not left men to their helplessness in the understanding of His unfolding of future things. Among the things which the Holy Spirit has been appointed to accomplish for those in whom He dwells is to show the "things to come" (John 16:13). In the light of this provision and its practical outworking only wonder can be entertained concerning the real relation to the Holy Spirit of those who, professing to be saved, are not interested in God's proclamation of "things to come." Since the knowledge of the future so determines the right understanding of past and present, no man is prepared to "preach the word" who habitually ignores divine prediction. The claim that the prophetic Scriptures cannot be understood is never made by those who give due attention to them. No more difficulty has been encountered in interpreting the Scripture bearing on Eschatology than the Scripture bearing upon Soteriology. The supposed trouble respecting the interpretation of Eschatology originates in the fact that many theologians have from the first given themselves to the study of Soteriology almost exclusively, to the all-but-complete neglect of Eschatology. Since Eschatology bulks so largely in the text of the Bible—sixteen Old Testament books being universally classed as prophetic and from one-fourth to one-fifth of the whole Sacred Text appearing as prediction when written—Bible expositors who are free to move outside the bounds of static theological dicta have discovered vast fields of revelation in the prophetic Scriptures, which doctrine of necessity determines the direction of right Biblical interpretation. Because of this discovery, there is an ever-growing school of premillennial interpretation and a fast-ripening division between otherwise orthodox men.

The primary division in all prophecy lies between that which is now fulfilled and that which is unfulfilled. This division has never been stabilized, of course. The time word *now* is ever changing. Things that were future yesterday may be fulfilled by tomorrow. No Eschatology is complete which concerns itself only with that which is future at a given time. Since all prediction was future at the time it came to be written, a complete Eschatology should account for all that is fulfilled and unfulfilled.

Naturally enough, prophecy may be divided again between that which is found in the Old Testament and in the New Testament. At this point, however, it is essential to observe the doctrinal rather than the structural division between the Testaments. This doctrinal cleavage occurs between the Gospels of Luke and John. In other words, the Synoptic Gospels continue and consummate the unfulfilled portions of the Old Testament. Malachi had ended with expectation of Israel's King and His kingdom. The Synoptics relate the coming of the King and the offer of His kingdom to that nation, which kingdom was, according even to divine purpose, rejected by the nation and its realization assigned to the second advent. A far-reaching error of theologians generally is to relate the promised kingdom—in so far as they apprehend it at all—to the first advent, whereas it is always linked to the second advent except as it was offered and rejected in the days of the first coming. The development of any earthly kingdom in this age and by virtue of forces released at the first advent is a theological fiction.

It becomes imperative, if any right understanding of Scripture is to be gained, to trace the distinctive order of events as set forth in Judaism to their divinely appointed completion. This the Synoptic Gospels do. Beginning with John and continuing to the end of Revelation, a new people composed of both Jews and Gentiles, a new divine purpose in a hitherto unrevealed age, with new predictions bearing upon a heavenly glory, are introduced, though—usually by way of contrast—much is added respecting the divine purpose for Israel.

Under Eschatology in its larger treatment as presented in Volume IV, the major prophetic themes of the Old Testament and of the New Testament are outlined. It may be restated here that, in general, prophecy can be classified as pertaining to Israel, Gentiles, and the Church. To this large threefold division may be added predictions respecting angels, heaven, and the new earth. Israel from her beginning in Abraham continues as a divinely preserved people through this age of the Church on into her kingdom, and finally appears with her eternal glory in the new earth that is to be. That nation never loses its identity and in fulfillment of everlasting covenants and predictions is blessed on the earth. That nation, as such, is never seen in heaven. The Gentiles from Adam on, continuing through Israel's Old Testament history, through "the times of the Gentiles," through the present age of Gentile privilege in the outcalling of the Church, even through the coming Messianic kingdom age as sharers in that kingdom, are finally seen in relation to the new earth and the city which comes down from God out of heaven (cf. Rev. 21:24, 26). Very extensive portions of Scripture carry prediction regarding the Gentiles. Reference is made here only to Gentiles as a continuing body of people quite apart from those individuals among their number who are saved in the present age. The Gentiles as such remain Gentiles into eternity to come. Finally, the Church from her beginning at Pentecost is seen as a pilgrim people on the earth, and later as partakers of the heavenly glory.

ETERNITY

Under this general theme consideration is properly given to eternity itself, eternity in relation to God, to time, and to "the gift of God [which] is eternal life."

1. DEFINITION. No thought ever confronts the finite mind which is less intelligible than that of eternity, and it is probable the idea that eternity will never end is more comprehensible than that it never had a beginning. In fact, the human mind cannot grasp the extent of that which is eternal. Philosophers and theologians alike have met with defeat when attempting to portray eternity. A slight increase of apprehension may be secured when it is contemplated in its relation to the eternal God.

2. IN RELATION TO GOD. Little will be gained in attempting to contemplate eternity as a mere negative idea, the absence of time. It is best considered as the mode of existence of the eternal God. Abundant testimony has been given in the Scriptures respecting the eternal character of God. He is never presented in the Bible as circumscribed by time. He may conform to time with its character of successions, but His own mode of existence is from everlasting to everlasting. He is Sovereign Designer and Ruler over all ages of time. Referring to Christ as very God and Creator of all things, Hebrews 1:2 declares that He *programmed the ages.* There is no reference here to Christ as Creator of material things, as later in verse 10, but rather to the fact that He originated and ordered the progression of all time-periods. The mode of existence which belongs to God is fundamental and basal, compared to which any other manner of existence such as that related to time may be considered something unusual or exceptional. To the finite creature, however, who is homed in time there is no other fashion of life than his own which is comprehensible to him. Such natural limitations should not blind the mind to divine revelation or to those conclusions which may be reached at least by the help of reason. It should be recognized that there are other modes of existence than that which is related to time, even though these cannot be comprehended in their essential features. An eternal existence belongs to the Creator; hence to that mode of life alone belongs ascendancy and supremacy. Thus the occurrence of a period of time with its finite creatures and its successions is properly to be rated as exceptional or inferior.

3. IN RELATION TO TIME. The prevalent notion that time represents an intercalation which has interrupted the flow of eternity, that it is "a narrow neck of land between two shoreless seas of eternity," seems much at fault. Such a conception involves the absurdity that eternity too may have an ending and a beginning. Whatever time may be and whatever its relation is to eternity, it must be maintained that no cessation of eternity has occurred or will. God's mode of existence remains

unchanged. Time might be thought of as something superimposed upon eternity were it not that there is ground for question whether eternity consists of a succession of events, as is true of time. The consciousness of God is best conceived as being an all-inclusive comprehension at once, covering all that has been or will be. The attempt to bring time with its successions into a parallel with eternity or to give time the character of a segment in the course of eternity is to misconceive the most essential characteristic of eternal things.

4. ETERNAL LIFE. A sharp distinction must be made between human existence which by its nature continues forever and the gift of God which is eternal life. In the last analysis, humanity is not wholly conformed to time. Every human being will be living on forever, even after it has been decreed that time shall be no more. Thus humanity intrudes into eternity and must, in the end, conform to the eternal mode of existence. Each human being has a beginning. In this he is unlike God. Each human being, however, has no end of his existence. In this respect he is to some extent like God. That human beings have no end is a solemn thought; but on those who receive God's gift of eternal life the very life of God is bestowed. That life is a partaking of the divine nature. It is no less than "Christ in you, the hope of glory." Thus by regeneration all who believe become possessors of that which in God is itself eternal. In 1 Corinthians 13:12 it is declared, accordingly, that the believer one day will know even as now he is known of God, that is, the finite mind will be superseded by the mind of God. Even now it is said that he has the mind of Christ (1 Cor. 2:16). Little, indeed, may be anticipated respecting the coming transcendent experience of those who now possess eternal life when they shall enter into the experience of eternal life in full.

EVANGELISM

Evangelism and evangelists are peculiar to the New Testament. They belong to God's great plan for calling out the elect who are His heavenly people. Israel had her prophets who were patriots and reformers, but no one of their number undertook a ministry comparable to the New

Testament evangelist. At the same time, there was no gospel message whatsoever sent from God to the Gentiles (cf. Eph. 2:12).

1. DEFINITION. Evangelism is the act of presenting to the unsaved the evangel or good news of the gospel of God's saving grace through Christ Jesus. It may be a dealing with individuals or with groups and congregations. In any case, the one ideal prevails. Probably the most arresting fact related to this ministry is that it has been committed to every individual who may be saved. The Apostle writes that "God . . . hath given to us the ministry of reconciliation . . . and hath committed unto us the word of reconciliation. Now then we are ambassadors for Christ, as though God did beseech you by us: we pray you in Christ's stead, be ye reconciled to God" (2 Cor. 5:18-20). This commission rests on all believers alike. In agreement with this universal commission is the revelation presented by Ephesians 4:12. Following upon enumeration of the ministry or leadership gifts—apostles, prophets, evangelists, pastors and teachers—the truth has been asserted that the responsibility of the pastor and teacher is to perfect the saints in their own work of the ministry, along with edifying of the Body of Christ. Thus is restated the thought that to every believer has been committed the evangelizing ministry. Each believer is, upon being saved, constituted a witness to the unsaved; but all believers are in need of such instruction, counsel, and direction as a God-appointed and well-trained pastor and teacher may impart. It is presupposed that the pastor and teacher has himself been fully trained for this leadership service. Courses which anticipate such a ministry are wanting in theological seminaries generally and therefore graduates who assume pastorates are not promoting evangelism through the God-intended agency of the whole company of believers. By so much the New Testament ideal of evangelism is failing. Instruction, nevertheless, should include discipline in the plan of salvation, the terms of the gospel, the use of the Scriptures, and the manner and method of effective work. Here Christians may well study to show themselves "approved unto God," workmen that need "not to be ashamed, rightly dividing the word of truth" (2 Tim. 2:15). It can thus be demonstrated that personal evangelism on the part of all who are saved is the New Testament plan of evangelism.

This New Testament purpose in which it is anticipated that each believer shall, after due instruction, have the high privilege of leading souls to Christ happens to be closely related to the believer's spiritual life; and since no effective service for God can ever be rendered apart from a right adjustment of the life to the holy will of God, extended instruction respecting a spiritual life must be incorporated as a part of the teaching undertaken in the training of believers. Soul-winning work, like all Christian service, depends upon the imparted power and direction of the Holy Spirit. The very desire for the salvation of the lost is not a human trait but the manifestation of divine love working through the believer. It is the love of God shed abroad in the heart out from the Holy Spirit, whom every believer has received. The believer must be guided in respect to those unto whom he speaks and directed in the manner of his approach to the unsaved.

Especial care must be exercised by preachers who are called upon to preach the gospel to groups and congregations. The gospel must be presented in its purity and no requirement laid upon the unsaved respecting works they might perform. Public methods often imply that there is saving value in something the unsaved are asked to do. God not only calls out His elect people through gospel preaching, but He ever cares for those whom He saves. If evangelizing methods do not contradict these great truths, there will be less unhappy results.

Two widely different programs for soul-winning have been pursued in the last century, namely, those adjusted to Arminian beliefs and those agreeable to Calvinistic views. The Arminian practices, being aggressive and conspicuous, may be unfortunately deemed more faithful and zealous in character. It should be recognized, however, that there are extremes both in the direction of zeal and of overcaution. The issue here being considered relates to practices followed by sincere and earnest men who deplore every extreme method. The Arminian theology forms the basis for one method of evangelism; so likewise the Calvinistic theology forms the basis for another. Arminian theologians declare that although men are born in depravity an enabling ability is given to them at birth whereby they may cooperate in their salvation if they will. This notion, unsupported by Scripture, lends encouragement to the evangelist to press people for decisions and assumes that all individuals could accept Christ if they but will to do so. It follows that, if pressed hard enough, any unregenerate person might be saved. That most mass evangelism has conformed to some degree to this Arminian theory is evident. Over against this, Calvinistic theologians contend on the authority of the Scriptures that all men are born depraved and that they remain so, being incapable of accepting Christ apart from the enlightening, drawing, calling work of the Holy Spirit. The following Scriptures, among many, sustain this conception:

"No man can come to me, except the Father which hath sent me draw him: and I will raise him up at the last day. . . . And he said, Therefore said I unto you, that no man can come unto me, except it were given unto him of my Father" (John 6:44, 65); "But the natural man receiveth not the things of the Spirit of God: for they are foolishness unto him: neither can he know them, because they are spiritually discerned" (1 Cor. 2:14); "But if our gospel be hid, it is hid to them that are lost: in whom the god of this world hath blinded the minds of them which believe not, lest the light of the glorious gospel of Christ, who is the image of God, should shine unto them" (2 Cor. 4:3–4); "For by grace are ye saved through faith; and that not of yourselves: it is the gift of God" (Eph. 2:8).

Language cannot be more explicit; and in truth were it not for the enlightening work of the Spirit by which He convicts of sin, of righteousness, and of judgment (John 16:7–11), no unregenerate person would ever turn to Christ for salvation. The point at issue is that, when the Spirit undertakes His work of bringing men to Christ, there will be little need of persuasive methods. The Holy Spirit uses the Word of God on the lips of a devoted servant of God or on a printed page, and men hearing the truth and believing are saved. From that time forth all who are saved occupy the Christian's position and have a definite responsibility to witness, not to the end they may thereby be saved but because they are saved.

2. EVANGELISTS. Of three times in which the word *evangelist* occurs within the New Testament, its place in Ephesians 4:11 is the most significant. The use of the term in this passage is with reference to the pioneer missionary who takes the message of salvation to regions beyond, where it has never gone. The revivalist laboring among churches and evangelized fields which are more or less spiritually dormant has no recognition as such in the Bible, though there is no Scripture against that type of ministry. A peculiar unreality must be seen in any spasmodic reviving when it is certain that the church thus stimulated will, for want of right direction and discipline thereafter, return at once to its unspiritual state. The evangelist's message by its very nature should be addressed to the unsaved and restricted to the theme of salvation. Should themes related to Christian living be introduced, the attention of the unsaved is at once removed from the one and only issue which concerns them to another and wholly irrelevant proposition, namely, whether they will adopt some manner of life which they, by reason of being unsaved, are utterly disqualified to consider. No minister needs more to possess the full knowledge of God's truth than does

the evangelist or the one who attempts to preach the gospel of saving grace.

EVOLUTION

Evolution is a humanly devised theory which has no truly scientific basis or evidence upon which to rest, but is all the same believed by college and university professors and in general the intellectual class. No thoughtful person can avoid the problem of the origin of all things, and the evolutionary theory is perhaps the best theory that unregenerate man can conceive. The unsaved cannot take God and His revelation into their thoughts. He certainly is not in all their thoughts (Ps. 10:4). The divine seeming so unreal to them, the concept of deity has not provided a reasonable enough basis for their minds when it is declared that God did anything. Therefore, being unable to believe the Genesis account of creation and not having any ability to believe that there is a God who created all things, they have devised the best theory that they can, but still with great inconsistency. As avowedly scientific men, they must refuse to accept anything which is unproved; yet in this theory of evolution they accept every word of testimony regardless of a lack of proof, and of course no effectual line of proof has been constructed or discovered. Such men in their unregenerate limitation are to be pitied. No Spirit-taught person will have trouble with the Genesis account of creation. Having nothing to put in its place, however, the evolutionist must devise the best theory that he can with which to satisfy the mind on the vexing problem of origins. Further discussion of this particular problem will be found in former volumes of this work, especially Volume II. See the index.

FAITH

According to the simplest conception of it, faith is a personal confidence in God. This implies that the individual has come to know

God to some degree of real experience. Not all men have faith, so the Apostle declares (2 Thess. 3:2). Thus lying back of faith is this determining factor, namely, *knowing God*. Regarding the personal knowledge of God, Christ said: "All things are delivered unto me of my Father: and no man knoweth the Son, but the Father; neither knoweth any man the Father, save the Son, and he to whomsoever the Son will reveal him" (Matt. 11:27). This statement is decisive. No one knows the Father except the Son and those only to whom the Son may reveal Him. However, with that divinely wrought knowledge of God in view, the invitation is immediately extended by this context for all the world-weary to come unto Him and there, and only there, find rest for the soul. Since God is not fully discerned by the human senses, it is easy for the natural man in a day of grace to treat the Person of God and all His claims as though they did not exist, or, at best, as if a mere harmless fiction. Faith accordingly is declared, in one aspect of it, to be "the gift of God" (Eph. 2:8). Utter want of faith is the condition of unregenerate men (1 Cor. 2:14) until God be revealed to them by the Son through the Spirit. The following quotation from the *International Standard Bible Encyclopaedia* states the simple facts about that faith which is confidence in God (Handley Dunelm, *s.v.*, "Faith"):

It is important to notice that Hebrews 11:1 is no exception to the rule that "faith" normally means "reliance," "trust." There "Faith *is* the substance [or possibly, in the light of recent inquiries into the type of Greek used by New Testament writers, 'the guaranty'] of things hoped for, the evidence [or 'convincing proof'] of things not seen." This is sometimes interpreted as if faith, in the writer's view, were, so to speak, a faculty of second sight, a mysterious intuition into the spiritual world. But the chapter amply shows that the faith illustrated, e.g. by Abraham, Moses, Rahab, was simply *reliance* upon a God known to be trustworthy. Such reliance enabled the believer to treat the future as present and the invisible as seen. In short, the phrase here, "faith *is* the evidence," etc., is parallel in form to our familiar saying, "Knowledge *is* power." A few detached remarks may be added: (*a*) The history of the use of the Greek *pistis* is instructive. In the LXX it normally, if not always, bears the "passive" sense, "fidelity," "good faith," while in classical Greek it not rarely bears the active sense, "trust." In the *koinē*, the type of Greek universally common at the Christian era, it seems to have adopted the active meaning as the ruling one *only just in time*, so to speak, to provide it for the utterance of Him whose supreme message was "reliance," and who passed that message on to His apostles. Through their lips and pens "faith," in that sense, became the supreme watchword of Christianity. . . . In conclusion, without trespassing on the ground of other articles, we call the reader's attention, for his Scriptural studies, to the *central place of faith in Christianity*, and its significance. As being, in its true idea, a reliance as simple as possible upon the word, power, love, of Another, it is precisely that which, on man's side, *adjusts him* to the living and merciful presence and action of a trusted God. In its nature, not by any mere arbitrary arrangement, it is his one possible receptive attitude, that in which he brings nothing, so that he may receive all. Thus "faith" is our side of union with Christ. And thus it is our means of possessing all His benefits, pardon, justification, purification, life, peace, glory.—II, 1088

In its larger usage, the word *faith* represents at least four varied ideas: (1) As above, it can be personal confidence in God. This the most common aspect of faith may be subdivided into three features: (a) Saving faith, which is the inwrought confidence in God's promises and provisions respecting the Savior that leads one to elect to repose upon and trust in the One who alone can save. (b) Serving faith, which contemplates as true the fact of divinely bestowed gifts and all details respecting divine appointments for service. This faith is always a personal matter, and so one believer should not become a pattern for another. That such faith with its personal characteristic may be kept inviolate, the Apostle writes: "Hast thou faith? have it to thyself before God" (Rom. 14:22). Great injury may be wrought if one Christian imitates another in matters of appointment for service. (c) Sanctifying or sustaining faith, which lays hold of the power of God for one's daily life. It is the life lived in dependence upon God, working upon a new life-principle (Rom. 6:4). The justified one, having become what he is by faith, must go ahead living on the same principle of utter dependence upon God. (2) It can also be a creedal or doctrinal announcement which is sometimes distinguished as *the faith*. Christ propounded this question: "When the Son of man cometh, shall he find faith on the earth?" (Luke 18:8; cf. Rom. 1:5; 1 Cor. 16:13; 2 Cor. 13:5; Col. 1:23; 2:7; Titus 1:13; Jude 1:3). (3) It may signify faithfulness, which implies that the believer is faithful toward God. Here is an inwrought divine characteristic, for it appears as one of the nine graces which together comprise the fruit of the Spirit (Gal. 5:22–23). (4) It may prove a title belonging to Christ, as in Galatians 3:23, 25 where Christ is seen to be the object of faith.

While faith, basically considered, must be divinely inwrought, it is ever increasing as the knowledge of God and experience in His fellowship advances. It is natural for God not to be pleased with those who distrust Him (Heb. 11:6). Faith, indeed, vindicates the character of God and frees His arm to act in behalf of those who trust Him. Thus because of the heaven-high riches which reliance secures, it is termed by Peter once, "precious faith" (2 Pet. 1:1).

FALL

A lapsarian is one who believes that man fell from his first estate of innocence by sinning. This position adheres to the record which the Bible presents. If men do not receive that record it is because they fear not to reject the testimony of God. When the natural man, who has no confidence in the Word of God, would attempt to account for the origin of things in the universe, as his reason impels him to do, he turns to the best solution of the problem that his imagination can devise, namely, the evolutionary theory. He should well know that there is no worthy basis of fact upon which this theory may rest. He rejects the Genesis account on which all subsequent Scripture will depend only because an unregenerate man cannot know God and his mind cannot recognize that God if such there be is able to do anything. Not only should evolutionary theory be called into question because of the utter lack of foundation on which it might rest, but the condition in which humanity is finding itself in the world demonstrates that the divine record is true. Writing on the theme of man's fall in the *International Standard Bible Encyclopaedia,* Herman Bavinck states it thus:

Indirectly, however, a very powerful witness for the fall of man is furnished by the whole empirical condition of the world and humanity. For a world, such as we know it, full of unrighteousness and sorrow, cannot be explained without the acceptance of such a fact. He who holds fast to the witness of Scripture and conscience to sin as sin (as ἀνομία, *anomía*) cannot deduce it from creation, but must accept the conclusion that it began with a transgression of God's command and thus with a deed of the will. Pythagoras, Plato, Kant, Schelling, Baader have all understood and acknowledged this with more or less clearness. He who denies the Fall must explain sin as a necessity which has its origin in the Creation, in the nature of things, and therefore in God Himself; he justifies man but accuses God, misrepresents the character of sin and makes it everlasting and indefeasible. For if there has not been a fall into sin, there is no redemption of sin possible; sin then loses its merely ethical significance, becomes a trait of the nature of man, and is inexterminable. . . . From the standpoint of evolution, there is not only no reason to hold to the "of one blood" of Acts 17:26, A.V., but there has never even been a first man; the transition from animal to man was so slow and successive, that the essential distinction fails to be seen. And with the effacing of this boundary, the unity of the moral ideal, of religion, of the laws of thought and of truth, fails also;

the theory of evolution expels the absolute everywhere and leads necessarily to psychologism, relativism, pragmatism and even to pluralism, which is literally polytheism in a religious sense. The unity of the human race, on the other hand, as it is taught in holy Scripture, is not an indifferent physical question, but an important intellectual, moral and religious one; it is a "postulate" of the whole history of civilization, and expressly or silently accepted by nearly all historians. And conscience bears witness to it, in so far as all men show the work of the moral law written in their hearts, and their thoughts accuse or excuse one another (Rom. 2:15); it shows back to the Fall as an "Urthatsache der Geschichte."—II, 1093

The message of the Bible is one of redemption from that estate in sin which, according to the Sacred Text, must be due to the fall. Thus the whole Biblical revelation comes to be without reason or reality when the fall of man is denied. The record of the fall which the Scriptures present is one of great simplicity. A man and woman are brought into being as innocent and as upright as the creation of a holy God could make them. They know God's mind since they commune with Him. An arbitrary command is given that they abstain from eating the fruit of one certain tree. To disobey God is to repudiate Him and to adopt a course of independent action which must be wholly foreign to the proper relation which should exist between a creature and Creator. The warning had been duly given that, as a result of disobedience or independent action, "dying they would die." The reference is to perishing, both physical and spiritual, with its consummation in the second death. By the immediate experience of spiritual death man's first parents were converted downward and became a kind of being wholly different from that which God created. As in all nature, they could propagate henceforth only after their kind. The offspring did not receive the unfallen nature with which their parents were created; they received the fallen nature that the parents had acquired. Proof of this is found in the record that the first-born was a murderer, and in the intimation that Abel recognized his own sin when he presented a slain lamb as his offering to Jehovah. From that fall of the first parents every member of the human race is blighted and they, each one for himself, must accept God's redeeming grace or go on to the consummation of spiritual ruin, which consummation is known as the second death (cf. Rev. 2:11; 20:14; 21:8). Thus the effect of the fall is universal. Men are not in need of the saving grace of God merely because of the sins they have committed as fruitage of the fallen nature; they are in need of a complete regeneration and eventual release from every effect of the fall. Such blessing, with vastly more, is the portion of all who are divinely saved.

FATHERHOOD OF GOD

While it is not given to the finite mind fully to comprehend the infinite God, it may be observed that some knowledge of Him is available and to enter into it becomes a privilege and duty. He is revealed through nature as its Designer and Creator. God is revealed also through the Scriptures, which directly testify of Him, and through the Person of the Lord Jesus Christ, who came to reveal Him (John 1:18) and to introduce men to Him (Matt. 11:27). God is to be recognized both as Creator and Father. The human mind seems to comprehend God as Creator more readily than it does as Father. It is more common to investigate the creative activities of God, therefore, than to consider His Fatherhood. In spite of this tendency, there is an extended body of truth bearing on the Fatherhood of God. He has been presented by the Sacred Text as Father in four respects.

1. OF THE LORD JESUS CHRIST. At this point the phrase, "the God and Father of our Lord Jesus Christ," used three times (cf. John 20:17; 2 Cor. 11:31; Eph. 1:3; 1 Pet. 1:3), should be considered. It is quite unlike the more common phrase with which the Apostle opens nearly every one of his Epistles, namely, "Blessed be God, even the Father of our Lord Jesus Christ" (cf. 2 Cor. 1:3). In the latter passage only the Fatherhood in respect to Christ is asserted, while in the former declaration Christ has been said to sustain a twofold relationship which is first to God and second to the Father. These distinct relationships are not the same. On the side of His humanity, the First Person is said to be His God. On the side of His Deity, the First Person is declared to be His Father. The connection in which the First Person is set forth as His God began with the incarnation and continues as long as His humanity continues. The connection in which the First Person is mentioned as His Father has continued from all eternity and will ever remain as it has been. The First Person is never the God of the Second Person, but His Father in a peculiar sense which belongs more to other spheres of existence than it does to this earthly sphere. The thought of inferiority or succession is not to be included in a divine Father and Son relationship. It is more nearly that of manifestation. There appears to be that in the unique, eternal affiliation between the First and Second

Persons of the Godhead which may best be conveyed to the human mind by the pattern of the appellations used for an earthly father and his son. Whenever Christ addressed the First Person as *God,* it is clearly indicated by so much that He spoke out from His humanity (cf. Matt. 27:46; Heb. 10:7).

The Arian dishonor to Christ raised the contention that Christ, although unique, was inferior to the Father. This evil conception is now perpetuated by Unitarian theology and doubtless is the conviction of most so-called modernist theologians today. Rejection must also be accorded the four beliefs: (a) that Christ became a Son by His incarnation (Luke 1:35), (b) that He became one by the resurrection (Rom. 1:4), (c) that He is one only by virtue of office, and (d) that He is one only by title. It rather was a Son whom God sent into the world, whom He "gave" (cf. Isa. 9:6; John 3:16). The Second Person did become a human son by assumption of human form and He was begotten in His humanity by the Holy Spirit, but that is all far removed from the fact that He was forever the Son of the Father. He was the eternal Son before He came into the world. Other titles—*Only Begotten* and *First Begotten*—speak of His Deity and are also eternal in their reference. Christ, being God, is sent forth the Son that He was and is, not however in order to become a Son.

2. OF ALL WHO BELIEVE. A fact infinitely true, yet difficult to believe, is that all who receive Christ (cf. John 6:53), or believe on His name (cf. John 1:12-13), become legitimate offspring of God; they become conformed eventually to the image of God's Son—Christ, which truth requires that they have become actual sons of God, else Christ would not be able to call them *brethren* (cf. Rom. 8:29), nor could they be heirs of God and joint heirs with Christ except they be constituted *actual* sons of God (Rom. 8:17). To the one thus recreated, the measureless value of his estate does not appear in the present world. It will be the major distinction characterizing throughout eternity those who are sons of God. As His present supreme purpose, God is now "bringing many sons unto glory" (Heb. 2:10).

3. OF ISRAEL. Several times God addresses the nation of Israel as a father or as his sons (cf. Ex. 4:22; Deut. 32:6; Isa. 63:16; 64:8). The latter designation when applied to Israel does not intimate that individual Israelites were regenerated sons of God. The term appears to connote national solicitude or fatherhood by reason of parental care for all, much as Jehovah declared Himself to be a husband unto Israel (cf. Jer. 31:32).

4. OF ALL MEN. In tracing the genealogy of Christ back to Adam, Luke accounts for Adam's existence by declaring him to be a son or creation of God (Luke 3:38). This, most evidently, is sonship by right of creation—the only conception of divine fatherhood which an unregenerate person can entertain. The Apostle similarly quotes the pagan poets as asserting that all men are the offspring of God thus (cf. Acts 17:28). All men may indeed be considered sons of God inasmuch as they owe their existence to Him. This greatly restricted conception has been seized upon by modern men, however, as a basis for a supposed universal sonship and universal fatherhood of God on intimate terms. It should be remembered, contrary to such an assumption, that Christ told the very authorities of the Jewish nation how they were children of the devil (cf. John 8:44). Hence sonship that is based on mere existence, which existence but links man to God as Creator, must be far removed from a sonship which is the estate of each believer—regenerated, born of God, and member of the family and household of God as he is.

FIRST-FRUITS

One of Israel's feasts appointed by Jehovah was the feast of first-fruits. The feast centered about the waving of a sheaf of first-fruits which was waved before Jehovah at the time of harvest. It was a representative sheaf and contemplated all the sheaves of the whole harvest, since unto Jehovah must thanks be given for the increase which sowing and reaping secured. The term *first-fruits* is used variously in the Bible and each one of several applications should be considered:

1. CHRIST. Twice is Christ said to be First-Fruits and that in His resurrection (1 Cor. 15:20, 23). With His glorified human body Christ appeared in heaven immediately after resurrection. His appearance in the realm above became a representation of the vast harvest of those who are to follow in glorified bodies like His body of resurrection glory (Phil. 3:20–21). None of His people who have died are yet in possession of their resurrection bodies. The acquiring of that body awaits the coming of Christ. Thus it is true that He "only hath immortality, dwelling in the light . . ." (1 Tim. 6:16). He died and was buried, and because

of this experience it would be natural to say that He put on incorruption as all who are resurrected will do (1 Cor. 15:51–52); but still Christ did not see corruption (cf. Ps. 16:10; Acts 2:25–28). Therefore, He as no other put on immortality in His resurrection. Christ as one glorified in His resurrection human body is the Antitype of the Old Testament wave sheaf.

2. EARLY CHRISTIANS. Christ alone is the First-Fruits in heaven. James, however, declared: "Of his own will begat he us with the word of truth, that we should be a kind of firstfruits of his creatures" (1:18). This declaration recognizes both the sovereign election of God—for it is by His own will that He was directed—and the fact of the regenerating power of the Spirit. The latter is achieved by the agency of the Word of Truth. That the ones said to be begotten are first-fruits can be pressed no further than that they were first in order among the vast company of redeemed belonging to the Church which no man can number. That they were "a kind of firstfruits" evidently recognizes the truth of Christ alone being the First-Fruits, strictly speaking.

3. BLESSINGS. As an earnest, a foretaste, of that which awaits the child of God in glory, the blessings which are now realized by the believer because of the presence of the Spirit in his heart constitutes what is called first-fruits. The Apostle said: "And not only they, but ourselves also, which have the firstfruits of the Spirit, even we ourselves groan within ourselves, waiting for the adoption, to wit, the redemption of our body" (Rom. 8:23). Thus a reckoning may be made to some extent of the experience in glory for all who are now among the saved, if the Holy Spirit is the first-fruits.

4. FIRST BELIEVERS IN A LOCALITY. Quite similar to the preceding classification is another whereby when the gospel is first preached in a locality there are those who believe and become the first-fruits of that locality. Twice the Apostle refers to the spiritual first-fruits of Achaia thus (Rom. 16:5; 1 Cor. 16:15).

5. ISRAEL. Jeremiah stated: "Israel was holiness unto the LORD, and the firstfruits of his increase: all that devour him shall offend; evil shall come upon them, saith the LORD" (2:3). As Israel is the first in order of the unfolding of divine purpose for this world, that people became a first-fruits on an extended scale of the whole divine program. It will be observed how warning is given here to all peoples respecting the grievous punishment that shall fall on those who persecute Israel.

6. REVELATION 7 AND 14. Twice is reference made in Revelation to a company numbering 144,000. In the first instance (Rev. 7:1–8) they

are identified as from the tribes of Israel—which identification should direct all attempts at interpretation. These individuals are sealed with the protective and selective seal of God. In Revelation 14:1-5 this same company—being sealed, their number cannot be increased or decreased —are seen to be the first-fruits of the coming kingdom age wherein the King shall reign from Zion.

FLESH

It has been generally recognized that the Christian is in unceasing conflict with three major foes, namely, the world, the flesh, and the devil. The combats with the world and the devil are waged from without, but the strife opposing the flesh operates from within. A more extended contemplation of the doctrine of flesh is presented in Volume VI. It may be restated, however, that the Greek word $\sigma\acute{a}\rho\xi$ with its various forms appears in the New Testament under two general meanings. It, like its synonym $\sigma\hat{\omega}\mu\alpha$, may refer to no more than the physical body. Christ accordingly declared, "That which is born of the flesh is flesh," and this birth He held in distinction from that which is wrought of the Spirit (John 3:6; cf. 6:51; 1 Cor. 15:39; Eph. 5:31). The second and more vital meaning of this term carries with it an ethical import. When thus used, the word may embrace all—spirit, soul, and body—or that which is the entire being of unregenerate man. It includes thereby the fallen Adamic nature. The Apostle has written of the sin nature which is found in the flesh (Rom. 8:3). The Scriptures are exceedingly clear in teaching that the flesh with its sin nature is still a living, vital part of every believer and that he will continue in possession of the flesh and its fallen nature until the body is redeemed at the coming of Christ or until he leaves this earthly frame behind in death. Notions are entertained that the sin nature which is in the flesh can be eradicated now by some supposed divine achievement. But the truth obviously remains that the world, the flesh, and the devil are never removed; they are overcome by the superior power of the Holy Spirit in response to an attitude of faith. Thus it may be seen that even were the sin nature eradicated the believer's three major conflicts abide, and it is not only revelation but reason that the divine method of overcoming them must be that which alone succeeds when dealing with the sin nature—which nature happens to be only an integral part of the flesh anyway: hence this nature is always to be governed by the power of God rather than eradicated.

The essential evil character of the flesh is seen from the direct assertions of the New Testament that it is "enmity against God" (Rom. 8:7–8), that it is "contrary" to the Spirit (Gal. 5:17); of it the Apostle testified: "In me (that is, in my flesh,) dwelleth no good thing" (Rom. 7:18). God faithfully declares that this mighty opposing factor is present in every believer, nor does He withhold the revelation that it may be held in subjection by the power of the Holy Spirit, who indwells the believer to this end. This evil nature which is termed "sin in the flesh" (Rom. 8:3) and "sin that dwelleth in me" (cf. Rom. 7:17, 20–21, 23) has already been brought into judgment by Christ in His death. The judgment is set forth in Romans 6:1–10, which context has no bearing upon the great fact of salvation from the penalty of sin or upon that of the believer's justification before God (cf. Col. 2:11–12). In this connection the Apostle declares: "And they that are Christ's have crucified the flesh with the affections and lusts" (Gal. 5:24). The statement thus presented is not only true but becomes fundamental to any right understanding of this great theme. The judgment of the flesh with its lusts was achieved perfectly by Christ in His death unto the sin nature. This judgment is referred to in Romans 8:3, where the Apostle says that Christ "condemned [or, judged] sin in the flesh." Paul does not imply that the flesh and its lusts were rendered inactive or destroyed, as the A.V. translation in Romans 6:6 suggests. A judgment rather is gained against the flesh and its lusts by Christ and so the "old man's" power may by the Spirit be disannulled for such time as victory is claimed by means of the Spirit. The objective is that sin (the nature) should not be served. This particular judgment makes it righteously possible for the indwelling Spirit to hold the sin nature in check. Were it not for this judgment of the cross, the Spirit could not thus deal with the nature, and it is equally evident that He could not dwell where an unjudged sin nature reigns. Deliverance from the flesh and its lusts, then, is by the Spirit on the ground of Christ's death. This deliverance is assured on the fulfillment of three conditions hinging on as many verbs: (1) "reckon," which means to count on the plan and provisions of God to be sufficient therefor (Rom. 6:11), (2) "let not," which command points to a conflict and implies that the power of the flesh will be disannulled if this foe is fought in the way and with the resources that God has provided (Rom. 6:12), and (3) "yield," which word directs the human will how to walk in the path of God's holy ways (Rom. 6:13). Were the theory of eradication of the sin nature found to be true, all this Scripture with its extended analysis of the life under the enabling power of the Spirit would be rendered both aimless and useless.

The word σαρκικός (or σάρκινος) used eleven times in the New Testament is a reference to that which may be characterized by the flesh, usually with an uncomplimentary signification. The Apostle declares himself to be σαρκικός (Rom. 7:14). Here the evil character of the flesh residing within is seen, as also in 1 Corinthians 3:1–4, in which context this word has been used four times. *Things* may be fleshly (1 Cor. 9:11), *wisdom* (2 Cor. 1:12) and Christian *weapons* (2 Cor. 10:4) and *commandments* (Heb. 7:16) and *lusts* too (1 Pet. 2:11).

The spelling σάρκινος, strictly speaking, indicates that of which a thing is made. In 2 Corinthians 3:3 reference is made accordingly to the "fleshy tables of the heart."

Psuchē and *psuchikos* are held in distinction from *sarkikos*. The former refers to the natural unregenerate person as such or to that which is soulish in character. The present body, in contrast to the future "spiritual body," is a natural or *psuchikos* entity (1 Cor. 15:44, 46). Its limitations, both natural and spiritual, are indicated thereby (cf. 1 Cor. 2:14; James 3:15; Jude 1:19).

Pneuma and *pneumatikos* complete the triad of word roots related to spirituality in the New Testament. Under these special terms the Spirit-filled life is in view. Reference is made hereby to a life dominated and directed by the Holy Spirit.

In the Apostle's threefold division of humanity with respect to their attitude toward the Word of God—"the natural man," "he that is spiritual," and "carnal"—the unregenerate persons are *natural* as being spiritually unchanged (1 Cor. 2:14), the saved ones who are walking in the Spirit are by so much *spiritual* (1 Cor. 2:15), while believers who are influenced by the flesh and its lusts are accounted *carnal* (1 Cor. 3:1–4).

Two different "walks," then, are possible to the believer: one "after the flesh" and one "after the Spirit." The saved person is never considered to be longer within the sphere of the flesh, though he may be fleshly in conduct (Rom. 8:9).

FOREKNOWLEDGE

The foreknowledge which God possesses must be distinguished from mere prescience or knowledge of future events. Prescience may depend upon the will of creatures for its immediate execution or for its expectation, but foreknowledge in God is that which He Himself purposes to bring to pass. In this way, then, the whole order of events from the least detail unto the greatest operates under the determining decree of God so as to take place according to His sovereign purpose. By so much, divine foreknowledge is closely related to foreordination. Likewise, foreknowledge in God should be distinguished from omniscience in that the latter is extended sufficiently to embrace all things past, present, and future, while foreknowledge anticipates only the future events. Again, foreknowing in God should be distinguished from His knowledge of events which are merely possible. It is in the range of divine understanding to foresee what would happen under certain circumstances but in His providence never does occur. Manifesting this so-called hypothetical prescience, Christ declared: "Woe unto thee, Chorazin! woe unto thee, Bethsaida! for if the mighty works, which were done in you, had been done in Tyre and Sidon, they would have repented long ago in sackcloth and ashes" (Matt. 11:21).

The doctrine of divine foreknowledge is, as regards the evidence upon which it rests, confined to the Sacred Text. In that Text it will be found that God is working according to His own eternal purpose, and that this purpose includes all that comes to pass; therefore, foreknowledge in God as presented in the Scriptures must be contemplated, not as a mere preview of events that blind fate might engender or that are supposed to arise in the will of men and angels, but as a program incorporated in the decree of God respecting all things. Theories and notions which introduce hypothetical issues foreign to this Biblical conception must be treated as unrelated to the scope of the doctrine. Such a side to this theme is well stated by Dr. Caspar Wistar Hodge in the *International Standard Bible Encyclopaedia:*

Now while the writers of the Old Testament and the New Testament do not write in an abstract or philosophical manner nor enter into metaphysical explanations of the relation between God's foreknowledge and foreordination, it is perfectly evident that they had a clear conception upon this subject. Although anthropomorphisms are used in regard to the manner in which God knows, He is never conceived as if He obtained His knowledge of the future as a mere onlooker gazing down the course of events in time. The idea that the omnipotent Creator and sovereign Ruler of the universe should govern the world and form His plan as contingent and dependent upon a mere foresight of events outside His purpose and control is not only contrary to the entire Scriptural idea of God's sovereignty and omnipotence, but is also contrary to the Scriptural idea of God's foreknowledge which is always conceived as dependent upon His sovereign purpose. According to the Scriptural conception, God foreknows because He has foreordained all things, and because in His providence He will certainly bring all to pass. His foreknowledge is not a dependent one which must wait upon events, but is simply the knowledge which God has of His own eternal purpose. Dillmann has called this "a productive foreknowledge" (*Handbuch d. alttest. Theol.*, 251). This is not exactly correct. The Old Testament does not conceive God's foreknowledge as "producing" or causing events. But when Dillmann says that in the Old Testament there is no hint of an "idle foreknowledge" on God's part, he is giving expression to the truth that in the Old Testament God's foreknowledge is based upon His foreordination and providential control of all things. The Divine foreknowledge, therefore, depends upon the Divine purpose which has determined the world plan (Amos 3:7), and all its details (Job 28:26–27). Before man is born God knows him and chooses him for his work (Jer. 1:5; Job 23:13–14), and God's thorough knowledge of man in Psalm 139 is made to rest upon the fact that God has determined man's lot beforehand (Ps. 139:14–16).

The same thing is true of the New Testament teaching on this subject. The Divine foreknowledge is simply God's knowledge of His own eternal purpose. This is especially clear in those cases where God's eternal purpose of redemption through Christ is represented as a mystery which is known by God and which can be known by man only when it pleases God to reveal it (Eph. 1:9; 3:4–9). —II, 1129–30

Referring to the central passage on foreknowledge (Rom. 8:28–29), Dr. Hodge continues:

In Romans 8:29–30 the word "foreknow" occurs in immediate connection with God's predestination of the objects of salvation. Those whom God foreknew, He also did predestinate to be conformed to the image of His son. Now the foreknowledge in this case cannot mean a mere prescience or foresight of faith (Meyer, Godet) or love (Weiss) in the subjects of salvation, which faith or love is supposed to determine the Divine predestination. This would not only contradict Paul's view of the absolutely sovereign and gracious character of election, but is diametrically opposed to the context of this passage. These verses form a part of the encouragement which Paul offers his readers for their troubles, including their own inward weakness. The apostle tells them that they may be sure that all things work together for good to them that love God; and these are defined as being those whom God has called in accordance with His purpose. Their love to God is evidently their love as Christians, and is the result of a calling which itself follows from an eternal purpose, so that their Christian love is simply the means by which they may know that they have been the subjects of this call. They have not come within the sphere of God's love by their own choice, but have been "called" into this relationship by God, and that in accordance with an eternal purpose on His part.

What follows, therefore, must have as its motive simply to unfold and ground this assurance of salvation by tracing it all back to the "foreknowledge" of God. To regard this foreknowledge as contingent upon anything in man would thus be in flat contradiction with the entire context of the passage as well as its motive. The word "foreknowledge" here evidently has the pregnant sense which we found it to have in Peter. Hence those whom God predestinates, calls, justifies and glorifies are just those whom He has looked upon with His sovereign love. To assign any other meaning to "foreknowledge" here would be out of accord with the usage of the term elsewhere in the New Testament when it is put in connection with predestination, and would contradict the purpose for which Paul introduces the passage, that is, to assure his readers that their ultimate salvation depends, not on their weakness, but on God's sovereign love and grace and power.—*Ibid.*, p. 1130

Any right comprehension of divine foreknowledge, then, must see it as the Biblical and reasonable recognition on the part of God concerning that which He has made certain by His all-inclusive decree. In the Old Testament such foreknowledge is indicated in Job 23:13–14; Psalm 139:1–24; Jeremiah 1:5; and in the New Testament in Acts 2:23; 15:18; Romans 8:28–29; 11:2; 1 Peter 1:2, all of which Scripture should be attended with care.

FOREORDINATION

The entire field of God's revealed purposes will be seen only when all the various approaches to His decree have been noted. This theme includes the doctrine of decrees, of election, of predestination, of foreordination or divine choice, of foreknowledge, of efficacious call, and of the free will of man. In its simplest form, the one phase of foreordination means ascribing to God the ability and sagacity to provide with infinite precision the things which form the ongoing of the universe He has created. That the theme extends into realms of other worlds and contemplates that in God which His creatures may not now understand is readily conceded. There is probably little difficulty in the mind of any serious person who holds God in due respect over the issue of His right and accompanying necessity to plan the course of His universe before He brings it into being. Difficulty may arise with respect to the evil that is present now in that which a holy God designed, created, and is executing. Pious souls, however, will not allow that evil is engendered by God, and a reasonable person will not claim that evil is present because God could not prevent it, nor will thoughtful, observing men conclude that the universe is a gigantic accident moving ungoverned to its own destruction. It must be recognized that in some way quite beyond man's comprehension the permission and presence of evil in God's universe is consistent with His holy character and cannot be linked with Him as in any wise responsible for it. This principle is to be seen operating in another and more attractive form when it is observed that, though all fruitful service is being wrought by the enabling power of the Holy Spirit, God does not withhold or claim for Himself any reward for that service when the believer stands before the judgment seat of Christ. The Christian is then rewarded as though he had by himself achieved all that may have been done in the overcoming power of the Spirit.

The doctrine of foreordination, then, is almost identical with that of predestination. The former term doubtless has a wider significance in that it may include all things within the scope of God's purpose, while the latter is usually employed only of people and restricted to the predetermined destiny of those who are saved, with the exception of Acts 4:27-28 which is a reference to that determined respecting the sufferings of Christ (cf. Rom. 8:29-30; 1 Cor. 2:7; Eph. 1:5, 11).

FORGIVENESS

The correct understanding of the teaching of Scripture on forgiveness will go far in the direction of clarifying other doctrines of the Bible. Because of the fact that this theme is so constantly misunderstood, special attention should be given to it. Forgiveness on the part of one person toward another is the simplest of duties, whereas forgiveness on the part of God toward man proves the most complicated and costly of undertakings. As seen in the Bible, there is an analogy between forgiveness and debt and, in the case of that forgiveness which God exercises, the debt must be paid—though it be paid by Himself—before forgiveness can be extended. Thus it is learned that while human forgiveness only remits a penalty or charge divine forgiving must require complete satisfaction for the demands of God's outraged holiness first of all. This doctrine may be divided into seven important particulars.

1. IN THE OLD TESTAMENT. This aspect of divine forgiveness, though rich in typical significance, is nevertheless a complete forgiveness in itself. The all-important feature which enters into all divine remission, namely, payment of every obligation to injured holiness as the preliminary to forgiving, is included in the offering of animal sacrifices. First, the sacrifice itself was deemed by the one who offered it a substitute in that upon it fell the just penalty of death. It was only when a sacrifice had thus been presented that the offender could be forgiven. Accordingly, it is declared in Leviticus 4:20, as always in the Old Testament: "The priest shall make an atonement for them, and it shall be forgiven them." But, since the sacrifice served only typically and as a covering of sin until the appointed time when God should deal finally or righteously with sin in the death of Christ, the transaction was incomplete on the divine side, sin necessarily being pretermitted. However, divine forgiveness as such was extended to the offender perfectly. Two New Testament passages shed light upon the nature and fact of this temporary divine dealing with sin. In Romans 3:25 reference is made by the word πάρεσις to the pretermitting or passing over of sins aforetime, that is, before the cross; likewise in Acts 17:30 by the word ὑπερεῖδον—translated "winked at"—reference is made to the fact that in times past God did not then fully judge sin. It should be remembered, however, that the vast array of divine promises for full and perfect dealing with every sin thus passed over was all gathered up and accounted for by Christ on the cross eventually.

2. FOR THE UNSAVED. In this aspect of the general doctrine of forgiveness there is need for emphasis on the truth that forgiveness of sin is extended to the unsaved only as an integral part of the whole divine undertaking called salvation. Of the many transformations wrought by God in response to simple faith in Christ, the remission of sin is but one. Hence it should be observed that the forgiveness of sin can never be claimed by itself on the part of those who are unregenerate. Forgiveness is provided for them to infinite completeness, but may be

secured only as a phase of God's whole work in salvation. Though too often supposed to be the truth, remission of sin for the unsaved is not equivalent to salvation. Forgiveness connotes subtraction, indeed, whereas all else in salvation is glorious addition. It is therefore written, "I give unto them eternal life" (John 10:28), and in Romans 5:17 reference is made, for example, to "the gift of righteousness."

3. FOR CHRISTIANS WHO SIN. The foundational truth respecting the believer in relation to his sins is the fact that when he was saved all his trespasses (the past, present, and future)—so far as condemnation may be concerned—were forgiven. This must be the meaning of the Apostle's word in Colossians 2:13, "having forgiven you all trespasses." So complete proves this divine dealing with all sin that it can be said, "There is therefore now no condemnation to them which are in Christ Jesus" (Rom. 8:1). The believer is not condemned (John 3:18), and therefore shall not come into judgment ("condemnation," John 5:24). It need only be remembered that, since Christ has borne all sin and since the believer's standing is complete in the risen Christ, he is perfected forever by reason of being in Christ. As a member in the household and family of God, the Christian—should he sin—of course is, as any child, subject to chastisement from the Father, but never to be condemned with the world (1 Cor. 11:31–32).

The cure for the effect of his sin upon himself is confession thereof to God. By this he is returned to agreement with God respecting the evil character of all sin. It is written: "If we confess our sins, he is faithful and just to forgive us our sins, and to cleanse us from all unrighteousness" (1 John 1:9). The simple act of penitent confession results with absolute divine certainty in the forgiveness and cleansing of the sin. The believer thus exercised about evil conduct should not wait until some change of feeling respecting the sin is experienced; it is his privilege to accept by faith that restoration which God so certainly promises as following at once. It may be added here that, though confession is always directed to God (cf. Ps. 51:4; Luke 15:18–19), there are times and situations when such admission should be extended to the person or persons wronged also. This will be especially true when those wronged are aware of the evil. However, it must be emphasized that confession is primarily made unto God and should in the vast majority of experiences go no further.

As for the effect of the believer's sin upon God, it may be observed how, were it not for that which Christ has wrought and that which He undertakes when the Christian sins, the least sin would have the power to hurl the one who sins from the presence of God and down to eternal ruin. In 1 John 2:1 it is asserted that Christ advocates before God for the believer without delay at the very time that he sins. By so much it is revealed that He enters a plea before God the Father in the court of heaven that He bore that very sin in His body on the cross. This is so complete an answer to the requisite divine judgment which otherwise must fall upon the believer that by such advocacy He wins here the exalted title, "Jesus Christ the righteous." There was a specific and separate dealing by Christ on the cross with those sins which the believer would commit. It is written, consequently, "He is the propitiation for our sins" (1 John 2:2). It is true, also, that he has become the propitiation "for the sins of the whole world." However, in any right understanding of the doctrine of divine forgiveness, a wide difference will be observed between the propitiation which Christ became for Christians and that which He became for the world of the unsaved.

4. IN THE COMING KINGDOM. Being itself the manifesto of the King respecting the terms of admission into the Messianic kingdom as well as of conditions which are to obtain in that kingdom, the Sermon on the Mount (Matt. 5:1—7:27) affords a specific indication of the terms on which divine forgiveness may be secured during the extended period. This indication is found in the prayer (Matt. 6:9–13) which Christ taught His disciples to pray during the period of His kingdom preaching to Israel—a time when His ministry was wholly confined to the proclamation of that kingdom. It is therefore imperative, if any semblance of a right interpretation is to be preserved, that this prayer, including the disclosure respecting divine forgiveness, be confined in its doctrine and application to the age unto which it belongs. In that age much is made of man's relationship to his fellow man. It is then that what has become known as the Golden Rule (Matt. 7:12) has its proper place. The specific phrase in the prayer which discloses the terms of divine forgiveness reads: "And forgive us our debts, as we forgive our debtors." No misinterpretation should be permitted here regardless of sentiment or custom pertaining to this prayer formula. The passage conditions divine forgiveness upon human alacrity to forgive. This could not apply to one who as a believer has been forgiven all trespasses already—past, present, and future; nor could it apply to the Christian who has sinned and who is subject consequently to chastisement, since of him it is written that if he but confesses his sin he will be forgiven and cleansed. The acts of confession and of forgiving others have no relation to each other whatsoever. This is the one petition in the prayer

which Christ took up afterwards for a special comment and interpretation. It is as though He anticipated the unwarranted use of the prayer in this age and sought to make its character all the more clear. The comment of Christ reads: "For if ye forgive men their trespasses, your heavenly Father will also forgive you: but if ye forgive not men their trespasses, neither will your Father forgive your trespasses" (Matt. 6: 14–15). No unprejudiced contemplation of this petition or of Christ's interpretation of it has ever rescued it from being in complete disagreement with the fact of divine forgiveness in the grace age. It is written, for example, in Ephesians 4:32: "And be ye kind one to another, tenderhearted, forgiving one another, even as God for Christ's sake hath forgiven you." Here a contrast between law and grace is again set up. To be forgiving because one has already been forgiven of God for Christ's sake is quite removed from the condition wherein one will be forgiven only in the measure in which he himself forgives. The latter belongs to a merit system such as will obtain in the kingdom; the former is in harmony with the present riches of divine grace.

5. THE OBLIGATION BETWEEN MEN. Though, as stated above, the terms upon which divine forgiveness may be secured in the kingdom is that of having forgiven others, the motive for forgiving others in the kingdom proves similar to that under the present reign of grace, namely, the fact that one has been forgiven. This principle of action as one related to the kingdom requirements is declared by Christ in Matthew 18:21–35. A certain king forgave a debt of ten thousand talents—an enormous sum of money, whereupon the one thus forgiven refused to cancel a debt in the paltry amount of one hundred pence. That such an incident could have no place in the life of all who are perfected in Christ and therefore secure forever is learned from the closing verses of this portion, which reads: "And his lord was wroth, and delivered him to the tormentors, till he should pay all that was due unto him. So likewise shall my heavenly Father do also unto you, if ye from your hearts forgive not every one his brother their trespasses" (Matt. 18:34–35). The believer who belongs to this age is enjoined to be kind unto other believers, tenderhearted, and forgiving to one another even as God "for Christ's sake hath forgiven you."

6. THE UNPARDONABLE SIN. When Christ was on earth ministering in the power of the Holy Spirit, a peculiar sin was possible and might have been committed, namely, attributing to Satan the power of the Spirit thus manifested. For this sin there could be no forgiveness either in the age then present or the age immediately following (Matt. 12:22–32).

It is evident that no such situation exists in the world now. It is wholly without warrant to suppose that any human attitude toward the Holy Spirit is a duplication of this evil and hence as unpardonable as the one sin of which Christ gave warning. An unpardonable sin and a "whosoever will" gospel cannot coexist. Were there an unpardonable sin possible today, every gospel invitation in the New Testament would have to exclude specifically those who had committed that sin.

7. A SIN UNTO DEATH. The Apostle John writes of a sin resulting in physical death which believers may commit. The passage reads, "If any man see his brother sin a sin which is not unto death, he shall ask, and he shall give him life for them that sin not unto death. There is a sin unto death: I do not say that he shall pray for it" (1 John 5:16). It will be remembered that, according to John 15:2 and 1 Corinthians 11:30, God reserves the right to remove from this life a believer who has ceased to be a worthy witness in the world. Such a removal does not imply that the one thus removed is lost; it only means a form of drastic chastisement and to the end that such may not be condemned with the world (1 Cor. 11:31–32).

GENEALOGY

The *International Standard Bible Encyclopaedia* presents an exhaustive listing of forty-one genealogies all of which, excepting two of Christ, are in the Old Testament. To the historian as well as to the theologian these genealogies contribute much, especially in tracing the line of the seed from Adam to Christ. In the wording of these genealogies a phrase like "the son of" should be interpreted according to the custom in force at the time that the genealogy was written. The Jews, for instance, in reckoning a genealogy counted grandsons and great grandsons as if *sons*. This fact is of real importance when tracing a recorded lineage.

Turning to the all-important genealogies of Christ—one by Matthew (1:1–16) tracing the line of Messianic seed from Abraham to Christ, and one by Luke (3:23–38) tracing the lineage of the seed from Christ back to Adam—it will be seen that the important point is that the virgin birth with its divine character and the fact of Christ's lineage through

David are established, whatever may be the variations or omissions in these two records.

In the conclusion of an article on these particular genealogies for the *International Standard Bible Encyclopaedia* Dr. Louis M. Sweet presents the following pertinent material:

> It is clear, therefore, from the general trend as well as from specific statements of both Gospels, that the genealogies and the birth-narratives were not floating traditions which accidentally touched and coalesced in mid-stream, but that they were intended to weld inseparably the two beliefs that Jesus was miraculously conceived and that He was the heir of David. This could be done only on the basis of Joseph's genealogy, for whatever the lineage of Mary, Joseph was the head of the family, and the Davidic connection of Jesus could only be established by acknowledgment of Him as legal son by Joseph. Upon this basis rests the common belief of the apostolic age (see Zahn, *ibid.*, 567, note references), and in accordance with it all statements (such as those of Paul, Rom. 1:3; 2 Tim. 2:8) must be interpreted.
>
> For it must be remembered that, back of the problem of reconciling the virgin birth and the Davidic origin of Jesus, lay the far deeper problem—to harmonize the incarnation and the Davidic origin. This problem had been presented in shadow and intimation by Jesus Himself in the question: "David himself calleth him Lord; and whence is he his Son?" It is further to be noticed that in the annunciation (Lk. 1:32) the promised One is called at once Son of God and Son of David, and that He is the Son of God by virtue of His conception by the Spirit—leaving it evident that He is Son of David by virtue of His birth of Mary. With this should be compared the statement of Paul (Rom. 1:3-4): He who was God's Son was "born of the seed of David according to the flesh, and declared to be the Son of God with power, according to the spirit of holiness, by the resurrection from the dead." This is at least most suggestive . . . , for it indicates that as Paul and Luke were in very close sympathy as to the person of Our Lord, so they are in equally close sympathy as to the mystery of His origin. The unanimity of conviction on the part of the early church as to the Davidic origin of Jesus is closely paralleled by its equally firm conviction as to His supernatural derivation. The meeting-point of these two beliefs and the resolution of the mystery of their relationship is in the genealogies in which two widely diverging lines of human ancestry, representing the whole process of history, converge at the point where the new creation from heaven is introduced.—II, 1198-99

Because of the twofold fact that Christ on His human side was the Son of David and on the divine side was Messiah, Jehovah incarnate, Emmanuel, as such David's Lord, the problem posed to finite minds was beyond solution by the Jewish rulers (Matt. 22:41–46). It may be noteworthy also that the pronoun *whom* of Matthew 1:16 is feminine in gender, thus relating the child as a son to Mary.

The Apostle Paul warns against inordinate expenditure of time upon genealogies (1 Tim. 1:4; Titus 3:9) as being for the people of little value.

GENTILES

The Bible presents the origin, present estate, and destiny of four classes of rational created beings in this universe: the angels, the Gentiles, the Jews, and the Christians. Of these, the angels and the Christians have previously been considered. Nothing is more germane to a true Biblical interpretation than observance of the truth that these specific classes continue what they are—except that in the present age individual Jews or Gentiles may by faith in Christ become Christians— throughout their history, which history in each instance extends into eternity.

As for their racial stock, the Gentiles had their origin in Adam and consequently their natural headship in him. They have partaken of the fall; and, though they are the subjects of prophecy which predicts that some of them will yet share, as a subordinate people, with Israel in her coming kingdom glory (Isa. 2:4; 60:3, 5, 12; 62:2; Acts 15:17), they, as respects their estate in the period from Adam to Christ, rested under a fivefold indictment: "without Christ, being aliens from the commonwealth of Israel, and strangers from the covenants of promise, having no hope, and without God in the world" (Eph. 2:12). With the death, resurrection, and ascension of Christ together with the descent of the Spirit, however, the door of gospel privilege was opened unto the Gentiles (Acts 10:45; 11:17–18; 13:47–48), and out of them God is now calling an elect company (Acts 15:14). The new proffered blessings for this age do not consist in being permitted to share in Israel's earthly covenants, all of which even Israel is not now enjoying, but rather, through riches of grace in Christ Jesus, in being privileged to be partakers of a heavenly citizenship and glory. It is revealed too that the mass of Gentiles will not in the present age enter by faith into these heavenly riches.

Therefore, Gentile people, designated as "the nations," go on until at the end of their stewardship as earth-rulers, which spells a final termination for "the times of the Gentiles" (Luke 21:24; cf. Dan. 2:

36–44), they of that particular generation will, at the end of the tribulation period (cf. Matt. 24:8–31 with 25:31–46), be called upon to stand before the Messiah King seated on the throne of His glory (Matt. 25:31–32) here upon earth. At that time, some who are set on the left hand and designated "the goats" will be dismissed into "everlasting fire, prepared for the devil and his angels," but others who are stationed on His right and designated "sheep" will be ushered into "the kingdom" prepared for them from the foundation of the world (Matt. 25:31–46). The basis of such judgment and its disposition of each of these groups, who together represent the sum total of that generation from among the Gentile nations, will be what is meritorious to the last degree. For the "sheep" enter the kingdom and the "goats" ultimately a lake of fire on the sole issue of their treatment of a third group whom Christ designates "my brethren." The context does not bear out the usual interpretation that this is a description of a last and final judgment when all people of all the ages are ushered into either judgment or heaven, because the saved, each one, when departing this world are translated so as to be immediately present with the Lord in heaven (Acts 7:55–56; 2 Cor. 5:8; Phil. 1:23); and furthermore, who, according to such an exegesis, would answer to "my brethren"? The scene is at the close of the great tribulation (Matt. 24:21), after removal of the Church from the earth, and at a time when nations will be divided over the Semitic question. The issue is concerned with what nations will be chosen to enter Israel's Messianic kingdom on the earth.

The destiny of the Gentiles has been further revealed when it is declared concerning the city which, after creation of the new heavens and the new earth, comes down from God out of heaven (Rev. 3:12; 21:2, 10) that "the nations of them which are saved shall walk in the light of it: and the kings of the earth do bring their glory and honour into it. . . . And they shall bring the glory and honour of the nations into it" (Rev. 21:24–26). The terminology *the nations of them which are saved* could not refer to the Church when her destiny is not earthly; neither is she ever termed *the nations,* nor does she include the kings of the earth in her number. In this same context, the city itself is said to be "the bride, the Lamb's wife," which means the Church (Rev. 21:2, 9–10). Thus it is disclosed how, in spite of the fact that a dispensation of world rule was committed unto them, that in the present age the gospel is preached unto them with its offers of heavenly glory, that in the coming age they share the blessings of the kingdom with Israel, and that they appear in the eternal glory, they remain Gentiles in contradistinction with the one nation Israel onward to the end of the picture; and so there is no defensible ground for diverting or misapplying this great body of Scripture bearing on the Gentiles.

Gentiles in their relation to God are never placed by Him under the Mosaic Law. Likewise, the direction for life which has been addressed to Christians is never applicable to Gentiles as such. Almost no Scripture is written to Gentiles, though much Scripture has to do with them (cf. Ps. 2:10–12).

GENTILE TIMES

A prediction to Israel of the long period in which their possession of Jerusalem should be released to Gentiles and Jerusalem be in the hands of Gentiles, as now, is the measurement of that period known as Gentile times. Christ termed this era "the times of the Gentiles." What He said is recorded in Luke 21:24: "And they shall fall by the edge of the sword, and shall be led away captive into all nations: and Jerusalem shall be trodden down of the Gentiles, until the times of the Gentiles be fulfilled." Thus is introduced one of the most important time-periods in human history. Over against "the times of the Gentiles" is a phrase— *the times and the seasons*—which refers to God's dealing with Israel (cf. Acts 1:7; 1 Thess. 5:1). Under what is contemplated by these two prophetic indications, "the times of the Gentiles" and "the times and the seasons," the entire prophetic prospect of the Old Testament as well as of the New Testament largely is accounted for well.

The times of the Gentiles measure foreign dominion over Jerusalem, evidently began with the Babylonian captivity, and continue until the present hour and will do so on until Israel is returned to possession of her own land. However, another period unforeseen in Old Testament prediction has intervened meanwhile, leaving Israel's "times and seasons" and Gentile times as well yet to be consummated.

It follows, then, that measurements have been divinely indicated both for the duration of Jewish times and of Gentile times. There is no occasion for misunderstanding about these periods. To Daniel it was disclosed that 490, which is a matter of 70 sevens, would intervene before Israel's kingdom bringing in "everlasting righteousness" might be set up: "Seventy weeks are determined upon thy people and upon thy holy city, to finish the transgression, and to make an end of sins, and to make reconciliation for iniquity, and to bring in everlasting righteousness, and to seal up the vision and prophecy, and to anoint the most Holy" (Dan. 9:24). Till the cutting off of Messiah would be 483 years, or a total of 69 sevens. Only *one* seven or week of years remains unfulfilled, but between the sixty-ninth seven and the seventieth seven very much is still to be fulfilled. The intercalatory period is left indefinite in extent, nevertheless the seventieth seven of years has yet to run its course. Daniel declares: "And the people of the prince that shall come shall destroy the city and the sanctuary; and the end thereof shall be with a flood, and unto the end of the war desolations are determined" (9:26). Thus it is suggested respecting Jewish times and seasons that an indefinite period must be anticipated to occur between the cutting off of Messiah in death and the consummation of the whole 490-year period. A Gentile intercalation was inserted in the Jewish calendar and in this time no Jewish purpose or prediction is being fulfilled; all the same, a seven-year period yet remains to run its course. In like manner, Gentile times which began with the captivity of Babylon about 600 years before Christ may be measured by two periods. One of these is a time of seventy years during which Jerusalem remained in complete desolation. Of this period Jeremiah had predicted: "And this whole land shall be a desolation, and an astonishment; and these nations shall serve the king of Babylon seventy years. And it shall come to pass, when seventy years are accomplished, that I will punish the king of Babylon, and that nation, saith the LORD, for their iniquity, and the land of the Chaldeans, and will make it perpetual desolations" (Jer. 25:11–12). This time of ruin Daniel discovered to be near its termination once when he was in the spirit of prayer. He records his experience: "In the first year of his [Darius'] reign I Daniel understood by books the number of the years, whereof the word of the LORD came to Jeremiah the prophet, that he would accomplish seventy years in the desolations of Jerusalem" (9:2).

The second subdivision period is indicated not by precise measurement of years, as with the two Jewish times, but by the succession of world empires. These empires are indicated by the colossal image— made from gold, silver, brass, and iron—of Daniel, chapter 2. History revealed the gold to be Babylon, the silver to be Media-Persia, the brass to be Greece, and the iron to be Rome. The same four great empires are anticipated in Daniel, chapter 7, under the characters of nondescript beasts. Since Rome was the fourth, the period covered by this empire is that of its predicted end. The metallic image had feet of iron and clay and these apparently by so much removed from the legs of iron, so that in Rome between the legs of iron and the feet there is again an indefinite period extending onward; but the time of the feet and toes must still run its course to complete Gentile times. That hour evidently corresponds to the seventieth week in Jewish times. Both Jewish times and Gentile times anticipate the era known as the great tribulation.

Gentile times are therefore inclusive of about 600 years before Christ and will end seven years after this age of grace is completed. The present age while concerned with both Jews and Gentiles in the earth is neither advancing Jewish times nor Gentile times. It is quite unrelated to any other time.

GLORY

Since glory is one of the greatest themes related to God and to heaven, it is important that its outreach should be understood so far as human minds may proceed to comprehend. It would be natural enough to conceive of glory as some supernal illumination with an appeal to the range of human vision, but it rather includes the ecstatic state of mind and physical enjoyment which belong to celestial realms.

In the case of the boundless glory of God, it is said to be both essential or intrinsic and declarative. As for that glory which is called intrinsic or essential, it may be observed that, regardless of any recognition of it on the part of creatures, God is Himself a glorious being. Glory belongs to Him as light and heat belong to the sun. It therefore becomes a misrepresentation of infinite proportions to withhold from God a worthy acknowledgment of His glory. An injustice is forced upon Him if the entire universe of created beings does not ascribe to Him that essential glory. To fail to do so is to "lie, and do not the truth" (cf. 1 John 1:6). The declarative glory of God, on the other hand, is that which His creatures may accord to Him. Unfallen angels and the redeemed in heaven declare His praises forever. Only fallen angels and members of this fallen race withhold glory from God. Such indignity and insult shall be accounted for to Him alone. It is this rebellion within God's universe which the Son of God will judge in time to come.

Of the essential glory of God, again, it may be said that His glory is concentrated in Himself. It is because of what He is that glory belongs to Him and only Him. Respecting the declarative glory, furthermore, it may be stated that all His creation, as all His works, declare to a certain degree that glory—"The heavens declare the glory of God" (Ps. 19:1). However, that which concerns the child of God more particularly is the essential glory itself for it will be that which he must ascribe to Him as rightfully His, and this is not difficult to do at all in the light of what He is and has revealed Himself to be.

Beyond all that Solomon's glory typified, Christ's earthly glory will be supreme when He sets up the kingdom on earth.

Essentially, the New Testament use of the word *glory* is of a place and not an estate. God, for example, is now "bringing many sons unto glory" (Heb. 2:10). When Christ shall appear in glory, then shall His Bride appear with Him all glorious herself (Col. 3:4). Doubtless glory is the same location as that to which Christ referred when He said in John 14:1-3, "I go to prepare a place for you."

GOD

As in any usual composition the personality of the author is taken for granted, so a knowledge of God is secured by induction of all passing intimations about the writer to be found in the Sacred Text which He wrote.

Many efforts have been made to define God, but perhaps none more satisfactory than that of the *Westminster Larger Catechism,* which reads: "God is a Spirit, in and of himself infinite in being, glory, blessedness, and perfection; all-sufficient, eternal, unchangeable, incomprehensible, every where present, almighty, knowing all things, most wise, most holy, most just, most merciful and gracious, long-suffering, and abundant in goodness and truth" (Question 7).

As good an analysis of this whole theme as might be had anywhere would be secured if each one of the descriptive terms in the Catechism statement were treated by itself.

The doctrine of God in the Old Testament is set forth in three primary names which He bears. These are:

1. EL, meaning strength, and its two cognates—Elah, meaning a covenant-keeping God, and Elohim, a plural name that is used constantly as if a singular grammatical form. It seems evident that the doctrine of the Trinity is foreshadowed in this plural name. The one passage—Deuteronomy 6:4—is most revealing and might be translated: "Jehovah [a singular form] our Elohim [a plural] is one Jehovah." The word for *one* here may signify an integration of constituent parts as for instance when it is said, "And the evening and the morning . . . one day," "And they [two] shall be one flesh" (Gen. 1:5; 2:24).

Many modern scholars assert that the plural form of *Elohim* does not intimate the Trinity. Oehler, for one, asserts that it is a case of the plural of *majesty*—some kind of attempt to multiply the force of the title. However, he gives no sufficient reason, nor do others succeed in proving that a trinitarian thought is not present. It all seems, then, to be a form of unbelief. The Old Testament certainly does not lack for emphasis upon the majesty of God. (The triune mode of existence has had its treatment earlier in Volume I.)

2. JEHOVAH. The meaning of this term is 'Self-Existent One.' As an exalted title it was so sacred to the Jew that use of it was avoided by the people for many generations. The moral implications of God seen in this name are dwelt upon by T. Rees in his article "God" written for the *International Standard Bible Encyclopaedia:*

> The most distinctive characteristic of Jehovah, which finally rendered Him and His religion absolutely unique, was the moral factor. In saying that Jehovah was a moral God, it is meant that He acted by free choice, in conformity with ends which He set to Himself, and which He also imposed upon His worshippers as their law of conduct.
>
> The most essential condition of a moral nature is found in His vivid personality, which at every stage of His self-revelation shines forth with an intensity that might be called aggressive. Divine personality and spirituality are never expressly asserted or defined in the Old Testament; but nowhere in the history of religion are they more clearly asserted. The modes of their expression are, however, qualified by anthropomorphisms, by limitations, moral and physical Jehovah's jealousy (Ex. 20:5; Deut. 5:9; 6:15), His wrath and anger (Ex. 32:10–12; Deut. 7:4) and His inviolable holiness (Ex. 19:21–22; 1 Sam. 6:19; 2 Sam. 6:7) appear sometimes to be irrational and immoral; but they are the assertion of His individual nature, of His self-consciousness as He distinguishes Himself from all else, in the moral language of the time, and are the conditions

of His having any moral nature whatsoever. Likewise, He dwells in a place and moves from it (Judg. 5:5); men may see Him in visible form (Ex. 24:10; Num. 12:8); He is always represented as having organs like those of the human body, arms, hands, feet, mouth, eyes and ears. By such sensuous and *figurative language* alone was it possible for a personal God to make Himself known to men.—II, 1256

3. ADONAI, meaning 'Master'; used of God and of men.

The New Testament presents God as Father of all who believe and as one to be known through His personal interrelations. The name of God in the New Testament is again a threefold revelation: Father, Son, and Holy Spirit. Not just one of these but all are required to present the one God.

Though God exists in a threefold mode of being, He is represented in the New Testament as one God, and so the Christian is as much under obligation to defend the doctrine of one God as the Unitarian, the Jew, or the Mohammedan.

GOSPEL

The word εὐαγγέλιον means 'good news' and was fully appreciated when all the news of the day had to be carried by couriers. To bear good news was a high honor. Four different messages of good news have been rightly identified and set forth by Dr. C. I. Scofield:

(1) The Gospel of the kingdom. This is the good news that God purposes to set up on the earth, in fulfillment of the Davidic Covenant (2 Sam. 7:16 . . .), a kingdom, political, spiritual, Israelitish, universal, over which God's Son, David's heir, shall be King, and which shall be, for one thousand years, the manifestation of the righteousness of God in human affairs. . . .

Two *preachings* of this Gospel are mentioned, one past, beginning with the ministry of John the Baptist, continued by our Lord and His disciples, and ending with the Jewish rejection of the King. The other is yet future (Matt. 24:14), during the great tribulation, and immediately preceding the coming of the King in glory.

(2) The Gospel of the grace of God. This is the good news that Jesus Christ, the rejected King, has died on the cross for the sins of the world, that He was raised from the dead for our justification, and that by Him all that believe are justified from all things. This form of the Gospel is described in

many ways. It is the Gospel "of God" (Rom. 1:1) because it originates in His love; "of Christ" (2 Cor. 10:14) because it flows from His sacrifice, and because He is the alone Object of Gospel faith; of "the grace of God" (Acts 20:24) because it saves those whom the law curses; of "the glory" (1 Tim. 1:11; 2 Cor. 4:4) because it concerns Him who is in the glory, and who is bringing the many sons to glory (Heb. 2:10); of "our salvation" (Eph. 1:13) because it is the "power of God unto salvation to every one that believeth" (Rom. 1:16); of "the uncircumcision" (Gal. 2:7) because it saves wholly apart from forms and ordinances; of "peace" (Eph. 6:15) because through Christ it makes peace between the sinner and God, and imparts inward peace.

(3) The everlasting Gospel (Rev. 14:6). This is to be preached to the earth-dwellers at the very end of the great tribulation and immediately preceding the judgment of the nations (Matt. 25:31 . . .). It is neither the Gospel of the kingdom, nor of grace. Though its burden is judgment, not salvation, it is good news to Israel and to those who, during the tribulation, have been saved (Rev. 7:9–14; Luke 21:28; Ps. 96:11–13; Isa. 35:4–10).

(4) That which Paul calls, "my Gospel" (Rom. 2:16 . . .). This is the Gospel of the grace of God in its fullest development, but includes the revelation of the result of that Gospel in the outcalling of the church, her relationships, position, privileges, and responsibility. It is the *distinctive* truth of Ephesians and Colossians, but interpenetrates all of Paul's writings.

. . . There is "another Gospel" (Gal. 1:6; 2 Cor. 11:4) "which is not another," but a perversion of the Gospel of the grace of God, against which we are warned. It has had many seductive forms, but the test is one—it invariably denies the sufficiency of grace alone to save, keep, and perfect, and mingles with grace some kind of human merit. In Galatia it was law, in Colosse fanaticism (Col. 2:18, etc.). In any form its teachers lie under the awful anathema of God.—*Scofield Reference Bible,* p. 1343

Strong objection is offered by Covenant theologians to a distinction between the gospel of the kingdom as preached by John the Baptist, Christ, and the other disciples and the gospel of the grace of God. One of them states that to make such a distinction is "unfortunate" and "dangerous." He with others contends that the kingdom gospel is identical with the gospel of divine grace. Here nevertheless will arise an absurdity which does not deter this type of theologian, namely, that men could preach the grace gospel based as it is on the death and resurrection of Christ when they did not believe Christ would die or be raised again (cf. Luke 18:31–34).

GOVERNMENT

Authority for human government dates from the flood when God expressly established it on the earth. This is well indicated, again, by Dr. C. I. Scofield:

"The Third Dispensation: Human Government. Under Conscience, as in Innocency, man utterly failed, and the judgment of the Flood marks the end of the second dispensation and the beginning of the third. The declaration of the Noahic Covenant subjects humanity to a new test. Its distinctive feature is the institution, for the first time, of human government—the government of man by man. The highest function of government is the judicial taking of life. All other governmental powers are implied in that. It follows that the third dispensation is distinctively that of human government. Man is responsible to govern the world for God. That responsibility rested upon the whole race, Jew and Gentile, until the failure of Israel under the Palestinian Covenant (Deut. 28:1 —30:10) brought the judgment of the Captivities, when 'the times of the Gentiles' (See Luke 21:24; Rev. 16:14) began, and the government of the world passed exclusively into Gentile hands (Dan. 2:36–45; Luke 21:24; Acts 15:14–17). That both Israel and the Gentiles have governed for self, not God, is sadly apparent" (*Ibid.*, p. 16).

The government of God must be supreme since His authority over the universe is that of Creator. His plans must usually be realized through providence. The Christian is called upon, then, to recognize human government as of God (Rom. 13:1–7; 1 Pet. 2:13–17; cf. Matt. 22:21). Any organized people must have some form of government, as did Israel in the Old Testament and the local church in New Testament times.

There are three forms of church government which correspond to the familiar three forms of civil administration: strictly democratic, government by the voice of the people as in the congregational form of church organization; monarchial, government by chosen leaders as in the Methodist and Episcopal Churches; and republican, or government by representation as in those churches governed through elders and deacons.

In Luke 4:5–6 it is clearly indicated that the governments of this world system (cf. Matt. 4:8–9) are under Satan's authority. So also in John 5:27 and in 1 Corinthians 15:27 it is revealed that all authority has been committed to Christ by the Father. Eventually, Christ will put down all finite rule and authority (1 Cor. 15:25, 28).

GRACE

Grace—a much misunderstood feature of God's ways with lost men —is itself a revelation and all human hearts not having this truth of Scripture revealed will be unable to comprehend it or to adjust themselves to its provisions.

Grace is not mercy or love. In Ephesians 2:4–5 these three doctrinal words appear severally and in their individual, specific manner: "But God, who is rich in mercy, for his great love wherewith he loved us, even when we were dead in sins, hath quickened us together with Christ, (by grace ye are saved;)." Speaking first of mercy, it is defined as that compassion in God which moved Him to provide a Savior for the lost. If He had been able to save even one soul on the basis of His sovereign mercy alone, He could have saved every person on that basis and the death of Christ would have been rendered unnecessary. As for divine love, it is an emotion of infinite character, the motivating purpose back of all that God does in saving a soul. But since God is holy and righteous too and the sinner's sins are an offense to Him, He might perfectly desire to save a soul and still be utterly helpless to do so in the light of the claims which divine righteousness make against the sinner. Not until those claims are met can God's infinite love realize its desire. Therefore, to come now to the third definition, grace is what God may be free to do and indeed what He does accordingly for the lost after Christ has died on behalf of them. "By grace are ye saved" (Eph. 2:8). When thus released from His holy demands against the sinner by the sacrificial death of Christ, and that sacrifice is accepted intelligently, the love of God will never be satisfied until He has done all He can do for such a one. The greatest thing God can do, reverently speaking, is to make someone like His Son. Such, then, will be the destiny of everyone who believes (Rom. 8:29; 1 John 3:2).

Since grace only represents what God can and will do for those who trust the Savior, it must needs function apart from all human works or cooperation. It calls for no more than confidence in the only One who can save.

The Scriptures assign to the operating of grace the only salvation now offered to sinful men. God's grace also provides security for the saved one. This is done by continuing the grace work of God with the individual in spite of his imperfections. Grace also undertakes to direct the saved one in the new manner of his daily life after he has been saved. A new motive for this is set up by the fact that the one saved was perfected forever in the sight of God as being in Christ, therefore partaking of His merit and standing forever. Nothing of merit need be added to that which is perfected forever (cf. John 1:16; Rom. 5:1; 8:1; Heb. 10:14). Hence the obligation to gain merit is removed completely, and the whole law system with its merit ceases to be applicable to the saved one under grace. He is no longer under law, but under grace (Rom. 6:14). The new problem becomes that of how a perfected person should walk in this world. Grace teaches the saved one concerning his holy walk in daily life. The standard is as high as heaven itself. God requires, and with reason, that the saved one, by reason of being a citizen of heaven, should live according to the standards of heaven (cf. John 13:34; Eph. 4:1, 30; 1 Thess. 5:19).

GUILT

The divine disposition of guilt proves to be one of the great triumphs won by grace. For sin, which must be charged against all individuals, is rebellion itself against God and His authority. There are two aspects of guilt: (1) Personal guilt, which is nothing other than the historical fact of committing sin. That will be a fact which abides forever though the guilt may be lifted through forgiveness. Personal guilt is not transferable. (2) Guilt as an obligation to justice. In so far as another may bear the penalty, this type of guiltiness becomes transferable. Christ as Substitute once did bear the obligation of the world to justice. Therefore, the substitution on Christ's part engenders a universal obligation to acknowledge and to stand before God under this gracious provision. For anyone thus to recognize his obligation would be an act of faith— "by grace are ye saved through faith" (Eph. 2:8).

HADES

Like all otherwise unknown truths, the doctrine of a future state depends wholly on what is declared in the Sacred Text. It is usually asserted that the word *Sheol* of the Old Testament finds its equivalent in *Hades,* but Dr. E. W. Bullinger objects to such a conclusion in the following note: "This [Gen. 37:35] being the first occurrence of the word *Sheol,* the R.V. gives a note in the margin, 'Heb. *Sheol,* the name of the abode of the dead, answering to the Greek Hades, Acts 2:27.' This note is altogether wrong. (1) It is *interpretation* and *not translation.* (2) It prejudges the word from the outset, fixing upon it the word 'abode,' which has a technical meaning applicable only to the living: thus anticipating the conclusion, which cannot be arrived at until we have obtained all the evidence, and have it before us. (3) *Sheol* has nothing in it 'answering to the Greek *Hades.*' Hadēs must have the same meaning as Sheōl; and must answer to that. It must have the meaning which the Holy Spirit puts upon it, and not the meaning which the heathen put on it" (*A Critical Lexicon and Concordance to the English and Greek New Testament,* 6th ed., revised, p. 368). A study of these words is at once required.

1. OLD TESTAMENT TEACHING. Having cited the use of *Sheol* in sixty-five passages and pointed out that it is usually translated *grave,* sometimes *pit,* and sometimes *hell,* Dr. Bullinger declares:

On a careful examination of the above list, a few facts stand out very clearly. (i.) It will be observed that in a majority of cases *Sheōl* is rendered "the grave." To be exact, 54 per cent.: while "hell" is 41½ per cent.; and "pit" only 4½ per cent. *The grave,* therefore, stands out on the face of the above list as the best and commonest rendering. (ii.) With regard to the word "pit," it will be observed that in each of the three cases where it occurs (Num. 16:30, 33; and Job 17:16), *the grave* is so evidently meant, that we may at once substitute that word, and banish "pit" from our consideration as a rendering of *Sheōl.* (iii.) As to the rendering "hell," it does *not* represent

Sheōl, because both by Dictionary definition and by colloquial usage "hell" means the place of future *punishment*. *Sheōl* has no such meaning, but denotes the *present state of death*. "The grave" is, therefore, a far more suitable translation, because it visibly suggests to us what is invisible to the mind, *viz.*, the state of death. It must, necessarily, be misleading to the English reader to see the former put to represent the latter. (iv.) The student will find that "THE grave," taken literally as well as figuratively, will meet all the requirements of the Hebrew *Sheōl:* not that *Sheōl* means so much specifically A grave, as generically THE grave. Holy Scripture is all-sufficient to explain the word *Sheōl* to us. (v.) If we enquire of it in the above list of the occurrences of the word *Sheōl*, it will teach (a) That as to *direction* it is down. (b) That as to *place* it is in the earth. (c) That as to *nature* it is put for *the state of death*. Not the *act* of dying, for which we have no English word, but the *state* or duration of death. The Germans are more fortunate, having the word *sterbend* for the act of dying. *Sheōl* therefore means *the state of death;* or *the state of the dead*, of which *the grave* is a tangible evidence. It has to do only with the dead. It may sometimes be personified and represented as speaking, as other inanimate things are. It may be represented by a coined word, Grave-dom, as meaning the dominion or power of *the grave*. (d) As to *relation* it stands in *contrast* with the state of the living, see Deut. 30:15, 19, and 1 Sam. 2:6-8. It is never once connected with the living, except by contrast. (e) As to *association*, it is used in connection with mourning (Gen. 37:34-35), sorrow (Gen. 42:38; 2 Sam. 22:6; Ps. 18:5; 116:3), fright and terror (Num. 16:27, 34), weeping (Isa. 38:3, 10, 15, 20), silence (Ps. 31:17; 6:5; Eccles. 9:10), no knowledge (Eccles. 9:5-6, 10), punishment (Num. 16:27, 34; 1 Kings 2:6, 9; Job 24:19; Ps. 9:17, R.V., RE-turned, as before their resurrection). (f) And, finally, as to *duration*, the dominion of *Sheōl* or the grave will continue until, and end only with, *resurrection*, which is the only exit from it (see Hos. 13:14, etc.; and compare Ps. 16:10 with Acts 2:27, 31; 13:35).—*Ibid.*, pp. 368-69

2. NEW TESTAMENT TEACHING. Here three words are present: *Gehenna* used eight times, *Hades* eleven times, *Tartaros* once. (a) Gehenna is a place of future punishment. (b) To quote Bullinger again, this time on Hades:

"If now the *eleven* occurrences of Hadēs in the New Testament be carefully examined, the following conclusions will be reached: (a) *Hadēs* is invariably connected with *death;* but *never with life:* always with *dead* people; but never with the *living*. All in *Hadēs* will 'NOT LIVE AGAIN,' until they are raised from the dead (Rev. 20:5). If they do not 'live again' until after they are raised, it is perfectly clear that they cannot be *alive* now. Otherwise we do away with the doctrine of resurrection altogether. (b) That the English word 'hell' by no means represents the Greek *Hadēs;* as we have seen that it does not give a correct idea of its Hebrew equivalent, *Sheōl*. (c) That *Hadēs* can mean only and exactly what *Sheōl* means, *viz.*, the place where 'corruption' is seen (Acts 2:31; compare 13:34–37); and from which, *resurrection* is the only exit" (*Ibid.*, p. 369).

So also on (c) Tartaros: "Τάρταρος is not Sheōl or Hadēs, . . . where all men go in death. Nor is it where the wicked are to be consumed and destroyed, which is Gehenna . . . Not the abode of *men* in any condition. It is used only here, and here only of 'the angels that sinned,' (*see* Jude 6). It denotes the bounds or verge of this material world. The extremity of this lower air—of which Satan is 'the prince' (Eph. 2:2) and of which Scripture speaks as having 'the rulers of the darkness of this world' and 'wicked spirits in aerial regions.' Τάρταρος is not only the bounds of this material creation, but is so called from its coldness" (*Ibid.*, p. 370).

HEADSHIP

As the human head governs the body to which it belongs, so authority is vested in the headship relation wherever it exists.

1. Christ sustains at least five such relations, as: (a) Head of the corner (Acts 4:11; 1 Pet. 2:7). See Ephesians 2:19–22, where the whole company of believers is seen as a building of God, Christ being the Headstone of the corner. (b) Head over every man (1 Cor. 11:3; cf. Eph. 5:23). Whether recognized or admitted by men, Christ is ruling over all of them. To Him they must one day render an account. (c) Head over the mystic Body of Christ, the Church (Eph. 4:15; Col. 1:18; 2:19). This figure is used more than any other to represent the service and manifestation of Christ by or through the members of His Body. (d) Head over the Bride (Eph. 5:23–33). Here again the Church is in view with a unique relationship, which relationship is to be realized fully after the marriage of the Lamb. (e) Head of principalities and powers (Eph. 1:21; Col. 2:10). Christ has universal authority over all angelic hosts.

2. The Head of Christ is God (1 Cor. 11:3). The authority which Christ exercises was given Him by the Father (John 5:27; Acts 17:31; 1 Cor. 15:25–28).

3. Adam is the natural head of the race, which race fell in him (Rom. 5:12).

4. Christ ranks as Head over the New Creation, which creation is in Him and partakes of His resurrection life (Eph. 1:19–23).

5. Man is head over the woman (1 Cor. 11:3; Eph. 5:23). Exceptions due to personalities and unusual situations make this a difficult phase in the doctrine of headship. Nevertheless, by divine arrangement the man is set over the woman in authority and conditions are never happy when this divine order has been ignored. The woman is not made with ability to exercise authority and often becomes eccentric or out of balance.

HEALING

Spiritual believers in all past generations have experienced divine favor, healing included. The claims of so-called divine healers, however, assume and imply that to secure such healing it is needful to go to them. At least seven errors are nevertheless to be found in their teaching, and these should be taken up separately.

1. "Healers" alone control God's healing of the body. But any company of spiritual believers, if asked to do so, would testify of divine curing far beyond the claims of professional healers.

2. Healing was provided in the atonement. It is taught that Christ bore diseases as He bore sins on the cross and therefore healing may be claimed absolutely by faith and without fail. Such error will mislead for few are prepared to refute these fantastic claims. So great an issue should be fully sustained by Scripture, doubtless, but it is not. It rather should be recognized that the body is not yet redeemed. The believer awaits a redeemed body. Romans 8:23 clearly states this: "And not only they, but ourselves also, which have the firstfruits of the Spirit, even we ourselves groan within ourselves, waiting for the adoption, to wit, the redemption of our body." The physical man will be redeemed at the return of Christ, as the Scripture foretells: "And God shall wipe away all tears from their eyes; and there shall be no more death, neither sorrow, nor crying, neither shall there be any more pain: for the former things are passed away" (Rev. 21:4). Extremists do not dare claim

redeemed bodies for themselves, when they all increase in age and limitations.

If Christ bore all sickness the healing in answer to true faith should of course never fail, but it does. Isaiah 53:5 in this connection reads: "But he was wounded for our transgressions, he was bruised for our iniquities: the chastisement of our peace was upon him; and with his stripes we are healed." Reference here may well be to spiritual healing. The Old Testament, indeed, teaches both spiritual healing and physical healing (cf. Ps. 103:3). In Matthew 8:16–17 reference is made to Isaiah 53:4, for Christ healed because He bore all afflicted ones on His heart of compassion.

Divine healers base their authority to heal the sick on Matthew 10:8, which reads: "Heal the sick, cleanse the lepers, raise the dead, cast out devils: freely ye have received, freely give," but there the command is given as well to raise the dead, heal leprosy, and cast out demons. The kingdom gospel was to be accompanied with wonders and miracles like these, but no such command for the supernatural ever came with the gospel of grace.

It remains to be noted that Paul's thorn in the flesh was not healed in spite of all his faith (2 Cor. 12:1–9), and that he with sadness left Trophimus sick at Miletum (2 Tim. 4:20). Epaphroditus, however, was healed as a direct mercy of God (Phil. 2:26–30; cf. Ps. 41:3; Gal. 4:13).

3. Sickness is from Satan and never in the will of God (cf. Deut. 32:39; Job 1–2; Hos. 6:1). By their taking this position the whole field of divine chastisement is rejected. But a man was blind from his birth that the glory of God might be seen in him, and Paul had a thorn in the flesh which was sent directly from God. It cannot be proved that Satan is the one cause of sickness or that disability may not be the will of God in some instances.

4. Anointing from the healer is as essential as faith. In all His healings, nonetheless, Christ anointed but once in so far as the record goes (Mark 6:13), and it is not mentioned again for curative purposes in the New Testament except in James 5:14. The Jewish rite of laying on of hands seemed to be observed at times. Peter cast a shadow and some were healed, but he never went into the shadow-casting business. Multitudes are healed today because it is directly in the will of God for His children apart from anointings, laying on of hands, or Peter's shadow.

5. Remedies are against the will of God. This assertion would change all medical missions and the work of Christian physicians and hospitals.

Medicine, to be sure, is usually the supply of elements needed in the system for its recovery. Hence to use remedies for healing is no different in principle than to feed the body with food or to clothe it for warmth.

Healing for the believer is within the Father's care of His child as also all financial support, or for that matter every good and perfect gift.

Two Old Testament types are evidence of divine cure. Each secured physical healing and for a reason: (1) leprosy (Lev. 14:1–57) and (2) the serpent bite (Num. 21:5–9). The healing in both cases was absolute and becomes clearly a type of the remedy for sin, which healing is in the death of Christ and never fails in answer to faith.

6. Christ must heal because He is the same yesterday, today, and forever. He may be the same Person, beyond all question, but not always have the same purpose. The Apostle, if his example means anything, prescribed wine for Timothy (1 Tim. 5:23).

7. Personal faith is required. This demand provides the divine healer's way out of difficulty when he fails to help. To put it back on the afflicted for lack of faith, however, is cruel and unscriptural. Many sufferers are driven insane by this treatment. In the Bible faith is required likewise on the part of the one who heals. One instance is actually recorded where healing failed because of unbelief on the part of those who would cure (cf. Matt. 17:14–21).

In conclusion, it may be asserted that it pleases God to heal His children of physical diseases when it is in the way of His parental dealing with them. It was said by David: "This poor man cried, and the LORD heard him, and saved him out of all his troubles" (Ps. 34:6). The death of Christ provides no absolute cure for physical ills, though it does so provide for spiritual ills. As well might one claim financial prosperity from the death of Christ according to 2 Corinthians 8:9, as to claim present-day physical healing from the Scriptures on the basis of the death of Christ.

HEART

Like *soul* and *spirit*, *heart* is a Biblical term which may represent the individual (Gen. 18:5; Lev. 19:17; Ps. 104:15; cf. Matt. 13:15 with 1 Cor. 2:10).

The meaning of the term has never been fully defined. This can be done only by a complete induction of all Scripture bearing upon the subject.

By referring to the heart as an organ of the physical body attention can be drawn to human emotions—courage, anger, fear, joy, sorrow, devotion, hatred (Deut. 19:6; 1 Sam. 25:37; Ps. 4:7; 12:2; 27:14). A man may love God with all his heart.

HEAVEN

The Scriptures appear to indicate that there are three heavens. The first and second are not specifically mentioned as such, but "the third heaven" is declared to exist (2 Cor. 12:2). It is evident that there cannot be a third heaven without also a first and second heaven.

a. The first heaven must be the atmosphere which surrounds the earth. Reference is certainly made to the fowls of heaven (Hos. 2:18) and to the clouds of heaven (Dan. 7:13). Herein is the native abode of human beings and all created life upon earth.

b. The second heaven may be the stellar spaces (cf. Gen. 1:14-18 for stars of the heaven) and so is the abode of all supernatural angelic creatures.

c. The third heaven (its location however wholly unrevealed) is the abode of God—the Father, the Son, and the Holy Spirit, and until this age has never been entered by any created being—angel or human. The present divine purpose is to populate the third heaven. It is called *glory* (Heb. 2:10) and represents a place rather than a state of mind or being (John 14:1-3). Those who enter will be "made meet" (Col. 1:12). More specifically, they will become actual sons of God (John 1:12; 3:3). They will be perfected forever (Heb. 10:14), justified (Rom. 5:1), and made partakers of Christ's $\pi\lambda\acute{\eta}\rho\omega\mu a$ (John 1:16), which is all fullness (Col. 1:19), the very nature of the Godhead bodily (Col. 2:9).

Similarly, the Scriptures employ the word *heaven* itself in a threefold usage:

a. *The kingdom of heaven* is a phrase peculiar to Matthew's Gospel (3:2, etc.) and indicates the earthly Messianic reign of Christ. Any rule of God over the earth is a form of the kingdom of heaven (cf. Dan. 2:44).

b. *The heavenly,* a phrase peculiar to the Epistle to the Ephesians (1:3, etc.), is a reference to the sphere of present association between believers and Christ, a copartnership in various respects. It signifies, therefore, not some favored place on the earth, but anywhere this communion with Christ may exist.

c. *Heaven* may represent the abode of the Godhead and of the redeemed forever.

As in many instances, knowledge about this place is wholly a matter of the testimony of the inspired Bible. It has been said that men really know nothing of heaven from experience since none have returned to tell of it. There are, however, three experienced witnesses:

a. Christ. Heaven was His abode for all eternity. He discloses more regarding it than does any other person in Scripture.

b. The Apostle Paul, who—probably when stoned to death in Lystra —was caught up to the third heaven (Acts 14:19–22; 2 Cor. 12:1–9). He was prohibited, however, from disclosing what he saw and heard. A thorn in the flesh was given to remind him to keep this mighty secret.

c. John the Apostle, who was called into heaven (Rev. 4:1), and then given instruction to write a book (Rev. 1:11) and record all that he saw and heard. If it is asked why Paul could not report but John was told to report, it may be observed that Paul's experience was typical of a believer at present departing by death while John's experience was more like that common to all believers at the rapture in a future day. After his experience and in spite of prohibition the Apostle Paul wrote: "To depart and to be with Christ is far better" (Phil. 1:23).

One has well said, "Heaven is a prepared place for a prepared people." Very definite preparation is required of those who would enter that celestial sphere (cf. Col. 1:12). They must be like Christ both in standing and state (Rom. 8:29; 1 John 3:2).

It remains to observe that heaven is a place of beauty (Rev. 21:1— 22:7) with various inhabitants (Heb. 12:22–24), of life (1 Tim. 4:8), holiness (Rev. 21:27), service (Rev. 22:3), worship (Rev. 19:1–3), fellowship with God (2 Tim. 4:8), glory (2 Cor. 4:17. See Revelation 21:4–5).

HOLINESS

Whether found in the Hebrew of the Old Testament or the Greek of the New Testament, three words arise from the same root, namely, *holy, saint, sanctify* (see SANCTIFICATION). No induction of holiness truth will be complete, therefore, which does not include all passages where these three words appear.

A thing may be holy because of its relation to God—for example, the holy place, the holy of holies. A thing may be holy because of actual association with Him or divine purpose—for instance, a holy nation, holy brethren.

Those who would live unto God and in fellowship with Him are enjoined to be holy in life. Since the Creator is holy in Himself, quite apart from all evil (Ps. 22:3; 1 John 1:6; James 1:17), the obligation to be holy—simply of course because He is holy—rests alike upon all God's creation. To sum it all up:

a. God is holy (Ps. 99:1–9; Isa. 6:2–3; Hab. 1:13; 1 John 1:5).

b. Being set apart or sanctified, some men are holy (Heb. 3:1).

c. Some angels are holy, being separate from evil (Matt. 25:31).

An unusual text appears in the words: "Ye shall be holy; for I am holy" (Lev. 11:44; cf. 1 Pet. 1:16). Man the creature is plainly required to be like his Creator. This obligation is unusual and constitutes an inherent or intrinsic law, binding on all created beings. After one is saved and brought into vital union with Christ a new responsibility is engendered to walk worthy of salvation, and this means to be as He was in this world.

The holiness of man is subject to a threefold consideration:

a. What is known as positional (Luke 1:70; Acts 20:32; 1 Cor. 1:2; 6:11; Eph. 4:24; Heb. 3:1; 10:10, 14).

b. Experimental (Rom. 6:1–23).

c. Ultimate (Rom. 8:29; Eph. 5:27; 1 John 3:1–3).

HOPE

Hope is expectation directed toward that which is good. Sometimes in Scripture the word is translated *trust*. Christ never used the term as such. There was of course certainty in all that He said. Two aspects of the doctrine may be noted:

a. Israel's hope (Luke 1:54, 67–79; 2:38; Acts 26:6–7; 28:20; Eph. 2:12) is of their coming Messiah and His kingdom on the earth.

b. Hope for the Christian is centered on the soon return of Christ (Titus 2:13–15; 1 John 3:2–3).

Bishop H. C. G. Moule lists seven elements when discussing Christian hope in general, as follows:

a. The return of Christ.

b. The resurrection body.

c. Being presented spotless before Christ.

d. Rewards.

e. Deliverance from Satan, sin, and death.

f. Companionship with saints.

g. Endless life with God.

The believer's hope, which operates as an anchor of the soul, is that he will one day join our great High Priest within the veil (Heb. 6:10 –20).

HORN

The term *horn* is a symbol of power and authority. Reference is made in Scripture to the following:

1. "The horn of David" (Ps. 132:17; cf. 92:10).

2. "The horn of the house of Israel" (Ezek. 29:21).

3. "A little horn"—the man of sin yet to appear with all his signs and lying wonders (Dan. 7:8, 11, 20–21; 8:5, 8–9, 21; Mic. 4:13; Zech. 1:21; 2 Thess. 2:9).

HUMILITY

Humility is a divine characteristic to be found in human hearts only as inwrought by the Spirit of God. It is far removed from self-depreciation or an inferiority complex. Perhaps no better word has been written on the subject than that of Archbishop Fénelon (1651–1715), himself a most holy and spiritual man, which runs as follows:

"He who seeks not his own interest, but solely God's interest in time and eternity, he is humble. . . . Many study exterior humility, but humility which does not flow from love is spurious. The more this exterior stoops, the loftier it inwardly feels itself; but he who is conscious of stooping does not really feel himself to be so low that he can go no further. People who think much of their humility are very proud" (cited by F. E. Marsh, *Emblems of the Holy Spirit,* p. 173). Archbishop Fénelon thus declares humility to be the effect of yieldedness to God's will.

In the Old Testament this word appears as a noun 3 times and in all its forms about 40 times. It is found in the New Testament some 15 times. It always has the meaning of true piety (cf. Deut. 8:2–3; 1 Kings 21:29; 2 Chron. 7:14). Such virtue was anticipated under the law (Mic. 6:8). Humility as a virtue occupies a large place in the coming kingdom (Isa. 57:15; Matt. 5:3; 11:25; 18:4; 23:12; Luke 10:21; 14:11; 18:14). As a fruit of the Spirit it is wrought in the believer today (Gal. 5:22–23; cf. 1 Cor. 13:4; 1 Pet. 5:5–6).

Since man has no merit in himself before God but receives all that he has, humility is only the right and natural attitude. Christ was humble, still not because He was a sinner or meritless. To become conscious of humility is its utter ruin.

IMMORTALITY

Three important statements will serve to clarify this doctrine concerned with the future life. (1) Immortality is not endless existence or mere existence after death (for dying does not terminate human life). The unsaved go on living after death as do the saved, too. (2) Immortality likewise is not the same as the gift of eternal life, that which is bestowed on all who believe in Christ. (3) Immortality is something related to the material part of man rather than the immaterial. The commonly used phrase *immortality of the soul* is most unscriptural. The soul is never considered mortal by Scripture.

Immortality and incorruption, however, are companion terms. As there are two ways of leaving earth for heaven—by death and resurrection or by translation directly from the living state, at the coming of Christ—so many will see corruption and through resurrection put on incorruption, while others because alive when Christ comes shall put on immortality. In the end both groups reach the same estate, that is, a "body like unto his glorious body" (Phil. 3:21).

It remains to be declared that no believer has yet an immortal body. Only one such body actually exists and is in heaven. Christ it was who did not see corruption (Ps. 16:10; Acts 2:31). He therefore put on immortality over a mortal (dead) body. He is now the only one who has immortality, dwelling in the light (cf. 1 Tim. 6:16), "and hath brought life and immortality to light through the gospel" (2 Tim. 1:10).

IMPUTATION

The word *impute* means to reckon over unto one's account, as the Apostle writing to Philemon regarding whatever Onesimus might owe Philemon declared: "Put that on mine account" (1:18). Because of the various phases of doctrine involved, imputation becomes at once one of the major or fundamental doctrines of Christianity. On this account great care is enjoined, that the student may comprehend the teaching perfectly. There are three major imputations set forth in the Scriptures, as will be seen below.

Imputation may either be real or judicial. A real imputation calls for the reckoning to one of what is antecedently his own, while a judicial imputation for the reckoning to one of what is not antecedently his own.

1. OF ADAM'S SIN TO THE RACE. The central passage bearing on im-

putation is found in Romans 5:12–21. In verse 12 it is declared that death as a penalty has come upon all men in that all have sinned. This does not refer to the fact that all men sin in their daily experience, but as the verb *sinned* is in the aorist tense it refers to a completed past action. That is, all men sinned when Adam sinned, and thereby brought the penalty of physical death upon themselves by so doing. That this evil may not be deemed personal sins, the Apostle points out how all died in the period between Adam and Moses, or before the Mosaic Law was given (which law first gave to sin the heinous character of transgression), and likewise how all irresponsible persons such as infants and imbeciles died although they have never sinned willfully, as in the case of Adam's transgression. Since God reckons each member of the race to have sinned in Adam's sin, this becomes the one case of real imputation, that is, a reckoning to each person that which is antecedently his own. An illustration of like seminal action may be seen in the record that Levi, who was supported by tithes, paid tithes while being in the loins of his great grandfather Abraham (Heb. 7:9–10, meaning when Abraham gave tithes to Melchizedek).

2. OF THE SIN OF THE RACE TO CHRIST. In this particular field of truth the whole gospel resides. Though the word *impute* is not used, similar terms are to be found such as "made him to be sin," "laid on him," "bare our sins" (Isa. 53:5–6, 11; 2 Cor. 5:21; 1 Pet. 2:24). Here is a judicial imputation since the sin was never antecedently Christ's, for when laid upon Him it became His in an awful sense.

3. OF THE RIGHTEOUSNESS OF GOD TO THE BELIEVER. This third imputation constitutes the Christian's acceptance and standing before God. It is the only righteousness that God ever accepts for salvation and by it alone may one enter heaven. The entire book of Romans is more or less occupied with setting forth the doctrine respecting the imputed righteousness of God, and as the purpose of the Romans Epistle is to reveal the truth concerning salvation it follows that the imputed righteousness of God must be a most important factor therein. The apostolic phrase *the righteousness of God* (Rom. 1:17; 3:22; 10:3), then, means a righteousness from God rather than the mere fact that God Himself is righteous. In Romans 3:10 it is declared that none among men are in the sight of God righteous; hence an imputed righteousness is the only hope for men on this earth. Regarding the hope of imputed righteousness, the Apostle wrote: ". . . not having mine own righteousness, which is of the law, but that which is through the faith of Christ, the righteousness which is of God by faith" (Phil. 3:9). To be fitted for

the presence of God is of immeasurable importance (Col. 1:12). This calls for a righteousness which is made over to the believer even as Christ was made to be sin for all men (2 Cor. 5:21). Obviously here must be a judicial imputation as this righteousness is not antecedently the believer's. Nevertheless, when imputed to him by God he will possess it forever.

This imputation which provides the believer with all he needs before God forever is so important that its basis is revealed in the Scriptures, and so it is quite essential for each believer to understand the revelation. It is made unto him a legal bestowment through the death of Christ and is applied by the Holy Spirit through His baptism of the believer into Christ.

a. Such imputation is constituted legal before God since Christ offered Himself without spot to God (Heb. 9:14). This is to say, Christ not only was made a sin offering by His death, by which remission of sin is legally possible on the ground of the truth that He substituted for those who believe, but also He presented Himself without spot as an offering well-pleasing to God, thus providing a release of all that He is in infinite merit and making His merit available for those who had no merit. As God goes to the cross for the legal basis to remit sin, so He goes to the same cross for the legal basis to impute righteousness. All of this is typically presented in the five offerings of Leviticus, chapters 1–5, where Christ's death may be seen both as a sweet savor and a non-sweet savor in the estimation of the Father. There is that in His death which was not a sweet savor to God as seen in the words of Christ, "My God, my God, why hast thou forsaken me?" (Matt. 27:46; cf. Ps. 22:1). Similarly, as cited above, Hebrews 9:14 suggests a sweet savor offering to God. He offered Himself without spot to God not merely to inform the Father of Himself, but in behalf of others. Here also He served as a Substitute. When others did not have and could not secure a standing and merit before God, He released His own self and all its perfection for them. Nothing could be more needed on the part of meritless sinners.

b. Imputed righteousness is applied directly on the ground of the pivotal fact that the believer is in Christ. By the baptism of the Spirit, being joined thereby to Christ, one is in Christ as a new Headship. As hitherto that one was in the first Adam, fallen and undone, now in the resurrected Christ he partakes of all that Christ represents, even the righteousness of God which Christ is. Christ is thus made unto the believer righteousness (1 Cor. 1:30), and being in Him the believer is "made" the righteousness of God (2 Cor. 5:21). Unto this marvelous standing the Great Apostle aspired when he wrote: "And be found in him, not having mine own righteousness, which is of the law, but that which is through the faith of Christ, the righteousness which is of God by faith" (Phil. 3:9).

The extent of this position in Christ cannot be estimated or understood. In Hebrews 10:14, however, it is declared: "For by one offering he hath perfected for ever them that are sanctified," and in John 1:16 reference is made to the πλήρωμα or fullness of Christ which the believer has received. That fullness is described in Colossians 1:19: "For it pleased the Father that in him should all fulness dwell," and again in 2:9: "For in him dwelleth all the fulness of the Godhead bodily," while verse 10 repeats the message of John 1:16, namely, that the believer is filled with the πλήρωμα (or, is complete) in Him.

The legal basis for the imputing of God's righteousness to the believer is found, then, in the sweet savor offerings and the application is accomplished by his being placed in union with Christ through the working of the Holy Spirit.

The three imputations named above prove foundational to all that enters into Christianity. They are wholly foreign to the Mosaic system and never mentioned in any Scriptures related to the coming kingdom. This teaching, along with other foundational doctrines such as propitiation, accordingly should be comprehended by every student at any cost.

INCARNATION

Because of the immeasurable truths involved, the incarnation—whereby a member of the Godhead is entering permanently into the human family and becoming part of it—proves one of the seven greatest events in the history of the universe, as follows: (1) creation of angels, (2) creation of material things including all life on the earth, (3) the incarnation, (4) death of the Incarnate One, (5) His resurrection, (6) His coming again to reign on the earth, and (7) His reign on the earth forever and ever. Naturally two questions will arise: Who is this incarnate Person? and What can be His mode of existence?

a. The identification is complete. He must be the Second Person or

Son who became incarnate, not the Father or the Spirit. It remains true that Christ was and is God in the mystery of the Godhead Three; but He alone of the Three became flesh and took upon Him the form of man. He therefore is unique. There has never been and never will be again one like this theanthropic Person. Nor should there be surprise that He is different from all other human beings. The Scriptures are ever concerned to set forth in knowable terms the eternal character of the One who became incarnate. In the opening of John's Gospel it is written: "In the beginning was the Word, and the Word was with God, and the Word was God. The same was in the beginning with God. All things were made by him; and without him was not any thing made that was made. . . . And the Word was made flesh, and dwelt among us, (and we beheld his glory, the glory as of the only begotten of the Father,) full of grace and truth" (1:1–3, 14). The attempt by John through the Spirit of God in the opening verses of his Gospel is to de-clare the eternal character of the One who became flesh and dwelt among us. The term *logos* (see LOGOS) refers to the preincarnate Christ and embodies a truth far too little employed by theologians. The "be-ginning" of John 1:1 must go back before all creation came into ex-istence and therefore far antedates the "beginning" of Genesis 1:1. John is saying of the dateless past that the Person who became incarnate *was* existent already. He then existed as old and as wise as now. He did not sometime begin to be; He *was* in the beginning. The Logos is and always has been the expression of God, the Manifester. Those who de-sire to know what God is like need only to behold the Son of God as He showed Himself to the world. Of this the Apostle John writes: "No man hath seen God at any time; the only begotten Son, which is in the bosom of the Father, he hath declared him" (John 1:18).

Though no man ever spoke as that One spoke, He did not come into the world merely to manifest the wisdom of God. Though no man could do the miracles which He wrought except God be with him, He did not come to manifest the power of God. He came rather to manifest the love of God, and not in a whole lifetime of compassion for us but rather in one event of His life especially. Of this it is written: "But God com-mendeth his love toward us, in that, while we were yet sinners, Christ died for us" (Rom. 5:8); "Hereby perceive we the love of God, because he laid down his life for us: and we ought to lay down our lives for the brethren" (1 John 3:16).

b. Christ entered the human family that He might be a kinsman and thus meet the requirements laid down for a kinsman redeemer. According to the type seen in the Old Testament, especially the Book of Ruth (cf. Lev. 25:49; Isa. 59:20), no one could redeem except he be a near kinsman not involved in the condition from which he wished to rescue. He must also be willing as well as able to redeem. All this Christ fulfilled perfectly when He became a kinsman by being born into the human family.

Through His incarnation Christ combined both the perfect, divine nature of God and human nature in one Person. He was no less God because of His humanity and no more than human as respects humanity because of the divine being which He was.

If the Logos was to become "flesh" and as Immanuel be one of the human family, there was but one way it could be done. He must submit to a human birth. Had He suddenly appeared on earth among men as if one of them or even been seen descending from heaven, the identity of His Person—without a human body, soul, and spirit all of His own—could never have been established satisfactorily.

It is too often assumed that Christ began to be at the time of His birth of the virgin, whereas He was from all eternity. From the standpoint of fact, then, humanity was only added to Deity.

INFANT SALVATION

Many and varied problems are discovered in a study of the doctrine of infant salvation. Like all salvation issues, the doctrines here involved must ever be correctly stated and harmonized—election, Anthropology, the fall of the race, Soteriology, together with redemption. The entire field of sovereign grace toward a lost world is in view. No theology is established or complete which does not account for the salvation of those who die in infancy. This company is great numerically, and without this group some representation from every tribe and nation might not be included among the redeemed. Being unable to respond to God's proffered grace in Christ, the child, if saved at all, must be saved on other terms than those imposed upon the adult portion of humanity. God's freedom to save the lost in righteousness is evidently at stake.

It will be recognized that when a disproportionate emphasis on the lost estate of men is present there may well be a tendency to think of all children as if they were born reprobate. That they are unregenerate at birth is certain; yet God likewise has in great mercy provided for the unsaved whom it is His purpose to save. Earlier, extreme Calvinists asserted that hell is a place paved with infants not over a span long; because of this sort of teaching and as a heritage from Rome came about the belief in baptismal regeneration. To such a position, of course, the Word of God gives no sanction either directly or indirectly.

In *The Sunday School Times* (beginning November 10, 1928) was published a symposium by well-known Bible teachers and theologians on the subject of infant salvation; and it was the expressed opinion of all who wrote articles that infants are saved in and through the death of Christ for them, that Christ's sacrifice provided righteous freedom on God's part to save all for whom Christ died and that, since He died for all mankind, God is free to save whom He will and upon such terms as He may elect to impose. As infants cannot possibly respond to the terms of faith imposed upon the adult portion of the race, God may and does act directly in behalf of those who die in infancy. No unrighteousness can be found in this outworking of God's purpose and will.

The whole subject of infants being saved, though it introduces many and varied theological problems, is first of all somewhat established by the fact that in Scripture little ones are seen in heaven and are recognized as being there (cf. 2 Sam. 12:23; Matt. 18:3–5, 10; 19:14).

In an article for *Bibliotheca Sacra,* furthermore, at the beginning of his discussion on the doctrine, Dr. Alan H. Hamilton states:

> The entire program of Christian religious education will be built upon the educator's answer to these three questions: (1) What is the spiritual state of the child as he comes into the world? To this, two contrasting answers have been given, the one that he is born with a spiritual life which must be carefully cultivated and directed, the other that he inherits the curse of a fallen race and is born devoid of spiritual contact with God or of ability within himself to make that contact. (2) What are the spiritual needs of the child? The school of thought following the first concept given above will respond with a training designed to enhance and bring into full fruition the essence of spiritual life which the child possesses. Those who are convinced of the second concept will lay major emphasis upon the child being brought, as early as possible, to a saving relationship with God through Christ. As we will see, ecclesiastical bodies differ as to the manner in which this relationship is thought to be effected; but the general agreement is there, nonetheless, that in some manner a spiritual life must be imparted. This will lay the foundation upon which Christian character can be built and from which Christian virtue will flow. (3) What are the spiritual possibilities of the child? To the first group the child, already in possession of spiritual life, may be so enlightened and hedged about that he can retain his original spiritual life and develop from

birth to manhood without interruption. Should he turn aside to actual sin, of course, that life is lost and a subsequent conversion experience is necessary. To the second group it is not considered possible that the appreciation and appropriation of spiritual things can be realized prior to the time of regeneration. No lack of emphasis upon moral training is to be noted among this group, neither is there, generally, a failure to present Scripture truths; but all of this is done with the realization that there is no spiritual life to develop until the occurrence of the new, spiritual birth. Since, however, this school of thought conceives of regeneration as a sovereign act of God, it is able to expect (where thinking along this line is consistent) that salvation can occur very early in the child's life and need not tarry until a period of greater intellectual comprehension is reached.

Both of these schools of thought have developed within evangelical Christianity. The first, as will be readily recognized, has grown out of a rationalism which has tended toward universalism. It began to gain prominence in the latter half of the nineteenth century with the writings of Horace Bushnell (*Christian Nurture*, 1847), F. G. Hibbard (*The Religion of Childhood*, 1864), R. J. Cooke (*Christianity and Childhood*, 1891), and C. W. Rishell (*The Child as God's Child*, 1904). The title of a pamphlet by J. T. McFarland from this period indicates the trend of thought. It is called *Preservation versus the Rescue of the Child* (see Hastings' *Encyclopaedia of Religion and Ethics, s.v.,* "Childhood").

The second school has followed more closely the supernaturalism presented by the Scriptures. It represents the view taken in this study, in which the authority of the Bible is assumed and which, it is hoped, will be shown to be the only system of thought which can stand the tests of the Scriptures, of consistency, and of the approval of the Christian consciousness.

It is of interest to note that the findings of the child study movement, not following the teachings of Scripture but instead the tenets of psychology, have given support to the view taken here by asserting that religion is something external to the child. It is usually considered as being imparted to him by his environment.

There has been also, during the past twenty years especially, a growing conviction in the hearts of the Christian public that the little child is a proper object for the simple teaching of the gospel. This movement finds its roots in the view presented here: the complete depravity of every member of the human race, and the absolute possibility of regeneration, even for the very young child, because of the supernatural operation of God in saving grace.

With these three values in view, therefore, the study of the doctrine of infant salvation is undertaken: (1) its practical value in bringing a certain and Scriptural answer to the questionings of those whose lives are touched by the death of an infant; (2) the theological value in providing a test of current theological systems; and (3) the contribution which it may make, in a foundational way, to the construction of a proper program of evangelism and education for the child.—CI, 343–45

Dr. Hamilton goes on to quote from the early Fathers and to demonstrate that this doctrine did not then have the place of importance theologically which it has now. Its present significance was well declared by Dr. B. B. Warfield when he said: "No system of theological thought can live in which it [the doctrine of infant salvation] cannot find a natural and logical place" (*Two Studies in the History of Doctrine*, p. 239, as cited by Hamilton, *ibid.*, p. 343).

Certain problems require consideration.

a. That infants are saved by reason of being innocent. This is a universal belief, especially being entertained by parents of a deceased child; but innocence can save no one when all are born depraved (see DEPRAVITY).

b. That proper baptism will save all so presented. But if baptism can save any or at all, Christ's death is in vain. Why should He die?

c. That in so far as Christ died for all, all are saved thereby. This is the viewpoint which Richard Watson declares upon the supposed authority of Romans 5:17–18 (see Watson's *Theology*, II, 57 ff.), where the gift of righteousness extends to those who "receive abundance of grace." But here God speaks to reasonable adult persons; still, He is nonetheless free to save as He will.

d. That infants belong to the election. Are infants who die in infancy necessarily of the elect? It is evident that they are if saved at all. Is a child fortunate, then, who dies in infancy because more sure of heaven than if he were to continue and perhaps be unwilling to be saved even in late years? Of that none can speak. God guides and works out His own plan in every life which is lived on earth. It is probable that the elect company, in order for it to be from every kindred, tribe, and people, will be built up in part out of those who die in infancy.

It may be definitely asserted, in conclusion, that infants who die before accountability begins are saved through the redemption which is in Christ Jesus.

INFINITY

The doctrine of infinity, such as it is, will be contained in the one word *infinite*. It represents only that which is of God, since His power and resources and mode of being are infinite (Ps. 147:5). Due to the poverty of human language and a disposition oftentimes to speak in superlatives, this particular term, which in itself is most restricted, has become to many a mere form of exaggeration (cf. Job 22:5; Nah. 3:9). *Infinite* occurs three times in Scripture, as indicated above.

INHERITANCE

As an Old Testament doctrine, the theme of inheritance begins with Jehovah's partitioning of the promised land to tribes and families (Lev. 25:23–28; Num. 26:52–56; 27:8–11). When no heir existed the estate went to the nearest kinsman. God's way of preserving these properties in line with their original grants was to cause that all estates should be restored in the year of jubilee or every fifty years.

The New Testament doctrine is to the effect that the believer has an inheritance in God (Rom. 8:16–17; Eph. 1:14; 1 Pet. 1:4) and God a heritage in the believer (Eph. 1:18; cf. Rom. 5:8–10).

INNOCENCE

The term *innocent* implies only absence of evil (Matt. 27:4, 24). It is thus altogether negative. By so much it corresponds with the legal words *not guilty*.

A child is an example of innocence (Matt. 18:3). Adam as created was innocent; but the term does not describe the Last Adam's life on earth. He on the contrary was holy and undefiled and separate from sinners (Heb. 7:26). Here, then, is another term which should be used with care and discrimination.

INSPIRATION

As applied to Scripture, the term *inspiration* means 'God-breathed' (2 Tim. 3:16–17) and more particularly that the words of Holy Writ are derived from God. *All* Scripture is said to be God-breathed, not as the Revised Version might suggest: "Every scripture inspired of God [or, God-breathed] is also profitable . . ." Regarding the Scriptures and plenary, verbal inspiration, it may be said that no other explanation has been the belief of the church from the beginning.

The English word *inspiration* is from the Latin root *spiro,* which means 'to breathe,' translating the Greek word θεόπνευστος (used but once in the New Testament, 2 Tim. 3:16) that means 'God-breathed or inbreathed of God.' Scripture did not originate with men, but with God. It is one of God's most wonderful actions. 2 Peter 1:21 has to do with the counterpart to this divine work respecting human reception of the God-directed words. The Bible authors were moved or borne along as a ship by the wind. Each word of the Bible is, therefore, to a certain degree of dual authorship—both from the Holy Spirit and its human authors.

Men of serious mind have sought to prove the authoritative character of the Scriptures by declaring that only some parts are inspired; but this approach leaves to man the responsibility of determining how much is inspired, and man indeed may as well be sole author of the text if he can pass such a discriminating judgment.

No progress has ever been made in formulating doctrine from the Bible when men have doubted the inspiration of the Scriptures in all its parts. This work on Systematic Theology, then, is based on a complete credence respecting the plenary, verbal inspiration of the Bible, the very position which has been defended on earlier pages.

INTERCESSION

Interceding is a form of prayer sufficiently particular to justify separate consideration apart from the general doctrine of prayer (see PRAYER).

Intercession contemplates the ministry of one who stands between God and some great need, as in the case of Abraham interceding for the cities of the Jordan plain. Rightfully it is said in Romans of all praying: "We know not what we should pray for as we ought," when so much is involved in God's purpose and plan for each human life. Only "Thy will be done" (Matt. 6:10) can be the final attitude of all who intercede. The Christian cannot himself know the scope and force of prayer; however, in this respect God makes provision. The one central passage on intercession (Romans 8:26–27), therefore, reads: "Likewise the Spirit also helpeth our infirmities: for we know not what we should pray for as we ought: but the Spirit itself maketh intercession for us with groanings which cannot be uttered. And he that searcheth the hearts knoweth what is the mind of the Spirit, because he maketh intercession for the saints according to the will of God." The Spirit knows omnisciently (cf. 1 Cor. 2:10–11), then, and God who searches the heart knows the mind and language of the Spirit. This portion of Romans is a peculiar passage in that it records communication between the Father and the Spirit. Prayer in all its forms has adequate enablement. It is to be offered to the Father (Matt. 6:9), in the name of the Son (John 16:23–24), and in the power of the Spirit's enablement (cf. Eph. 6:18; Jude 1:20).

INTERMEDIATE STATE

The doctrine of an intermediate state concerns the estate of the redeemed between death and resurrection of the body. Some treatment of this theme is usually incorporated into works on Systematic Theology as a phase of Eschatology.

There is little or no direct teaching on this doctrine in the Old Testament; yet when the Synoptic Gospels are considered as a continuation of the Old Testament revelation, as indeed they should be considered, much light is thrown on the Hebrew Scriptures respecting the intermediate state. Two important passages may be cited for illustration: "And in hell he lift up his eyes, being in torments, and seeth Abraham afar off, and Lazarus in his bosom" (Luke 16:23); "And Jesus said unto him, Verily I say unto thee, To day shalt thou be with me in paradise" (Luke 23:43). These verses are revealing in respect to the estate of the Old Testament saints. Christ Himself, in the former, pictures the rich man suffering torment and the beggar enjoying Abraham's bosom. To a Jew, Abraham's bosom is the sublime place of rest and peace; but of course this is far removed from the believer's place in this age, for the Apostle Paul says that "to depart and to be with Christ is far better" than anything the world may afford.

The body rests in the grave, accordingly, and must see corruption. There is no Scripture which justifies the notion that the soul and spirit sleep in unconsciousness during the interval between death and resurrection. The dying thief, as noticed above, was assured of a place in paradise the day that he died. It is probable that paradise—now the place of waiting for the blessed dead before they rise—was at the resurrection of Christ moved into heaven; for Paul, likely when stoned to death at Lystra (2 Cor. 12:1-10), was caught up into a paradise located in the third heaven. God does not reveal further the estate of those with Christ in paradise.

2 Corinthians 5:1-8 may promise an intermediate body for those believers who die lest they be found disembodied. It is a body "from heaven," not indeed the resurrection body from the grave.

In answer to the question whether those now with Christ know of conditions on earth and whether they know each other, no revelation is given; and here, as always, the silence of God should be respected.

INTERPRETATION

The doctrine of interpretation contemplates the science of discovering the exact meaning of the Spirit Author as this is set forth in a given Scripture passage. Such a science may be described theologically as *hermeneutics*. To fathom this doctrine it is necessary to know and follow the recognized rules of Scripture interpretation. In his classroom textbook on hermeneutics Dr. Rollin T. Chafer advances the following four major rules, to which less important rules may be added:

1. "The first rule of Biblical interpretation is: Interpret grammatically; with due regard to the meaning of words, the form of sentences, and the peculiarities of idiom in the language employed. The sense of Scripture is to be determined by the words; a *true* knowledge of the words is the knowledge of the sense. . . . The words of Scripture must be taken in their common meaning, unless such meaning is shown to be inconsistent with other words in the sentence, with the argument or context, or with other parts of Scripture.

. . . The true meaning of any passage of Scripture, then, is not every sense which the words will bear, nor is it every sense which is true in itself, but that which is intended by the inspired writers, or even by the Holy Spirit, though imperfectly understood by the writers themselves" (Angus-Green, *Cyclopedic Handbook of the Bible*, p. 180).

Out of the multitude of examples cited in the various texts, one from Lockhart on Ephesians 2:8 may be cited. "For by grace are ye saved through faith; and that not of yourselves: it is the gift of God." He says: "We may ask, what is the gift of God? Many would answer, 'grace'; many others, 'faith'; some, 'salvation.' But what does the grammar require?" After eliminating "grace" and "faith" as the antecedents of "that," he proceeds: "The only other possible antecedent is the salvation expressed by the verb 'saved.' Some have objected that the Greek noun for salvation is feminine; but we must notice that salvation is here expressed . . . by the verb, and Greek grammar again requires that a pronoun which refers to the action of a verb for its antecedent must be neuter. This exactly suits the case; and the meaning is, Ye are saved by grace through faith; but the salvation is not of yourselves, it is the gift of God. Here the interpretation that accords with the grammar is reasonable and satisfactory" (*Principles of Interpretation*, p. 85–86). I have pointed out before, however, that the observance of all grammatical requirements often leaves one short of the meaning of the doctrinal contents of the text. Cellérier has this in mind when he says: "Suppose that he [an interpreter] undertakes to explain the words of Jesus to the paralytic: 'My son, thy sins be forgiven thee' (Mark 2:5), Grammatical Hermeneutics may readily do its work, but it will not fathom the depth of meaning which these words contain" (*Biblical Hermeneutics*, Elliott and Harsha, translators, p. 53).

2. The second rule of interpretation is: "Interpret according to the context." "The meaning of a word, again, will often be modified by the connexion in which it is used. . . . This rule is often of great theological importance" (Angus-Green, *op. cit.*, p. 186–87). (Examples: Various meanings of *Faith, Flesh, Salvation, Grace*, etc.). "The study of the context is the most legitimate, efficacious, and trustworthy resource at the command of the interpreter. Nothing can be more convenient, more logical than to explain an author by himself, and to have recourse to the entire train of thought. It is much less easy for sophism to abuse this mode of interpretation than that of dealing with etymology, philology, and exceptions of syntax" (Cellérier, *op. cit.*, p. 101). Although these latter are often valuable aids, they may also be pushed to harmful effects. (Example: The etymological study of some words indicates that their significance has entirely departed from the root meaning. On the ground of etymology, therefore, it would be misleading for an interpreter to hold to the root meaning in such cases.) One of the most helpful results of contextual study is furnished by the definitions of the author's own terms. (Examples: "That the man of God may be perfect, thoroughly furnished unto all good works." 2 Tim. 3:17. By *perfect* here is meant: "Thoroughly furnished" for service. There are a number of contexts in which the word *perfect* needs the light from the context for its exact meaning. In such passages the thought is not perfection in its widest sense, but maturity in a specified line of experience or endeavor.)

3. Sometimes the context does not give all the light needed to determine the meaning of a word or a phrase. In such cases a third rule is necessary, namely: "Regard the scope or design of the book itself, or of some large section in which the words and expressions occur" (Angus-Green, *op. cit.,* p. 192). The purpose in writing a book is often clearly mentioned, especially in the N.T. Epistles. This avowed purpose will often throw light on passages otherwise obscure. Terry gives the following example: "There can be no doubt, . . . that, after his opening salutation and personal address, the apostle [Paul] announces his great theme [of Romans] in verse 16 of the first chapter. It is *the Gospel considered as the power of God unto salvation to every believer, to the Jew first, and also to the Greek. . . .* It manifestly expresses, in a happy personal way, the scope of the entire epistle." After an analysis of the entire epistle, he says: "It will be found that a proper attention to this general plan and scope of the Epistle will greatly help to the understanding of its smaller sections" (*Biblical Hermeneutics,* p. 111–12).

4. "The fourth and most comprehensive rule of Biblical interpretation is: Compare Scripture with Scripture. . . . A Scripture truth is really the consistent explanation of all that Scripture teaches in reference to the question examined; and a Scripture duty is the consistent explanation of all the precepts of Scripture on the duty" (Angus-Green, *op. cit.,* p. 195). As has already been noted, this procedure was not employed until the Reformation; and sound hermeneutics was not developed until this method was adopted. It results in "the analogy of faith which regulates the interpretation of each passage in conformity with the whole tenor of revealed truth." Under this general head Cellérier also says: "To admit a positive revelation and to reject things positively revealed is a great inconsistency" (*Op. cit.,* p. 19). This inconsistency is not uncommon. Some interpreters who claim to accept the Bible as the revealed Word of God, reject specific revelations in it because these do not fit into the framework of their preconceived theology.—*The Science of Biblical Hermeneutics,* pp. 75–78

Since every student of Scripture, especially the one who would attempt to expound the Word of God, is confronted with the problem of giving to the Sacred Text its precise meaning, the need of following these rules is imperative.

ISRAEL

An elect, sacred, and everlasting nation is the plan or purpose of God for Israel. This people came into being miraculously as the seed of Abraham through Isaac and Jacob. They are the object of immeasurable covenants and promises and this becomes their major identification or destination, for the covenants are secured or sealed by the act of Jehovah. Israel stands alone, in distinction from all other nations combined. Those many nations are known as Gentiles, but Israelites as Jews. Individual Jews are such because of the fact that they were born into covenant relations with God by a physical birth. Herein lies a great contrast, since Christians are such because they were born by a spiritual birth into right relations with God. Because Israel sustains a covenant relationship to God, He gave them a specific rule of life through Moses. Keeping the rule of life, however, did not and could not make them children of Jehovah's covenant. They were to keep the rule of life because they were already in the covenant. The believer has a rule of life secured by his position under grace today and so keeping this or any rule will not make him a child of God, although being a child of the Father above he should walk according to His revealed will.

Israel's relationship to Jehovah remained unchanged until the present age, in which time God has ordained that there should be "no difference" between Jew and Gentile (Rom. 10:12). All alike are under sin (Rom. 3:9; Gal. 3:22), and the individual Jew like the Gentile may be saved alone through faith in Christ. In similar manner, all Jews are now subject to divine judgment, which is something eternal if they continue as Christ rejecters. When the present age is completed, Israel will return to Jehovah's purpose for her and will enter, properly purged, the long-promised and anticipated kingdom glory. God must yet deal specifically with Israel in judgment (Ezek. 20:33-34). So also all the nations shall stand before the throne of Christ's glory to be judged respecting their treatment of Israel as a people (cf. Matt. 25:31-46).

In a manner and to an extent quite impossible of comprehension by the finite mind, Israel is appointed to glorify God. This truth must not be slighted. God speaks of the elect nation as "Israel my glory" (Isa. 46:13), and indeed He has chosen that nation above all nations for His glory (Gen. 12:1-3). He loves them with an everlasting love (Jer. 31:3). When the Christian loves with a divine compassion he will acknowledge what God loves. Therefore, he too must love Israel.

JEHOVAH

As an introduction to the name *Jehovah*—one of the three primary Old Testament names for God—and its import, two paragraphs from the article by Dr. T. Rees on "God" in the *International Standard Bible Encyclopaedia* may well be quoted:

Jehovah (Yahweh).—This is the personal proper name *par excellence* of Israel's God, even as Chemosh was that of the god of Moab, and Dagon that of the god of the Philistines. The original meaning and derivation of the word are unknown. The variety of modern theories shows that, etymologically, several derivations are possible, but that the meanings attached to any one of them have to be imported and imposed upon the word. They add nothing to our knowledge. The Hebrews themselves connected the word with hāyāh, "to be." In Exodus 3:14 Jehovah is explained as equivalent to *'ehyeh*, which is a short form of *'ehyeh 'ăsher 'ehyeh*, translated in R.V. "I am that I am." This has been supposed to mean "self-existence," and to represent God as the Absolute. Such an idea, however, would be a metaphysical abstraction, not only impossible to the time at which the name originated, but alien to the Hebrew mind at any time. And the imperfect *'ehyeh* is more accurately translated "I will be what I will be," a Semitic idiom meaning, "I will be all that is necessary as the occasion will arise," a familiar Old Testament idea (cf. Isa. 7:4, 9; Ps. 23).

This name was in use from the earliest historical times till after the exile. It is found in the most ancient literature. According to Exodus 3:13 f., and especially 6:2–3, it was first introduced by Moses, and was the medium of a new revelation of the God of their fathers to the children of Israel. But in parts of Genesis it is represented as being in use from the earliest times. Theories that derive it from Egypt or Assyria, or that would connect it etymologically with Jove or Zeus, are supported by no evidence. We have to be content either to say that Jehovah was the tribal God of Israel from time immemorial, or to accept a theory that is practically identical with that of Exodus—that it was adopted through Moses from the Midianite tribe into which he married. The Kenites, the tribe of Midianites related to Moses, dwelt in the neighborhood of Sinai, and attached themselves to Israel (Judg. 1:16; 4:11). A few passages suggest that Sinai was the original home of Jehovah (Judg. 5:4–5; Deut. 33:2). But there is no direct evidence bearing upon the origin of the worship of Jehovah: to us He is known only as the God of Israel.
—Pp. 1254–5

The various compounds with *Jehovah* being used in the Old Testament are:

Jehovah-jireh—'Jehovah sees' (Gen. 22:13–14),
Jehovah-nissi—'Jehovah is my banner' (Ex. 17:15),
Jehovah-shalom—'Jehovah is peace' (Judg. 6:24),
Jehovah-shammah—'Jehovah is there' (Ezek. 48:35),
Jehovah-tsidkenu—'Jehovah our righteousness' (Jer. 23:6),
Jehovah-rā-ah—'Jehovah my shepherd' (Ps. 23:1),
Jehovah-rapha—'Jehovah that healeth' (Ex. 15:26).

In the light of the plural form of *Elohim*, Deuteronomy 6:4 is significant, also the collective use there of the word *one*. The text reads:
"Hear, O Israel: The LORD our God is one LORD." A translation just as
acceptable might read: "Jehovah [note the name is singular] our
Elohim [now it is plural] is one [several entities united in one] Jehovah." What, therefore, must be the significance of Christ's reference
to Himself as Jehovah or the "I am" (John 8:58)?

JERUSALEM

The International Standard Bible Encyclopaedia (p. 1596) declares:
"The earliest mention of Jerusalem is in the Tell el-Amarna Letters
(1450 B.C.), where it appears in the form of Uru-sa-lim . . ." The
earthly Jerusalem, sometimes called Zion because such was the name
for the city's ancient citadel, is referred to as the city of David (cf.
2 Sam. 5:6–12) and the city of the great king (Matt. 5:35). It is indeed
a city of an incomparable history and of a marvelous destiny. It will yet
be the capital of the whole earth. Out from it Messiah's law and rule
shall go, for Isaiah 2:1–4 declares: "The word that Isaiah the son of
Amoz saw concerning Judah and Jerusalem. And it shall come to pass in
the last days, that the mountain of the LORD's house shall be established
in the top of the mountains, and shall be exalted above the hills; and all
nations shall flow unto it. And many people shall go and say, Come ye,
and let us go up to the mountain of the LORD, to the house of the God of
Jacob; and he will teach us of his ways, and we will walk in his paths:
for out of Zion shall go forth the law, and the word of the LORD from
Jerusalem. And he shall judge among the nations, and shall rebuke
many people: and they shall beat their swords into plowshares, and their

spears into pruninghooks: nation shall not lift up sword against nation, neither shall they learn war any more."

During the time of Messiah's absence now, Jerusalem is a sign; for as long as it is under the leadership of foreign powers, as today, Gentile times are unfulfilled, though Gentile times are to be fulfilled at once when the city is returned to Israel's ownership or authority: "And they shall fall by the edge of the sword, and shall be led away captive into all nations: and Jerusalem shall be trodden down of the Gentiles, until the times of the Gentiles be fulfilled" (Luke 21:24). The city of the future will have a specific religious character: "Thus saith the LORD of hosts; It shall yet come to pass, that there shall come people, and the inhabitants of many cities: and the inhabitants of one city shall go to another, saying, Let us go speedily to pray before the LORD, and to seek the LORD of hosts: I will go also. Yea, many people and strong nations shall come to seek the LORD of hosts in Jerusalem, and to pray before the LORD. Thus saith the LORD of hosts; In those days it shall come to pass, that ten men shall take hold out of all languages of the nations, even shall take hold of the skirt of him that is a Jew, saying, We will go with you: for we have heard that God is with you" (Zech. 8:20-23). Again, Isaiah declared regarding the filth of the city: "And it shall come to pass, that he that is left in Zion, and he that remaineth in Jerusalem, shall be called holy, even every one that is written among the living in Jerusalem: when the Lord shall have washed away the filth of the daughters of Zion, and shall have purged the blood of Jerusalem from the midst thereof by the spirit of judgment, and by the spirit of burning. And the LORD will create upon every dwelling place of mount Zion, and upon her assemblies, a cloud and smoke by day, and the shining of a flaming fire by night: for upon all the glory shall be a defence. And there shall be a tabernacle for a shadow in the daytime from the heat, and for a place of refuge, and for a covert from storm and from rain" (4:3-6; cf. Jer. 31:6-14; Mic. 4:6-7).

While the name *Jerusalem* may likely mean 'city of peace,' it has in its history been the location of more wars than any other locality in the world. It proves indeed the symbol of Israel dwelling in the land, so that as long as Israel is living out of the land and scattered among the nations there can be no world peace, as there is none today.

The present situation, with many nations aroused to action as in the United Nations Council, has not been duplicated before since Jerusalem was destroyed by Titus in 70 A.D. It is to be observed, certainly, that action could be taken at any time which would restore the promised land to Israel. It assuredly is a land of promise and Jehovah's covenant respecting it cannot be broken.

The new Jerusalem is a city yet to be (Rev. 21:1–2). It was the hope of Old Testament saints (cf. Heb. 11:10). According to the present plan of spiritual citizenship it is described in Hebrews 12:22–24. This description conforms completely to the one given in Revelation 21:2—22:5. According to Revelation 22:5 the heavenly city endures forever. This city is not the new heaven, for it comes down out of heaven (Rev. 21:10). See Zion.

JESUS

Jesus, the human name for the Son of God, is really the Greek form of the Hebrew name *Joshua* (cf. Acts 7:45; Heb. 4:8). The incarnate One was named by God, His full title being *Lord Jesus Christ. Lord* relates Him to His eternal Deity and *Christ* to His threefold office in relation to Israel, that of prophet, priest, and king, as the Messiah.

The name *Jesus,* bestowed according to divine command, means "He shall save his people from their sins" (Matt. 1:21), as Joshua meant "Jehovah is salvation." This signification has given a very important and far-reaching meaning to the cognomen *Jesus.*

In Revelation 19:11–16 the last and final description of Christ's second advent is given. In this passage He appears under four titles. Three are revealed and one is withheld. He is Faithful and True (vs. 11), which characterization relates Him in language chosen by the Spirit to the Gospel by Mark. He is the Word of God (vs. 13), which relates Him to the Gospel by John. He is King of kings and Lord of lords (vs. 16), which relates him to the Gospel by Matthew. The name "that no man knew" (vs. 12) is likely one related to the Gospel by Luke, speaking of His humanity. *Jesus* is the human name, of a certainty, and what is involved thereby in His people being removed from their many sins is not knowable. The time will nevertheless come when, according to Philippians 2:9–10, "at the name of Jesus" every knee is forced to bow.

JUDAISM

There is no revelation of any distinctive relationship being set up either between God and the angels or between God and the Gentiles which partakes of the character of a true religion, but God has entered into relations with the Jew which results in Judaism, or what the Apostle identifies as the religion of the Jews (Acts 26:5; Gal. 1:13; cf. James 1:26–27), and with the Christian which results in Christianity, or what the New Testament writers designate as "the faith" (Jude 1:3) and "this way" (Acts 9:2; 22:4; cf. 18:26; 2 Pet. 2:2). Judaism and Christianity have much in common, for each is ordained of God to serve a specific purpose. They incorporate similar features in the realm of religion—God, man, righteousness, sin, redemption, salvation, human responsibility, and human destiny; but these similarities do not establish identity since the dissimilarities far outnumber the similarities. There are also remarkable points of likeness between the laws of Great Britain and the statutes of the United States, but this fact does not constitute the two nations one.

A complete religious system provides at least seven distinctive features, all of which accordingly are present both in Judaism and Christianity. These elements are: (1) an acceptable standing on the part of man before God, (2) a manner of life consistent with that standing, (3) a divinely appointed service, (4) a righteous ground whereon God may graciously forgive and cleanse the erring, (5) a clear revelation of the responsibility on the human side upon which divine forgiveness and cleansing may be secured, (6) an effective basis upon which God may be worshiped and petitioned in prayer, and (7) a future hope.

It should be made emphatic that to observe distinction between Judaism and Christianity is the beginning of wisdom in understanding the Bible. Theologians of past generations have made no greater mistake than to suppose, despite all the evidence to the contrary, that Judaism and Christianity are one and the same, or as some have said: "One is the bud and the other is the blossom." Judaism has not merged into Christianity. This is a colossal error of Covenant Theology perpetuated to the present day. Inasmuch as the Bible contains both these systems and any comprehensive theology which is systematic at all will distinguish between the two systems, it is to be reckoned but incidental that both are found in the one divine revelation or volume. Howbeit, admittedly they have much in common.

These systems doubtless set up conflicting and opposing principles, but since these difficulties appear only when an attempt is made to coalesce systems, elements, and principles which God has separated the conflicts really do not exist at all outside the unwarranted unifying efforts of theologians; in fact, they rather demonstrate the *necessity* of a due recognition of all God's different and distinct administrations. The true unity of the Scriptures is not discovered when one blindly seeks to fuse these opposing principles into one system, but rather when God's plain differentiations are observed. The dispensationalist does not create the great differences as he is sometimes accused of doing. The conflicting principles, such as may be found in the text of Scripture, are observable by all who penetrate deep enough to recognize the essential features of divine administration. Instead of creating the problems, the dispensationalist is actually the one who has a solution for them. If the ideals of an earthly people for long life in the land which God gave unto them (Ex. 20:12; Ps. 37:3, 11, 34; Matt. 5:5) does not articulate with the ideals of a heavenly people who, while on the earth, are but "strangers and pilgrims" and enjoined to be looking for and loving the imminent appearing of Christ (2 Tim. 4:8; Titus 2:13; 1 Pet. 2:11), the problem is easily solved by the one whose system of interpretation will be proved rather than distressed by such distinctions. A plan of interpretation which, in defense of an ideal unity of the Bible, contends for a single divine purpose, ignores drastic contradictions, and is sustained only by occasional or accidental similarities, must be doomed to confusion when confronted with the many problems which such a system imposes on the text of Scripture, which problems are recognized by the dispensationalist only as he observes them in such a system as would create them.

All Scripture "is profitable for doctrine, for reproof, for correction, for instruction in righteousness" (2 Tim. 3:16), but all Scripture is not of primary application to a particular person or class of persons which the Bible designates as such. All Scripture is not about the angels nor about the Gentiles. In like manner, all Scripture is not addressed to the Jew nor to the Christian. These are obvious truths, and the dispensationalist's plan of interpretation is none other than an attempt to be consistent in following these distinctions in the primary application of Scripture as far as, and no further than, the Bible carries them. However, all Scripture is profitable just the same, that is, it has its moral, spiritual, and secondary application. To illustrate this: Much valuable truth may be gained from the great body of Scripture bearing on the Jewish Sabbath; but if that body of Scripture has a primary application to the Church, then the Church has no Biblical ground for observance of the first day of the week (which she certainly has) and she could offer no excuse for her disobedience respecting the Sabbath, and her individual members, like all Sabbath breakers, should be stoned to death (Num. 15:32–36). In like manner, if all Scripture is of primary application to believers of this age, then they are in danger of hell fire (Matt. 5:29–30), of unspeakable plagues, diseases, and sicknesses, and by reason of these to become few in number (Deut. 28:58–62), and of having the blood of lost souls required at their hands (Ezek. 3:17–18). Moral and spiritual lessons are to be drawn from God's dealing with Israelites quite apart from the necessity being imposed upon Christians to comply with all that a primary application of the Scriptures which are specifically addressed to Israel would demand. Of the believer of this age it is said: "He shall not come into condemnation [judgment, R.V.]" (John 5:24) and "There is therefore now no condemnation to them that are in Christ Jesus" (Rom. 8:1, R.V.). These precious promises are disannulled by diametrically opposite declarations if all Scripture applies primarily to the Christian. Arminianism is the legitimate expression of all this confusion, to be sure, and the would-be Calvinist who ignores the plain distinctions of the Bible has no defense against Arminian claims.

Both Christianity and Judaism have their separate histories and are in existence at the present time. So, likewise, they have their separate eschatologies, all of which the student should recognize and study.

JUDGMENT

Again, many theologians have erred greatly in contending that there is one judgment and in seeking to merge several other judgments into this particular one. For instance, they are convinced that the judgment of the nations (Matt. 25:31–46) is the same as the judgment of the great white throne (Rev. 20:11–15). One Christian young man when asked concerning the judgment of the nations precisely who the sheep were said in reply: "The saved people, of course." To the next question —"And who are the goats?"—he replied: "Those are the unsaved people." When asked who are the ones called "my brethren," he was helpless to answer. This problem drove him to the study of the Scripture and made him a most exceptional and useful Christian. Inattention to the details of Scripture is without excuse in the light of the disclosure that there are at least eight well-defined judgments presented by the Word of God. These are:

1. OF THE CROSS. Sin has been judged by Christ as Substitute for all on behalf of whom He died. The believer has been in court, condemned, sentenced, and executed in the Person of his Substitute (John 5:24; Rom. 5:9; 8:1; 2 Cor. 5:21; Gal. 3:13; Heb. 9:26–28; 10:10, 14–17; 1 Pet. 2:24). In this connection it may be said that Satan has been judged at the cross (John 16:11; Col. 2:14–15), which judgment evidently consists in taking from him much of the authority he had over the unsaved in keeping them from knowing the gospel of grace (cf. Isa. 14:17 with 61:1). The cross completed this judgment upon sin. "It is finished" (John 19:30). It therefore becomes something to believe for salvation.

2. OF SELF. The warning to judge self is addressed directly to those who are saved: "For if we would judge ourselves, we should not be judged. But when we are judged, we are chastened of the Lord, that we should not be condemned with the world" (1 Cor. 11:31–32). Here chastisement of the believer is contemplated as a judgment from God which will not occur if the believer will be faithful in judging himself before God. Hence the promise of 1 John 1:9 is to be included with thought of this warning. Forgiveness and cleansing are assured once the believer has made confession to God, since that really means self-judgment.

3. OF BELIEVERS. As stated above, this kind of judgment is experienced by believers and only when confession or self-judgment is lacking. It is a most real and practical thing in daily experience and underlies all Christian spirituality. Right relations with God can be maintained only as one is attentive and faithful in the matter of confession to God covering all known sin. The extreme form of chastisement is removal of the believer from this life through death (John 15:2; 1 Cor. 11:30–32; 1 John 5:16). The central passage on chastisement is found in Hebrews 12:3–15.

4. OF THE BELIEVER'S WORKS. According to 2 Corinthians 5:10 —"For we must all appear before the judgment seat of Christ; that every one may receive the things done in his body, according to that he hath done, whether it be good or bad"—all who are saved must come before the βῆμα or judgment seat of Christ. This experience occurs in spite of the assurance given by John 5:24 that the child of God shall not come into judgment. Although his sins have been judged at the cross and will not be brought up again, at the judgment seat of Christ his works or service must be judged. This distinction is made clear in 1 Corinthians 3:9–15. "If any man's work shall be burned, he shall suffer loss: but he himself shall be saved; yet so as by fire" (vs. 15). See Romans 14:10; 1 Corinthians 4:5; Ephesians 6:8; 2 Timothy 4:8; Revelation 22:12.

5. OF ISRAEL. That Israel must come into judgment is most clearly taught, and indeed before they enter the kingdom or more specifically at the end of the great tribulation. The central passage is Ezekiel 20: 33–44, with added confirmation from the parable of the ten virgins (see likewise all of Matt. 24:9—25:30; cf. Joel 3:11–15).

It would seem probable that there will be a resurrection of all Israel of the past dispensation in connection with this special judgment and that the nation shall awake to its national importance and past greatness then. Those who lived with the kingdom in view are to rise and enter the earthly glory (cf. Ezek. 37:1–14; Dan. 12:1–3).

6. OF THE NATIONS. At the close of the great tribulation and at the time when the nations will have taken sides, as they must do during the tribulation, for or against Israel, the Semitic question will be the problem of those days. All nations then living and immediately involved in their relation to Israel will be judged. That judgment will consider every nation on the earth at the time, some peoples to be dismissed unto the lake of fire to which they by reason of their actions were destined to go, others to enter the kingdom with Israel. The latter are the sheep nations and the former—those on the left hand—are the goat nations (cf. Matt. 25:31–46). The issue is the kind of treatment accorded Israel during the tribulation period. Prophecy has indicated that certain Gentile nations will share the coming kingdom with Israel (cf. Isa. 60:3; 61:6; 62:2). These nations shall serve Israel (cf. Isa. 14:1–2; 60:12). The Gentile nations are declared to be present in the earth when the new city comes down from God out of heaven (cf. Rev. 21:24, 26).

The astonishing thing is that, when the King-Messiah tells the sheep nations of their faithfulness to Him through kind treatment of Israel (Matt. 25:35–36), they do not recognize they have done these things (cf. vss. 37–39). Likewise, when the goat nations are informed regarding their failure toward Christ through harsh treatment of Israel (Matt. 25:41–43) they are also unaware of having done anything amiss and must, as the sheep nations, ask "When . . . ?"

The question may therefore be raised: Is there an issue in the world so great that it determines the destiny of nations, yet the nations do not know about it? Yes there is, and that issue must be Israel, the elect, sacred nation. Of a truth, the nations of the earth cannot understand how God has an elect people in Israel, a chosen stock. But "I have chosen thee above all the nations of the earth for my glory" (cf. Deut. 7:6; Isa. 46:13) is not said of any other people, nor can it easily be understood by the nations of the earth.

At the beginning of their history as a people, God gave to Abraham a warning in which he said: "I will bless them that bless thee, and curse him that curseth thee" (Gen. 12:3). It is not accidental that the word "curse" appears in both the Genesis and Matthew passages. At the time when God is anticipating the period of Israel's life among the nations, He said: "I will bless them that bless thee," while at the end of this period He in the Person of His Son also said: "Come, ye blessed of my Father." Likewise, at the beginning: "I will curse him that curseth thee," whereas at the end it must be said: "Depart from me, ye cursed, into everlasting fire, prepared for the devil and his angels." And all of this judgment comes because of Christ's "brethren"—Israel.

7. Of Angels. The central passage here (1 Cor. 15:24–26) indicates that during the kingdom reign of Christ angelic powers must be judged, and among them as a last enemy death must be destroyed. There are also fallen angels to be judged (cf. 1 Cor. 6:3; 2 Pet. 2:4; Jude 1:6; Rev. 20:10).

8. Of the Great White Throne. The major passage for this last judgment is Revelation 20:11–15, which reads: "And I saw a great white throne, and him that sat on it, from whose face the earth and the heaven fled away; and there was found no place for them. And I saw the dead, small and great, stand before God; and the books were opened: and another book was opened, which is the book of life: and the dead were judged out of those things which were written in the books, according to their works. And the sea gave up the dead which were in it; and death and hell delivered up the dead which were in them: and they were judged every man according to their works. And death and hell were

cast into the lake of fire. This is the second death. And whosoever was not found written in the book of life was cast into the lake of fire." This is God's final dealing with all the wicked dead. That all unsaved humanity must be raised to judgment is taught by Christ in John 5:28-29. Nobody has any authority to modify the terrible revelation that God has made in connection with the final reckoning. The Word of God must stand as it is. But a moment's comparison between the events enumerated in relation to the judgment of the nations (Matt. 25:31-46) as contrasted with those of the great white throne (Rev. 20:11-15) ought to show that they are utterly incomparable.

THE JUST

The just is a distinctive phrase peculiar to the Old Testament where men are classed as either wicked or just. In Psalm 37:12, for example, it is written: "The wicked plotteth against the just, and gnasheth upon him with his teeth." This term *just* is applied to individual men like Noah (Gen. 6:9). The terminology refers to the qualities in a person of justice, reasonableness, righteousness in life and compliance with all the law of God. Bildad asked the question: "How then can man be justified with God?" (Job 25:4). Micah came nearer than any other to answering this question according to the Old Testament when he said: "He hath shewed thee, O man, what is good; and what doth the LORD require of thee, but to do justly, and to love mercy, and to walk humbly with thy God?" (6:8).

The student should distinguish between the just man of the Old Testament who manifestly was constituted such by his own good works, on the one hand, and the justified man of the New Testament who is constituted thus by faith in Christ (Rom. 5:1), on the other hand.

JUSTICE

Justice refers to a virtue which doubtless has its only perfect manifestation in God, although He cleanses the sinful and forgives. The gospel of God's grace is the solution to the problem of how God can remain the just One and yet pardon sinners (Rom. 3:25–26). See the doctrines of Gospel, Government, Grace, Guilt, Holiness, Judgment, Punishment, and Righteousness.

JUSTIFICATION

Those who would discern the important facts and force of Christian doctrine do well to distinguish between the things which God does for the Christian and the things which the Christian may do for God. The wide difference in activities is obvious. What God does is usually His to do of necessity since no one else could do it, and what the Christian may do for God may be superhuman and thus dependent on an enabling power of the indwelling Spirit of God.

The things which are wrought of God on behalf of the Christian in his salvation are, again, to be grouped into two classes: those which are done when one believes and is saved and those which are done when Christ comes to take His own unto Himself. So much is accomplished in the first undertaking that he may well say in the words of the Apostle: "Giving thanks unto the Father, which hath made us meet to be partakers of the inheritance of the saints in light" (Col. 1:12). In the second undertaking the body will be changed (cf. 1 Cor. 15:51–54; Phil. 3:21), and the saved one will pass out of all limitations of knowledge into the immeasurable knowledge of God. This is indicated in 1 Corinthians 13:12: "For now we see through a glass, darkly; but then face to face: now I know in part; but then shall I know even as also I am known."

Manifestly, to be justified before God is His own undertaking. It appears as the consummation of God in the work of salvation—not chronologically, however, but logically. That is, it does not occur after some other features of His saving work, only because of those features. The Apostle has indicated certain achievements of God in logical order. It is written then: "For whom he did foreknow, he also did predestinate to be conformed to the image of his Son, that he might be the firstborn among many brethren. Moreover whom he did predestinate, them he also called: and whom he called, them he also justified: and whom he justified, them he also glorified" (Rom. 8:29–30). In this passage justification is named as the last and consummating work for the believer while still in the world. In so justifying God does not legalize a fiction or make-believe. He must and does have a righteous ground on which to justify the ungodly (cf. Rom. 4:5). A distinction must be observed here between just men of the Old Testament and those justified according to the New Testament. According to the Old Testament men were just because they were true and faithful in keeping the Mosaic Law. Micah defines such a life after this manner: "He hath shewed thee, O man, what is good; and what doth the LORD require of thee, but to do justly, and to love mercy, and to walk humbly with thy God?" (6:8). Men were therefore just because of their own works for God, whereas New Testament justification is God's work for man in answer to faith (Rom. 5:1).

Throughout past generations the theologians have striven to form definitions of justification but perhaps with uniform incompleteness and failure. So great and valuable a theological treatise as the *Westminster Shorter Catechism* presents the following effort: "Justification is an act of God's free grace, wherein he pardoneth all our sins, and accepteth us as righteous in his sight, only for the righteousness of Christ, imputed to us, and received by faith alone" (Question 33). Yet there is no Biblical ground whatever for this reference to divine pardon of sin in connection with justification, for justifying has not anything to do with pardon or forgiveness though it is true that none are forgiven who are not justified and none justified who are not forgiven. To forgive means subtraction while to justify means addition. Justification is a declaration by God respecting the Christian that he has been made forever right and acceptable to Himself. For so much as this to be declared there must be an unalterable reality on which it may rest. This basis is the position to which the Christian has been brought through God's grace. All whom God has predetermined are called, and all who are called are justified, and all who are justified are now (logically speaking), and to be (chronologically speaking), glorified (Rom. 8:29–30). God cannot afterwards condemn the one that He has before justified (Rom. 8:33). In fact, four great supporting realities are to be named at this point. "Who is he that condemneth? It is Christ that died, yea rather, that is risen again, who is even at the right hand of God, who also maketh intercession for us" (Rom. 8:34). Thus a justified state must be unchangeable since the ground upon which it rests is so secure forever. There is no justification provided for man which is not eternal in character. Because the actual standing of the Christian before God is so little understood, justifying is also misunderstood. Of the Christian, however, it is revealed that:

1. HE IS A NEW CREATION. "Therefore if any man be in Christ, he is a new creature: old things are passed away; behold, all things are become new. And all things are of God, who hath reconciled us to himself by Jesus Christ, and hath given to us the ministry of reconciliation" (2 Cor. 5:17–18). The old things which have passed away are not habits or failures in daily life, but positions, which positions were cared for by God—being reconciled of God by Jesus Christ.

2. HE IS MADE THE RIGHTEOUSNESS OF GOD through being in Christ. —"But of him are ye in Christ Jesus, who of God is made unto us wisdom, and righteousness, and sanctification, and redemption" (1 Cor. 1:30); "For he hath made him to be sin for us, who knew no sin; that we might be made the righteousness of God in him" (2 Cor. 5:21). Observe accordingly the ambition of the great Apostle at the time when he was saved and had abandoned all his former confidences for the sake of Christ: "But what things were gain to me, those I counted loss for Christ. Yea doubtless, and I count all things but loss for the excellency of the knowledge of Christ Jesus my Lord: for whom I have suffered the loss of all things, and do count them but dung, that I may win Christ, and be found in him, not having mine own righteousness, which is of the law, but that which is through the faith of Christ, the righteousness which is of God by faith" (Phil. 3:7–9).

3. HE IS PERFECTED FOREVER. According to Hebrews 10:14 the Christian is perfected forever in position though not yet in daily life. In this passage the word *sanctify* must be given its true meaning, 'to set apart or classify' as all are so grouped by themselves who are in Christ. It therefore relates to every Christian. The passage reads: "For by one offering he hath perfected for ever them that are sanctified" (Heb. 10:14).

4. HE HAS THE FULLNESS OF CHRIST. Furthermore, to be in Christ,

as all saved persons are by the baptism of the Spirit, means that the fullness or *plērōma* of Christ becomes their unchangeable portion. Consider with special care the amazing declarations bearing upon this: "And of his fulness have all we received, and grace for grace" (John 1:16); "For it pleased the Father that in him should all fulness dwell" (Col. 1:19); "For in him dwelleth all the fulness of the Godhead bodily. And ye are complete in him, which is the head of all principality and power" (2:9–10). To be "complete in him" is but a restatement of John 1:16. The words *ye are complete* are translated from the same root as yields the form πλήρωμα, since all that Christ is—the πλήρωμα of the Godhead bodily—becomes the Christian's possession because of the fact that he lives in Him. One cannot be thus perfectly in Christ (1 Cor. 12:13) and not partake of all that Christ is.

It is this complete standing which belongs to every believer, which position God recognizes whether anyone on earth recognizes it or not. And it is such a one that God justifies. Indeed, He defends that justification as faithfully and as definitely as once He condemned man as ungodly.

The conclusion of the whole matter is that God undertakes by His Spirit and through His Son to make all He saves meet to be partakers of the inheritance of the saints in light, and because of the perfection or quality of the imputed merit of the Son of God He accepts them and is free to justify them forever. If God could be just Himself in justifying His own Son who is the embodiment of divine righteousness, He will be just likewise when He justifies the ungodly who through the mighty changes achieved by salvation appear before Him in the imputed merit of His Son. This is not legalizing a mere fiction nor is it any form of pardon and forgiveness only.

A notable passage is properly considered here, namely: "Even the righteousness of God which is by faith of Jesus Christ unto all and upon all them that believe: for there is no difference: for all have sinned, and come short of the glory of God; being justified freely by his grace through the redemption that is in Christ Jesus" (Rom. 3:22–24). A righteousness from God is said to be received and possessed on a faith principle in answer to faith in Christ Jesus, and it reaches unto and comes down upon all who believe—that must signify "being justified freely," not hoping to be because of a good manner of life. The word translated *freely* presents a peculiar meaning and revelation here. It does not mean without hesitation on God's part or any expense on the part of the one who is justified. It means here *without a cause*, no otherwise than the same word does in John 15:25 where Christ is reported as saying: "They hated me without a cause." There was no basis in Him for their hatred. Thus the thought in Romans is: "Being justified without a cause for justification in the one who is justified." None could find a cause in Christ for any hate against Him, so none could find a cause for justification in those who have come short of the glory of God through sin.

If it be inquired how God can justify the ungodly and sinful, the answer is to be found in the last part of Romans 3:24. It is all by His grace. But how can God exercise such matchless grace and achieve so much for the ungodly by grace? Verse 24 answers this query also: "through the redemption that is in Christ Jesus." Then Paul's great verse may well be read in reverse order: Because of the redemption which is secured in Christ Jesus, God is free to exercise His grace toward the ungodly sinner, even justifying him eternally, though finding no cause for justification in the sinner outside of the fact that the righteousness of God has been bestowed upon all who believe. In verse 26 it is declared too that God is Himself just and righteous when He justifies the one who does no more than to believe on Jesus. The verse reads: "To declare, I say, at this time his righteousness: that he might be just, and the justifier of him which believeth in Jesus." Let no one, therefore, add to or take from the sole fact that ungodly sinners are saved—even to eternal justification—who only believe.

Justification rests on the redeeming death of Christ and not, as sometimes supposed, on His resurrection. When it is believed that it depends on the resurrection, it is usually because of some misunderstanding of Romans 4:25, which reads: "Who was delivered for our offences, and was raised again for our justification." He was raised again, however, not to the end that justification might be possible, but because the free grant of it had been secured by His death. When the thing which completes the whole basis of justification was achieved, Christ came out of the realms of death. His great redemption work was thus shown to be something perfectly done.

Justification causes no one to be righteous. It is not the bestowment as such of righteousness. It rather proclaims one to be justified whom God sees as perfected in His Son. Therefore, this may be stated as the correct formula of justification: The sinner becomes righteous in God's sight when he is in Christ; he is justified by God freely, or without a cause, because thereby he is righteous in His sight.

KING

The term *king* is used of one who rules over a people and is in possession of a dominion. It is applied as a concept first of all to God (1 Sam. 8:7), for He is sovereign over all. Secondly, the term is applied to Christ. Every Old Testament prophecy of the kingdom anticipates His kingly office: (a) Christ will yet sit on the Davidic throne as David's heir (2 Sam. 7:16; Ps. 89:20–37; Isa. 11:1–16; Jer. 33:19–21). (b) He came as a King (Luke 1:32–33). (c) He was rejected as a King (Mark 15:12–13; Luke 19:14; cf. Gen. 37:8; Ex. 2:14). (d) He died as a King (Matt. 27:37). (e) When He comes again, it is as a King (Rev. 19:16; cf. Luke 1:32–33).

A complete induction should be made here of all the Scripture bearing on David's throne and David's Son. Christ combined the offices of King and Priest (which latter office is found in connection with the Church as well as Israel; cf. Heb. 7 where Christ is a priest after the order of Melchizedek). His reign is mediatorial in that God will reign through Christ. The mediatorial feature which contemplates victory over all enemies, angelic and human, will cease eventually (1 Cor. 15:25–28). However, His reign is eternal nonetheless (2 Sam. 7:16; Ps. 89:36–37; Isa. 9:6–7; Luke 1:33), for He continues to reign by the same authority of the Father (cf. 1 Cor. 15:28).

KINGDOM

Two specific realms are in view as the doctrine of kingdom receives consideration:

1. THE KINGDOM OF GOD, which includes all intelligences in heaven or on earth who are willingly subject to God.

2. THE KINGDOM OF HEAVEN, which embraces any sort of empire that God may have on earth at a given time. The kingdom of heaven appears then in various aspects through the centuries, as—

a. THEOCRATIC. First the rule was exercised by divinely appointed leaders, judges, and patriarchs.

b. COVENANTED. It thus became the national hope of Israel (2 Sam. 7).

c. PREDICTED. Much prophecy anticipates a glorious kingdom for Israel on the earth.

d. ANNOUNCED. The ministry of John the Baptist, Christ, and the Apostles was to announce the kingdom unto the nation as at hand. That offer, however, was rejected.

e. POSTPONED UNTIL CHRIST RETURNS. One of the greatest errors of theologians is an attempt, as essayed now, to build a kingdom on the first advent of Christ as its basis, whereas according to the Scriptures it will be realized only in connection with the second advent. All Scriptures conform to this arrangement, strange though it may look.

f. MYSTERY. According to Matthew 13:11 the present conditions in Christendom are a mystery form of the kingdom. Since the kingdom of heaven is no other than the rule of God on the earth, He must now be ruling to the extent of full realization of those things which are termed "the mysteries" in the New Testament and which really constitute the new message of the New Testament.

g. REALIZED. Not until the millennium will the kingdom of heaven come to realization.

A distinction should be made between the kingdom of God and the kingdom of heaven. It is to be observed that Matthew employs the terminology *kingdom of heaven* and that Mark and Luke, when presenting much of the same teaching, use the phraseology *kingdom of God*. Some have assumed on this basis that the two kingdoms are one and the same. However, the differences seem more important than the similarities. Entrance into the kingdom of God is by a birth from above (John 3:3), for instance, whereas to the Jew of Christ's day and in anticipation of His earthly kingdom entrance to the kingdom is based upon righteousness. Matthew 5:20 declares this: "For I say unto you, That except your righteousness shall exceed the righteousness of the scribes and Pharisees, ye shall in no case enter into the kingdom of heaven."

As for another impressive difference, Matthew 8:12; 24:50–51; 25:28–30 declare that "the children of the kingdom" may be cast out. This retribution cannot be applied to the kingdom of God and its members (John 3:18). The parable of the wheat and the tares (Matt. 13: 24–30, 36–43) and that of the good and bad fish (Matt. 13:47–50), significantly enough, are spoken only of the kingdom of heaven. However, the parable of the leaven (Matt. 13:33; Luke 13:21) is predicated of both kingdoms. Leaven represents evil doctrine rather than evil persons, and evil doctrine may and does corrupt both kingdoms.

LAW

Law is a term used about 200 times in the Bible, meaning a rule which regulates human conduct. Six subdivisions of the Bible doctrine of law follow:

1. NATURAL, INHERENT, OR INTRINSIC. That which God requires of every creature because of His own character, as it is written: "Be ye holy; for I am holy" (Lev. 11:44; 1 Pet. 1:16). This law was binding upon all, from Adam to Moses (cf. Gen. 26:5; Rom. 2:14–15; 5:12–14).

2. PRESCRIBED BY MAN (Gen. 9:6; Matt. 20:15; Luke 20:22; Acts 19:38; 1 Tim. 1:8–10; 2 Tim. 2:5). That which human government requires of its subjects.

3. OF MOSES. A rule divinely given through Moses to govern Israel in the land of promise. It was commended to them because they were a covenant people. Thus it defined the manner of their daily life. It was itself a covenant of works (Ex. 19:5–6). This covenant they soon broke. It will yet be superseded by the New Covenant (Jer. 31:31–34; Heb. 8:8–13). This agreement will include the former Law of Moses (Deut. 30:8).

The Law of Moses is recorded in three parts:

a. COMMANDMENTS. Embrace the moral government of Israel (Ex. 20:1–17). They are condensed and summarized in Matthew 22:36–40; fulfilled by love (Rom. 13:10; Gal. 5:14; James 2:8); proved to be law in character (Rom. 7:7–14).

b. JUDGMENTS. Embrace the social requirements (Ex. 21:1—23:33).

c. ORDINANCES. Regulate the worship (Ex. 25:1—31:18).

These three forms of law satisfied all of Israel's requirements before God. But the entire system, including the commandments as a rule of life, ceased with the death of Christ (John 1:17; Rom. 10:4). The Law of Moses, to be sure, was an ad interim dealing in effect only until Christ should come. For the time being it gave to sin the character of transgression (Rom. 5:13; Gal. 3:19). It was preceded (Ex. 19:4) and followed (John 1:17) by grace.

4. REVEALED WILL OF GOD IN ANY FORM. That which has been disclosed in addition to law codes. Observe the definite article with *law* in Romans 7:15–25 because thus Paul may refer to something besides the Law of Moses. The law as the will of God includes all His revealed orders for any people at any time. The word *law* in Romans, then, is used nine times without the article and many more times with the article (cf. Rom. 8:4), and not always referring to Moses.

5. MESSIANIC RULE OF LIFE FOR THE KINGDOM. That which governs the millennium (Matt. 5:1—7:29). Proof that the Messianic rule is pure law may be gained in the following tests: (1) any action is legal which aims to secure merit (Matt. 6:14–15); (2) any action is legal which has been wrought in reliance upon the flesh (Rom. 6:14).

6. OF CHRIST. That which now governs the Christian (1 Cor. 9:20–21; Gal. 6:2). Observe the term "my commandments" which was used by Christ only in the upper room (John 14:15, etc.). This form of life-direction includes all the teachings of grace addressed to the Christian, who is not himself under law since grace has provided all the merit that ever could be required (John 1:16; Rom. 5:1; 8:1; Col. 2:10). The saved one is "inlawed to Christ" (1 Cor. 9:20–21, lit. rendering). The believer is not without law to govern his conduct when "inlawed" to Christ.

LIFE

Life represents something mysterious and undefined, but more especially that which is consciousness, energy, and existence. No one has comprehended even what animates the smallest insect. A man might be weighed a few moments before he dies and the same body also be weighed immediately after death. The weight would be the same, yet something most essential—though little understood—has evidently departed. Life is that which gives sensation to the whole body whereby all functions of the body continue in their orchestration. With the passing of life, however, every function of the natural body ceases.

From a Biblical viewpoint, life may signify: (1) that which is natural and animal or (2) what is divine and eternal.

1. NATURAL. This form of life is subject to death and is derived by human generation. It is nevertheless endless in every human being, that is to say, a continuing on forever in the future of everyone born into this world. Natural life has a beginning, but no end.

2. ETERNAL. This priceless treasure, which is the gift of God, should not be confused with the mere endless existence which all possess. It is a life added to that which has been experienced before by itself. Christ said: "I am come that they might have life, and that they might have it more abundantly" (John 10:10). This life is no less than "Christ in you, the hope of glory" (Col. 1:27). It comes free because a gift of His love. It at once relates the one who has received it to God and to things eternal. Christ likened it to a birth from above (John 3:3, R.V. margin) "for those which were born . . . of God" (John 1:13).

Thus all depends upon receiving Christ and being saved through Him. John has said so again: "He that hath the Son hath life; and he that hath not the Son of God hath not life" (1 John 5:12).

LOGOS

Logos is a term which John by the Holy Spirit applies to Christ as a cognomen six times (John 1:1, etc.). The same word was especially employed by Philo (c. 40 A.D.) to mean something in God corresponding to *reason* in man as well as something emanating from Him corresponding to *speech* in man. Though used by the Holy Spirit to designate Christ in His preincarnate state, there is no record that Christ ever applied the term to Himself. It is probable that the name should have a more general use even within the bounds of Christ's preincarnate state.

In the blessed Trinity of Persons, Christ has always been the revealer; hence the Angel of Jehovah is Christ. He came into the world, the incarnate One, in order to reveal God as perfectly as possible. This is declared in John 1:18, which reads: "No man hath seen God at any time; the only begotten Son, which is in the bosom of the Father, he hath declared him."

Though Christ manifested both the wisdom and the power of God, He came principally to declare the bosom of the Father, that is, His love. Christ as Logos is to the Father what speech is to reason. He declares the love of God. Not throughout all His life on earth nor even in all His healings, but particularly in one event of His first coming does He tell out the divine love. It accordingly is written: "But God commendeth his love toward us, in that, while we were yet sinners, Christ died for us" (Rom. 5:8); "Hereby perceive we the love of God, because he laid down his life for us: and we ought to lay down our lives for the brethren" (1 John 3:16).

As the written Word declares God to man, so Christ the living Word perfectly declares God to man. Both are said to be truth (John 14:6; 17:17), everlasting (Ps. 119:89; John 8:58), life-giving (John 14:6; James 1:18), saving (Acts 16:31; 1 Cor. 15:1–2), purifying (Titus 2:14; 1 Pet. 1:22), sanctifying (John 17:17; Heb. 10:14), glorifying to God (Acts 13:48; Rom. 15:9), judging (John 5:27; 12:48), living (John 11:25; 1 Pet. 1:23).

LORD'S DAY

The Lord's Day does not represent merely a change from the Sabbath, but a new day belonging to a new order. It celebrates the New Creation with Christ Himself resurrected as its Head, whereas the Sabbath was related to the old creation (Ex. 20:8–11; 31:12–17; Heb. 4:4). The new day, to be sure, was anticipated in prediction (cf. Lev. 23:11; Ps. 118:22–24 with Acts 4:11–12; Matt. 28:1). It is the first day or, as following seven days before, the eighth day after a completed week (cf. Col. 2:12).

The day began with a normal appreciation of the resurrection of Christ and His work. It has been signally blessed of God throughout the present age. True to its character as a day of rest, however, the Sabbath came at the end of a week of labor. That is the order expected under the law. Under grace the week begins with its day of privilege, which properly enough is the order for grace.

The Lord's Day belongs only to Christians; it is not for all men, nor for creation as a whole. Hence the day should not be legislated upon an unwilling public; indeed, for its keeping no rules are recorded, which is fitting enough to the order and character of grace. Men are not justified in returning to the rules provided for the Sabbath in order to secure directions for observance of the Lord's Day. When Christ came from the grave, He said to His friends: "Rejoice" (cf. Ps. 118:24) and "Go tell . . ." (Matt. 28:9–10, lit. rendering). These words may well be taken as wise direction respecting observance of the day. The Lord's Day, moreover, can be extended to all days as the Sabbath could not be (cf. Rom. 14:5–6).

LORD'S SUPPER

The ordinance of the Lord's Supper is a divinely appointed testimony from the believer's heart to God respecting his trust in Christ's efficacious death. As such it has nevertheless been greatly perverted, the Church of Rome having developed the unwarranted doctrine of transubstantiation. The Lutheran doctrine is to the effect that Christ must be present by omnipotent power in the elements—a blessing to believers and a condemnation to others.

The words, "as often as ye eat this bread, and drink this cup" (1 Cor. 11:26), indicate the liberty under grace in any matter of times and seasons, that is, relative to frequency in partaking of the Lord's Supper. Here, then, is a testimony from the heart to God by which the Lord's death is shown forth, and one to continue "till he come" again (1 Cor. 11:26), as the Jewish altar set forth Christ's death until He came the first time.

As the resurrection is celebrated by fitting observance of the Lord's Day each week, so it seems probable that it is well to celebrate Christ's death just as often (as some Christians make a practice of doing today).

LOVE

Love must be what Dr. Henry Drummond chose to term it, "the greatest thing in the world" (the title of his addresses on 1 Cor. 13). It is that which God is like to infinity. To realize the personal, unchanging love of God is a supreme experience.

There is everywhere a very real human love; but all Christian love, according to the Scriptures, is distinctly a manifestation of divine love operating through the human heart. A statement of the difference is found in Romans 5:5, ". . . because the love of God hath been shed abroad ['poured out,' margin] in our hearts through [as produced, or caused, by] the Holy Spirit which was given unto us" (R.V.). This activity, then, is not the working of human affection; it is rather the direct manifestation of the "love of God" passing through the heart of the believer out from the indwelling Spirit. It is realization of the last petition in the High Priestly prayer of Christ: ". . . that the love wherewith thou hast loved me may be in them, and I in them" (John 17:26). It is simply God's love working within and out through the believer. Such a feeling could not be humanly produced or even successfully imitated, for it, of necessity, goes out to the objects of divine affection and grace rather than to the objects of human desire. A human heart cannot *produce* divine love, but it can *experience* it. To have a heart that feels the compassion of God is to drink of the wine of heaven. In considering this imparted love of God, it should be noted:

1. The love of God being imparted is not experienced by the unsaved: "But I know you, that ye have not the love of God in you" (John 5:42).

2. The love of God reaches out to the whole world: "For God so loved the world . . ." (John 3:16); ". . . that he by the grace of God should taste death for every man" (Heb. 2:9); "And he is the propitiation for our sins: and not for our's only, but also for the sins of the whole world" (1 John 2:2). This is a divine love for the world of lost men. It indicates how God's affection knows no bounds. What is sometimes called "the missionary spirit" is none other than that compassion which brought the Son of God from heaven "gushing forth" or overflowing from a human heart. Interest in lost men is not secured by any attempted development of human affections; it however will be immediately

realized in a Christian heart when there is a right relationship to the Spirit of God. A desire for the salvation of others becomes the first thought of many after they are born again.

3. The love of God abhors the present world system: "Love not the world, neither the things that are in the world. If any man love the world, the love of the Father is not in him. For all that is in the world, the lust of the flesh, and the lust of the eyes, and the pride of life, is not of the Father, but is of the world" (1 John 2:15–16). Such purified feeling will always be the experience of the one to whom the love of God is imparted.

4. The love of God is directed especially toward His Spirit-born children: "Much more then, being now justified by his blood, we shall be saved from wrath through him. For if, when we were enemies, we were reconciled to God by the death of his Son, much more, being reconciled, we shall be saved by his life" (Rom. 5:9–10); ". . . Christ also loved the church, and gave himself for it" (Eph. 5:25). He loves His own even though they are wandering away, for so it is revealed in the return of the "prodigal son" (Luke 15:11–32). Furthermore, "If we love one another, God dwelleth in us, and his love is perfected in us" (1 John 4:12). By divine compassion, then, the Christian proves his reality before the world. As also in another place: "A new commandment I give unto you, That ye love one another; as I have loved you, that ye also love one another. By this shall all men know that ye are my disciples, if ye have love one to another" (John 13:34–35). Such divine love is also the test of our brotherhood in Christ: "Hereby perceive we the love of God, because he laid down his life for us: and we ought to lay down our lives for the brethren. But whoso hath this world's good, and seeth his brother have need, and shutteth up his bowels of compassion from him, how dwelleth the love of God in him?" (1 John 3:16–17); "We know that we have passed from death unto life, because we love the brethren" (1 John 3:14).

5. The love of God continues without end: ". . . Having loved his own which were in the world, he loved them unto the end" (hence, eternally, John 13:1). Of the love of God operative in the believer it is said that it "suffereth long" and then still "is kind" (1 Cor. 13:4).

6. The love of God is exercised toward Israel: ". . . Yea, I have loved thee with an everlasting love" (Jer. 31:3). So the Spirit-filled believer will learn to rejoice in the great prophecies and purposes of God for that people with whom He is in everlasting covenants and for whom He has correspondingly an everlasting love.

7. The love of God is sacrificial: "For ye know the grace of our Lord

Jesus Christ, that, though he was rich, yet for your sakes he became poor, that ye through his poverty might be rich" (2 Cor. 8:9). Such an attitude on the part of the Son of God toward the eternal riches must, if reproduced in the Christian, affect largely his attitude toward earthly wealth.

Not only is the love of God sacrificial respecting all riches, it is sacrificial in regard to life itself: "Hereby perceive we the love of God, because he laid down his life for us." It therefore follows: "and we ought to lay down our lives for the brethren" (1 John 3:16-17). The Apostle Paul testified: "I say the truth in Christ, I lie not, my conscience also bearing me witness in the Holy Spirit, that I have great heaviness and continual sorrow in my heart. For I could wish that myself were accursed from Christ for my brethren, my kinsmen according to the flesh" (Rom. 9:1-3). The Apostle knew full well that there was no occasion for him to be accursed since his Lord had been made a curse for all; but the fact remains how he could still be *willing* to be made a curse. This kind of experience is the direct outworking in a human life of the divine love which gave Jesus to die under the curse or judgment of all the sin of the world. When this divine compassion for lost men is reproduced in the believer, it becomes the true and sufficient dynamic for soul-saving work.

Thus the mighty heart of God may be manifested in a human life, and the one word, "love," together with the other eight words which indicate all the fruit of the Spirit, be a representation of true Christian character (Gal. 5:22-23). The other eight words, when traced in the Scriptures, will also prove to be divine graces which can be realized in the human heart only as they are *imparted;* for example, ". . . that my joy might remain in you," ". . . My peace I give unto you" (John 15:11; 14:27). These divine graces are not produced in every Christian's heart. They will be achieved only within those who are "by the Spirit walking" (cf. Gal. 5:16).

MAN OF SIN

Two important personages appear in the anticipations which prophecy of evil places before the Bible student—the man of sin as mentioned by

Paul in 2 Thessalonians 2 and the first beast of Revelation 13. The man of sin is identified throughout the Bible by his blasphemous assumption that he is God. He looms as the political ruler who will yet head up the nations. He indeed is designated in the Old Testament "the prince of Tyrus" (Ezek. 28:1–10), the "little horn" (Dan. 7:8), the desolator (Dan. 9:27), the willful king (Dan. 11:36), and in the New Testament "the abomination of desolation" (Matt. 24:15), "that man of sin" (2 Thess. 2:3–10), the "white horse" rider (Rev. 6:2), and probably also the first-named beast (Rev. 13:1–10). It is indicated too that he will federate the ten divided kingdoms of the Roman world and rule over them during the great tribulation. His coming and rule will be "after the working of Satan with all power and signs and lying wonders, and with all deceivableness of unrighteousness . . ." (2 Thess. 2:9–10). He becomes the embodiment of Satan's power (Luke 4:5–6). He is Satan's masterpiece and counterfeit of Christ as King, indeed a counterfeit of the Second Person in Satan's aping of the Trinity. He is included with Satan in those revelations which reach back to Satan's creation (Isa. 14:12–17; Ezek. 28:1–19). He shares the lake of fire with Satan (Rev. 20:10). His earth-rule is terminated by the glorious coming of Christ (2 Thess. 2:6–8). He must appear, however, before the Day of the Lord (2 Thess. 2:2–4, R.V.). This order of events is maintained in each important Scripture bearing on the theme (cf. Dan. 7:8–9; Matt. 24:15–31; 2 Thess. 2:1–10, R.V.; Rev. 13 and 19). He continues "forty and two months" (Rev. 13:5). Christ indicates that the man of sin, when standing in the holy place, is the sign to Israel of the end of their age (Matt. 24:14–19). He is known especially by his blasphemous assumption to be God (Ezek. 28:1–10; John 5:43; 2 Thess. 2:4; Rev. 13:5–6). His character is estimated in the Scripture from the divine standpoint of God's holiness and purpose.

MARRIAGE

Marriage is one of the oldest institutions in the world. It was established by God in the Garden of Eden (Gen. 2:21–25), was blessed by the presence of Christ in the wedding at Cana of Galilee (John 2:1–11), and is declared by the Apostle to be honorable in all men (Heb. 13:4).

The Old Testament records plural marriages, and that with the most prominent of the saints. However, according to the record in the primeval Garden of Eden, it was doubtless God's intention that a man should have one wife and the wife but one husband. It was clearly taught in the New Testament that, because of an advance in the relationship between God and His saints, there should be the most careful recognition of this more exalted ideal of one wife and one husband (Eph. 5:22–33).

According to the New Testament, then, the husband is to function as the head of the wife, to love his wife and cherish her even as Christ loved the Church. So, also, the wife is to reverence her husband and be obedient to his wishes. There will be little difficulty about the wife so adjusting herself to her own husband if he is carrying out the instructions for him by loving her as Christ loved the Church.

Certain questions arise which are not easily answered. Is marriage a rite binding upon unregenerate people? May divorced people be married again? If so, then under what conditions? So, also, there is a problem which appears on mission fields: Should any man who is the husband of plural wives abandon all of them excepting one if he were to become a Christian? Is this requirement altogether necessary? One thing is certain: a believer should never be married to an unbeliever. All such practices ought to be discouraged on every hand. The reason, too, is obvious: God cannot bless one in a household without blessing all, but the blessing He would design for a believer cannot rightfully be extended to an unbeliever. If the saved person proposes to marry an unsaved person, let them first consider whether they are pleased to live on such limited blessing as God might extend to the unsaved person of the couple.

MEDIATION

A major aspect of Christology, the doctrine of mediation is spoken of as such only once in the Old Testament (Job 9:33) and six times in the New Testament—Galatians 3:19–20; 1 Timothy 2:5; Hebrews 8:6; 9:15; 12:24. Mediation is the work of one who reconciles persons at variance with one another. Sin set man at odds with God. An "at-one-ment" based upon divine satisfaction was therefore required. Accordingly, "there is one . . . mediator between God and men, the man Christ Jesus" (1 Tim. 2:5). The fact of His two natures is required for such a responsibility. In Him both Deity and humanity do meet, of course, and in Him the full representation of each is secured or perfected. He must be a sinless man on whom no charge rests, first of all, otherwise He needs a mediator Himself. He must be actually God likewise, not a mere agent of representation. Job's "daysman" then is the precise thought—one who has a right to lay His hand on God in behalf of man and to lay His hand on man in behalf of God. This indeed was Job's cry of appeal unto God, according to Job 9:33.

The mediation of Christ is to be observed in three aspects. (1) As a prophet (Heb. 1:1 ff.). Here He represents God to man. (2) As a priest. Here He especially represents man to God (Heb. 9:15). (3) As a king (Ps. 2). In this particular He reigns as God's choice of king over the earth. His kingdom will be mediatorial, in which time every enemy must be destroyed, even death. That kingdom reign lasts forever and forever (1 Cor. 15:24–28). Christ is the Interpreter of God to man and the Door of access for man to God (John 1:18; 10:7).

MERCY

Three words need especially to be distinguished, namely, *love, mercy,* and *grace* (Eph. 2:4 ff.). Love is that in God which existed before He would care to exercise mercy or grace. Mercy, on the other hand, is that in God which duly provided for the need of sinful man, while grace is that in Him which acts freely to save because all the demands of holiness have been satisfied. Salvation is as much adjusted to justice (Rom. 3:26), then, as to love (John 3:16). Sinners are not actually saved by mercy but by grace. Mercy only provides a Savior and draws the sinner to Him. God's mercy alone goes out to every living creature, not His active grace.

Mercy is the Old Testament equivalent of the New Testament word, *grace.* Men, furthermore, are especially enjoined to be merciful (Deut. 25:4; Ps. 37:21; 109:16; Prov. 12:10; Dan. 4:27; Mic. 6:8; Matt. 5:7; James 3:17).

MERCY SEAT

The doctrine of mercy seat is divided into two parts, that related to the Old Testament and that related to the New. In the Old Testament the lid of the ark found in the holy of holies which covered the broken Law and which was overshadowed by the cherubim—protectors of the holiness of God—was the mercy seat (Ex. 25:17-22). It became a seat of mercy thus when sprinkled with typical blood. The animal blood was efficacious in that it looked on typically to the death of Christ. The high priest—a sinful man needing to offer sacrifice for himself as much as for others—went in before the mercy seat once a year (Lev. 16:2-15) on behalf of the people and there found mercy from God for them.

In the New Testament (Rom. 3:25; Heb. 9:5) the mercy seat is identified with its antitype, the body of Christ which hung on the cross, sprinkled upon as it were by His own blood. It becomes thereby the place where God can meet the sinner in saving favor. The justifying grace of God is only possible through the redemption that is in Christ (Rom. 3:24). The importance of this theme is not seen in the Old Testament type of the ark and its covering, but rather in the antitype or New Testament doctrine of propitiation (which doctrine see).

MESSIAH

The word *Messiah* contemplates Christ as the final or greatest Prophet, the final Priest, and the final King. In Psalm 2:2 indeed two Persons of the Godhead are distinguished—Jehovah and His Messiah. The New Testament rendition of the word, *Messias* (A.V.), used twice (John 1:41; 4:25), no less than its Old Testament predecessor means 'anointed.' The common and real Greek equivalent in the New Testament is the title translated *Christ*. The entire field of prediction relative to Jehovah's coming one whom He would send to redeem man is involved in this Messianic theme. The Messiah is Israel's one hope. As the Anointed or Sent One, it is said of Christ that God gave the Spirit to Him without measure (John 3:34). In Him, to be sure, all the fullness of the Godhead dwelleth bodily (Col. 2:9). Both the priestly and the kingly aspects of Messiah continue forever, if not the prophetic.

MILLENNIUM
(See KINGDOM)

The term *millennium* is used to indicate the period of Christ's reign on the present earth which Revelation 20 foretells. It is far more accurate and satisfactory to speak of this period as the kingdom, however, than to indicate merely the time during which it continues (as with the terminology, *millennium*).

The early church was concerned with the doctrine of *chiliasm* (which term is drawn from the Greek word for thousand, as *millennium* from the Latin). The fact of a millennium indeed was held by all evangelical teachers until recent centuries, when the teachings of postmillennialism and amillennialism came to be received by some.

There are now, in consequence, three millennial theories, generally speaking. (1) Postmillennialism began to take theological shape with the teaching of Daniel Whitby in England, who lived two centuries ago (1638–1726). Though believing with the Early Church that the kingdom would come at the second advent of Christ, Whitby went on to state that by the present gospel agencies every evil in the world would be corrected until Christ should have a spiritual reign over the earth and continue that reign for a thousand years, at which time His second advent would occur and He come back to set up the judgment and close the present order. The supposed progress of righteousness in the world has been hindered so much, however, that this theory has proved a dead issue for upwards of twenty-five years. Men who held this view have largely drifted into (2) amillennialism or nonmillennialism, which theory teaches that there will be no millennium other than that which supposedly is in progress at the present time. Its advocates believe that, since the thousand-year period is mentioned only in Revelation 20, and this chapter looks (?) obscure, and fulfillment of the prediction concerning the thousand-year period as found in the chapter can be placed back into the past as already accomplished, there remains no earthly kingdom reign whatever for Christ in the body. Such a theory is born out of the theology of Rome which teaches that the church is the kingdom and therefore is reigning or should be reigning now. Men holding this viewpoint are obliged to contend that Satan is bound at present, or at least that he is bound with regard to believers if not with regard to the unsaved. That very position was espoused by the late B. B. Warfield of Princeton and is held doubtless by many teachers of theology in seminaries today.

(3) Premillennialism teaches that the present age increases with evil and ends in judgment at the second advent of Christ, when He will set up His kingdom and reign with righteousness for a thousand years. The length of the reign is not the important thing, but the fact that the Church will reign with Him as His Bride. When it is contended that there is only one reference to a kingdom lasting one thousand years, it should be remembered that in connection with the Day of the Lord, which is terminology equivalent to the kingdom age, Peter said a day with the Lord seems a thousand years and a thousand years a day (2 Pet. 3:8). That Day begins with Christ's coming as a thief in the night and ends with fire descending from heaven (2 Pet. 3:10).

It should be remembered that the millennium is not heaven. On the contrary, it is to be characterized by a limited amount of evil which Christ the King will judge perfectly and immediately (Isa. 11:1–16). Neither is it that new earth which God will yet create (Isa. 65:17; 66:22; 2 Pet. 3:13; Rev. 21:1) for therein righteousness dwells, which is something not true of the millennium.

MINISTRY

In Old Testament times spiritual ministry was for the most part limited to prophets and priests, and was largely a temple ritual. Christ's ministry is a perfect example of what such work should be like, for He said, "I am among you as he that serveth" (Luke 22:27; cf. John 13: 15). The ministries in the Church hinge upon a gifted leadership (Eph. 4:11) which is unto the service and edification of the Body of Christ (Eph. 4:12–16). "The work of the ministry," it will thus be seen, is committed to the whole company of believers (Eph. 4:12). Those who serve with definite responsibility in the church are known as deacons and elders. The deacons are usually responsible for the temporalities while the elders are responsible for the spiritualities (see Elders or Bishops). Rewards are promised to such as minister and prove faithful in service. This does not entail the adding of merit to salvation, but simply a recognition of man's faithfulness on the part of God (see Rewards).

MIRACLE

In God's universe He is both immanent and transcendent. The powers of nature are limited, but God is able to introduce unto infinity therein whatever He wills to do. His own works as manifest in creation and providence are hardly to be classed as miracles. They are rather the normal works of God in His own particular sphere of action. What is natural with God may be supernatural with man.

Theology properly distinguishes the miracles of the Old Testament from the marvels of the New Testament. The latter are characterized by the fact that they were wrought either by Christ personally or by others whose undertakings were accomplished in the name of Christ.

The evidence supporting miracles as a reality is the same as for any supernatural feature of divine revelation.

Consideration should be given to the supernatural power of Satan (Rev. 13:13–15; cf. Isa. 14:12, 16–17). That Satan has power to perform supernatural things is clearly indicated in the Scripture (2 Thess. 2:9).

MYSTERY

The ancient meaning of the word *mystery* is related to the cults of Babylon and Rome, and to imparting of the knowledge of these secrets as in the modern lodges or fraternal orders where secrets are considered essential. The popular use of the word applies it to that which is mysterious or unknowable.

The New Testament use of the term relates it to some work or purpose of God hitherto unrevealed. It may be related to something which needs to be understood but must have a key (Rev. 1:20). The word is employed in the New Testament twenty-seven times excluding 1 Corinthians 2:1 (where see R.V. margin). Paul used it twenty-one times himself. The "mysteries" comprise practically all the added truth found in the New Testament supplementing that of the Old Testament, apart from its history (Deut. 29:29).

The New Testament mysteries are not indeed secrets to be withheld, but to be published (1 Cor. 4:1). "Woe is unto me, if I preach not the gospel" (1 Cor. 9:16), said Paul, in contrast to the anathema falling upon the member of a lodge or cult who divulges their secrets.

NAME

Bible names usually have a significant meaning and often represent the precise character of the person named, as in the case of Jacob (Gen. 27:36).

The names of God declare His character: *El* or *Elohim* meaning 'the strong one and the covenant-keeping one'; *Jehovah*, 'the self-existing one or the God of redemption'; *Adonai*, 'master.' There are about four hundred different names and titles of Deity in the Old Testament. *Lord*, when referring to Christ, intimates His Deity and eternal being. The name *Jesus* points to His humanity. *Christ* refers to the anointed one who was expected throughout the Old Testament. No names are given for the Holy Spirit. There are, however, about forty-four descriptive titles used of Him.

The name may even represent the person (Matt. 10:22; 19:29; John 20:31; Acts 5:41). To believe on Christ's name means to believe on Him and to be saved through His name. Works wrought in His name are done by His immediate power (Acts 16:18; 19:11–17; cf. Luke 24:47). Prayer in His name is as though Christ Himself spoke through the believer (John 14:14; 16:23; cf. Rom. 10:13).

NATURAL MAN

The Greek word—ψυχικός—for *natural man* is used six times in the New Testament. In 1 Corinthians 15:44, 46 reference is made to a *psuchikos* body, an organism adapted to the soul, in contrast to a *pneumatikos* body, an organism adapted to the spirit. In 1 Corinthians 2:14, James 3:15, and Jude 1:19 the whole self is in view or the natural man's limitations are indicated by means of this terminology. One of the designations used by Paul for the unregenerate indeed is to be found in this term (1 Cor. 2:14). They are described accordingly as unchanged from their original fallen and depraved state. Distinctions must be drawn between the natural man and the spiritual as well as between the natural and the carnal. (See Flesh.)

NUMBERS

From all indications certain numbers are significant as they have been occasionally used in Scripture. *One* denotes unity (Eph. 4:3–6). *Two* denotes diversity or difference one from another—"two witnesses," "doubletongued" (1 Tim. 3:8; Rev. 11:3), etc. *Three* relates to things sacred and things of heaven, as for example three heavens and three persons of the Godhead (Matt. 28:19; 2 Cor. 12:2). It is one of the numbers suggesting completeness. *Four* speaks of the earth and creative works; for instance, the four points of the compass, the four phases of the moon, the four seasons, and the four corners of the earth (Rev. 7:1; 20:8). *Five* appears to be of divine grace (5 offerings of Lev. 1–7). *Six* is a human number, as may be seen from the six days of creation, man's work week of six days, or 666 in Revelation 13:18. *Seven* is the second number to suggest fullness or completion (not, perfection), e.g., Revelation 1:4. Its multiples (also its half) are: 7×2 or 14, which intimates genealogy (Matt. 1:17); 70 (Luke 10:1); 70×7 (Matt. 18:

22); 77 (Gen. 4:24); 7×7 or 49, which led to the year of jubilee (Lev. 25:8 ff.); 3½, which is also expressed by the phraseology "a time, and times, and half a time" (Rev. 11:9; 12:14). Seven appears in all parts of divine revelation—with special significance in Genesis 36 times, in Exodus 17 times, in Leviticus 20 times, in Numbers 23 times, in Deuteronomy 14 times, in John 7 times, in Ephesians 9 times, and in Revelation 29 times. *Eight* may be the number of resurrection, of the putting off of the flesh by circumcision (Gen. 17:12; Matt. 28:1). *Nine* seems to be the number suggesting finality of judgment or 3×3 (Gen. 17:1). *Ten* is the third number to intimate completeness and indeed is the beginning of a new series of numerals (Matt. 25:1). *Eleven* signifies disorder, because it stands for 12 minus 1 (Acts 1:26). *Twelve* is the fourth and last number of completeness. It indicates election, e.g., 12 tribes, 12 apostles, 12×2 or 24, which yields the number of elders seated round about the throne (Gen. 49:28; Matt. 10:2; Rev. 4:4). *Thirteen* is perhaps the number of calamity (Gen. 14:4). The number 2520 is the most remarkable number of all to be considered. It is the product of the four completeness numbers (3, 7, 10, 12) taken together, and the lowest common denominator for all ten digits, as it can be divided by all or any of them. It indeed is a most complete chronological number, being 7×360 (Dan. 9:25).

OBEDIENCE

Old Testament obedience was directed, speaking doctrinally and in general, to God (cf. Abraham, Gen. 22:18; Saul, 1 Sam. 15:22; 28:18). It was a national issue with Israel (Isa. 1:19; Zech. 6:15).

Certain distinctions occur in the New Testament statement of the doctrine. First, there is the personal obedience of Christ to the Father (Phil. 2:8)—a great Bible theme—which served as a test of His true humanity (Heb. 5:8). In the accomplishing of salvation Christ's obedience is also prominent (Rom. 5:12–21). "Children of obedience" (1 Pet. 1:14, R.V.) are such because they stand in the obedience of the Last Adam; "children of disobedience" (Eph. 2:2) are such because they have to do with the disobedience of the first Adam. It is necessary for the unsaved to be obedient to the gospel (Acts 5:32; 2 Thess. 1:8) if they would be redeemed. Christians are to be obedient both before God and man (Acts 5:29; 1 Pet. 1:22). Children are to be subservient to parents (Eph. 6:1; Col. 3:20). Servants are to obey their masters (Col. 3:22) and wives to submit to husbands (Eph. 5:22). No word is addressed to unregenerate people regarding obedience to God, apart from the gospel. Obedience for the Christian is equivalent to abiding in Christ (John 15:10).

OMNIPOTENCE

Omnipotence is an attribute belonging to God alone. It speaks of His unlimited power (Gen. 18:14; Ps. 115:3; 135:6; Isa. 43:13; Jer. 32:17; Matt. 19:26; Mark 10:27; Luke 1:37; 18:27).

The Greek term παντοκράτωρ, used ten times, is translated *omnipotent* only once (Rev. 19:6; cf. 2 Cor. 6:18; Rev. 1:8; 4:8; 11:17; 15:3; 16:7, 14; 19:15; 21:22, where the translation is *Almighty*). In the Old Testament the wording *El Shaddai* meaning 'the Almighty God' is used forty-seven times (Gen. 17:1). God's limitless power is exercised under the control of His holy will. He may be expected to do, and for moral reasons will do, only that which is in harmony with His character. He will not do wrong nor act foolishly (Gen. 1:1–3; 17:1; 18:14; Isa. 44:24; Matt. 3:9; 19:26; Rom. 4:17; 2 Cor. 4:6; Eph. 1:11, 19–21; 3:20; Heb. 1:3). Note all passages wherein the word *able* appears, for example, "God is able" (2 Cor. 9:8). God can do all that He wills to perform, but He may not will all that He can do.

OMNIPRESENCE

Though not a Biblical word, *omnipresence* suggests quite well how God fills the scene personally everywhere, not merely with His power or authority (1 Kings 8:27; 2 Chron. 2:6; Ps. 139:12; Isa. 66:1; Acts

17:28). This particular doctrine indicates that the whole of God is in every place, which cannot be pantheism and its denying the personality of God. There is also a more localized conception of the Godhead—for instance, "Our Father which art in heaven," "And is set down at the right hand of the throne of God," "An habitation of God through the Spirit" (Matt. 6:9; Eph. 2:22; Col. 3:1; Heb. 12:2; cf. Ps. 113:5; 123:1; Rom. 10:6–7). God was especially in Christ (2 Cor. 5:19). The Son indwells the believer (John 14:20; Col. 1:27); the Spirit dwells within the believer (1 Cor. 6:19); the Father, the Son, and the Spirit are all in an undiminished and an undivided sense indwelling every believer (Rom. 8:9; Gal. 2:20; Eph. 4:6).

OMNISCIENCE

Omniscience, again, is not a Bible word, though it customarily will refer to the fact that God knows to an infinite degree and eternally all that is knowable whether actual or possible. God's actual knowledge may be specified in the following passages of Scripture: Psalm 33:13–15; 139:2; 147:4; Isaiah 44:28; 46:9–10; Malachi 3:16; Matthew 6:8; 10:29–30; Acts 2:23; 15:8; Hebrews 4:3. God's knowledge of things ideally possible is to be seen in Isaiah 48:18 and Matthew 11:21. His knowledge is eternal (Acts 15:18), incomprehensible (Ps. 139:6), and all-wise (Ps. 104:24; Eph. 3:10).

There are three aspects to divine knowledge: (a) self-knowledge, which includes all things, even Himself; (b) omniscience, which includes all things in creation whether ideally possible or real; and (c) foreknowledge, which relates only to things divinely determined or foreseen.

The knowledge of God is not subject to increase or decrease, nor subject to reason, is not distressed by regretting, memory, or foreboding. As an anthropomorphism, God is represented as attaining to knowledge and as repenting (Gen. 6:6; 11:5).

Omniscience is the cognition linked with omnipresence. The practical value thereof is important: (a) to those in testing and trial, (b) to those who are tempted to sin in secret, for it is all known by God, and (c) from the infinite resources of God to supply the lack of wisdom in man's case (Ps. 19:12; 51:6; 139:23–24; James 1:5).

ONLY-BEGOTTEN

The Greek term for *only-begotten*, μονογενής, is used nine times altogether in the New Testament (Luke 7:12; 8:42; 9:38), on five occasions of Christ (John 1:14, 18; 3:16, 18; 1 John 4:9) and once of Isaac (Heb. 11:17).

When used of Christ two ideas inhere: (a) that He is the Son of the Father and (b) that He ranks in a unique way as such. He is a Son of His as none other could be because the only one begotten as He was, or while in the perfected state that He enjoys eternally. Christians are not begotten on the same plane (Heb. 1:6). He is unique in that He alone can be the full revealer of the Father to men (John 1:14–18) and the Mediator between God and men (John 3:16, 18; 1 John 4:9).

The only begotten Son is that association in the Godhead which can be best illustrated to man by the relationship of father and son. Certain theories are to be rejected, namely, that Christ is a begotten Son because of the incarnation, that Christ became a begotten Son by the resurrection, that Christ is the begotten Son only by title, or that He can be the begotten Son by official position. He is the first of those begotten by God and therefore pre-eminent or before all others who ever will be begotten.

ORDAIN

'Ordain' is the English translation of ten Greek words: διατάσσω (1 Cor. 7:17), *to arrange throughout, arrange fully in order;* καθίστημι (Titus 1:5; Heb. 5:1; 8:3), *to set down, constitute;* κατασκευάζω (Heb. 9:6), *to prepare fully;* κρίνω (Acts 16:4), *to separate, come to a decision;* ὁρίζω (Acts 10:42; 17:31), *to determine;* ποιέω (Mark 3:14), *to make;* προορίζω (1 Cor. 2:7), *to predetermine, mark out before;* τάσσω (Acts 13:48; Rom. 13:1), *to appoint;* τίθημι (John 15: 16; 1 Tim. 2:7), *to lay, place;* χειροτονέω (Acts 14:23), *to hold out the hand as in voting.*

In ecclesiastical usage it refers to setting men apart unto a particular service (Mark 3:14; John 15:16; Acts 6:1–6; 13:2, 4; Gal. 1:1; 1 Tim. 4:14; Titus 1:5).

The Bible does not teach that ordination by men is an indispensable provision affording divine grace. The authority to ordain men seems vested in the company which carries on the ministry (Acts 1:15–26; 6:1–6). There is always grave danger that men will assume more at such a point than the Scriptures allow. That ordinances are in the sole care of ordained men is an attempt to safeguard these ordinances, of course, but there is no authority for it in the New Testament (1 Cor. 14:26).

ORDINANCE

'Ordinance' is the rendering of five words in the Greek New Testament:

διαταγή—*a disposing in order* (Rom. 13:2; cf. Acts 7:53).

δικαίωμα—*legal statutes* (Luke 1:6; Heb. 9:1; cf. Rom. 1:32; 2:26; 5:16–18; 8:4; Heb. 9:10; Rev. 15:4; 19:8).

δόγμα—*an opinion* (Eph. 2:15; Col. 2:14; cf. Luke 2:1; Acts 16:4; 17:7).

κτίσις—*a founding* (1 Pet. 2:13; cf. Mark 10:6). Sixteen times it is used to signify *creature* or *creation,* including Hebrews 9:11.

παράδοσις—*delivery, instruction* (1 Cor. 11:2; cf. Matt. 15:2). The word is translated thirteen times as *tradition.*

There are certain actions ordained and commanded of God as well as there are traditions of men which have been imposed as binding. The term *ordinance,* or *ordinances,* however, is limited by ecclesiastical usage to marriage, baptism, and the Lord's Supper. (See each of these doctrines at the proper place.)

PARACLETE

Paraclete is an untranslated Greek word peculiar in the New Testament to John. It refers to the work of the Spirit (John 14:16, 26; 15:26; 16:7), when translated *Comforter,* and also to the personal work of Christ in heaven (see 1 John 2:1, where it is translated *advocate*). The literal meaning of the verb root is 'to call to one, call for.' Once it is used in the LXX when Job speaks of "miserable comforters" (Job 16:2).

There are three significant meanings in the word: (1) legal advocate, (2) intercessor, and (3) helper in general. The first and second are found in the work of Christ the Advocate, while the last is discernible in the work of the Holy Spirit. See Advocacy.

PARADISE

In Greek the meaning of the term *paradise* is 'garden' or 'park,' and so it can be used of Eden in the LXX (cf. Gen. 13:10; Isa. 51:3; Ezek. 28:13; 31:8–9). The word is found three times in the New Testament (Luke 23:43; 2 Cor. 12:4; Rev. 2:7).

The Jewish teaching made paradise that part of hades which was reserved for the blessed. An illustration of this belief is given by Christ in the account of the rich man and Lazarus (Luke 16:19–31).

Paradise is now, since the resurrection of Christ (Eph. 4:8–10), removed from hades and located where Christ sits enthroned (2 Cor. 12:4), the third heaven. Revelation 2:7 promises, as opposed to the theory that would deny consciousness to the departed at present: "To him that overcometh will I give to eat of the tree of life, which is in the midst of the paradise of God." The wresting of Scripture by the advocates of soul sleeping is well illustrated in their treatment of the doctrine of paradise (e.g., a verse like Luke 23:43).

For the present abode of the spirits of departed believers, see 2

Corinthians 5:8 and Philippians 1:23. For the present abode of the bodies of departed believers, see Romans 8:23; 1 Corinthians 15:35–57; Philippians 3:20–21. Sheol as declared in Old Testament speech and hades as in New Testament represent the abode of the departed spirits of unregenerate mankind.

When stoned to death at Lystra, though the time element cannot be finally established, Paul was caught up to paradise—the third heaven, but afterwards was not permitted to recount what he saw or heard. Nevertheless he wrote this much about it: "To depart and to be with Christ . . . is far better" (Phil. 1:23).

PAROUSIA

Parousia is a Greek word for the 'coming' of someone or 'being present by reason of coming' (cf. 2 Cor. 7:6–7; Phil. 2:12). It is not restricted to either form of Christ's appearing but is used both of His return for and with His saints (cf. Matt. 24:3 with 1 Cor. 15:23). It is used twenty-four times in the New Testament. Other terms to be distinguished from it are: *apokalupsis*—'manifestation' or 'revelation' (used eighteen times in the New Testament, five at least referring to Christ's return, e.g., 1 Cor. 1:7; 2 Thess. 1:7; 1 Pet. 1:7); *epiphania*—'appearance' (used six times and always of Christ's first or second coming—2 Thess. 2:8; 1 Tim. 6:14; 2 Tim. 1:10; 4:1, 8; Titus 2:13); *Day of the Lord*—signifying the time of His judgments at the second coming (2 Thess. 2:2, R.V.).

PAULINE THEOLOGY

Pauline theology is a modern classification in theological study, usually made in contrast to that of Christ, John, or Peter.

Paul was the divinely chosen agent to develop the Christian system for New Testament readers since previously it had appeared only in part with the teachings of Christ. To the Apostle was given two distinct revelations: (1) that of the way of salvation and of life under grace (*International Standard Bible Encyclopaedia*, p. 2291; cf. Gal. 1:11–12) and (2) that of the doctrine of the Church, which is Christ's Body (Eph. 3:1–6). These two bodies of truth include the great New Testament message which is Christianity, something Paul termed "my gospel" (Rom. 2:16). For a time he stood alone in the defense of the new system of Christianity (Gal. 2:11–14).

PEACE

Peace is the opposite of anxiety in the heart and of either discord or enmity between individuals and nations. Four aspects of peace should be considered:

1. WITH GOD (Rom. 5:1). That means the believer is now and forever on a peace footing in his relation to God, because he was justified. This aspect of peace is never an experience. It is wholly positional.

2. OF GOD (Phil. 4:7; Col. 3:15; cf. Heb. 13:20). Referring not to position but to an experience, Christ said: "My peace I give unto you" (John 14:27). Here is inwrought peace, part of the fruit of the Spirit (Gal. 5:22).

3. IN THE COMING KINGDOM (Isa. 9:6–7). The two great kingdom words for Israel are *righteousness* and *peace*. Note in proof of this statement the whole Sermon on the Mount (Matt. 5:1—7:27).

4. IN ONE BODY. The agelong enmity between Jew and Gentile likened to a middle wall of partition is broken down when Jews and Gentiles are joined now to each other in one Body, the Church (Eph. 2:14–18; Col. 1:20).

5. IN GENERAL. Observe the following points: (a) There can be no peace in this Christ-rejecting world (Isa. 57:20–21). (b) 1 Thessalonians 5:3 indicates that the nations will have reached a time of temporary truce or peace before Christ comes. (c) No strife is to characterize the coming kingdom reign of the Prince of Peace, for peacefulness shall cover the earth as the waters cover the sea (Isa. 11:9). At that time a blessing is to be pronounced upon all who are peacemakers (Matt. 5:9).

PERFECTION

This subject should be considered under seven aspects.

1. IN THE OLD TESTAMENT (Gen. 6:9; Job 1:1, 8). Israel as a nation might be required to be perfect (Deut. 18:13). Men likewise were said to be perfect relatively (Ps. 37:37). (See the doctrines of The Just and Justification.) Old Testament saints are seen in heaven as "spirits of just men made perfect" (Heb. 12:22–24). Paul was blameless before the law (Phil. 3:6).

2. PROGRESSIVE. New Testament saints may progress relative to spiritual maturity, which refers to being more or less full grown and not to sinless perfection (1 Cor. 2:6; cf. 13:11; 14:20; Phil. 3:15; 2 Tim. 3:17).

3. AND THE FLESH. "Are ye so foolish? having begun in the Spirit, are ye now made perfect by the flesh?" (Gal. 3:3).

4. IN SOME PARTICULAR. (a) Obeying God (Col. 4:12). (b) Imitating God (Matt. 5:48). (c) Service (Heb. 13:21). (d) Patience (James 1:4).

5. POSITIONAL. Positional perfection is due to the believer's standing in Christ (Heb. 10:14). In this respect the believer is seen to be absolutely and infinitely perfect, indeed as perfect as Christ Himself, but it is altogether due to the fact that he is in Christ and partaking of what Christ is, not to any perfection of his own.

6. ULTIMATE (INDIVIDUAL). Scripture contemplates that at some future time the believer will be conformed to the image of Christ (Col. 1:28; cf. vs. 22; Phil. 3:12; 1 Thess. 3:13; 1 Pet. 5:10).

7. ULTIMATE (CORPORATE). The whole body of believers will be perfected as such (John 17:23; Eph. 4:12–13; 5:27; Jude 1:24; Rev. 14:5).

Scripture gives no basis for the extreme doctrines of personal holiness or sinless perfection advocated by some Christians.

POWER

The natural divisions of this subject are:

1. OF GOD. (a) Over all spiritual beings and realms as Creator, Preserver, and Consummator. (b) Over physical realms likewise in respect to creation, cohesion, and consummation (Col. 1:16–17). The Old Testament name of *El Shaddai* reveals God as the "Strong One" become the Strength-Giver and Satisfier of His people (Gen. 17:1); by this means He would incite man's confidence and reliance upon Himself.

2. OF ANGELIC HOSTS. The angelic beings are referred to in the Scripture as principalities and powers. Illustrations of Satan's might (second only to the divine) may be observed in Job, chapters 1–2, and Isaiah 14:12–17.

3. OF NATURE. The power of nature is to be seen in the wind, tide, sun, beasts, ability in all lower forms of life to grow, to form life or reproduce (Gen. 1:22).

Two important Greek words for *power* are found in the Scriptures. The first, δύναμις, is used 130 times by the New Testament, and from it the following English words are derived: dynamic, dynasty, dyne, dynamometer, dynamite, dynamo, etc. It connotes any power at work (Rev. 5:12). The second word, ἐξουσία, employed 104 times by the apostolic writers, has reference to the power of choice or liberty of doing as one pleases, physical and mental power, the ability or strength with which one is endued which he either possesses or exercises, the power of authority and right, the power of rule or government (e.g., Matt. 28:18).

4. OF MAN. The realization of power for a believer may be noted in five different respects, pertaining to (1) victory over inherent sin (Gal. 5:16), (2) manifestation of Christ's virtues (Gal. 5:22–23), (3) service (Phil. 2:13), (4) God (Gen. 32:28), and (5) people unto the glory of God (Ex. 3:10). Cf. 2 Corinthians 11:13–15; 2 Thessalonians 2:8–10.

PRAISE

Praise is a word used in the Old Testament about 300 times and in the New Testament about 34 times. This term indeed has the same root as *price,* meaning to ascribe value and worth to another. It far exceeds mere gratitude for any blessings received (e.g., Rev. 4:11; 5:12).

Praise is a great Old Testament theme, especially in the Psalms. Laudation of God is found also in the following New Testament passages: John 9:24; 12:43; Ephesians 1:6, 12, 14; Philippians 1:11; 4:8; Hebrews 2:12 (cf. Psalm 22:22); 1 Peter 4:11. Praise is sometimes applied to men (Matt. 6:1–4; John 12:43; 1 Cor. 4:5; Gal. 1:10).

The Bible is the one and only book of inspired praise. Praise accordingly is made therein a duty (Ps. 50:23).

There is a progressive order climbing from (a) thanksgiving to (b) adoration and finally to (c) worship, which last-named is expressed not only verbally as appreciation but also bodily as dedication (Rom. 12:1).

PRAYER

Six aspects of prayer are to be considered here:

1. In the Old Testament. Prayer in the Old Testament was based on the divine covenants and on the character of God, hence its phraseology "according to thy word" or "for thy great name's sake" (Gen. 18:23–32; Ex. 32:11–14; 1 Kings 8:22–53; Neh. 9:4–38; Dan. 9:4–19). Prayer followed blood sacrifice usually (Heb. 9:7).

2. For and in the Kingdom. This aspect of prayer is based on God the Father's care, though still very largely conditioned on human merit (Ps. 72:15; Matt. 6:5–15; 7:7–11).

3. Under Grace. The basis now is that of the believer's position and privilege in Christ. It is offered in the name (i.e., as vitally linked with

the Person) of Christ (John 14:14; 16:23–24). Prayer under grace proves to be a ministry of the believer in his priestly office. The Believer is seen thus to be in partnership with Christ (cf. 1 Cor. 1:9). The "greater works" of John 14:12–14 are accomplished by the new partnership of Christ with the believer. Christ in fulfillment of this alliance accomplishes the "greater works," as the believer in fulfillment of his responsibility does the praying (John 14:14). The supreme objective in all such work and prayer is "that the Father may be glorified in the Son" (John 14:13). Here the sole condition for prayer to be answered is praying in "my name." This is the new grace ground of prayer. It means praying from the vantage ground of the believer's position in Christ. He may of course make a foolish and unworthy prayer from that ground, but he never departs from the ground. The words *in my name* may signify that in this partnership Christ identifies Himself as the real one who is petitioning. It is as though He signed the petition along with the believer. John 15:7 declares that as the Word of Christ abides in the believer, and as the believer is obedient to that Word, which connotes abiding in Christ (John 15:10), he may "ask what he will" (cf. two reasons for unanswered prayer given in James 4:2–3). The all-inclusive "whatsoever" (John 14:13) should be considered in its relation to the name through which prayer is offered, that is, it must designate whatsoever may be agreeable and suitable to Christ.

There is a divine order prescribed for prayer under grace. This is set forth by the words: "In that day ye shall ask me nothing. Verily, verily, I say unto you, Whatsoever ye shall ask the Father in my name, he will give it you" (John 16:23). Also, judging from another Scripture, prayer is to be offered in the Holy Spirit (Jude 1:20). By use of the phrase "in that day," then, reference is made to the time immediately after Christ's resurrection and the Day of Pentecost, or the dawning of the new age of grace. In other words, this is the prescribed arrangement of prayer for the day in which Christians live and it is distinctly declared that in the present time they are not to pray directly to Christ, but to the Father in the prevailing name of Christ with assurance that the Father will answer their prayer. Praying to the Father in the name of the Son and in the power of the Holy Spirit is an order which has not been arbitrarily imposed. The reason for this order is quite obvious. To pray to Christ would mean to abandon His mediation; it would not be praying *through* Him but rather *to* Him, thereby sacrificing the most vital feature of prayer under grace—prayer *in His name*. It is equally out of order to pray to the Holy Spirit for by so doing Christians imply that they do not need His help; instead of proceeding by His help, they would be ignoring the need of Him.

It is not difficult to adjust one's self to these requirements and to be intelligent in the order of prayer. Let it be restated that prayer in the present dispensation is to the Father and in the name of the Son and the power of the Holy Spirit.

4. BY CHRIST. Christ prayed, and properly so (Heb. 5:7), directly to the Father without mediation or dependence upon the Holy Spirit, so far as any revelation on the subject goes.

5. BY THE SPIRIT. In Romans 8:26-27 and concerning the Spirit's help in intercession, it is observed how when praying (even for others) one cannot know all that may be involved: "We know not what we should pray for as we ought: but the Spirit . . . maketh intercession for us with groanings which cannot be uttered." It is probably true that He "maketh intercession" not only directly to the Father, but also through the believer by inspiring and enlightening him respecting that for which he should pray.

6. BY MOSES AND PAUL. The prayers of Moses for Israel and of Paul (e.g., Eph. 3:14-21) for the saints of this age should be studied carefully.

PREACHING

Preaching is referred to 20 times in the Old Testament and 250 times in the New Testament. It may be defined as that service wherein man is entrusted with the proclamation of God's message to men. It is the present-day method, with its ramifications, of completing "all that Jesus began both to do and teach" (Acts 1:1).

Ephesians 4:11 contemplates several distinct forms of preaching in this age: *apostle* (ἀπόστολος, used 80 times), *prophet* (προφήτης, used 160 times), *evangelist* (εὐαγγελιστής, used 3 times), *pastor* (or shepherd, ποιμήν, used 17 times), and *teacher* (διδάσκαλος, used 60 times). *Pastor* and *teacher*, however, seem to designate one and the same ministry.

There are various gospels or messages in Scripture, of course: (1) that of the kingdom (Matt. 4:23 ff.), (2) of God (Rom. 1:1, 15), (3) of

Christ (Rom. 1:16; 15:19 ff.), (4) of peace (Rom. 10:15), (5) of grace (Acts 20:24), (6) of salvation (Eph. 1:13), and (7) one called "everlasting" (Rev. 14:6).

There are six words in the New Testament meaning to *speak, preach,* or *proclaim:* (1) διαγγέλλω (Luke 9:60); (2) διαλέγομαι (Acts 17: 2); (3) εὐαγγελίζω (Acts 8:40); (4) καταγγέλλω (Acts 15:36); (5) κηρύσσω (Rom. 10:8); (6) λαλέω (Matt. 10:19; in all, used 210 times), the more general words being λαλέω, 'to speak'; κηρύσσω, 'to herald'; and εὐαγγελίζω, 'to evangelize.' In contradistinction, according to their distinctive natures, the kingdom gospel is heralded (κηρύσσω); the good news of salvation preached (εὐαγγελίζω).

According to Ephesians 4:12 all believers are called upon to "preach" or deliver the good news somehow. It is "the work of the ministry," to be sure, for which the pastor and teacher is meant to equip them (John 17:18; 2 Cor. 5:18–20).

PREDESTINATION

In its doctrinal significance, predestination is almost identical with foreordination (see at the proper place). Predestination accordingly speaks of the divine purpose as related to men and angels. God's decrees, however, relate to all things, material and immaterial. Sin then is decreed, the saved one's destiny is predestinated. The word *predestinate* means 'to mark off,' but the doctrine relates only to certain functions of the divine purpose. Salvation is according to election. Certain things that belong to such as may be saved are predestined (Rom. 8:29–30; Eph. 1:4–5, 9; 3:11; cf. Acts 4:28). Note the absence of all conditional features here. Predestination is more of persons than their actions, and not merely of persons as such but their destiny.

Predestination witnesses to divine certainty but not compulsion. There obviously are different ways of making things certain. It may be done by moral influence or by control of the human will. God chooses to accomplish His purpose by guiding and inclining human wills. This truth should prevent misrepresentations of predestination. Two Greek words are translated *predestinate:* προορίζω (cf. the derivative *horizon* —'that which lies beyond or before,' also a word like *provide;* see Acts

4:28; Rom. 8:29–30; 1 Cor. 2:7; Eph. 1:5, 11) and προγίνωσκω, 'to know beforehand' (Acts 2:23; 26:5; Rom. 8:29; 11:2; 1 Pet. 1:2, 20; 2 Pet. 3:17).

Predestination is in harmony with all Scripture, decrees, election, covenants, and human experience. It is more than almightiness or resistless divine will. God weighs every moral feature of every problem. Predestination in consequence is always agreeable to the holy nature of God.

Since predestination is never said to control the destiny of the unsaved, any suggestion that its provisions are for the unsaved must be resisted.

PRIESTHOOD

The priest is man's representative before God as the prophet is God's representative sent to man.

1. IN THE OLD TESTAMENT. (a) The patriarch was priest over his household (Gen. 8:20; 14:17–20; Job 1:15). (b) Melchizedek as a priest became the type of Christ's priesthood both in person and order (Gen. 14:17–20; Ps. 110:1–4; Heb. 6:20—7:28). Israel was in no way prepared to recognize the priesthood of a Gentile like Melchizedek. (c) Aaron and his sons offered both atoning sacrifices and intercession. Aaron is a type of Christ and His priesthood in service, as Christ offered Himself to God (cf. Heb. 8:3) and carried His own blood into the heavenly sanctuary on high. This is an important point in the message of the letter to the Hebrews.

2. FOR CHRIST. This aspect of the doctrine must contemplate Christ's service here on earth both in sacrifice and intercession and also His present priesthood in heaven. In baptism He was evidently set apart by John under a special, divinely arranged provision (Heb. 5:1–2; 7:23–25; 9:24). Hebrews 5:1–2 declares the full qualifications of a high priest. Observe how and in what particulars Christ fulfilled these. No priest of Israel was ever to come from the tribe of Judah and no high priest would have consecrated a priest out of any family but Levi's. John the Baptist, of course, was a priest in his own right and divinely appointed to consecrate Christ though He did come from the tribe of Judah.

3. IN THE NEW TESTAMENT (1 Pet. 2:5, 9; Rev. 1:6). As the Old Testament high priest is a type of Christ, so the Old Testament priest is a type of the believer. The priest of both Testaments is (1) born to his office, (2) properly inducted into service by a full bath, (3) serving under divine appointment. Israel had a priesthood in one family only; all the Church is a priesthood.

The New Testament priest offers no efficacious sacrifices, but is unceasingly responsible in matters of worship, sacrifice, and intercession (Rom. 12:1-2, etc.). A distinction must be observed between the priestly office of the believer which all share alike and equally, on the one hand, and gifts for service which differ among Christians though to each believer some gift is given, on the other (1 Cor. 12:4).

PROPHECY

Prophecy is a distinct and unique feature of revelation wholly foreign to human ability. It amounts to history being prewritten, therefore must prove a great phenomenon. Its fulfillment in the past is unquestionable, standing as indisputable evidence for inspiration.

1. As PREDICTION. Predictive prophecy is to be distinguished from preaching or forthtelling, itself a kind of prophetic ministry.

2. ITS EXTENT. Predictive prophecy occupies almost one quarter of the text of Scripture. It reaches out indeed to practically all aspects of human life and history. The main classifications are: (a) that which is fulfilled and unfulfilled; (b) that of the Old Testament and the New Testament; (c) that concerning Israel, Gentiles, and the Church; (d) that concerning Christ in His first advent and His second advent (the latter extending over about eight times more Scripture than the former); (e) that before, during, and after the Jewish exile; (f) messages to the northern kingdom and the southern kingdom.

3. IN THE MINISTRY OF CHRIST. The unique prophetic ministry of Christ is the consummation of all prophecy, for He came as the greatest Prophet, Priest, and King. He at last fulfilled Deuteronomy 18:15 (the student is urged to compare all New Testament references to this passage).

4. ITS STUDY. The study of prophecy is especially anticipated in this age; it will, however, be understood only by the enabling power of the Holy Spirit (John 16:13).

PROPITIATION

The Greek words employed in the doctrine of propitiation are: ἱλασμός, signifying that which Christ became for the sinner (1 John 2:2; 4:10), ἱλαστήριον, the place of propitiation (Rom. 3:25; Heb. 9:5), ἵλεως (Matt. 16:22; Heb. 8:12), and ἱλάσκομαι (Luke 18:13; Heb. 2:17).

'Ιλάσκομαι indicates that God has become *gracious, reconciled*. In profane Greek the word means "to render propitious by prayer and sacrifice." But from the Biblical standpoint God is not of Himself alienated from man. His sentiment does not, therefore, need to be changed. Still, in order that He may not for righteousness' sake be necessitated to comport Himself otherwise, an infinite expiation is necessary, which to be sure He Himself in His love institutes and gives. Man, all exposed to wrath, could neither venture nor find an expiation. But then God, in finding it, anticipates and meets the demands of His own righteousness. Nothing happens to change God, as in the heathen view. Therefore it is never read that God must be reconciled. Rather something happens to man, who now escapes the wrath to come. A call for mere mercy would require use of the cry 'Ελέησον. When guilt and its punishment need to be acknowledged, however, the word ἱλάσκομαι is used (Luke 18:13; Heb. 2:17).

Christ became the Propitiator and thus the Father is propitiated. The terminology in Hebrews 9:5 for *mercy seat* corresponds to the LXX translation of the word, namely, ἱλαστήριον.

1. IN THE OLD TESTAMENT. The mercy seat is a throne of grace because of there being propitiation. Sacrificial blood sprinkled on the lid of the ark, where Jehovah's presence was to be found, changed what would otherwise be a scene of awful judgment to one filled with mercy, making it in a measure the mercy seat. However, animal blood was efficacious only to the extent that it provided a just ground on which God could pass over the sins until Christ should come and shed His own

blood for them. God was propitiated aforetime merely to the extent of
deferring judgment. For this measure of grace nevertheless it was reasonable to pray (cf. Luke 18:13).

2. IN THE NEW TESTAMENT. Christ by having His own blood
sprinkled, as it were, over His body at Golgotha, becomes the Mercy
Seat in reality. He is the Propitiator and has made propitiation by so
answering the just demands of God's holiness against sin that heaven
is rendered propitious. This fact of propitiation existing is to be believed. Certainly the adjustment is not to be asked for if it has already
been accomplished. The flood-gates of divine mercy are open, the flow
coming however only through that channel which Christ as Propitiator
is.

Propitiation is the Godward side of the work of Christ on the cross.
The death of Christ for the sin of the world changed the whole position
of mankind in its relation to God, for He recognizes what Christ did in
behalf of the world whether man enters into it or not. God is never said
to be reconciled, but His attitude toward the world is altered when the
world's relation to Him becomes radically changed through the death
of Christ.

God is propitious toward the unsaved and toward the sinning saint:
"And he is the propitiation for our sins: and not for our's only, but also
for the sins of the whole world" (1 John 2:2). Attention should be
called to the fact that God saves a sinner or restores a saint without
striking a blow or even offering a word of criticism. It is too often supposed that human repentance and sorrow soften the heart of God and
render Him propitious. This cannnot be true. It is the legal fact that
Christ has borne all sin which renders God propitious.

The most determining truth to which all gospel preaching should be
harmonized is that God is propitious; thus all the burden is taken off
sinner or Christian, only leaving him to believe that through Christ's
bearing his sin God is propitious.

The publican went up to the temple to pray after having presented
his sacrifice, which was the custom (Luke 18:13). The Authorized Version reports him to have said: "God be merciful to me a sinner." What
he really prayed was (R.V. marg.): "God, be thou propitiated to me the
sinner." He did not ask for mercy as though he must persuade God to
be propitious, but in full harmony with the relationship existing between
the Old Testament covenant people and God, and on the ground of his
offering or sacrifice, he did ask God to be propitious on that special basis.
Such a prayer ever since Christ has died is wholly wrong. In the present

age of grace one need not ask God merely to be merciful toward sin, for that He cannot be, and furthermore since Christ's death has rendered God propitious there is no occasion even to ask God to be propitiated. In fact, to do so becomes rank unbelief and unbelief can save no one. The mercy seat in the Old Testament could be made a ἱλαστήριον by sacrifice (Heb. 9:5), but the blood-sprinkled body of Christ on the cross has long ago become the mercy seat for the sinner once and for all. It is there accordingly that God in righteousness can meet the sinner with salvation and restore the saint to communion. The mercy seat becomes a perpetual throne of grace. What otherwise would be an awful judgment throne is changed to one of infinite mercy.

PROVIDENCE

The Greek word for *providence* is πρόνοια, translated thus but one time in Scripture (Acts 24:2) and then of a Gentile king. The theological term suggests (cf. *provide*) the directing care of God over things animate and inanimate—embracing things both good and evil—especially over those who are yielded to His will.

Providence is the divine outworking of all decrees, the object being the final manifestation of God's glory. He directs all things perfectly, no doubt, yet without compelling the human will. He works in man the desire to do His will (Phil. 2:13). The doctrine accordingly is full of comfort. Providence should be distinguished of course from mere preservation.

PUNISHMENT

1. FUTURE. Future, eternal punishment must have an adequate cause or reason therefore. The Bible is the only authority on this determining theme. It declares that sin is infinite because of being against God. His character is outraged by it and His authority resisted.

The doctrine of punishment, then, contends that men exist forever and must because of the unavoidable divine judgment against them for sin (in its every form) forever be separated from God in a state which is conscious torment. Some have speculated on what that torment is. It has been asserted that it is (a) remorse due to failure to secure the blessings of heaven when they were offered, (b) suffering of the soul which can best be described to the human mind by the figures employed in the Scriptures—a lake of fire, a bottomless pit, or a worm that does not die, (c) a literal fire, pit, and undying worm.

The doctrine is more emphasized by Christ than by any other in the Bible. He taught that, apart from His own saving power, men die in their sins (John 8:24) and are raised again to judgment (John 5:28-29; cf. Matt. 5:22, 29-30; 10:28; 18:9; 23:15, 33; 25:41, 46; Luke 12:5).

In the Old Testament the Hebrew word *sheol* (sometimes translated "grave," "pit," and "hell"), like the New Testament Greek work *hades* (translated "hell," and "grave"), refers to the place of departed spirits, and three shades of meaning are given to it: (1) the grave where activity ceases (Ps. 88:3), (2) the end of life so far as mere human knowledge can go (Eccles. 9:5, 10), (3) a place of conscious sorrow (2 Sam. 22:6; Ps. 9:17; 18:5; 116:3).

In the New Testament the Greek words γέεννα, ἅιδης, and τάρταρος (this term in verbal form) are translated "hell." Γέεννα is a name which speaks of human sacrifice and suffering (Matt. 5:29), ἅιδης indicates the place of departed spirits (Luke 16:23), while τάρταρος refers to the lowest abyss, and to it the wicked spirits are consigned (2 Pet. 2:4).

Additional English words concerned with this theme to be found in the New Testament are: (1) "perdition," meaning utter loss and ruin (1 Tim. 6:9); (2) "damnation," which is often more accurately translated *judgment* or *condemnation* (Matt. 23:14); (3) "torment," which speaks of physical pain (Luke 16:28); "the second death," which is synonymous with the "lake of fire" (Rev. 20:14); "everlasting fire" (Matt. 18:8) and "everlasting punishment" (Matt. 25:46). The Greek for *everlasting*—more often translated *eternal*—is αἰώνιος; although it may be used to indicate mere ages of time, implying an end or termination, this word is almost universally found in the New Testament to express that which is eternal. The new life which the believer has received is forty-seven times said to be "eternal" or "everlasting." Mention is likewise made of the "eternal Spirit," the "everlasting God," "eternal salvation," "eternal redemption," "eternal glory," "everlasting kingdom," and the "everlasting gospel." Seven times this word is used in connection with the destiny of the wicked (Matt. 18:8; 25:41, 46; Mark 3:29; 2 Thess. 1:9; Heb. 6:2; Jude 1:7).

Some assert that αἰώνιος is limited in duration when referring to the suffering of the lost; but, if this were true, every promise for the believer and the very existence of God would doubtless have to be limited as well. See Hades.

2. PRESENT. (a) God punishes nations (note e.g., Egypt, Ex. 7–12) and (b) He punishes individuals as He may decree it necessary (Acts 12:23). The saints, for instance, are both chastened and scourged (Heb. 12:6).

RECONCILIATION

The chief Greek words concerned with reconciliation are: καταλλαγή (Rom. 5:11; 11:15; 2 Cor. 5:18–19), καταλλάσσω (Rom. 5:10; 1 Cor. 7:11; 2 Cor. 5:18–20), and ἱλάσκομαι (Heb. 2:17). Reconciliation means that someone or something is thoroughly changed and adjusted to something which is a standard, as a watch may be adjusted to a chronometer. The doctrine may be considered in as many as three aspects:

1. OLD TESTAMENT USE. In the Old Testament reconciliation speaks of atonement or a covering for sin (Lev. 8:15).

2. OF THE WHOLE WORLD TO GOD (2 Cor. 5:19). The need of this adjustment is expressed in Romans 5:6–11, where the doctrine with its universal scope appears. Note four expressions in use there: *ungodly, without strength, sinners, enemies.*

By the death of Christ on its behalf, the whole world is thoroughly changed in its relation to God. But God is never said to be reconciled to man. The world is so altered in its position respecting the holy judgments of God through the cross of Christ that God is not now imputing their sin unto them. The world is thus rendered savable.

3. OF EACH INDIVIDUAL (2 Cor. 5:20). Distinguish three changes connected with reconciliation in 2 Corinthians 5:17–20: (a) that which is positional or structural, wherein a soul is seen to be in Christ (vs. 17), (b) that of a general relationship, or the basis on which salvation may be offered to all mankind (vs. 19), and (c) that which is a mental attitude or the trust of the individual heart when one sees and accepts the

value in the death of Christ for him (vs. 20). Consider likewise the passages: Matthew 5:24; 1 Corinthians 7:11; Ephesians 2:16; Colossians 1:21.

Since the position of the world before God is completely changed through the death of Christ, God's own attitude toward man cannot longer be the same. He is prepared to deal with souls now in the light of what Christ has accomplished. This seems to be a change in God, of course, but it is not a reconciliation. God, on the contrary, believes completely in the thing which Christ has done and accepts it, so as to continue being just, although able thereby to justify any sinner who accepts the Savior as his reconciliation.

REDEMPTION

The doctrine of redemption is set forth by the precise meaning of the original words: (1) λυτρόω, λύτρον, λύτρωσις. This word root in all three forms is used eight times and only of the one who *received* redemption (cf. Luke 1:68—"redeemed his people"). (2) ἀγοράζω, used thirty-one times, meaning to be in the 'agora' or place of assembly and market, hence to buy for one's self by a *price* freely paid (cf. Rev. 5:9— ". . . hast redeemed us to God by thy blood out of every kindred, and tongue, and people, and nation"). (3) ἐξαγοράζω, used four times, meaning to purchase *out of* the market not to return (cf. Gal. 3:13— "redeemed us from the curse of the law"). (4) ἀπολύτρωσις, used eight times, meaning a *full* deliverance of the soul from sin and of the body from the grave (Rom. 3:24; 8:23; 1 Cor. 1:30; Eph. 1:7, 14; 4:30; Col. 1:14).

1. IN THE OLD TESTAMENT. (a) Israel is redeemed as a nation out of Egypt (Ex. 6:6; cf. Isa. 63:4). (b) One animal should be redeemed by another (Ex. 13:13). (c) A lost estate could be redeemed by a kinsman (Lev. 25:25). This practice becomes a type of Christ's redemption. There were four requirements in the type as likewise four with the antitype: (1) A redeemer must be a near kinsman. To fulfill this Christ took upon Himself the human form, entered the race. (2) He must be able to redeem. The price of redemption must needs be paid, which in the antitype was the blood of the Son of God (Acts 20:28; 1 Pet. 1:18– 19). (3) He must be willing to redeem (cf. Heb. 10:4–10). (4) He

must be free from the calamity which occasioned the need of redemption, that is to say, he could not redeem himself. This was true of Christ, for He needed no redemption. According to the type of the high priest on the Day of Atonement, then, Christ offered sacrifice but not for Himself (Luke 1:35; Heb. 4:15).

Of the above, (1) and (2) are related more especially to Christ's humanity and (3) and (4) to His Deity.

2. IN THE NEW TESTAMENT. a. THE NEED OF REDEMPTION. All are slaves because sold under sin (Rom. 7:14; 1 Cor. 12:2; Eph. 2:2) and helplessly condemned to die (Ezek. 18:4; John 3:18; Rom. 3:19; Gal. 3:10).

b. THE SAME PRICE FOR ALL. To redeem from sin called for death by blood-shedding. A substitute, however, may take the sinner's place. (Heb. 9:27–28).

c. NO RETURN. When spiritually redeemed, as disclosed by ἐξαγοράζω, the emancipated one never returns as such to his former slavery. The Redeemer will not sell a slave He has bought (John 10:28).

d. EMANCIPATION. So, also, the redeemed are loosed from bondage—not even bound as slaves to the Redeemer. They are set free. The Redeemer will not own a slave who is not one by choice (John 8:36; Rom. 8:19–21; Gal. 4:31; 5:13). The slave may become a willing bondslave (Ex. 21:5–6; Ps. 40:6–8; 1 Cor. 9:18–19; 2 Cor. 5:14–15).

e. THE GOSPEL APPEAL. (1) God has undertaken for the needs of lost men. (2) Christ became a kinsman redeemer. (3) Man's lost estate ends in eternal woe or the second death. (4) Christ, however, has now paid all demands against sin. (5) Ἀγοράζω—'to purchase in the market' —may become something experimental through ἐξαγοράζω and ἀπολύτρωσις. Observe that one may realize what is signified by ἐξαγοράζω only through the immediate application of redemption, which follows upon personal faith since it is *something to believe*.

REGENERATION

The Greek for *regeneration* is παλιγγενεσία (πάλιν, 'again, once more' and γένεσις, 'birth, creation').

The general use of the word (i.e., of the noun as such) is found concerning the kingdom only in Matthew 19:28 and concerning those regenerated by the Spirit only in Titus 3:5 (cf. Ezek. 37:1–10; Matt. 17:11; John 1:13; 3:6–7; Acts 3:21; Rom. 8:21; 1 Cor. 15:27; 1 Pet. 1:3, 23; 1 John 2:29; 3:9; 4:7; 5:1, 4, 18; Rev. 21:1).

The doctrine of individual regeneration is obscure in the Old Testament, but in the New Testament it becomes definite (John 3:1–6). Regeneration proves to be the imparting of the divine nature (cf. Titus 3:5; 1 Pet. 1:23; 2:2). All believers, then, have divine sonship (Gal. 3:26, R.V.).

Five facts concerning the nature of regeneration need to be stated: (1) a new life has been thereby begotten which is eternal; (2) that life is the divine nature; (3) the believer is begotten by the Spirit; (4) God the Father becomes his legitimate Father; (5) therefore, all believers are heirs of God and joint heirs with Christ. On the human side, regeneration is conditioned simply on faith (John 1:12–13; Gal. 3:26).

REPENTANCE

Quite contrary to the impression which the usual theology has spread abroad is the correct definition of repentance, the usual idea being that it means sorrow or agony of heart respecting sin and wrongdoing. The true meaning of the word shows that it is a change of mind; and although there may be nothing to preclude that change being accompanied by grief, yet the sorrow itself is not repentance. Instead, it is the reversal of mind.

Another serious Arminian error respecting this doctrine occurs when repentance is added to faith or believing as a condition of salvation. It is true that repentance can very well be required as a condition of salvation, but then only because the change of mind which it is has been involved when turning from every other confidence to the one needful trust in Christ. Such turning about, of course, cannot be achieved without a change of mind. This vital newness of mind is a part of believing, after all, and therefore it may be and is used as a synonym for *believing* at times (cf. Acts 17:30; 20:21; 26:20; Rom. 2:4; 2 Tim. 2:25; 2 Pet.

3:9). Repentance nevertheless cannot be added to believing as a condition of salvation, because upwards of 150 passages of Scripture condition salvation upon believing only (cf. John 3:16; Acts 16:31). Similarly, the Gospel by John, which was written that men might believe and believing have life through Christ's name (John 20:31), does not once use the word *repentance*. In like manner, the Epistle to the Romans, written to formulate the complete statement of salvation by grace alone, does not use the term *repentance* in relation to salvation.

Again, confusion over this doctrine arises when it is not made clear that covenant people such as Israel or Christians may repent as a separate act. Throughout the time when the gospel of the kingdom was preached by John the Baptist, Christ, and the Lord's disciples, there issued a call to repentance which was for none other than the anticipated repentance of that Jewish nation, as Matthew 3:2 has indicated: "Repent ye: for the kingdom of heaven is at hand." This is not a gospel call, but one leading to restoration of a covenant people into its right and original relationship to God (cf. Matt. 4:12–17). In like manner, a Christian, once having sinned, may repent as a separate act, which is something far removed from being saved over again (cf. 2 Cor. 7:8–11).

Repentance itself is one act only and not two. This observation is well illustrated by 1 Thessalonians 1:9–10, ". . . how ye turned to God from idols."

RESURRECTION

The Greek for *resurrection* is ἀνάστασις, used forty-three times; note also: ἐξανάστασις of Philippians 3:11, meaning a *resurrection out from among the dead*, ἐξεγείρω (1 Cor. 6:14), and ἔγερσις (Matt. 27:53).

The doctrine is twofold, pertaining to (1) the resurrection of Christ and (2) the resurrection of humanity, including both saved and unsaved.

1. OF CHRIST. a. THE OLD TESTAMENT DOCTRINE. (1) This may be found in prophecy (Ps. 16:9–10; 22:22–31; 118:22–24; David's conception can be seen in Acts 2:25–31). (2) It may also be observed in

type (the two birds of Leviticus 14:4–7; the "firstfruits" of Lev. 23: 10–11). (3) Christ's resurrection is not directly related to Israel's program or the earth, for it belongs only to the New Creation doctrinally (Col. 2:9–15).

b. THE NEW TESTAMENT DOCTRINE. (1) Resurrection for Himself was predicted by Christ (Matt. 16:21; 17:23; 20:19; Luke 18:33; 24:7). (2) It was subject to absolute proof (1 Cor. 15:4–8). (3) It was an actual resurrection and therefore cannot be illustrated by eggs, bulbs, chrysalises, etc. (Luke 24:39). (4) It resulted in a new order of being quite incomparable (1 Tim. 6:16; 2 Tim. 1:10), not the mere reversal of death. (5) There are seven reasons given for the resurrection of Christ. He arose (a) because of what or who He is (Acts 2:24), (b) to fulfill prophecy (Acts 2:25–31; Rom. 1:4; cf. Jer. 33:20–21; Luke 1:31–33)—Is David's Son dead? (c) to become the Bestower of life (Rom. 7:4; 1 Cor. 15:45; cf. John 20:22), (d) to impart power (Eph. 1:19–20; cf. Matt. 28:18–20; Rom. 6:4), (e) to be Head over all things to the Church (Eph. 1:22–23), (f) on account of a justification ground being accomplished by His death (Rom. 4:25), (g) to be the First-Fruits (Phil. 3:21; cf. 1 Cor. 15:22–23). (6) The resurrection of Christ is the standard of divine power in this age (Eph. 1:19–20; cf. Israel's deliverance out of Egypt for that of the past age and out of the present dispersion for that of the kingdom, Jer. 23:7–8). (7) The Lord's Day is the commemoration of Christ's resurrection, so is observed fifty-two times each year at the beginning of each week.

2. OF HUMANITY. a. THE OLD TESTAMENT DOCTRINE. Old Testament saints anticipated a resurrection of their bodies (Job 19:26; John 11: 24; Heb. 6:2).

b. THE NEW TESTAMENT DOCTRINE IN GENERAL. (1) Three resurrections are to occur successively in the order named (1 Cor. 15:20–24): Christ (His was fulfilled already), the saints, and "the end" (resurrection). Note the time relationships here indicated. (2) Christ taught the universality of resurrection (John 5:25–29; cf. Dan. 12:2; Matt. 11:22, 24; 12:41–42; Luke 10:14; 11:32; Acts 24:15; 1 Cor. 15:22). (3) Resurrection is not to be thought of as if the same as restoration; cf. all so-called resurrections which have been recorded in Scripture (2 Kings 4:32–35; 13:21; Matt. 9:25; Luke 7:12–15; John 11:44; Acts 9:36–41; 14:19–20). (4) The believer's body is much like seed which has been sown (1 Cor. 15:35–44). (5) There is one grand exception to the universality of death and resurrection (1 Cor. 15:51–52).

c. PRESENT PARTICIPATION. The believer has now been raised as respects his spirit (Col. 2:12; 3:1).

d. PAUL'S PREACHING. The resurrection both of Christ and believers forms a part of Paul's gospel (1 Cor. 15:1–4).

REVELATION

The Greek for *revelation* is ἀποκάλυψις (cf. the cognate verb, ἀποκαλύπτω, *to reveal*). The words *revelation* and *reveal* imply an unveiling or disclosing of things unknown—a coming into view. It is reasonable to suppose that God would speak to His creatures whom He has made quite capable of such communion. He has spoken in various ways:

1. BY THE CREATION. This is declared in Psalm 19:1–6 and Romans 1:19–20.

2. BY THE WRITTEN WORD. The Bible claims to be (2 Tim. 3:16), and is, God's written Word. In every particular it has proved to be His message to man. It treats faithfully and truthfully of things whether in heaven or on earth. Indeed, it discloses things otherwise unknown.

3. BY THE LIVING WORD. While the written Word unveils many things, the one message to come pre-eminently through the Son (Heb. 1:1–2) is that which declares the Father. John 1:18 states that no full revelation of Him had been given until Christ came (see Logos). Christ unveiled the wisdom of God (John 7:46; 1 Cor. 1:24) and the power of God (John 3:2), but the prime message disclosed is of God's love, and that unveiled not so much in His life and work as in His death (Rom. 5:8; 1 John 3:16). This is the essential meaning of Hebrews 1:1–2 (cf. John 3:16).

4. BY THE BOOK OF REVELATION. The Apocalypse is so named because it is an unveiling of the Lord Jesus Christ, a revelation which the Father gave His *Son* (not, first of all, John) to show unto His servants (Rev. 1:1).

REWARDS

God offers rewards to the believer as a recognition of whatever faithfulness may be shown to Him in service. This is the counterpart to all the doctrine of grace. Having saved a soul on the basis of grace so that there is for the Christian no obligation for afterpayments or building up of merit, God recognizes an indebtedness on His part to reward believers for their service to Him. It would be quite easy for man to say: "He has done so much for me, the most I can do in return would be little enough," but what He has accomplished under grace creates no real demand or obligation of repayment whatever, else it would not be grace. What the believer has achieved for God He recognizes in faithfulness with rewards at the judgment seat of Christ (Matt 16:27; Luke 14:14; Rom. 14:10; 1 Cor. 4:5; 2 Cor. 5:10; Eph. 6:8; 2 Tim. 4:8; Rev. 22:12).

All condemnation in the matter of guilt is forever past for the Christian. He shall not come into judgment respecting his sin (John 3:18; 5:24; 6:37; Rom. 5:1; 8:1, R.V.; 1 Cor. 11:32), therefore the judgment seat of Christ deals wholly with the matter of service and not with the question of sin.

The following note by Dr. C. I. Scofield (*Reference Bible,* p. 1214) is clearly stated: "God, in the New Testament Scriptures, offers to the *lost,* salvation, and, for the faithful service of the *saved,* rewards. The passages are easily distinguished by remembering that salvation is invariably spoken of as a free gift (e.g. John 4:10; Rom. 6:23; Eph. 2:8, 9); while rewards are earned by works (Matt. 10:42; Luke 19:17; 1 Cor. 9:24, 25; 2 Tim. 4:7, 8; Rev. 2:10; 22:12). A further distinction is that salvation is a present possession (Luke 7:50; John 3:36; 5:24; 6:47), while rewards are a future attainment, to be given at the coming of the Lord (Matt. 16:27; 2 Tim. 4:8; Rev. 22:12)."

The two extended Scripture passages bearing on the doctrine of rewards are 1 Corinthians 3:9–15 and 9:16–27 (cf. the passages on the various crowns: 1 Cor. 9:25; Phil. 4:1; 1 Thess. 2:19; 2 Tim. 4:8; James 1:12; 1 Pet. 5:4; Rev. 2:10; 3:11).

RIGHTEOUSNESS

The Greek word for *righteousness* is δικαιοσύνη. It becomes an absolute term when applied to God. Four general aspects of righteousness are to be noted:

1. God's. With respect to character, God is transparently holy and righteous in all His acts. When combined with love, His righteousness results in grace. God's righteousness is ever absolute and perfect to infinity: "In him is no darkness at all." God's righteousness is seen in two ways: (a) He is a righteous Person (James 1:17; 1 John 1:5) and (b) He is righteous in all His ways (Rom. 3:25–26).

2. Man's. This kind of righteousness is recognized only to show its inadequacy and ripeness for condemnation (Isa. 64:6; Rom. 3:10; 10:3; 2 Cor. 10:12).

3. Imputed. The imputed type of righteousness is not God's attribute as if that were bestowed on man, nor human goodness in any form. It is that which the believer becomes in virtue of his being in Christ. Jesus Christ represents the righteousness of God, and the believer becomes what Christ is at the moment of believing (2 Cor. 5:21). Righteousness was imputed likewise to Old Testament saints (cf. Abraham, Gen. 15:6; Rom. 4:3; Gal. 3:6; James 2:23).

4. Imparted. Romans 8:4 presents a righteous conduct as being possible on the part of each believer which is not the result of his own effort, but on the contrary that of the Spirit. This righteousness is produced not by the believer, then, but "in" him.

SABBATH

1. Meaning. The word *Sabbath* means cessation or complete rest, with no added implication relative to worship or spiritual activity. *Sabbath* is a transliteration from the Hebrew word for 'repose.'

2. GENERAL FACTS. a. The Sabbath originated with creation's work being completed (Gen. 2:2–3). b. There is no mention of a seven-day week between Genesis 2 and the giving of the Law in Exodus 20. Then it was made a part of the law system with extra Sabbaths, a Sabbatic year, and a year of jubilee (cf. Gen. 7:4, 10; 8:10–12; 29:27–28, 30; Ex. 16:1–30; Neh. 9:13–14). c. Prophets gave Sabbath observance the first place in Israel's duties (Isa. 58:13–14). They were judged for failure to keep it—even with a death penalty (Num. 15:32–36). As a nation, Israel so failed to keep the Sabbath that they were taken from the land that the land might have its Sabbath rest (Lev. 26:32–35; Ezek. 20:10–24). d. The inter-Testament period developed the synagogue which custom of meeting together introduced a form of Sabbath worship without any Old Testament authority. Traditions beside had been multiplied freely by the time of the first advent, but these Christ disregarded when the need arose (Matt. 12:1–14; Mark 2:23—3:6; Luke 6:1–11; 13:1–17; 14:1–6; John 5:1–18). e. There is no recorded observance by Christians of a Sabbath as such after Christ's resurrection and yet no one is termed a Sabbath-breaker; rather, Sabbath observance was condemned (Gal. 4:5, 10–11; Col. 2:16). f. Prophecy anticipates the termination of Sabbath observance for a time (Hos. 2:11; 3:4–5). g. Paul recognized Christian gatherings on the first day of the week (Acts 20:7; cf. Rom. 14:5–6). h. The Sabbath is to be restored in the tribulation (Matt. 24:20) and fully re-established in the kingdom (Deut. 30:8; Isa. 66:23; Ezek. 46:1). i. The Sabbath, after all, was Jehovah's perpetual covenant with Israel, excepting when under divine judgment (Ex. 31:16). j. It has never been given to Gentiles (Eph. 2:12; cf. 6:2–3).

SACRIFICE

In the Old Testament, sacrifices were an execution of the sentence of divine law upon the substitute. Ancient sacrifice, then, is of divine origin. In order to make it efficacious it was necessary that blood be shed (cf. Heb. 9:22).

1. SCOPE. There were sacrifices for the Jewish nation or congregation, for the family, and for the individual (Lev. 16).

2. BEFORE MOSES. Sacrifices were offered before the time of Moses by Abel, Noah, Abraham, Isaac, Job, and Jacob (Gen. 4:4; 8:20; 12:7; 26:25; 33:20; Ex. 12:3–11; Job 1:5; 42:7–9).

3. IN THE MOSAIC SYSTEM (Ex.–Deut.). Jewish sacrifices were always typical of Christ. Observe, for example, the five offerings of Leviticus 1:1—7:38.

4. OF CHRIST. The body of Christ was offered once-for-all (Heb. 10:1–12). The Father made the sacrifice (John 3:16; Rom. 8:32). Christ suffered *for*—ὑπέρ (Rom. 5:8), meaning 'for the benefit of'—man; also *in the stead of*—ἀντί (cf. ἀντίλυτρον, 1 Tim. 2:6)—him. The sacrifice of Christ is described as: a. Penal (2 Cor. 5:21; Gal. 3:13). b. Substitutional (Lev. 1:4; Isa. 53:5–6; 2 Cor. 5:21; 1 Pet. 2:24). c. Voluntary (Gen. 22:9, in type; John 10:18). d. Redemptive (1 Cor. 6:20; Gal. 3:13; Eph. 1:7). e. Propitiatory (Rom. 3:25; 1 John 2:2). f. Reconciling (Rom. 5:10; 2 Cor. 5:18–19; Col. 1:21–22). g. Efficacious (John 12:32–33). h. Revelatory (John 3:16; 1 John 4:9–10).

5. OF BELIEVERS. The Christian's sacrifice is but one of three functions of the priest (see Priesthood). a. Dedication of self as a reasonable sacrifice (Rom. 12:1–2). As Christ was both Sacrifice and Sacrificer, so the believer-priest may freely offer himself to God. b. The sacrifice of the lips. This means the voice of praise is to be offered continually (Eph. 5:20; Heb. 13:15). c. The sacrifice of substance (Phil. 4:18). Christians will certainly give more than the Jewish tithe.

6. IN THE KINGDOM. The anticipation of animal sacrifices in the kingdom (Ezek. 43:19–27) is naturally perplexing, yet evidently a memorial looking back to the cross (as the Lord's Supper does now) and no doubt one practice well enough adapted to an earthly people. No animal sacrifice ever has power to take away sin (Heb. 10:4).

SAINT

Saint is a word that comes from the same root in the original as *holy* and *sanctify*, referring as it does to what the believer is by virtue of his position in Christ. *Saint* is used fifty times in the Old Testament to denote Israel and sixty-two times in the New Testament to designate the believer.

The children of God are called *believers* about 50 times and *brethren* about 180 times, while the more common name of today, *Christian*, is used but 3 times in the apostolic writings.

The term never indicates personal character or worthiness. Being already set apart unto God in Christ, all Christians by so much are now saints from the moment they are saved. Sainthood, then, is not a future prospect. All believers are *saints*, positionally considered (1 Cor. 1:2, etc.).

SALVATION

The Greek for *salvation*, σωτηρία, is used about fifty times in the New Testament. It refers to the estate of one who has been *made whole*.

1. SCOPE. The general doctrine of salvation includes the following lesser dogmas: substitution, redemption, reconciliation, propitiation, conviction, calling, election, predestination, sovereignty, free will, grace, repentance, faith, regeneration, forgiveness, justification, sanctification, preservation, and glorification.

2. THE WORK OF GOD. Two Old Testament passages indicate that "salvation belongeth unto the LORD" (Ps. 3:8), "salvation is of the LORD" (Jonah 2:9). Any system which tends to combine human responsibility with this divine undertaking is wrong. Ephesians 2:8–10 relates good works to salvation wrought by grace as an effect thereof, and not a cause.

3. THREE TENSES. Salvation has reference to the believer's past, present, and future. (a) The past tense, which releases from the guilt and penalty of sin, is wholly accomplished for all who believe at the time when they believe (Luke 7:50; 1 Cor. 1:18; 2 Cor. 2:15; 2 Tim. 1:9). (b) The present tense, which releases from the power of sin, is being accomplished now in those who exercise faith for it (John 17:17; Rom. 6:14; 8:2; Gal. 5:16; Phil. 2:12–13). (c) The future tense releases from the very presence of sin (Rom. 13:11; Eph. 5:25–27; Phil. 1:6; 1 Pet. 1:3–5; 1 John 3:1–2).

4. ONE CONDITION. About 115 passages condition salvation on be-

lieving alone, and about 35 simply on faith. There are certain things, however, often added by man to this one and only condition, like the following: believe and repent, believe and be baptized, believe and confess sin, believe and confess Christ publicly, believe and promise a better manner of life, believe and pray for salvation.

5. Dispensational Aspects. A study of this division of the subject is best approached by considering the revealed purposes of God in each of the various dispensations. The present age-purpose as manifested in the heavenly people, for instance, calls forth an exalted, divine undertaking not seen before on the earth (Eph. 3:1-6).

6. Relationships, Factors, and Forces. Note in particular: (a) the work of the Father in salvation, (b) the work of the Son in salvation, (c) the work of the Spirit in salvation, (d) salvation in its relation to sin, (e) Satan's opposition to salvation, (f) salvation or deliverance out of the world, (g) salvation from the flesh, and (h) salvation in relation to heaven. All these are treated fully in Soteriology (Volume III).

7. Duration. There is no salvation offered under grace which stops short of being eternal in its character. This is due to the fact that it proves to be altogether a work of God, and His purpose and power never fail (Phil. 1:6).

SANCTIFICATION

It is particularly true that Bible doctrine suffers through misunderstanding and misstatement of the revealed facts about sanctification. Since one aspect of this doctrine deals with Christian living and experience, it is the more easily perverted and its exact statement the more imperative.

1. Essentials to a Right Understanding. Three general conditions govern a right conception of this subject.

a. Must Be Rightly Related to Other Bible Doctrines. Disproportionate emphasis on any one doctrine, or the habit of seeing all revealed truth in the light of one line of Bible teaching, leads to serious error. No person really understands a doctrine or is prepared to teach a Bible truth until he is able to see that truth in its right position, proportion, and relation to every other truth of the Word. Sanctification, like all other great doctrines of the Scriptures, represents and defines an exact field within the purpose of God. Since it aims at definite ends, it suffers as much from overstatement as from understatement. This doctrine must be considered, then, in its exact relation to all other aspects of truth.

b. CANNOT BE INTERPRETED BY EXPERIENCE. Some persons conclude they understand the doctrine of sanctification because it is their belief that they have been sanctified. Only one aspect of sanctification out of three, however, deals with the complexity of human experience in daily life. Therefore, an analysis of some personal experience must not be substituted for all the teaching of the Word of God. Even if sanctification were limited to the field of human experience, there would never be an experience that could be proved to be its perfect example, nor would any human statement of that experience exactly describe the full measure of the divine reality. It is the function of the Bible to interpret experience rather than the function of experience to interpret the Bible. Every experience which is wrought of God will be found to be in accord with the Scriptures. If not, it should be judged as a device of Satan. To some people an uncertain experience has become more convincing than the clear teaching of the Scriptures.

c. DEPENDS FOR A RIGHT UNDERSTANDING UPON CONSIDERATION OF ALL THE SCRIPTURE. The body of Scripture presenting this doctrine is much more extensive than appears to the one who reads only the English text, for the same root (Hebrew and Greek) words which are translated "sanctify," with its various forms, are also translated by two other English words, "holy" and "saint," with all their various forms. Therefore, to discover the full scope of this doctrine from the Scriptures, one must go beyond the passages in which the one English word "sanctify" is used and include, as well, the portions wherein the terms "holy" and "saint" are employed. Very much is thus added to the field of investigation.

Observance of these three general conditions just named will avoid practically every error connected with the doctrine of sanctification.

2. MEANING OF WORDS INVOLVED. a. "SANCTIFY," WITH ITS VARIOUS FORMS. This word, which is used 106 times in the Old Testament and 31 times in the New, means 'to set apart,' and then the state of being set apart. It indicates classification in matters of position and relationship. The basis of the classification is usually that the sanctified person (or thing) has been set apart, or separated, from others in his position and

relationship before God, that is, from that which proves unholy. This is the general meaning of the word.

It is also important to consider that there are three things which the word *sanctification,* in its general use, does not imply: (1) The Bible use of the word does not imply past improvement in matters of holiness, for God is said Himself to be sanctified, and He has experienced no improvement in holiness.

(2) The Bible use of the word does not necessarily imply a state of sinlessness. In the Old Testament it is stated that the people washed their garments and separated themselves from some defilement and so were sanctified before God. This is far from sinlessness. Even the Corinthian Christians, who were "utterly at fault," are said to be sanctified. Many inanimate things were sanctified, and these could not even be related to the question of sin.

(3) The Bible use of the word does not necessarily imply finality. Being sanctified once did not save the Israelites from needing to be sanctified again and again. They were for the time being set apart unto God. Hence there are aspects of this truth, it will be seen, which do not imply finality.

b. "HOLY," WITH ITS VARIOUS FORMS. This word, which is used about 400 times in the Old Testament and about 12 times of believers in the New Testament, refers to the state of being set apart, or being separate, from that which is unholy. Christ was "holy, harmless, undefiled, separate from sinners." Thus was He sanctified. Similarly, also, there are certain things which the word *holy* in its Biblical use does not imply:

(1) No past improvement need necessarily be implied, for God is Himself holy. It is the state itself which is indicated by this word, and not the process by which it has been attained.

(2) Sinless perfection is not necessarily implied, for one reads of a "holy nation," holy priests, "holy prophets," "holy apostles," "holy men," "holy women," "holy brethren," "holy mountain," and "holy temple." None of these was sinless before God. They were holy, nevertheless, according to some particular standard or issue that constituted the basis of their separation from others.

(3) The word does not necessarily imply finality. All these people just named were repeatedly called to higher degrees of holiness. They were set apart for some holy purpose; thus were they sanctified. Leviticus 21:8 illustrates the similarity of meaning between the words "sanctify" and "holy" as used in the Bible. Speaking of the priest, God said: "Thou shalt sanctify him therefore; for he offereth the bread

of thy God: he shall be holy unto thee: for I the LORD, which sanctify you, am holy." Here the root word, employed four times, is twice translated "sanctify" and twice "holy."

c. "SAINT." This term, used of Israel about 50 times and of believers about 62 times, is applied only to living persons and relates only to their position in the reckoning of God. It is never associated with the quality of their daily life. They are saints by reason of being particularly classified and set apart in the plan and purpose of God. Being sanctified thus, they are saints. In three Epistles, according to the Authorized Version, believers are addressed as those who are "called to be saints." Such a translation is most misleading. The words "to be" should be omitted; indeed, the fact that they are italicized in the A.V. only means the translators added this expression themselves. Christians *are* saints by their present calling from God. The passages, then, do not anticipate a time when they will be saints. They are already sanctified, set apart, classified, "holy brethren," who therefore may be called saints. Sainthood is not subject to progression. Every born-again person is as much a saint the moment he is saved as he ever will be in time or eternity. The whole Church, which is Christ's Body, proves to be a called-out, separate people. They are the saints of this dispensation. According to certain usages of these words, they are all sanctified. They are all holy.

The Spirit has chosen to give believers the title of "saints" more than any other designation except one. They are called "brethren" 184 times, "saints" 62 times, and "Christians" 3 times. It would not be amiss to attempt the rescue of such a divinely emphasized but misunderstood title from its present state of disuse and ruin. Many Christians do not believe they are saints because they do not know of their position in Christ.

The right understanding of the Bible doctrine of sanctification must depend, then, upon consideration of all the passages wherein the words "sanctify," "holy," and "saint" appear. Reference to all the passages, of course, is impossible in this limited study.

3. THE MEANS. a. GOD IS ETERNALLY SANCTIFIED. Because of infinite holiness, God Himself—Father, Son, and Spirit—is eternally sanctified. He is classified as distinct, set apart, and separate from sin. He is altogether holy. He is Himself sanctified (Lev. 21:8; John 17:19).

b. GOD SANCTIFIES PERSONS. God—Father, Son, and Spirit—is said to sanctify other persons. (1) *The Father Sanctifies.* "And the very God of peace sanctify you wholly" (1 Thess. 5:23). (2) *The Son Sanctifies.* "That he might sanctify and cleanse it with the washing of water by the word" (Eph. 5:26; cf. Heb. 2:11; 9:13–14; 13:12). (3) *The Spirit Sanctifies.* "Being sanctified by the Holy Ghost" (Rom. 15:16; cf. 2 Thess. 2:13). (4) *The Father Sanctified the Son.* "Whom the Father hath sanctified, and sent into the world" (John 10:36). (5) *God Sanctified Israel.* God sanctified the priests and people of Israel (Ex. 29:44; 31:13). (6) *Sanctification Is God's Will.* "For this is the will of God, even your sanctification" (1 Thess. 4:3).

(7) *The Believer's Sanctification Comes from God.* (a) *By Union with Christ.* "To them that are sanctified in Christ Jesus" (1 Cor. 1:2); Christ has been made unto believers their sanctification (1 Cor. 1:30). (b) *By the Word of God.* "Sanctify them through thy truth: thy word is truth" (John 17:17; cf. 1 Tim. 4:5). (c) *By the Blood of Christ.* "Wherefore Jesus also, that he might sanctify the people with his own blood, suffered without the gate" (Heb. 13:12; cf. 9:13–14); "The blood of Jesus Christ his Son cleanseth us from all sin" (1 John 1:7). (d) *By the Body of Christ.* "By the which will we are sanctified through the offering of the body of Jesus Christ once for all" (Heb. 10:10). The cross has separated believers from the world: "God forbid that I should glory, save in the cross of our Lord Jesus Christ, by whom the world is crucified unto me, and I unto the world" (Gal. 6:14). (e) *By the Spirit.* "God hath from the beginning chosen you to salvation through sanctification of the Spirit" (2 Thess. 2:13; cf. 1 Pet. 1:2). (f) *By Choice.* "Follow peace with all men, and holiness, without which no man shall see the Lord" (Heb. 12:14; cf. 2 Tim. 2:21–22). (g) *By Faith.* "Sanctified by faith that is in me" (Acts 26:18).

c. GOD SANCTIFIED DAYS, PLACES, AND THINGS (Gen. 2:3; Ex. 29:43).

d. MAN CAN SANCTIFY GOD. This he may do by setting God apart in his own thought as holy. "Hallowed be thy name." "But sanctify the Lord God in your hearts" (1 Pet. 3:15).

e. MAN CAN SANCTIFY HIMSELF. Many times did God call upon Israel to sanctify themselves. He likewise says to believers in this age: "Be ye holy; for I am holy." Also, "If a man therefore purge himself from these [vessels of dishonor so as to depart from iniquity], he shall be a vessel unto honour, sanctified, and meet for the master's use" (2 Tim. 2:21). Self-sanctification, however, can only be realized by the divinely provided means. Christians are asked to present their bodies a living sacrifice, holy and acceptable unto God (Rom. 12:1). They are to "come out from among them, and be . . . separate" (2 Cor. 6:17). Having the Christian's promises, they are to cleanse themselves "from

all filthiness of the flesh and spirit, perfecting holiness [i.e., sanctifica-
tion] in the fear of God" (2 Cor. 7:1). "This I say then, Walk in the
Spirit, and ye shall not fulfil the lust of the flesh" (Gal. 5:16).

f. MAN CAN SANCTIFY PERSONS AND THINGS. "For the unbelieving
husband is sanctified by the wife, and the unbelieving wife is sanctified
by the husband: else were your children unclean; but now are they
holy" (i.e., sanctified; 1 Cor. 7:14). "And Moses sanctified the people."
"So they sanctified the house of the LORD."

g. ONE THING CAN SANCTIFY ANOTHER. "For whether is greater, the
gold, or the temple that sanctifieth the gold? . . . For whether is
greater, the gift, or the altar that sanctifieth the gift?" (Matt. 23:17,
19).

From a very limited consideration of the Scriptures on the subject of
sanctification and holiness, it is evident that the root meaning of the
word is to set apart unto a holy purpose. The one set apart is sometimes
cleansed and sometimes not. Sometimes this one can partake of the
character of holiness and sometimes, as in the case of an inanimate
thing, it cannot. Yet a thing which of itself can be neither holy nor unholy is just as much sanctified when set apart unto God as the person
whose moral character is subject to transformation. It must also be
evident that where these moral qualities exist cleansing and purification
are sometimes required in sanctification, but not always.

4. THREE ASPECTS. Though the exact meaning of the words "sanctify," "holy," and "saint" is unchanged, there is a far deeper reality
indicated by their use in the New Testament than is indicated by their
employment in the Old. After all, the Old Testament is but a "shadow
of good things to come." The New Testament revelation, then, may be
considered in three divisions:

a. POSITIONAL. This is a sanctification, holiness, and sainthood which
comes to the believer by the operation of God through offering of the
body and shed blood of the Lord Jesus Christ. Those who are saved have
been redeemed and cleansed in His precious blood, forgiven all trespasses, made righteous through the new headship in Him, justified, and
purified. They now are the sons of God. All of this indicates a distinct
classification and separation, deep and eternal, achieved through the
saving grace of Christ. It is based on facts of position which are true of
every Christian. Hence, every believer is now said to be sanctified positionally, holy, and by so much a saint before God. This position bears
no relationship to the believer's daily experience more than that it

should inspire him to holy living. His position in Christ is, to be sure, according to the Scriptures, the greatest possible incentive to holiness of life.

The great doctrinal Epistles observe this order in teaching the truth. They first state the marvels of saving grace and then conclude with an appeal for a life corresponding to the divinely wrought position (cf. Rom. 12:1; Eph. 4:1; Col. 3:1). Christians are not now accepted in themselves; they are accepted in the Beloved. They are not now righteous in themselves; He has been made unto them righteousness. They are not now redeemed in themselves; He has been made unto them redemption. They are not now positionally sanctified by their daily walk; He has been made unto them a sanctification like that. Positional sanctification is as perfect as He is perfect. As much as He is set apart, believers, since they are found to be in Him, are set apart. Positional sanctification is as complete for the weakest saint as it is for the strongest. It depends only on one's union with and position in Christ. All believers are classified as "the saints." So, also, they are classed as the "sanctified" (cf. Acts 20:32; 1 Cor. 1:2; 6:11; Heb. 10:10, 14; Jude 1:1). The proof that imperfect believers are nevertheless positionally sanctified and therefore saints is discovered in 1 Corinthians. Corinthian believers were unholy in life (e.g., 1 Cor. 5:1–2; 6:1–8), but they are twice said to have been sanctified (1 Cor. 1:2; 6:11).

By their position, then, Christians are rightly called "holy brethren" and "saints." They have been "sanctified through the offering of the body of Jesus Christ once for all" (Heb. 10:10), and are new men by reason of now being "created in righteousness and true holiness" (Eph. 4:24). Positional sanctification and positional holiness are "true" sanctification and holiness. In his position in Christ the Christian stands righteous and accepted before God forever. Compared to this, no other aspect of the present truth can merit an equal recognition. But let no person go on from here to conclude that he is holy, or sanctified, in life because Christians are now said to be holy, or sanctified, in position.

b. EXPERIMENTAL. While all believers are said to be sanctified every whit positionally, there is never a reference in any of these Scriptures to their daily lives. Such an aspect of sanctification and holiness is found in another and entirely different body of truth which may be termed *experimental sanctification.* As positional sanctification is absolutely disassociated from the daily life, so experimental sanctification is absolutely unrelated to position in Christ. Experimental sanctification instead may depend (1) on some degree of yieldedness to God, (2) on some degree of separation from sin, or (3) on some degree of Christian growth to which the believer has already attained.

(1) *Result of Yieldedness to God.* Whole self-dedication to God is one's reasonable service: "Present your bodies a living sacrifice, holy, acceptable unto God, which is your reasonable service" (Rom. 12:1). By so doing the Christian is classified and set apart unto God through his own choice. There is an element of finality and completeness possible in this. Within the sphere of his own knowledge of himself, the believer may definitely choose the mind and will of God as the rule for his life. This yielding to the will of God may be accordingly complete and final. Herein is self-determined separation unto God, an important aspect of experimental sanctification. "Now being made free from sin, and become servants to God, ye have your fruit unto holiness" (or, sanctification; Rom. 6:22).

Sanctification cannot be experienced as a matter of feeling or emotion any more than justification or forgiveness can. A person may nevertheless be at peace and full of joy because he *believes* these things to be true in his life. So, also, by yielding unto God a new infilling of the Spirit may be made possible which will result in some blessedness in life hitherto unknown. This felicity might come either suddenly or gradually. In any case it is not the sanctification itself that is experienced: it is rather the blessing of the Spirit made possible through sanctification or a deeper life of separation unto God. Experimental sanctification works in such a way as to have its effect upon the daily life, and by so much acts in contrast to positions which are in no way related to daily living.

(2) *Result of Freedom from Sin.* The Bible takes full acount of the many sins of Christians. It does not teach that only sinless people are saved, or kept saved; on the contrary, there is faithful consideration of, and full provision made for, the sins of saints. These provisions are both preventive and curative. The question of sin in the believer is taken up exhaustively by 1 John. One passage (2:1-2) may be taken as a key to the Epistle. It begins: "My little children, these things write I unto you, that ye sin not." This much relates to the prevention of sin in the Christian. It continues: "And if any [Christian] man sin, we have an advocate with the Father, Jesus Christ the righteous: and he is the propitiation for our sins." This much refers to the cure of sin in Christians. Much Scripture indeed is written "that we be not sinning," but in addition believers are told that if they still fall into sin they have abundant provision from God for its cure. The things which are written

are not set down to encourage any believer to sin; they however are written "that we be not sinning" longer. "Shall we continue in sin, that grace may abound? God forbid." He alone can forbid, and if requested He will forbid—such are the marvelous provisions in grace for eternal keeping of the child of God.

It may be concluded from these and many other Scriptures that a son of God need not sin. To that end the Savior has died (Rom. 6:1–14). To that end Christians have a message written them (1 John 2:1–2). To that end they are indwelt by the Spirit of God (Gal. 5:16). It is the purpose of the Father that His children be free from sin in order that He may have fellowship with them, for "truly our fellowship is with the Father and with his Son Jesus Christ." The basis upon which Christians may have fellowship with the Father and His Son is specified: they must walk in the light as God is in the light (1 John 1:7), which means to live by the power of the Spirit and instantly to confess every known sin. Because of the Advocate's defense of him and because of the believer's confession of sin, God is free to forgive and cleanse from all unrighteousness. Christians then must not say they have no sin nature (1:8). This would be to deceive themselves. Such ones must not say, either, that they have not sinned (1:10). This would be to make Him and His testimony to what is in man untrue. It does not become a Christian to boast of himself, but instead every true victory should be acknowledged to the glory of the Lord Jesus Christ.

Has any child of God reached complete deliverance from sin? This question should never be confused with the facts concerning positional sanctification, nor with the truths connected with sanctification through yieldedness to God. The answer to this query may be stated as follows: While the believer is definitely trusting the sufficiency of the Spirit and fulfilling every condition for enablement, he will be divinely kept from sinning (Rom. 6:14; 8:2; Gal. 5:16). That statement is not based upon any personal experience; it rests on the Word of God. The Christian never reaches a place where he cannot sin. On the other hand, the Scriptures plainly teach that, in spite of the fallen nature, there is deliverance for the believer from bond-servitude to sin through union with Christ in His death and resurrection (Rom. 6:1–10) and through the power of the indwelling Spirit to enable (Rom. 8:2; Gal. 5:16). This victory will be realized just so long as it is claimed by faith. Such is the divinely provided preventative for sinning.

The old nature, with its incurable disposition to sin, remains in every believer so long as he is in his present body. He is therefore disposed to sin. The sin nature itself is never said to have died. It was crucified, put to death, and buried with Christ, but since this death was accomplished two thousand years ago the reference must be to a divine judgment against the nature which was gained by Christ when He "died unto sin." There is no Bible teaching to the effect that some Christians have died to sin and others have not. The passages involved must include *all* saved persons (Gal. 5:24; Col. 3:3). All believers have died unto sin in Christ's sacrifice, but not all have claimed the riches which were provided for them by that death. Saved people are not asked to die experimentally or to re-enact His death; they are urged only to "reckon" themselves to be dead indeed unto sin. This is the human responsibility (Rom. 6:1–14).

If through weakness, willfullness, or ignorance the Christian does sin, there is a cure provided. On the human side there must be a genuine confession and repentance of heart (2 Cor. 7:8–11; 1 John 1:9). On the divine side there is "an advocate with the Father," and the Father "is faithful and just to forgive us our sins, and to cleanse us from all unrighteousness." Experiences of failure and defeat should be growing less as the believer increasingly discovers the marvels of God's power and grace and the utter helplessness of his own strength. Every restoration, forgiveness, and cleansing is a renewal of experimental sanctification.

(3) *Result of Christian Growth.* Christians are immature in wisdom, knowledge, experience, and grace. In all such realms they are appointed to grow, and their growth should be manifest. They are to "grow in grace, and in the knowledge of our Lord and Saviour Jesus Christ." Beholding the glory of the Lord as in a glass, they are "changed into the same image from glory to glory, even as by the Spirit of the Lord." This transformation will have the effect of setting them more and more apart to God. They will, to that very extent, be more sanctified.

A Christian may be "blameless," though it could not be truthfully said of him that he is "faultless." The child laboring to form his first letters in a copybook may be blameless in the work he does, but the work is certainly not faultless. A believer may be walking in the full measure of what is his understanding today, yet he must know he is not now living in the added light and experience that will be his tomorrow through growth. There is a relative perfection, then, within imperfection. Christians who are quite incomplete, quite immature, and quite given to sin may nonetheless "abide" in the Vine. They may have fellowship with the Father and with His Son. There is also imperfection within perfection. Those saved ones who really are incomplete, immature, and given to sin, are even now positionally sanctified and complete "in Him" —the Lord Jesus Christ.

Christian growth and experimental sanctification are not the same, for one is a cause and the other its effect. The Christian will be more and more set apart as he grows into the image of Christ by the Spirit. To state that he will be more experimentally sanctified as he grows in grace and the knowledge of his Lord and Savior Jesus Christ does not necessarily question his present purity or victory in daily life; it is only to declare that he will be more set apart as he develops in the likeness of his Lord. This is to consider experimental sanctification in the broadest and most general meaning of the word.

c. ULTIMATE. The ultimate aspect of sanctification, which is related to the saved one's final perfection, will be his in the glory. By His grace and transforming power God will have so changed every child of His— in spirit, soul, and body—that each will be "like him" and "conformed to the image of His Son." He will then present them "faultless" before the presence of His glory. His Son's Bride will be free from every "spot or wrinkle." It therefore becomes all Christians to "abstain from all appearance of evil. And the very God of peace sanctify you wholly; and I pray God your whole spirit and soul and body be preserved blameless unto the coming of our Lord Jesus Christ."

5. THREE AGENTS. Three agents of sanctification are emphasized in Scripture: (a) the Holy Spirit (1 Cor. 6:11; 2 Thess. 2:13; 1 Pet. 1:2), (b) the Son (Heb. 10:10), and (c) the Truth of God (John 17:17; Eph. 5:26).

SATAN

1. HIS PERSONALITY. As in the case with Christ, the knowledge of Satan depends wholly on what the Scriptures declare. No more or better evidence even there will exist for belief in the personality of one than for the other.

2. HIS POWER. (a) As created his might was second only to God's. (Ezek. 28:11–16). (b) After his moral fall (cf. Job 2:7; Isa. 14:12–17; Luke 4:6; 22:31, R.V.; 1 Cor. 5:5; Heb. 2:14) and even after his

judgment in the cross (John 16:11; Col. 2:15) he continues to reign as a usurper (2 Cor. 4:4). Consider here all passages throughout Scripture on Satan's temptations and solicitations to evil.

3. HIS WORK. (a) Relative to God, his evil works are still permitted. (b) Relative to demons, they must do his will. (c) Relative to the unsaved, he is in authority over them (Isa. 14:17; 2 Cor. 4:3–4; Eph. 2:2; Col. 1:13; 1 John 5:19, R.V.). (d) Relative to the saved, he comes in conflict with them (Eph. 6:11–18). (e) Relative to truth, he is a liar (John 8:44) and author of "the lie."

4. HIS CAREER. (a) Past. (1) Satan experienced a moral fall (Isa. 14:12–17; Ezek. 28:15; 1 Tim. 3:6). (2) Satan's judgment was predicted in Eden (Gen. 3:15). (3) His judgment was accomplished at the cross (John 12:31–33).

(b) Present. (1) He is reigning as a usurper today (2 Cor. 4:4; Eph. 2:2; Rev. 2:13). (2) He gains the name *accuser of the brethren* for what he is doing now (Rev. 12:10). (3) He is father in a spiritual sense to all who accept his philosophy of independence from God (John 8:44; Eph. 2:2).

(c) Future. (1) He is one day to be cast out of heaven (Rev. 12:7–12; cf. Isa. 14:12; Luke 10:18). (2) He is to be confined to the abyss for one thousand years (Rev. 20:1–3, 7). (3) When released from the abyss, he will lead armies against God (Rev. 20:8–9). (4) His final doom is the lake of fire (Rev. 20:10).

SECURITY

Security as a doctrine comprehends only the continuation of salvation for those who are saved. It should be distinguished accordingly from the doctrine of assurance. Also, it has no relation to the unregenerate person or mere professor.

While Arminians make much of Christian experience as the proof of insecurity, they do employ a few Scriptures in addition. These are subject to the following classification: a. Passages dispensationally misapplied: Ezekiel 33:7–8; Matthew 18:23–35; 24:13. b. Passages related to false teachers of the last days of the Church: 1 Timothy 4:1–3; 2 Peter 2:1–22; Jude 1:17–19. c. Passages related to no more than moral reformation: Luke 11:24–26, for example. d. Passages related to profession which is proved to be such by its fruits: John 8:31; 15:6; 1 Corinthians 15:1–2; Hebrews 3:6, 14; James 2:14–26; 2 Peter 1:10; 1 John 3:10. e. Passages containing admonition of various kinds: Matthew 25:1–13; Hebrews 6:4–9; 10:26–31. f. Passages related to the loss of rewards, walking in the dark, and chastisement: John 15:2; 1 Corinthians 3:15; 9:27; 11:27–32; Colossians 1:21–23; 1 John 1: 5–9; 5:16. g. Passages related to falling from grace: Galatians 5:4, for instance.

The positive doctrine of security is based upon twelve undertakings of God for His people, four of which are related to the Father, four to the Son, and four to the Spirit.

1. Undertakings Related to the Father: (a) the sovereign purpose or covenant of God, which is unconditional (cf. John 3:16; 5:24; 6:37), (b) the infinite power of God set free to save and keep (cf. John 10:29; Rom. 4:21; 8:31, 38–39; 14:4; Eph. 1:19–21; 3:20; Phil. 3:21; 2 Tim. 1:12; Heb. 7:25; Jude 1:24), (c) the infinite love of God (cf. Rom. 5:7–10; Eph. 1:4), and (d) the influence on the Father of the prayer of the Son of God (cf. John 17:9–12, 15, 20).

2. Undertakings Related to the Son: (a) His substitutionary death (cf. Rom. 8:1; 1 John 2:2), (b) His resurrection, securing a resurrection unto life for believers (John 3:16; 10:28; Eph. 2:6), (c) His advocacy in heaven (cf. Rom. 8:34; Heb. 9:24; 1 John 2:1–2), (d) His shepherdhood and intercession (cf. John 17:1–26; Rom. 8:34; Heb. 7:23–25).

3. Undertakings Related to the Spirit: (a) regeneration (partaking of the divine nature is entrance into that which cannot be removed; cf. John 1:13; 3:3–6; Titus 3:4–6; 1 Pet. 1:23; 2 Pet. 1:4; 1 John 3:9), (b) indwelling (He is given to abide forever and certainly by His presence the believer will be preserved; cf. John 7:37–39; Rom. 5:5; 8:9; 1 Cor. 2:12; 6:19; 1 John 2:27), (c) baptism (by which the believer is joined to Christ so as to share eternally in the New Creation glory and blessing; cf. 1 Cor. 6:17; 12:13; Gal. 3:27), and (d) sealing (Eph. 1:13–14; 4:30).

Anyone of the twelve undertakings is sufficient to guarantee eternal security to the believer. There is no true distinction indeed between salvation and safekeeping, for God offers no salvation at the present time which is not eternal. When rightly understood, the effect of this doctrine of security will be such as to promote a holy life (cf. 1 John 2:1).

SEPARATION

Separation as a doctrine represents the human side of sanctification. Compare the meaning of the related terms *consecration* and *dedication*. Separation is *from* something *unto* something, consequently in doctrine it means going from evil unto Christ (not, unto right conduct merely).

1. OLD TESTAMENT TEACHING. Two examples come to mind here. Israel as a nation was separated from Egypt by the exodus. Abraham as an individual was separated from his homeland.

2. NEW TESTAMENT TEACHING. The study of this doctrine in the New Testament may be divided as follows:

a. POSITIONAL (John 17:14, 16, 21–23; Rom. 6:1–11; Gal. 6:14–15). The believer has been positionally set apart by virtue of being in Christ.

b. EXPERIMENTAL. (1) From evil. (a) Evil things (2 Cor. 6:14–18) must be left behind by Christians. They will not be taken out from the conditions of the *cosmos* world, but kept safely therein (John 17:15). (b) Likewise the believer must avoid unholy partnerships (2 Tim. 2:20–21; 2 John 1:9–11). God cannot bless both parties in an unequal partnership. (2) Unto God. This step ought to be taken by all believers through self-dedication.

3. THE DIVINE SIDE. For His part, God encourages separation by promising special felicity to the faithful (Ps. 50:7–15; 2 Cor. 6:17–18; Heb. 12:14–17).

SIN

1. DEFINITION. Sin is that which proves unlike the character of God. Three theories should be noted as inadequate because they define evil as no more than: (a) violation of divine law, (b) finiteness, or (c) selfishness.

2. ORIGIN. Being the opposite of virtue, wickedness was ever ideally

existing wherever virtue might be found. It could have no expression, of course, until beings capable of sin were created, hence in due course the sin of angels and later of men.

3. DIVINE PERMISSION. The following statements should be considered first when pondering the question of why God ever permitted sin to be expressed.

a. There is no revelation in answer to this question so far as it relates to the angels.

b. There is indeed but little revelation on the subject relative to men. The varied suggestions listed below, however, may be studied:

(1) Sin was allowed to intrude so as to secure a race possessed of that virtue which is due to a free-will decision for good rather than evil. God knows perfectly all things, but man must learn by means of experience or revelation (Gen. 3:22). Christ accordingly is said, on the human side, to have learned by experience (Heb. 2:10; 5:8). How, then, can man come to the possession of knowledge which sees a difference between good and evil? He evidently must learn what God knows in order to apprehend. How can man know what God recognizes about sin and its character without the appearing of sin? Is not this manifestation of evil a necessity if the divine ideal which man represents is to be realized? To what lengths of sin and its consequences must humanity go, however, for this end to be realized? Must evil still be condemned by God and judged? Should it be excused on the ground that God must permit it for a purpose of His, it no longer demonstrates the infinite character of evil; hence the full expression of sin is demanded and its eternal punishment as well.

(2) Holy angels may benefit from the tragedy of sin to be observed on the earth (Eph. 3:10–11; Heb. 12:1; 1 Pet. 1:12).

(3) The claims of evil principles demand experimental testing rather than mere denunciation from God, in order for every mouth to be stopped (cf. Rom. 3:19).

(4) Divine hatred of sin must be revealed (Rom. 9:22).

(5) To display the riches of divine grace in all the ages to come (Eph. 2:7–8; cf. Luke 7:47 as an illustration), sin had to come into manifestation.

c. What, then, is the moral relation which God sustained to the permission of sin? Evidently He must allow sin to be expressed that man, His unique creation, may become what God intended him to be.

d. What, consequently, is the moral relation of man to the evil which

God has permitted? It must be to him as wicked as revelation and experience disclose it to be.

4. IMPORTANT FACTS. a. God's own character is holy and everyone of His ways perfect (1 John 1:5).

b. Sin is exceedingly sinful. It proves infinite in its evil character since it is committed against the infinite God. Note here in proof: (1) Satan's first sin and its effects, (2) Adam's first sin and its effects, and (3) the infinite sacrifice of Christ as the requirement to cure sin.

c. God's purpose is not to avoid sin, but to secure blood-cleansed sinners in the glory.

5. DIVINE JUDGMENT. God's condemnation of evil covers four universal aspects thereof: a. Imputed sin with its penalty of death, which comes directly to each individual from God because of participation in Adam's sin (Rom. 5:12–21). This type of sin comes immediately to every individual and is the only cause for the universality of physical death.

b. The sin nature. Transmitted sin and its effects as manifest in a fallen nature, spiritual death, and depravity, are received mediately from Adam through physical generation.

c. The estate under sin. Herein God, for purposes of pure grace, refuses to receive any merit from man as a contribution to his salvation (Rom. 3:9; 11:32; Gal. 3:22). This aspect of sin is limited to one age only, the present era.

d. Personal sin. This kind of evil is cured by blood sacrifice alone. Three general divisions of the theme may be observed: (1) sins done *aforetime* or before the cross and *at this time* (Rom. 3:25–26), (2) sins of the unsaved and of the saved, (3) Christ's death *for* sins and His dying *unto* sin (Rom. 6:10; 1 Pet. 3:18).

Seven ways of divine dealing with the guilt of personal sin are to be noted: (1) it is removed from the condemned as far as the east is from the west (Ps. 103:12), (2) cast behind His back (Isa. 38:17), (3) sought for and not found (Jer. 50:20), (4) cast into the depths of the sea (Mic. 7:19), (5) forgiven, including all past, present, and future conduct (Col. 2:13), (6) remembered in heaven no more (Heb. 10:17), (7) removed by cleansing (1 John 1:7).

SONSHIP

1. Several factors appear when considering the doctrine of sonship. Sonship involves an actual begetting on the part of parents, resulting in legitimate sonship and legitimate parenthood if done lawfully. Note the latitude in Old Testament use of *son*.

2. Sonship represents that into which one enters when he is saved and admitted to the family of God (John 1:12–13; 3:5; Rom. 8:16–17, 29; Gal. 3:26; 2 Pet. 1:4). This is likewise a legitimate and actual generation.

3. Sonship may apply at times to no more than the creation (Ex. 4:22; 2 Sam. 7:14; Ps. 103:13; Mal. 2:10; Luke 3:38; Acts 17:29).

4. Observe, too, the five sonships of Christ. He was Son of God from all eternity, but He became Son of man by incarnation (John 20:17).

a. Son of God. This sonship declares Him the only begotten who is the unique Son, the first-begotten from all eternity (Matt. 16:16).

b. The Son of Adam, the Son of man. The human aspect of Christ's sonship is revealed here (Matt. 8:20).

c. The Son of Abraham. This sonship relates Him to the Abrahamic covenant (Matt. 1:1).

d. The Son of David. Thus is Christ related to the Davidic covenant (Matt. 21:9).

e. The Son of Mary. This sonship relates to the incarnation (Matt. 1:25).

SOUL AND SPIRIT

The truth respecting the immaterial part of man has to do with soul and spirit.

1. Origin. Three theories may be considered here:

a. Pre-existence. Transmigration of souls lies at the bottom of this view.

b. Creation. Soul and spirit of man are created at birth according to this position.

c. Traducian. Soul and spirit are generated the same as the body, this interpretation maintains.

2. DISTINCTIONS. *Soul* connotes that in the immaterial part of man which is related to life, action, emotion. *Spirit* is that part within related to worship, communion, divine influence.

a. Often interchangeable, as in the case of σῶμα and σάρξ too, πνεῦμα and ψυχή may be used thus.

(1) The same function may be ascribed to each (cf. Mark 8:12; John 11:33 and 13:21 with Matt. 26:38 and John 12:27; 1 Cor. 16:18 and 2 Cor. 7:13 with Matt. 11:29; 2 Cor. 7:1 with 1 Pet. 2:11; 1 Thess. 5:23 with Heb. 10:39; James 5:20 with 1 Cor. 5:5 and 1 Pet. 4:5).

(2) The departed are sometimes mentioned as *soul* and sometimes as *spirit* (Gen. 35:18; 1 Kings 17:21; John 10:17; Acts 2:27, 31; 20:10; Rev. 6:9; Rev. 20:4 with Matt. 27:50; John 19:30; Acts 5:5, 10; Heb. 12:23; 1 Pet. 3:18).

(3) God is said to be *soul* (Isa. 42:1; Jer. 9:9; Amos 6:8, Hebrew; Matt. 12:18; Heb. 10:38) and *spirit* (John 4:24).

b. *Soul* and *spirit* as synonymous terms are not always interchangeable. The soul is said to be lost, for example, but not the spirit. "The Spirit itself beareth witness with our spirit," not "soul." Note likewise *psuchikos* in 1 Cor. 2:14 and *pneumatikos* in 1 Cor. 2:15 (cf. 15:44; also, Jude 1:19 where "sensual" is from ψυχικός, defined as "having not the Spirit" or πνεῦμα).

c. When no technical distinctions are in view the Bible is dichotomous, but otherwise it is trichotomous (cf. Matt. 10:28; Acts 2:31; Rom. 8:10; 1 Cor. 5:3; 6:20; 7:34; Eph. 4:4; James 2:26; 1 Pet. 2:11).

SPIRIT, THE HOLY

The Holy Spirit is a designation applied to the third (equal) Person in the Trinity. Four general divisions for the doctrine of the Spirit vary according to time periods:

(1) The Old Testament. Characterized by sovereignty, the first pe-

riod begins with the opening of Genesis. A very wide range of activity is indicated by this characterization. (2) Christ's days of ministry. Characterized as progressive, the Spirit's operations in this period may properly be so described because He was now working together with and through Christ. (3) The present age. Now He is indwelling and ministering to the Church in various ways. He became resident in the world on the Day of Pentecost. He began to form the Church at the same time and filled subsequently all who were prepared for that climactic blessing. Seven different ministries of the Spirit in the present dispensation are to be noted: restraining (2 Thess. 2:7), convicting (John 16:8), regenerating (John 3:5), indwelling or anointing (1 John 2:27), baptizing (1 Cor. 12:13), sealing (Eph. 1:13), and filling (Eph. 5:18). Several details may be recalled concerning the filling of the Spirit from Pneumatology: (a) the seven manifestations which constitute the filling, (b) the three conditions upon which one may be filled, and (c) the Old Testament type to be seen in Abraham's servant (Gen. 24:1–67). (4) The kingdom age (Acts 2:16–21; cf. Joel 2:28–32), wherein His ministry will be characterized by widespread witnessing.

SPIRITUALITY

The Greek for "he that is spiritual"—πνευματικός—is found twenty-five times in the New Testament. As related to man, spirituality represents that manner of life which is wrought *in* (not, *by*) the believer by the unhindered, indwelling Spirit of God (Rom. 8:4).

Πνευματικός is to be contrasted with ψυχικός (6 times this term has been used), meaning the natural, unregenerate, soulish (i.e., "sensual," James 3:15 or "having not the Spirit," Jude 1:19) man; and with σαρκικός (used 11 times), meaning one whose life is characterized by emphasis on the σάρξ.

A Christian may be either σαρκικός or πνευματικός, but not ψυχικός any more. From the ψυχικός state he has been saved by Christ; from the σαρκικός state he may be delivered by dependence on, and right relation to, the indwelling Spirit (cf. 1 Cor. 2:14, ψυχικός; 2:15–16, πνευματικός; 3:1–4, σαρκικός).

An illustration of these spiritual truths may be found in 1 Corinthians

1:10—15:57. 1:10—11:34 has to do with the σαρκικός, while 12:1—
15:57 deals with the πνευματικός (cf. 12:1). In chapter 12 the term
πνευματικός concerns things like (1) baptism (vss. 12–13) and (2)
gifts conveyed by the Spirit (vs. 4), which gifts are bestowed in sovereign
grace, and all equally honorable because given by God and energized by
Him.

STANDING AND STATE

The two doctrines of Christian standing and daily life or state merge
into one important truth, hence may be treated here together.

Standing, as distinguished from state or daily contact with Christ, is
a reference to Christian position—the unchangeable and perfect work of
God for the believer, while *state* refers to the changing and imperfect
condition of his soul from moment to moment. Faith secures standing,
but adherence to all the laws governing a spiritual life must secure daily
benefits for the soul.

For Scriptures relating to the believer's standing consult: John 1:12;
Romans 5:1–2; 8:17; 1 Corinthians 6:19; 12:13; Ephesians 1:3, 6,
11, 13; 2:4–6; 5:30; Colossians 2:10; Hebrews 10:19; 1 Peter 1:4–5;
2:9; 1 John 3:2; 5:1, 13; Revelation 1:5–6. Compare 1 Corinthians
1:2–9 as a reference to standing with 1:11; 3:1–4; 4:18; and 5:2,
where state is revealed; 1 Corinthians 6:11 with 6:7; 1 Corinthians
6:15a with 6:15b; 1 Corinthians 16:23 with 16:17; Colossians 1:12–
13 with 3:8–9a.

All that enters into the believer's experience after he is saved—divine
training and development—is to the end that he may be more conformed in his state to what he possesses in standing from the moment
he is saved.

STEWARDSHIP

Stewardship is a New Testament doctrine governing benevolence,
and stands in sharp contrast to the Old Testament plan of tithing while

equally differentiated from mere random giving. The doctrine of steward-ship directs a Christian in matters of receiving, earning, and spending. It is an essential outworking of the principles of grace in contrast to those of law. Grace begets a family relationship in which all that is done by God to His child or by the child to God will be motivated only by love. The elements of bargain and trade, earnings and wages, or sup-posed just dues in return for service, are excluded when love consti-tutes the sole motive. The subject may be divided then as follows:

1. THREE GREEK WORDS. Bond servants in the Grecian home might be honored with high responsibilities, but they were never free from slavery, nor did they ever possess anything of their own. Three New Testament words for servant responsibility are:

a. παιδαγωγός (Gal. 3:24–25). This was a slave charged, not with the education, but the training and discipline of children of his master.

b. ἐπίτροπος (Matt. 20:8; Luke 8:3; Gal. 4:2); compare ἐπίσκοπος (Acts 20:28), a slave charged with the oversight of all his master's estate.

c. οἰκονομία (Luke 16:2–4; cf. *dispensation* in 1 Cor. 9:17; Eph. 1:10; 3:2; Col. 1:25). Compare also, οἰκόνομος (Luke 12:42; 16:1, 3, 8; Rom. 16:23; 1 Cor. 4:1–2; Gal. 4:2; Titus 1:7; 1 Pet. 4:10), a slave charged with the pecuniary affairs of his master.

There were stewards in the Old Testament (Gen. 15:2), but these did not represent the ideal of Old Testament benevolence (Gen. 24:2; 39:4). The tither of the Old Testament, having paid his tenth, was in sole authority over the remaining nine-tenths. The child of God under grace is a bondslave dispensing his Master's goods—"Ye are not your own" and "What hast thou that thou didst not receive?" (1 Cor. 4:7; 6:19–20; 1 Pet. 1:18).

2. THE DIVINE EXAMPLE. a. THE FATHER (John 3:16; Rom. 6:23; 8:32).

b. THE SON (John 6:32–33; 10:28; 15:13; Acts 20:35; 2 Cor. 8:2). Never is the divine giving an example of tithing or partial giving.

3. NEW TESTAMENT GIVING. Christ gave unstintingly (2 Cor. 8:9). The believer should be generous in the same way (2 Cor. 9:8). Such giving should be wrought by the Spirit, not legally or out of necessity —"for God loveth a cheerful [Greek, 'hilarious'] giver" (vs. 7). This is not difficult to do when it has been accepted and realized that all money is His and that the steward but administers the financial affairs of his Master. Note the motives implied in Ephesians 4:28 and 1 John 3:17.

4. PERSONAL ASPECTS. a. ACQUIRING MONEY. (1) The human con-

sideration—"The labourer is worthy of his hire" (Luke 10:7; 1 Tim. 5:18); "Be not slothful in business" (Rom. 12:11). (2) The divine consideration—"Whatsoever ye do, do all to the glory of God" (1 Cor. 10:31). Regardless of channels or agencies through which money is received, all the benefit comes directly from Him (1 Sam. 2:7; 1 Kings 3:11–13; Phil. 4:13–19; 1 Tim. 6:6–8; Heb. 13:5).

b. DISPENSING MONEY. The Spirit directs everything, even the use of money for one's personal needs or keeping it for some future need. Be led, then, of the Spirit. It is no longer to be a question like, What can I spare? but like, What is His will? The steward must decide for himself as led of the Spirit, and not by reason of solicitation or outside influence. To be a "hilarious" giver is indeed altogether possible (2 Cor. 9:7).

5. PROBLEMS IN FINANCE. a. SECURING FUNDS. Some counsel ought to be given. (1) The principle adopted may be one of solicitation or of "silent faith." (2) If solicitors are used, have due regard for the individual donor's rights to give or withhold as led by the Spirit. (3) In the method which chooses to receive offerings danger will not be absent. (4) As God hath prospered him, the believer should be told to share (1 Cor. 16:2).

b. DISPOSING OF FUNDS. A great trust is committed to the believers who dispose of funds.

6. DANGER OF RICHES. Those who long to be rich, lusting for possessions (Luke 12:16–21; 16:19–31; 18:18–30; 1 Tim. 6:6–10; James 5:1–6), run into serious danger. Compare other motives for seeking money such as to provide for others or to provide for self when pressed with large responsibilities.

7. TRUE RICHES. Note the following Scriptures on this point: Luke 12:21; 2 Corinthians 8:9; Ephesians 1:7; 3:16; 1 Timothy 6:18; James 2:5; Revelation 3:18. The central passage on New Testament stewardship is 2 Corinthians 8 and 9.

STONE

Stone is a symbol used of Christ. It may be applied to Him in three ways, as—

1. Related to the Gentiles in final judgment (Dan. 2:34).

2. Related to the Church by reason of being (a) her Foundation (1 Cor. 3:11) and (b) Chief Cornerstone (Eph. 2:20–22; 1 Pet. 2:4–5).

3. Related to Israel (Isa. 8:14–15; Matt. 21:44; Rom. 9:32–33; 1 Cor. 1:23; 1 Pet. 2:8). Note then in general: Since Christ did not come at first in the guise of an earthly king, He became a stumbling stone to Israel; the Church is built upon Christ as her foundation and cornerstone; the Gentiles will be broken by Christ in judgment. Past, present, and future aspects of the symbolism become apparent here.

SUBSTITUTION

Substitution is not a Biblical term (cf. Trinity, incarnation, etc.), but a Biblical doctrine nonetheless.

1. OLD TESTAMENT TYPE. a. In general, every animal sacrifice offered during Old Testament times substituted for the offender. All this was accordingly a type of Christ dying in the room and stead of the sinner.

b. The sweet savor and non-sweet savor offerings of Leviticus, chapters 1–5, indicate that two accomplishments are to be noticed in Christ's substitution:

(1) The non-sweet savor oblations were, first, the sin offering and, second, the trespass offering. In these the perfection of the offering itself had to be insisted upon since Christ the Antitype is perfect in Himself, but of course, at the same time, the offering is invested with the sin of the offerer. They are called non-sweet savor offerings since God cannot look upon sin with allowance whatsoever. In fulfilling this type of sacrifice Christ cried, "My God, my God, why hast thou forsaken me?" (Matt. 27:46).

(2) Sweet savor offerings were three in number: first, the burnt offering, second, the meal offering, and third, the peace offering. In these were depicted an aspect of Christ's death which was a delight to His Father, as it has been suggested in Hebrews 9:14: He "offered himself without spot to God." Here is substitution in the sense that God requires of the believer, not merely that he should have *no sins* (as typified by the non-sweet savor offerings), but that he indeed should have done *all good*. These three offerings, consequently, suggest how the perfection of

Christ may be accepted of God for a Christian. They are sweet to God since only Christ's perfections are in view, and manifestly as such they could apply to the elect alone.

2. NEW TESTAMENT DOCTRINE. Again the same twofold conception obtains. The Scriptures state the doctrine fully.

a. Sweet savor (Phil. 2:8; Heb. 9:11–14; 10:5–7).

b. Non-sweet savor (Rom. 3:23–26; 2 Cor. 5:21; 1 Pet. 2:24; 3:18; cf. Ps. 22:1; Matt. 27:46).

3. DETERMINING PREPOSITIONS. a. The Greek ὑπέρ often has a restricted meaning, as *for another's good, in another's behalf* (cf. Luke 22:19–20; John 10:15; Rom. 5:8; Gal. 3:13; 1 Tim. 2:6; Titus 2:14; Heb. 2:9; 1 Pet. 2:21; 3:18; 4:1). Actual substitution is not included at bottom in the word, but from usage it doubtless came to be so intended anyway.

b. ἀντί. Here the thought of substitution is clear (Matt. 20:28; Rom. 12:17; 1 Thess. 5:15; 1 Tim. 6:2; Heb. 12:2, 16; 1 Pet. 3:9).

SUFFERING

The doctrine of suffering divides naturally into two sections, one for each Testament. In the Old Testament division appear two main points: the sufferings of Christ as seen in type and prophecy and the sufferings of godly men as seen in the book of Job pre-eminently.

The Book of Job, earliest of all the books of the Bible perhaps to be written, is devoted to the knotty problem of suffering. Any little child who has had the advantage of discipline can tell why bad people suffer, but to tell why a good person suffers is a far different matter. Job did not suffer because he was sinful. This contention was the wrong interpretation placed on his sufferings by the three friends, Eliphaz, Bildad, and Zophar, their contention being that he was afflicted as a punishment for evil in conduct. When Job's sufferings were completed, Jehovah refused to have anything to do with the three friends until the patriarch lovingly offered sacrifices for them. Jehovah's declaration made it plain that they had not spoken the thing which was right (Job 42:7). In the light of the obvious fact that much interpretation of Job's affliction by the commentators has been to present him as an evil person needing to be punished, one wonders who will offer sacrifices for the commentators. It should not be forgotten that, at least three times, Jehovah testified to the spiritual maturity or perfection of His servant Job (1:1, 8; 2:3). To him therefore was given the high privilege of defending the worthiness of God apart from all benefits, as against the presumptuous claims of Satan to the contrary. Beginning with chapter 32, furthermore, in the progress of all the discussion presented, a young man named Elihu interrupts to set forth his theory that suffering is educational or a discipline; by it a good man, he said, may become a better man. Apparently this was quite all that Job ever recognized in the value of his suffering (Job 42:5–6). Right here the patriarch, to be sure, very closely approaches the New Testament doctrine of suffering, which may be divided as follows:

1. The sufferings of Christ were infinite. They came from two sources. a. What Christ suffered from the Father, in which no other can share (2 Cor. 5:21). b. What Christ suffered from men, in which others may share (John 15:18–20).

2. The believer may suffer with Christ (Matt. 10:25; John 15:18–19; Acts 9:15–16; Rom. 8:16–18; 9:1–3; Phil. 2:5–11; Col. 1:24; 2 Tim. 2:11–12; 1 Pet. 4:12–16). In Romans 9:1–3 suffering with Christ is seen to be a sharing of His burden for lost men. Suffering with Him proves a natural phase of a Christian's life and experience, for he is sojourning in an enemy's land, is called to be a witness against its sin, and is summoned to labor that souls may be saved from its evil and darkness. "If the world hate you, ye know that it hated me before it hated you. If ye were of the world, the world would love his own: but because ye are not of the world, but I have chosen you out of the world, therefore the world hateth you" (John 15:18–19). To those who did not believe on Him, on the other hand, it was said: "The world cannot hate you; but me it hateth, because I testify of it, that the works thereof are evil" (John 7:7). "It is enough for the disciple that he be as his master, and the servant as his lord. If they have called the master of the house Beelzebub, how much more shall they call them of his household?" (Matt. 10:25). "As thou hast sent me into the world, even so have I also sent them into the world" (John 17:18). "Beloved, think it not strange concerning the fiery trial which is to try you, as though some strange thing happened unto you: but rejoice, inasmuch as ye are partakers of Christ's sufferings; that, when his glory shall be revealed, ye may be glad also with exceeding joy" (1 Pet. 4:12–13).

So, also, as can be learned from these passages too, suffering with Christ here is the only possible path into the reward of being glorified together with Him over there. This does not mean working to earn salvation, for salvation cannot be gained by any degree of human suffering. It is rather that effort for which the glorious crown and reward will be given to the faithful because of their copartnership with Christ. Such a truth is brought out by the following passage: "Let this mind be in you, which was also in Christ Jesus: who, being in the form of God, thought it not robbery to be equal with God: but made himself of no reputation, and took upon him the form of a servant, and was made in the likeness of men: and being found in fashion as a man, he humbled himself, and became obedient unto death, even the death of the cross. Wherefore God also hath highly exalted him, and given him a name which is above every name: that at the name of Jesus every knee should bow, of things in heaven, and things in earth, and things under the earth; and that every tongue should confess that Jesus Christ is Lord, to the glory of God the Father" (Phil. 2:5–11).

Here it is implied, as the Apostle continues, that the believer should allow the mind of Christ to be reproduced in him by the power of God (Phil. 2:13), for the seven successive steps in the path of Christ from His native place in the glory to the felon's death on the cross were doubtless reviewed by Paul in order that such steps may be admitted in the Christian's life, as one who is to be "as his Lord" even in this world. It is also implied that, simply because of close relation to Jesus in suffering, there will be an identity with Him in all His glory. "The Spirit itself beareth witness with our spirit, that we are the children of God: and if children, then heirs; heirs of God, and joint-heirs with Christ; if so be that we suffer with him, that we may be also glorified together. For I reckon that the sufferings of this present time are not worthy to be compared with the glory which shall be revealed in us" (Rom. 8:16–18). "It is a faithful saying: For if we be dead with him, we shall also live with him: if we suffer, we shall also reign with him: if we deny him, he also will deny us" (2 Tim. 2:11–12).

Suffering was the ministry to which Paul was appointed by the Lord through the disciple Ananias, when the Lord commanded him to visit Paul: "Go thy way: for he is a chosen vessel unto me, to bear my name before the Gentiles, and kings, and the children of Israel: for I will shew him how great things he must suffer for my name's sake" (Acts 9:15–16).

Hence it may be concluded that, while all the mystery of suffering is not explained and probably cannot be, it is an essential part of the believer's life and union with Christ in this world and likewise of identification with Him in the glory.

3. The believer may suffer because of having to be chastened of the Father. This may be something

a. Preventative (2 Cor. 12:1–10; cf. Rom. 8:34).

b. Corrective (Heb. 12:3–15), having as possible results both holiness and the peaceable fruit of righteousness (cf. also John 15:2; 1 Cor. 11:29–32; 1 John 5:16).

c. Educational. Christians may be enlarged in their spiritual life by suffering (John 15:2). Even though a Son, Christ learned obedience by the things which He suffered (Heb. 5:8).

TABERNACLE AND TEMPLE

1. THE TABERNACLE. Moses' tabernacle presents the most exhaustive single item of Old Testament typology. Therefore, it figures largely in New Testament interpretation (cf. Heb. 9–10) with special reference to Christ and every feature of it important. Indeed it presents inexhaustible material for study as a type.

2. THE TEMPLE. a. No typology of the temple is expounded in the New Testament other than the following intimations or usage:

(1) *Temple,* or as some would translate—*sanctuary,* is used of the temple in Jerusalem (Matt. 23:16, etc.).

(2) *Temple* is also an expression used for the believer's body (1 Cor. 3:16–17; 6:19).

(3) The local church likewise is construed as a temple of God (2 Cor. 6:16).

(4) The true Church too is so reckoned (Eph. 2:21).

b. *Hieron* is distinguished from *naos* as a word for 'temple' as grounds are distinct from a residence built on them (John 2:14–15; cf. vss. 19–21).

c. The following data should also be observed:

(1) The Mosaic tabernacle (translated *temple,* 1 Sam. 1:9; 3:3) lasted around 500 years, right up to the time of the first Jewish temple which it replaced.

(2) Solomon's temple (1 Kings 6:1–38) lasted nearly 400 years and was destroyed finally by Nebuchadnezzar.

(3) Zerubbabel's temple (Ezra 6:15–18) lasted about 500 years and then was destroyed by Antiochus Epiphanes.

(4) Herod's Temple (John 2:19) was forty-six years in building and lasted eighty-five years. It was destroyed by Titus the Roman.

(5) The temple of God (2 Thess. 2:4) is to be built by Jews of the end times and occupied by the "man of sin."

(6) The millennial temple (Ezek. 40–44) is to be set up by the returning Messiah.

(7) The heavenly temple (Rev. 21:3, 22) is nothing but the presence of God in new Jerusalem.

(8) The human body (John 2:19–21; 1 Cor. 3:16–17; 6:19) is accounted a veritable temple.

(9) The living stones (Eph. 2:19–22) which believers are accounted forms a temple.

TEMPTATION

The Greek πειράζω means *to test* or *to make trial,* and is used about fifty times in the New Testament. It may signify probing to ascertain character and virtue (Matt. 6:13; Luke 4:2; John 6:6; 2 Cor. 13:5) or to reveal weakness and evil (Gal. 6:1). God cannot be tempted in the way of evil (note the negative compound *apeirastos* of James 1:13). The general classifications of testing in the Bible are:

1. OF MEN. a. Temptations may prove a solicitation to evil (1 Cor. 7:5; 10:13; Gal. 6:1; 1 Thess. 3:5; 1 Tim. 6:9; James 1:14).

b. Testing may also come in the direction of virtue itself (Gen. 22:1; Matt. 6:13; 26:41; Gal. 4:14; Heb. 11:37; James 1:2, 12; 1 Pet. 1:6; 2 Pet. 2:9; Rev. 3:10).

2. OF GOD. Scripture has declared it twenty-seven times that God was put to the test. God is not tempted by solicitation to evil (James 1:13), but He may be tried as happened in Acts 15:10 and as Christ was tested (which it will be shown was not to find evil in Him, but to prove His virtue).

a. God the Father (Matt. 4:7; Acts 15:10).

b. God the Son (Luke 4:1–13; Heb. 2:18; 4:15; cf. John 14:30).

c. God the Spirit (Acts 5:9).

3. OF CHRIST. a. Here it is necessary to distinguish between "able not to sin" and "not able to sin." Impeccability means the latter. Christ alone among men was not able to sin.

b. Christ was theanthropic, possessing both human and divine natures. The divine nature, to be sure, is neither peccable nor temptable (James 1:13). Some teach accordingly that the impeccability was due to His omnipotence and omniscience, or having infinite power and wisdom to maintain holiness. In other words, He was not able to sin because of the divine nature.

c. His other nature, by reason of being human, was both peccable and temptable, even apart from the influence of a fallen, sin nature which He necessarily did not share with the race (Heb. 4:15); but of course what His human nature might have produced had it been alone and unsupported by the divine is only conjecture. The human element in Christ certainly was never separated from the divine; still, the divine proved ever the dominant factor in His theanthropic being. He was not a man, then, to whom the divine nature had been added. He rather was God, who took upon Him by incarnation the form of a man. He became thereafter an indivisible Person. Whatever either nature did, His whole being did. No other such person ever existed and there will never be another. Because of the presence of His divine nature with manhood, then, He is incomparable. He could not be rendered peccable by the presence of His human nature: instead He was an impeccable, theanthropic Person. Had His humanity sinned, God would have sinned. A wire may be bent when alone, but not after it is welded into an unbendable bar of steel. His humanity could not contradict or dishonor His Deity.

d. If He, nevertheless in virtue of being both divine and human, was at the same time both omnipotent and impotent, omniscient and ignorant, infinite and finite, unlimited and limited, could it not be truthfully said that He was both impeccable and peccable? As human, it may be replied, He could be impotent, ignorant, finite, and limited without compromising Deity in the matter of sin; but He could hardly be peccable without so doing. And actually He did suffer weakness, pain, hunger, thirst, weariness, and even death, but without compromising Deity in sin.

e. An impeccable person can be tempted in the same sense that an unconquerable city may be attacked. Christ was tempted, but through it only proved to everyone His impeccability. Being God, after all, He *could not* sin (cf. John 14:30).

f. If peccable on earth, He would be peccable also in heaven (Heb. 13:8). How well, then, would the Christian's standing and security be grounded?

THRONE

The word *throne* comes from θρόνος (used fifty times) and from βῆμα (appearing once, Acts 12:21). For the other passages with βῆμα see Matthew 27:19; John 19:13; Acts 18:12, 16–17; 25:6, 10, 17; Romans 14:10; 2 Corinthians 5:10, all of which render it "judgment seat." Compare κριτήριον in James 2:6—"tribunal of judgment."

The various thrones of Scripture to be distinguished are those—

1. OF GOD (Matt. 5:34; Acts 7:49; Rev. 4:2). His government is like a mountain eminence (Isa. 2:2). There Christ is seated for the present (Heb. 8:1; Rev. 3:21).

2. OF DAVID (2 Sam. 7:16; Ps. 89:36; Luke 1:32). This is the earthly throne to which Christ has fallen heir and on which He will yet be seated (Ps. 2:6). Note its literal, earthly, and eternal character in Scripture. A throne of glory it is for Him (Matt. 19:28; 25:31). The Church will be seated with Christ on His throne (Rev. 3:21).

3. OF CHRISTIAN APPRAISAL. This judgment seat of Christ (Rom. 14:10; 1 Cor. 3:9–15; 2 Cor. 5:10) is needed to appraise the service which believers have rendered.

4. OF FINAL JUDGMENT (Rev. 20:11–15).

5. OF SATAN (Rev. 2:13—'seat' renders θρόνος; cf. Matt. 12:26; Col. 1:16). Note that Satan has an earthly throne.

6. OF THE TWELVE APOSTLES (Luke 22:30).

7. OF THE NATIONS (Luke 1:52).

8. OF GRACE (Heb. 4:16).

9. OF THE CHURCH (Rev. 4:4).

TITHING
(See STEWARDSHIP)

Tithing, or giving to God a tenth, is one practice antedating the law and still to this day a common usage.

1. BEFORE MOSES (Gen. 14:17–20; cf. Heb. 7:1–10).

2. IN THE LAW. The tithe became, in the main, God's method of support for the Levites and priests. Tradition added much more to the law of tithing than it required originally (Matt. 23:23; Luke 11:42).

3. IN CONTRAST TO GRACE. Under grace, benevolence will function "not of necessity" or because of any law requirement; rather does the Christian make his contribution "as he purposeth in his heart" (2 Cor. 9:7) and "as God hath prospered" (1 Cor. 16:2). Not all giving which avoids the mere tithe, however, is grace giving.

TONGUES

The doctrine of languages or tongues has several divisions, as follows:

1. BABEL. The first, universal language of man was confounded at Babel, from which event human languages sprang (Gen. 11:1–9). As another miraculous demonstration of His presence and power much later, God bestowed the gift of tongues, which appeared in the early church as recorded by the New Testament. The gift of tongues, however, the great Apostle predicted would cease (1 Cor. 13:8; cf. Mark 16:17; Acts 10:44–46; 11:15; 19:6; 1 Cor. 12–14).

2. REGULATIONS FOR GLOSSOLALIA. The divine directions given for the use of tongues are seven:

a. Tongues must be addressed to God (1 Cor. 14:2, 28).

b. The utterance must be prayer (1 Cor. 14:14).

c. The element of thanksgiving must be present (1 Cor. 14:15–17).

d. Tongues can be understood only by interpretation (1 Cor. 14:2, 5–6).

e. One must interpret—the complementary gift—if there is to be any use of the tongues gift (1 Cor. 14:28).

f. Only two at most at one service may exercise the gift (1 Cor. 14:27).

g. Women are to keep silent in church (1 Cor. 14:34).

During the history of the church there have been sporadic outbursts of a type of movement purporting to speak in tongues. This form of supernatural phenomena has sometimes been employed in order to establish serious error or false doctrine. It is so used by some, doubtless, at the present time.

3. PENTECOST. At Pentecost God had assembled Jews from all countries under heaven, for them to hear the gospel in their own tongue. The implication is that they returned to their own countries, bearing the message heard, thus obviating the long delay which a missionary's experience in learning the language of the people to whom he goes would have caused. It was in the power of God to reverse the experience of Babel, which He evidently did for a time in Jerusalem this day. Tongue gifts appeared in connection with the giving of the gospel to the Jews on Pentecost at Jerusalem (Acts 2:1-21), later at Samaria (Acts 8:14-17), and finally in giving the message to the Gentiles at Cornelius' house (Acts 10:44-48).

4. OF ANGELS. The Apostle speaks of the tongues of angels, of which, naturally, nothing can be known (1 Cor. 13:1).

TRANSFIGURATION

The word for *transfigure*—μεταμορφόομαι—is used both of Christ and Christians.

1. OF CHRIST. Jesus Christ's transfiguration is reported in each Synoptic Gospel (Matt. 17:1-13; Mark 9:2-13; Luke 9:28-36). Related to the prophetic office of Christ as it is, every report of this transfiguring records the command from heaven, "Hear ye him."

2. ITS MEANING. The record of Christ's transfiguration is preceded every time by the words: "There be some standing here, which shall not taste of death, till they see the Son of man coming in his kingdom"

(Matt. 16:28). Note as agreeable to this word Peter's interpretation of the meaning of the transfiguration episode (2 Peter 1:16–18). The elements of the Messianic kingdom were surely present for the transfiguration: (a) a glorified Christ, (b) glorified saints like Moses and Elijah—one having left the earth by death and one by the process of translation earlier, (c) Jews still on the earth but enjoying all the light of the glory—as seen in the three disciples.

3. ITS PURPOSE. As the kingdom preaching was coming to its end because of the rejection and imminent death of the King, it became necessary to encourage the disciples in the expectation that the Messianic kingdom would yet be set up according to covenant promise, later if not at once. The transfiguration bore out this certainty.

4. OF THE SAINTS. The word *transfigure* is used twice as an appeal to believers (Rom. 12:2; 2 Cor. 3:18). How is it to be distinguished from the word "transform"? A thing may be transformed by a light shining on it from without, of course, but a transfiguration is the shining forth of a light from within. The first appeal to believers, then, is for them to let the light of the divine nature shine forth unhindered (see Christology) from within, now that they have become partakers thereof. In the 2 Corinthians passage is revealed the nature of the divinely wrought change being enjoined.

TRIBULATION

The Greek for *tribulation*—θλῖψις—is used forty-two times in the New Testament. It has been translated by the words *tribulation* (21 times), *affliction* (17 times), *anguish* (1 time), *burden* (1 time), and *trouble* (3 times). There are two common meanings for the term: (1) trial of any kind and (2) the (great) tribulation. The tribulation indeed is one of the major highways of prophecy, which may be traced through Scripture as follows: Deuteronomy 4:29–30; Jeremiah 30:4–7; Daniel 12:1; Matthew 24:9–26; 2 Thessalonians 2:1–12; Revelation 3:10; 6:1—19:6. See also Psalm 2:5; Isaiah 2:10–22; 13:9–16; 24:21–23; 26:20–21; 34:1–17; 43:1–6; 49:15–24; Jeremiah 25:29–38; Ezekiel 30:3; Amos 5:18–20; Obadiah 1:15–21; Zephaniah 1:7–18; Zechariah 12:1–14; 14:1–4; Malachi 4:1–4.

The great tribulation is the period known as Daniel's seventieth week (Dan. 9:24–27), the order of events being the same in Daniel as in Matthew 24 and in 2 Thessalonians 2. The final week or heptad is seven years in duration, which is proved by the fact that it was exactly 69 ×7 years between the order to rebuild Jerusalem and the cutting off of Messiah. This remaining seventieth "week" of years belongs to Israel's age and will be characterized by the same general conditions as obtained in the past Jewish age. The time is to be shortened a little (Matt. 24:22). It is known as "the time of Jacob's trouble" (Jer. 30: 4–7) out of which Israel will be saved.

The great tribulation is the time of God's unavoidable judgments on a Christ-rejecting world (Ps. 2:5). It is characterized by:

1. The removal of the Holy Spirit together with the Church from the earth (2 Thess. 2:7).

2. The casting of Satan into, thus restricting him to, the earth (Rev. 12:9–12).

3. The development of sin which was hitherto restrained (2 Thess. 2:11).

4. The rule of the man of sin (John 5:43).

5. Termination by the second coming of Christ, the battle of Armageddon, and the smiting stone of Daniel 2.

TRINITY

The word *Trinity* is not a Bible term, though unquestionably a Bible truth. As a doctrine it divides thus:

1. IN THE OLD TESTAMENT. The emphasis of the Old Testament is upon divine unity. But even there a divine plurality may be seen in the meaning of *Elohim* (cf. Deut. 6:4), a plurality of persons and unity of essence.

2. IN THE NEW TESTAMENT. The New Testament lays its emphasis upon the individual Persons of the Trinity and their separate responsibilities for the purposes of redemption, yet here too there are occasional references to divine oneness of essence (cf. Matt. 28:19).

TYPES

The word *type* may be defined as "a divinely purposed illustration of some truth" (*Scofield Reference Bible*, p. 4), accordingly a prophetic act, institution, person, thing, or ceremonial. The words for *type* are:

1. τύπος, meaning "a blow, or the imprint thus made which may serve as a pattern." Note the various translations of this word root:

a. *Ensample* (1 Cor. 10:11; Phil. 3:17; 1 Thess. 1:7; 2 Thess. 3:9; 1 Pet. 5:3).

b. *Example* (1 Cor. 10:6; 1 Tim. 4:12; Heb. 8:5).

c. *Figure* (Acts 7:43; Rom. 5:14).

d. *Pattern* (Titus 2:7).

e. *Print* (of the nails, John 20:25).

2. ὑπόδειγμα. This word has the same resultant meaning in general as τύπος (John 13:15; Heb. 4:11; 8:5; 9:23; James 5:10; 2 Pet. 2:6).

3. DOCTRINAL IMPORT. (a) The great field of truth involved in types is full of instruction. (b) There must, however, be careful recognition of what makes something a true type. Only that so treated in the Bible can be received as typical beyond all question. Some things only illustrate truth, but do not foreshadow or serve as a type. Compare all that is mere congruity, analogy, or a parallel of truth.

4. VARIOUS CLASSIFICATIONS. A type may be:

a. A person (Rom. 5:14), as Adam, Melchizedek, Abraham, Sarah, Ishmael, Isaac, Moses, Joshua, David, Solomon.

b. An event (1 Cor. 10:11), as the preservation of Noah and his sons, redemption from Egypt, the Passover memorial, the exodus, the passage through the Red Sea, the finding of manna, securing the water drawn from the rock, lifting up the brazen serpent, and all the sacrifices blessed of God.

c. A thing of some kind (Heb. 10:20), as the tabernacle, the laver, the lamb of sacrifice, Jordan, a city like Babylon, or a nation like Egypt.

d. An institution (Heb. 9:11), as the Sabbath, animal sacrifice, Melchizedek priesthood, David's kingdom.

e. A ceremonial (1 Cor. 5:7), like all Old Testament appointments for the service of God.

5. IMPORTANT DISTINCTIONS. Careful distinctions must be drawn

so as to avoid mere flights of fancy. a. Types are found in the Old Testament, and there mostly in the Pentateuch; they cover the wide range of truth and subjects named above.

b. Strictly speaking, a type is that which has been so indicated in the Bible. 1 Corinthians 10:11, however, is of great import in this connection.

c. Types are one of three binding factors to link together the two Testaments: (1) types, (2) prophecies, and (3) continuity of truth.

d. Types are predictions because they foreshadow what was future at the time of the Old Testament.

e. Types are as much inspired as any of the Scriptures and are intended of God for either admonition or instruction.

f. Christ is the outstanding antitype in all typology.

WILL

Will is that faculty in a rational, conscious being by which he has power to choose a course of action and continue in it. Consideration should be given to two general divisions of the Bible doctrine.

1. OF GOD. The will of God is either what may be called directive or permissive.

a. Directive. This form of the divine will includes within its scope the doctrines of decree, election, predestination, and foreordination.

b. Permissive. In the permissive will of God He is seen allowing man his own choice of that which might be a mere second-best or even of what might be evil ways.

God's will is the standard with which to measure all that is esteemed right in motive, design, and execution. Man's highest end is realized when he conforms to God's will. Even Christ came not to do His own will, but only the will of the Father. There is nothing higher for man than to find and do the will of God. Heaven always has a specific purpose for the bringing of each person into the world, and that purpose comprehends every moment of life.

2. OF MAN. The major distinction between Calvinistic and Arminian systems of theology appears in their diverse understanding of man's will.

a. The will of man is but an instrument created by God and designed by Him for the execution of His own ends. The human will, accordingly, serves the divine purpose rather than hinders it.

b. The will is looked upon at times, on the human side, as sovereign and wholly accountable (John 7:17; cf. 6:44). For the exercise of the human will in the matter of salvation note Revelation 22:11, and for the use of the will in dedication, Romans 6:13. The will then is subject to various influences.

c. On the divine side, man's power to will is looked upon as under superior control, with the saved under the sovereign control of God (Phil. 2:13) and the unsaved under like control of Satan (Eph. 2:2).

3. GENERAL FACTS. Three facts of a general nature ought to be observed. a. There is little reference to the will of angels outside Satan (cf. Jude 1:6, 9).

b. Satan's initial sin is well summarized under five "I will's" (Isa. 14:13-14).

c. There are seven "I will's" of Jehovah in the Abrahamic covenant (Gen. 17:1-8), as elsewhere in the pledges made by God.

WOMAN

The origin of woman is given in Genesis 1:27 and 2:21-22, the reason for her creation in Genesis 2:18.

1. RELATION TO MAN. Woman is included in the doctrine of man in the generic sense, and furthermore both sinned in Adam's fall. She is not to be considered as less important than man, but only as a different form of human creation from him.

2. IN THE OLD TESTAMENT. Israel's women were honored above those of other nations, as may be learned from the commandment "Honour thy . . . mother." Considerable significance attaches to the great characters and names of Old Testament women like Sarah, Rebekah, Rachel, Miriam, Deborah, Hannah, Esther, Ruth.

3. IN THE NEW TESTAMENT. According to the New Testament the woman's place in relation to man calls for precise adjustment and recognition. Woman, as her position has been defined by the Scriptures, is in

great peril when out of her sphere, which never becomes that of leadership. Some outstanding New Testament women are: Elizabeth, Mary the mother of Christ, the other Marys, Lydia, Priscilla, etc.

WORLD

The English terminology *world* is a translation of four widely differing ideas in the Greek original:

1. Κόσμος, meaning order and arrangement as in contrast to chaos (cf. how creation was perfect once but ere long became chaotic, Isa. 24:1; Jer. 4:23). Though the Septuagint uses κόσμος for each of several Hebrew words, there is nothing strictly equivalent to the Greek term. It seems to be a new conception for world in the apostolic Word, employed with new force. It is conceived of now as separate from God, though orderly by way of arrangement.

a. Use in Peter. The Apostle Peter refers to the world in its past, present, and future, using this terminology: (1) "the world that then was" (2 Pet. 3:5-6) before the flood, (2) "the heavens and the earth, which are now" (2 Pet. 3:7), (3) "new heavens and a new earth" (2 Pet. 3:13; cf. Isa. 64:22; 65:17; Rev. 21:1).

b. General Meaning. At least three general senses attach to this expression. (1) The material earth as a creation of God (Acts 17:24). (2) The inhabitants of the world. These are the ones whom God loved and for whom Christ died (John 3:16). (3) The institutions of men as set up independent of God and headed by Satan, that is, the satanic system organized upon principles of self, greed, armament, and commercialism. This is the world that God does not love and the believer is warned against loving (1 John 2:15-17). The word *kosmos* is used 176 times in all.

2. Οἰκουμένη, meaning the inhabited world, in contrast to that part of the globe which is uninhabited or barbarian. Here accordingly is the field of prophetic meaning and kingdom preaching (Matt. 24:14). The word is used fifteen times.

3. Αἰών (Matt. 12:32; 13:22, 39-40, 49; 21:19; 24:3; 28:20), meaning an age or period of time. This term originally indicated the

span of man's life on the earth, later on any period of time, and even unbounded time, whether past or future. Its first New Testament connotation is of a definite period designed, adjusted, and executed by God, i.e., a dispensation (Heb. 11:3). God framed the ages (cf. Heb. 1:2). Note also αἰωνίοις as used in the phrases "since the world began" (Rom. 16:25) and "before the world began" (2 Tim. 1:9; Titus 1:2). This third expression for *world* is used about 100 times.

4. Γῆ, meaning earth or land (Matt. 6:10; 9:6; Mark 2:10; Luke 2:14), should also be considered. This term is used many times.

ZION

Zion was the ancient Jebusite stronghold in Jerusalem (see Jerusalem). It has a threefold significance in the Bible, including this original significance.

1. DAVID'S CITY. In the Old Testament the use of the term has reference to Israel and Jerusalem, the city of David (1 Chron. 11:5; Ps. 2:6; Isa. 2:3).

2. HEAVENLY CITY. The New Testament use has reference not only again to Israel (Rom. 11:26–27) but also to the new Jerusalem (Heb. 12:22–24). Into the latter the Church will be received.

3. MILLENNIAL CITY. The word as used in the following Scriptures has reference to the capital of the future kingdom age: Isaiah 1:27; 2:3; 4:1–6; Joel 3:16; Zechariah 1:16–17; 8:3–8; Romans 11:26.

LEWIS SPERRY CHAFER

SYSTEMATIC THEOLOGY

Volume Eight

BIOGRAPHICAL SKETCH & INDEXES

by

LEWIS SPERRY CHAFER
D.D., LITT.D., TH.D.

Late President and Professor of Systematic Theology
Dallas Theological Seminary

kregel PUBLICATIONS
Grand Rapids, MI 49501

Systematic Theology (eight volumes in four), by Lewis Sperry Chafer, © 1993 by Kregel Publications, a division of Kregel, Inc., P.O. Box 2607, Grand Rapids, Michigan 49501, by special permission of Dallas Theological Seminary. All rights reserved.

Cover Design: Alan G. Hartman

Library of Congress Cataloging-in-Publication Data

Chafer, Lewis Sperry, 1871-1952.
  [Systematic Theology]
  Chafer systematic theology / by Lewis Sperry Chafer.
     p.   cm.
  Originally published: Systematic theology. Dallas, TX.: Dallas Seminary Press, 1947-1948.
  Includes bibliographical references and indexes.
  Contents: v. 1   Prologomena, Bibliology, Theology Proper, Angelology, Anthropology and Harmatiology
             v. 2   Soteriology, Ecclesiology and Eschatology
             v. 3   Christology and Pneumatology
             v. 4   Doctrinal summarization, Biographical sketch and indexes
   1. Theology, Doctrinal. I. Title. II. Title: Systematic theology
BT75.C28   1993   230'.044—dc20   92-34956
                                                   CIP

ISBN 0-8254-2340-6 (deluxe hardback)

         1 2 3 4 5 Printing/Year 97 96 95 94 93

ACKNOWLEDGMENT

Grateful appreciation is extended for permission to use quotations from books copyrighted by the publishers and authors listed below:

D. Appleton-Century Company, Inc.—*The New Century Dictionary*.

John W. Bradbury—contribution written especially for this work.

Encyclopaedia Britannica, Inc.—*Encyclopaedia Britannica*.

Dr. E. Schuyler English—*Studies in the Gospel according to Matthew*.

Wm. B. Eerdmans Publishing Co.—*International Standard Bible Encyclopaedia*.

Funk & Wagnalls Co.—*New Standard Dictionary*.

Dr. Norman B. Harrison, The Harrison Service—*His Love*.

Loizeaux Brothers, Inc.—*Notes on Genesis*, by C. H. Mackintosh; *Notes on Exodus*, by C. H. Mackintosh; *Notes on Leviticus*, by C. H. Mackintosh; *Synopsis of the Books of the Bible*, by J. N. Darby; *Lectures on Daniel*, by H. A. Ironside; *Lectures on Revelation*, by H. A. Ironside; *Notes on Proverbs*, by H. A. Ironside; *Notes on the Minor Prophets*, by H. A. Ironside.

Moody Press—*Isaac and Rebekah*, by George E. Guille; *Scofield Correspondence Course*.

Dr. William R. Newell—*Romans Verse by Verse*.

Erling C. Olsen—*Meditations in the Psalms, Walks with Our Lord through John's Gospel*.

Our Hope—*Angels of God*, by A. C. Gaebelein; *Studies in Zechariah*, by A. C. Gaebelein; *Satan, His Person, His Work and His Destiny*, by F. C. Jennings; *Imperialism and Christ*, by Ford C. Ottman; *Unfolding the Ages*, by Ford C. Ottman.

Oxford University Press—*Biblical Doctrines*, by B. B. Warfield; *Christology and Criticism*, by B. B. Warfield; *Revelation and Inspiration*, by B. B. Warfield; *Studies in Theology*, by B. B. Warfield.

Fleming H. Revell Co.—*Christian Worker's Commentary*, by James M. Gray.

Charles Scribner's Sons—*The Sermon on the Mount*, by Martin Dibelius.

iv   ACKNOWLEDGMENT

The Sunday School Times Co.—*The Sunday School Times.*

Dr. John F. Walvoord—*Outline of Christology; The Doctrine of the Holy Spirit.*

Zondervan Publishing House—*The Critical and Explanatory Commentary,* by Jamieson, Fausset & Brown.

In the preparation of the indexes, the author was assisted by Mr. John A. Witmer, A.M., Th. M.

TABLE OF CONTENTS

BIOGRAPHICAL SKETCH

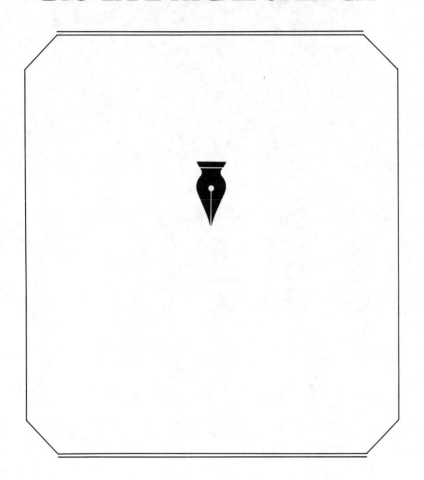

BIOGRAPHICAL SKETCH OF THE AUTHOR

By

C. F. LINCOLN, A.M., Th.D.

Treasurer and Professor of English Bible
Dallas Theological Seminary

The Reverend Lewis Sperry Chafer, D.D., Litt.D., was born at Rock Creek, Ashtabula County, Ohio, on February 27, 1871. He was reared in a devout Christian home, his immediate ancestors having been faithful ministers of the gospel.

His father, the Reverend Thomas Franklin Chafer, was graduated during the presidency of Jacob Tuckerman from Farmer's College, College Hill, Cincinnati, and from Auburn Theological Seminary with the class of 1864. He was born in the year 1829 and died during the fifty-third year of his life, in 1882, when Dr. Chafer was eleven years of age. William Chafer, the father of Thomas Franklin Chafer, and the paternal grandfather of Dr. Chafer, was born in York, England, and moved to the United States in the year 1837, when his son Thomas was eight years of age. He took up residence in the state of Kentucky and was long dedicated to farming in that section of the country.

Dr. Chafer's mother was Lois Lomira Sperry. She was born at Rock Creek, Ohio, on June 3, 1836, and died in the fall of the year 1915 at the age of seventy-nine when Dr. Chafer was forty-four years of age. Her father, Asa Sperry, was a licensed Welsh Wesleyan preacher, though he was a harness-maker by trade. Ann Sperry, of Irish descent, was the maternal grandmother of Dr. Chafer.

As a boy, Dr. Chafer attended the public schools of Rock Creek until he attained the age of twelve years. After that, from 1885 to 1888, he attended New Lyme Institute of New Lyme, Ohio. There was an orchestra or choral society at that institution and as a young student he was there first introduced to the serious study of music, in which art he became remarkably proficient. Later, when his widowed mother had removed to Oberlin, Ohio, for the education of her three children, as a young man Dr. Chafer attended Oberlin College and Conserv-

3

atory of Music from 1889 to 1892. It was at Oberlin that Dr. Chafer met Ella Loraine Case, a devoted student of music and a deeply spiritual-minded young lady who later became his beloved wife and faithful lifelong companion and coworker. At this time Dr. Chafer began travelling as a gospel singer with Evangelist Arthur T. Reed. This ministry continued for a period of about seven years, though during that time he was engaged to direct gospel music for other evangelists also. On April 22, 1896, Dr. Chafer was united in marriage to Miss Case whose home was in Ellington, Chautauqua County, New York. She at once took an active part in the ministry to which her husband was devoted, laboring with him as soloist and accompanist at the piano; in both of these services she was exceptionally gifted and thoroughly trained. In 1897, the year following his marriage, Dr. Chafer began his service as an evangelist, ministering in this work until the year 1914 both by preaching and singing. In the year 1900 Dr. Chafer was ordained to the gospel ministry by a Council of Congregational Ministers in the First Congregational Church of Buffalo. In 1903, due to his having taken up residence in East Northfield, Massachusetts, his ministerial relationship was removed to the Presbytery of Troy, New York. At that time Dr. C. I. Scofield was pastor of the Congregational Church of Northfield, which had been organized by D. L. Moody, and there was cemented between the two men a closeness of fellowship in the gospel that grew into an intimate companionship in the teaching ministry which lasted until Dr. Scofield's death in 1921. When Dr. Chafer moved to East Northfield he began at once his service as music leader, along with Ira Sankey, D. B. Towner, George Stebbins, and others, in the great Moody Summer Bible Conferences. Mrs. Chafer was official organist for the conferences. In the winter Dr. Chafer travelled out of Northfield in an ever widening evangelistic ministry, and his service in the Summer Conferences brought him into close touch with most of the great conservative Bible teachers of that period. In the year 1906 Dr. Chafer moved his ministerial relationship from the Troy Presbytery to that of the Orange Presbytery of North Carolina, and in the year 1916 he himself took up residence in East Orange, New Jersey. Some time after this, after a remarkable spiritual experience in the study of Dr. Scofield in Dallas, Texas, he definitely dedicated his life to an exacting study of the Bible. After an exceedingly fruitful Bible-teaching ministry which took him on repeated occasions to nearly every state in the union, Dr. Chafer removed to Dallas, Texas, in the year 1922, for the principal purpose of establishing the Dallas Theological Seminary. In the year 1924 the school was founded with the cooperation and advice of Dr. A. B. Winchester of Toronto, and Dr. W. H. Griffith Thomas of Philadelphia. Dr. Chafer was President of the Seminary from its beginning until the time of his death.

Dr. Chafer travelled in the ministry of Bible teaching in England, Scotland, Ireland, Belgium, and elsewhere. He always had a great missionary vision and served on various mission boards and visited mission fields in Europe, Mexico, and all of Central America where his counsel and ministry of Bible teaching and evangelistic service were of wonderful benefit to the missionaries and to the national churches.

Dr. Chafer was the author of many pamphlets and magazine articles and of the following books on Bible themes and doctrines: *Satan,* 1909; *True Evangelism,* 1911; *The Kingdom in History and Prophecy,* 1915; *Salvation,* 1916; *He That Is Spiritual,* 1918; *Grace,* 1922; *Major Bible Themes,* 1926; and *The Ephesian Letter,* 1935. These books have been before the Christian public in all English-speaking lands for many years and are still in constant and almost undiminished demand. Multiplied thousands have been blessed in spirit, instructed in the grace of God, and confirmed in the faith and in the assurance of salvation by the clear and forceful teaching set down by his able pen. A number of his books have been, or are being, translated on mission fields into several languages; thus a fruitful world-wide ministry has resulted.

From 1940 to 1952 Dr. Chafer was editor of *Bibliotheca Sacra,* the oldest theological quarterly in America.

The discipline and training which Dr. Chafer received as a background for the writing of this extensive work on Systematic Theology was that of many years of faithful study. In his early years he was known among Bible teachers as especially given to doctrine and was invited on several occasions to become teacher of Bible doctrine in leading institutes of this country.

When he undertook the professorship of Systematic Theology in the Seminary in Dallas, Texas, he at once gave himself to ceaseless study and reading in that division of ministerial training. He secured and became familiar with an exceedingly large library on Systematic Theology. The exercise of teaching this vast field of truth for many years required him to answer practically every question which students of serious mind could ask.

Dr. Chafer himself said that "the very fact that I did not study a prescribed course in theology made it possible for me to approach the subject with an unprejudiced mind and to be concerned only with what the Bible actually teaches." This independent research has resulted in this work which is unabridged, Calvinistic, premillennial, and dispensational.

In fulfillment of Ephesians 4:8, 11, God gave a beloved "teacher" unto the Church. We are sure that through this treatise on Theology God's purpose in such a gift, as expressed in verses 12–16, will be further fulfilled to the people of God for immense blessing in "the body of Christ."

———————

Dr. Chafer suffered a heart attack in California in the year 1935. Although that stroke was severe, by observing a careful regimen in his convalescence he recovered and gained strength for an active ministry until 1945 when again he was stricken in California. From this attack he did not have a full recovery, but after a period of time he was able to continue his classroom and platform ministry. A third attack in 1948 further weakened him, but he still continued his public work in a limited way until almost the close of his life.

In May, 1952, after his classes were finished at the Seminary he covered the cities in Pennsylvania known as the Harrisburg Circuit of Bible conferences and spoke at commencement and baccalaureate services at Grace Theological Seminary and Columbia Bible College. It seemed to us who were close to him that this pressing schedule with its nighttime train transfers and closely dated speaking engagements overtaxed his scant strength and carried him beyond the point of possible return to his normal ministry.

However, Dr. Chafer had often manifested that he desired to remain active in the Lord's work until the end. In June, 1952, following his custom in the summer, travelling alone he went to California to visit with friends and to minister with alumni of the Seminary. He reached Seattle and there, after an illness of about eight weeks, he died peacefully on August 22 in the home of his very dear friends, Mr. and Mrs. Robert O. Fleming. A long life of service had come to a close and the servant had gone into the presence of his waiting Lord.

Dallas, November 1953

TABLES OF CONTENTS

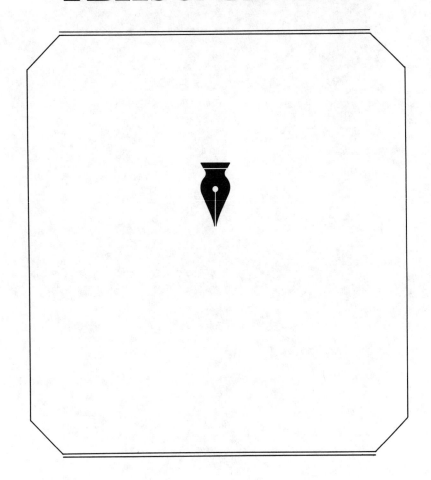

TABLE OF CONTENTS: VOLUME I

PROLEGOMENA

BIBLIOLOGY

TABLE OF CONTENTS: VOLUME II

ANGELOLOGY

ANTHROPOLOGY

TABLE OF CONTENTS: VOLUME III

SOTERIOLOGY

DIVINE ELECTION

TABLE OF CONTENTS: VOLUME IV

ECCLESIOLOGY

THE CHURCH AS AN ORGANISM

ESCHATOLOGY

GENERAL FEATURES OF ESCHATOLOGY

TABLE OF CONTENTS: VOLUME V

CHRISTOLOGY

TABLE OF CONTENTS: VOLUME VI

PNEUMATOLOGY

TABLE OF CONTENTS: VOLUME VII

DOCTRINAL SUMMARIZATION

AUTHOR INDEX

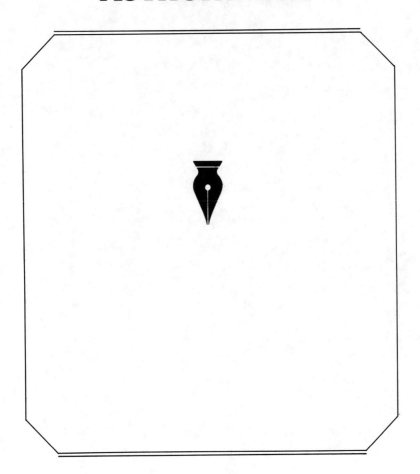

AUTHOR INDEX

A

Abbott, E. A.:
IV, 370—cited by Thiessen.

Alexander, A. B. D., "Logos," International Standard Bible Encyclopaedia; Howard-Severance Co., Chicago, 1915:
III, 13; V, 10.

Alexander, W. Lindsay, A System of Biblical Theology; T. & T. Clark, Edinburgh, 1888:
I, 6, 261, 267 f., 272, 284—citation of Calvin; I, 284 f.—citation of Swift; I, 285—citation of Pye Smith; I, 285—citation of Nicene Creed; I, 285—citation of Athanasian Creed; I, 285 f., 323—citation of Socinus; II, 215 f., 216—citation of Milton; II, 221, 221 f.—citations of Aristotle, Plutarch, Kant, Hahn; III, 13 ff., 68–72, 195, 198—citation of Owen; III, 199—citation of Owen; III, 212.

Alford, Henry, New Testament for English Readers; Lee and Shepard, Boston, 1872:
I, xii, 254 f.; II, 3, 69, 70, 72—citation of Chrysostom; II, 82 f.; III, 114 f.—citation of Delitzsch; III, 248, 325—citation of Chrysostom; III, 325 f.—citation of De Wette; IV, 362—cited by Thiessen; IV, 369 f.—cited by Thiessen; V, 10, 11, 27, 34 f., 60, 127, 196, 200 f., 210, 221 f., 271 f.; VI, 43, 143, 230.

Anderson, Sir Robert, The Coming Prince, 2nd ed.; Pickering & Inglis, London, 1909:
IV, 128, 130, 289, 338—cited by Thiessen.

Angus-Green, Cyclopedic Handbook of the Bible:
VII, 204 (twice), 205 (twice)—cited by Rollin T. Chafer.

Anselm, Cur Deus Homo:
III, 137—cited by Dale.

Aristotle:
I, 291—cited by Cooke; II, 221 f.—cited by Alexander; II, 294 f.

Atwood, John M., "Universalist Church," Encyclopædia Britannica, 14th ed., New York:
IV, 422.

Auberlen, C. A.:
II, 185—cited by Laidlaw; IV, 278—cited by Peters; V, 316—cited by Peters.

Augustine:
I, 6—cited by Shedd; I, 229—cited by Shedd; I, 282—cited by Harris; I, 284
—cited by Scofield; II, 29—cited by Gerhart; II, 31 f.—cited by Gerhart;
II, 212 f.; III, 57—cited by Shedd.

B

Barclay, Robert, Apology:
I, 13.

Bardesanes:
IV, 121.

Barnabas:
IV, 121.

Barnes, Albert:
IV, 262—cited by Peters; V, 374—cited by Peters.

Baur:
III, 145 f.—cited by Miley.

Bavinck, Herman, "The Fall," International Standard Bible Encyclopaedia;
Howard-Severance Co., Chicago, 1915:
VII, 149 f.

Baxter, Richard:
I, 289—cited by Watson.

Beecher, Henry Ward:
V, 287—cited by Peters.

Bengel:
IV, 278—cited by Brookes, in turn by Peters.

Besser:
II, 308—cited by Riddle.

Binney, Thomas:
III, 365 f.

Boettner, Loraine, The Inspiration of the Scriptures:
VI, 58—cited by Walvoord.

Bowne:
I, 150 f.—cited by Miley; I, 201 f.—cited by Miley.

C

Calvin, John:

I, 131—cited by Strong; I, 284—cited by Alexander; II, 283—cited by Shedd; III, 69—cited by Alexander; IV, 278—cited by Peters; IV, 279—cited by Haldeman; VI, 115—cited by Walvoord.

Carlyle, Thomas:

I, 176—cited by Strong; II, 280—cited by Shedd.

Carson, Alexander:

I, 83—cited by Manly.

Carver, William Owen, "Atonement," International Standard Bible Encyclopaedia; Howard-Severance Co., Chicago, 1915:

VII, 27.

Castenove:

I, 32—cited by Rogers.

Cellerier, J. E.:

VII, 204 (twice), 205—cited by Rollin T. Chafer.

Chafer, Rollin Thomas, The Science of Biblical Hermeneutics; Bibliotheca Sacra, Dallas, 1938:

V, 349 f.; VII, 203 ff.

Chalmers, Thomas, Natural Theology:

I, 182.

——, Institutes of Theology, Thomas Constable & Co., Edinburgh, 1852:

II, 221.

Channing, William Ellery:

I, 274; III, 62 f.—cited by Stock.

Charles:

IV, 362—cited by Thiessen.

Charnocke:

I, 193—cited by Shedd.

Chrysostom:

II, 72—cited by Alford; III, 325—cited by Alford.

Cicero:

I, 154—cited by Cooke; I, 292—cited by Cooke.

Clarke, Adam:

I, 195—cited by Cooke.

Denney, James:
I, 402 f.—cited by Warfield; II, 288 f.—cited by Thomas; V, 243—cited by Harrison.

——, The Atonement and the Modern Mind; A. C. Armstrong & Son, New York, 1903:
III, 43 f.

De Wette:
III, 325 f.—cited by Alford.

Dibelius, Martin, The Sermon on the Mount; Charles Scribner's Sons, New York, 1940:
V, 102, 113.

Dick, John, Lectures on Theology; Applegate & Co., Cincinnati, 1864:
I, 16, 16 f., 49—citations of Plato and Socrates; I, 161, 219, 220, 220 f.—citation of Samuel Clarke; I, 221 f., 242 f., 252, 283—cited by Wardlaw; I, 371; III, 300 f.

Dietrich:
I, 265—cited by Oehler.

Dillmann:
VII, 159—cited by Hodge.

Dods, Marcus:
III, 159 f.—cited by Warfield.

Doederlein, John C.:
I, 288—cited by Harris.

Dorner, I. A., History of Protestant Theology; T. & T. Clark, Edinburgh, 1871:
I, 377; II, 9; IV, 256.

Drummond, Henry, Addresses; Donohue, Henneberg & Co., Chicago:
VII, 230.

Dunelm, Handley:
See H. C. G. Moule.

Dwight, Timothy, Theology:
I, 144—cited by Watson; II, 221, 293.

E

Edwards, Jonathan:
I, 196—cited by Cooke; II, 164—cited by Watson; II, 170—cited by Laidlaw; III, 71 f.—cited by Alexander.

English, E. Schuyler, Studies in the Gospel according to Matthew; Fleming H. Revell Co., New York, 1935:
V, 106.

Eusebius:
IV, 120.

Everett, Theism and the Christian Faith:
I, 132.

F

Fairbairn, A. M., Christ in Modern Theology; Hodder & Stoughton, London, 1902:
II, 267.

Fairbairn, Patrick, The Typology of Scripture; Funk & Wagnalls, New York, 1900:
I, xxix; III, 116.

Fairchild, Edmund B.:
VI, 149—cited by Unger.

Fausset, Jamieson & Brown, The Critical and Explanatory Commentary; Zondervan Publishing House, Grand Rapids, 1934:
II, 301 f., 308 ff.; VI, 67.

Feinberg, Charles Lee, Bibliotheca Sacra; Dallas:
I, 379 ff., 394 f., 396.

Feltham, Owen:
I, 290—cited by Cooke.

Fenelon, Archbishop Francis S.:
VII, 190—cited by Marsh.

Fichte, I. H.:
I, 137—cited by Harris.

Fisher, George Park, The Grounds of Theistic and Christian Belief, rev. ed.; Charles Scribner's Sons, New York, 1902:
I, 165 f.

Flammarion, Camille:
II, 6—cited by Gaebelein.

Foster:
III, 158—cited by Warfield.

Foster, John:
I, 164—cited by Miley.

Foster, R. S.:
I, 159.

Fremantle:
III, 161—cited by Warfield.

G

Gaebelein, Arno C., Angels of God; Our Hope, New York, 1924:
II, 3, 6—citation of Flammarion; II, 7, 14, 19—citation of Bull.

——, Annotated Bible; Our Hope, New York:
IV, 57 f.

——, Studies in Zechariah; Francis E. Fitch, New York:
V, 186 f.

Gaussen, S. R. L., Theopneusty; John S. Taylor & Co., New York, 1842:
VI, 30 f.

Gerhart, E. V., Institutes of the Christian Religion; Vol. I published by A. C.
Armstrong & Son, New York, 1891; Vol. II published by Funk & Wagnalls,
New York, 1891:
II, 7—citation of Hooker; II, 9, 10—citation of Martensen; II, 25—citation
of von Gerlach; II, 25 f., 29—citation of Augustine; II, 29 f.—citation
of Hooker; II, 30—citation of Hooker; II, 31, 31 f.—citation of Augustine;
II, 33—citation of Meyer; II, 34 f., 83—citation of Pope & Moulton; II,
112.

Gieseler:
I, 283—cited by Harris.

Godet:
I, 205—cited by Vincent; IV, 89—cited by Thomas; VII, 159—cited by
Hodge.

Goff, John, How Was Jesus Baptized and Why?:
V, 64.

Good, Mason:
I, 174—cited by Cooke.

Gordon, A. J., The Ministry of the Spirit; American Baptist Publication Society, Philadelphia, 1894:
VI, 10 ff.

Gore, Charles, The Incarnation of the Son of God; Charles Scribner's Sons, New York, 1891:
I, 349 f.

Govett, R., Exposition of the Gospel of St. John; Bemrose & Sons, London:
V, 10 f., 35 f., 196.

Grant, F. W., The Numerical Bible; Loizeaux Bros., New York:
II, 307; III, 185; IV, 58 f.; V, 264 ff., 268.

Graves, Richard:
I, 280—cited by Watson.

Gray, James M., Christian Workers Commentary; Fleming H. Revell Co., New York, 1915:
VI, 67.

Gregory Nazianzen:
III, 136 f.—cited by Dale.

Green, W. H.:
II, 139—cited by Miley; II, 141—cited by Hodge.

Greene, Samuel, Present Day Tracts—Christology, "The Divinity of Jesus Christ":
I, 345.

Guille, George E., Isaac and Rebekah; Bible Institute Colportage Assn., Chicago, 1914:
VI, 55.

H

Hagenbach:
IV, 261—cited by Peters.

Hahn, G. L.:
II, 222—cited by Alexander.

Haldeman, I. M., History of Doctrine of Our Lord's Return; I. M. Haldeman, First Baptist Church, New York:
IV, 275 ff., 278—citation of Luther; IV, 279—citation of Calvin, Knox, Latimer.

——:
IV, 278—cited by Unger.

Hall, Robert, sermon on "The Spirituality of the Divine Nature":
I, 182.

Hamilton:
I, 138.

Hamilton, Alan Herbert, Bibliotheca Sacra; Dallas:
VII, 197 f., 198 f.

Hampden:
I, 22 f.—cited by Rogers.

Harnack, Adolf:
V, 53—cited by Warfield.

Harris, Samuel, God the Creator and Lord of All; T. & T. Clark, Edinburgh, Vol. I, 1896, Vol. II, 1897:
I, 184—citation of Voltaire; I, 216 f., 282—citation of Augustine; I, 282 f.—citation of Tertullian; I, 283—citation of Athanasian Creed; I, 283—citation of Gieseler; I, 283—citation of Westminster Larger Catechism; I, 283, 286—citation of Neander; I, 286 f.—citation of Orr; I, 288—citation of South; I, 288—citation of Doederlein; I, 309 f.—citation of Bushnell; I, 376 f.

——, The Philosophical Basis of Theism. rev. ed.; Charles Scribner's Sons, New York, 1883:
I, 133 f., 137—citation of Fichte.

——, The Self-Revelation of God; Charles Scribner's Sons, New York, 1892:
I, 133, 159 f.

Harrison, Everett F., Christian Doctrine of Resurrection, 1938, unpublished:
V, 241, 241 f.

Harrison, Norman B., His Love; The Harrison Service, Minneapolis:
VI, 203.

Hawes, E. E.:
VI, 150—cited by Unger.

Hawthorne, R. R., Bibliotheca Sacra; Dallas:
VI, 70.

Heard, J. B.:
II, 147—cited by Laidlaw.

Henry, Matthew, Commentary; Fleming H. Revell Co., New York:
II, 202; VI, 27, 68.

Hesiod:
II, 5—cited by Cooke.

Hibbard, F. G.:
VII, 198—cited by Hamilton.

I

Ignatius, Bishop of Antioch:
IV, 121.

Irenaeus, Bishop of Lyons:
IV, 121, 259 f.—cited by Peters from Neander.

Ironside, H. A., Lectures on Daniel; Loizeaux Bros., New York, 1920:
IV, 335 f., 348—cited by Thiessen; V, 294 f.

——, Lectures on Revelation; Loizeaux Bros., New York, 1919:
IV, 55 f.

——, Notes on the Minor Prophets; Loizeaux Bros., New York:
V, 187.

——, Notes on the Proverbs; Loizeaux Bros., New York, 1907:
V, 270 f.

J

Jamieson, Fausset & Brown, The Critical and Explanatory Commentary;
Zondervan Publishing House, Grand Rapids, 1934:
II, 301 f., 308 ff.; VI, 67.

Janet, Paul:
I, 152—cited by Miley; I, 152 f.—cited by Miley; I, 157—cited by Miley.

Jennings, F. C., Satan; A. C. Gaebelein, New York:
II, 44, 55 f., 97 f.

Justin Martyr:
IV, 121.

K

Kant, Immanuel:
II, 222—cited by Alexander; II, 295; VII, 91.

Keith, Sir Arthur, "Evolution of Man," Encyclopædia Britannica, 14th ed.,
New York:
II, 132 ff.

Kelly, William, Lectures Introductory to the Study of the Minor Prophets,
5th ed.; A. S. Rouse, London, 1906:
VI, 63.

Lightfoot, J. B., Epistle to the Philippians; Macmillan and Co., New York, 1890:
V, 38.

———, Epistle to the Colossians; Macmillan and Co., New York, 1886:
V, 10, 24.

Lindsay, James, "Biblical Theology," International Standard Bible Encyclopaedia; Howard-Severance Co., Chicago, 1915:
I, 4.

Locke:
I, 147—cited by Watson.

Lockhart, Clinton:
VII, 204—cited by Rollin T. Chafer.

Lucan:
I, 174—cited by Cooke.

Luering, H. L. E., "Blood and Water," International Standard Bible Encyclopaedia; Howard-Severance Co., Chicago, 1915:
VII, 54 f.

Luther, Martin, Commentary on Galatians; Robert Carter & Bros., New York, 1860:
V, 214 f.

———:

III, 138—cited by Dale; IV, 260—cited by Peters; IV, 278—cited by Peters from Walch and by Haldeman.

M

Mabie, Henry C., The Meaning and Message of the Cross, 2nd ed.; Fleming H. Revell Co., New York, 1906:
II, 271; III, 44—citation of Dale; III, 45, 46 f., 59 f.

MacDonald:
II, 136—cited by Laidlaw.

Mackintosh, C. H., Notes on Genesis, 4th Amer. ed.; Loizeaux Bros., New York, 1879:
VI, 53 f., 67.

———, Notes on Exodus; Loizeaux Bros., New York:
III, 119 f., 120 f.

Mackintosh, C. H., Notes on Leviticus; Loizeaux Bros., New York, 1879:
III, 39 f.; V, 267 f.; VI, 48.

Maclaren, Alexander:
III, 379—cited by Pierson.

Manly, Basil, Bible Doctrine of Inspiration; A. C. Armstrong & Son, New York, 1888:
I, 72—citation of Olshausen; I, 75, 75—citation of Schaff; I, 76, 76 f.—citation of Butler; I, 83—citation of Carson; I, 87—citation of Westcott & Hort; I, 87 f.—citation of Schaff.

Marais, J. I., "Psychology," International Standard Bible Encyclopaedia; Howard-Severance Co., Chicago, 1915:
II, 126 f., 185.

——, "Soul," International Standard Bible Encyclopaedia; Howard-Severance Co., Chicago, 1915:
II, 182 ff.

——, "Spirit," International Standard Bible Encyclopaedia; Howard-Severance Co., Chicago, 1915:
II, 184 f.

Marett, Ralph Ranulph, "Anthropology," Encyclopædia Britannica, 14th ed.; New York:
II, 126.

Marsh, F. E., Emblems of the Holy Spirit, late ed.; Pickering & Inglis, London, 1923:
VI, 52; VII, 190—citation of Fenelon.

Martensen, H. L., Christian Dogmatics, translated by Wm. Urwick; T. & T. Clark, Edinburgh, 1866:
V, 76 f.

——:
II, 9 f.—cited by Gerhart; II, 10—cited by Gerhart.

Masterman, E. W. G., "Jerusalem," International Standard Bible Encyclopaedia; Howard-Severance Co., Chicago, 1915:
VII, 208.

Mather, Cotton:
IV, 280—cited by Peters.

Matheson, George:
II, 283 f.—cited by Thomas.

Matthews, Burt L.:
III, 294.

Mauro, Philip, God's Gift and Our Response; Pickering & Inglis, Glasgow:
VI, 186.

Maury, Matthew Fontaine:
II, 127 f.—cited by Lewis.

McConnell, Francis J., "Sin," International Standard Bible Encyclopaedia;
Howard-Severance Co., Chicago, 1915:
II, 241 f.

McFarland, J. T.:
VII, 198—cited by Hamilton.

McTaggart, J. M. E., Some Dogmas on Religion:
II, 92.

Medley, Samuel:
V, 3.

Melanchthon:
II, 288—cited by Müller; IV, 262 f.—cited by Peters.

Meyer, H. A. W., Commentary on the New Testament (at John 11:49–52);
T. & T. Clark, Edinburgh, 1876:
V, 195.

——:
II, 33—cited by Gerhart; II, 347—cited by Moule; VII, 159—cited by Hodge.

Middleton:
III, 382 f.—cited by Dale.

Miley, John, Systematic Theology (II Volumes); The Methodist Book Concern, New York, 1892, 1894:
I, 150 f.—citation of Bowne; I, 152—citation of Janet; I, 152, 152 f.—citation
of Janet; I, 157—citation of Janet; I, 164—citation of John Foster; I, 170,
186, 201—citation of Miller; I, 201 f.—citation of Bowne; I, 218, 316, 387—
citation of Schaff; I, 388 f.; II, 138 f., 139 ff.—citation of Dawson; III, 146—
citation of Baur; III, 146–52.

Miller, Hugh:
I, 201—cited by Miley.

Milton, John:
II, 8—cited by Strong; II, 216—cited by Alexander.

Mivart, George, Lessons from Nature:
II, 147 f.

Moffat:
IV, 362—cited by Thiessen; IV, 370—cited by Thiessen.

Moorehead:
IV, 370—cited by Thiessen.

Morgan, G. Campbell, The Spirit of God; Fleming H. Revell Co., New York, 1890:
VI, 150.

Moule, H. C. G., Cambridge Bible, Romans; Cambridge University Press, 1908:
II, 274, 304 f., 346, 347; IV, 88 f.

——, Cambridge Bible, Colossians and Philemon; Cambridge University Press, 1906:
IV, 95 f.

——, Outlines of Christian Doctrine, 2nd rev. ed.:
VI, 294.

——, "Faith," International Standard Bible Encyclopaedia; Howard-Severance Co., Chicago, 1915:
VII, 147 f.

——:
I, 227; VII, 189.

Moulton and Pope:
II, 83—cited by Gerhart.

Müller, Julius, The Christian Doctrine of Sin; T. & T. Clark, Edinburgh, 1868:
II, 225, 237–41, 258 f., 266, 284, 288—citation of Melanchthon; II, 290 f.

——:
II, 166—cited by Laidlaw; II, 363—cited by Shedd; IV, 279—cited by Peters.

Müller, Max:
IV, 420—cited by New Standard Dictionary.

N

Nares, Edward:
I, 322 f.—cited by Watson.

Neander:
I, 286—cited by Harris; IV, 259 f.—cited by Peters; V, 85—cited by Peters; V, 374.

Newell, W. R., Romans Verse by Verse; Grace Publications, Inc., Chicago, 1938:
VI, 44 f.

Newton, Isaac:
I, 135 footnote—cited by Watson; I, 183 f.—cited by Watson.

Nitzsch:
IV, 425—cited by Van Oosterzee.

Nuelson, John L., "Regeneration," International Standard Bible Encyclopaedia; Howard-Severance Co., Chicago, 1915:
VI, 36.

O

Oehler, Gustav Friedrich, Old Testament Theology; Funk & Wagnalls Co.,
New York, 1883:
I, 263, 405; II, 167, 170—cited by Laidlaw.

Olsen, Erling C., Meditations in the Psalms (II Volumes); Fleming H. Revell
Co., New York, 1939:
V, 237, 269.

——, Walks with Our Lord through John's Gospel; Fleming H. Revell Co.,
New York, 1939:
V, 192 f.

Olshausen:
I, 71 f.—cited by Manly.

Orr, James, "Criticism of the Bible," International Standard Bible Encyclopaedia; Howard-Severance Co., Chicago, 1915:
VII, 103 f.

——:
I, 286 f.—cited by Harris.

Ottman, Ford C., Imperialism and Christ; Charles C. Cook, New York, 1912:
V, 328, 329–32.

——, Unfolding of the Ages; Baker & Taylor Co., New York, 1905:
IV, 354–57, 371; V, 310–314.

Ovid:
II, 194—cited by Vincent.

Owen, John:
I, 400—cited by Watson; III, 69 ff.—cited by Alexander; III, 198—cited by
Alexander; III, 199—cited by Alexander.

S

Sanger, James Mortimer, The Redeemed, Who Are They?:
III, 189.

Schaff, Philip:
I, 75—cited by Manly; I, 87 f.—cited by Manly; II, 83—cited by Gerhart.

——, Creeds of Christendom; Harper & Bros., New York, 1919:
I, 387.

Schleiermacher:
I, 70.

Schmiedel:
I, 345 f.—cited by Warfield.

Scofield, C. I., Scofield Reference Bible; Oxford University Press, New York:
I, 268 f., 284; II, 17 f., 18 f., 156 f.; III, 28, 32, 75 f., 93 ff., 122 f., 250, 302 f.;
IV, 4, 38, 60, 130 f., 286, 293, 311 f., 316, 357 f., 377, 397 f., 413 f.; V, 43 f.—
cited by Walvoord; V, 54 f., 88, 103, 127 f., 178, 181, 197, 226 f., 236, 303; VI,
86, 201 f.; VII, 11, 30, 58 f., 62, 114 f., 175 f., 177, 269.

——, Correspondence Course; Bible Institute Colportage Association, Chicago:
I, 284—citation of Augustine; IV, 149 f., 151 f.

Seneca:
I, 174—cited by Cooke; I, 198—cited by Cooke.

Shedd, W. G. T., Dogmatic Theology (III Volumes), T. & T. Clark, Edinburgh, 1889:
I, 6, 159 (twice), 193—citation of Charnocke; I, 236 f.—citation of Howe;
I, 393 f.; II, 174, 177, 211 f., 212 f.—citation of Augustine; II, 219, 280, 283,
285 f., 286 ff., 363—citations of Müller and Twesten; III, 59, 179 f., 182,
203 f.; VI, 115—cited by Walvoord; VI, 119—cited by Walvoord.

Sherlock, William:
I, 280 f.—cited by Watson.

Simpson, Carnegie:
II, 271—cited by Mabie.

Smeaton, George, The Doctrine of the Atonement; T. & T. Clark, Edinburgh, 1868:
III, 40 f.

Smith, J. Denham, The Brides of Scripture, 3rd ed.; Pickering & Inglis, Glasgow:
IV, 138 f., 141.

Smith, J. Pye, First Lines of Theology:
II, 221.

——:
I, 285—cited by Alexander; I, 299—cited by Watson; III, 153—cited by Dale.

Socinus, Faustus:
I, 323—cited by Alexander.

Socrates:
I, 49—cited by Dick.

South, Robert:
I, 288—cited by Harris.

Stearns:
II, 297—cited by Thomas.

Stephenson:
V, 374—cited by Peters.

Stock, John, Revealed Theology:
III, 62 f.—citation of Channing; III, 66—citation of Henry Rogers.

Storr:
V, 375 f.—cited by Peters.

Strong, Augustus H., Systematic Theology; A. C. Armstrong & Son, New York, 1899:
I, 6, 131—citation of Calvin; I, 157 f., 176—citation of Carlyle; I, 218 f., 283 f., 284—citation of Joseph Cook; I, 381—cited by Feinberg; II, 4, 8—citation of Milton; II, 17, 195 ff., 259; III, 68, 176 f.

Stuart:
I, 65—cited by Warfield.

Sunday School Times (The), Philadelphia:
VII, 197.

Sweet, Louis Matthews, "Satan," International Standard Bible Encyclopaedia; Howard-Severance Co., Chicago, 1915:
II, 37.

——, "Genealogy of Christ," International Standard Bible Encyclopaedia; Howard-Severance Co., Chicago, 1915:
VII, 166 f.

Swift:
I, 284 f.—cited by Alexander.

Trench, R. C., Notes on the Miracles of Our Lord, 2nd Amer. ed.; D. Appleton & Co., New York, 1857:
V, 174 ff.

——, Notes on the Parables of Our Lord, 9th ed.; D. Appleton & Co., New York, 1856:
V, 167.

——, Synonyms of the Greek New Testament; Kegan Paul, Trench, Trübner & Co., London, 1880:
III, 56.

Trumbull, Henry Clay, The Blood Covenant; Charles Scribner's Sons, New York, 1885:
VII, 54.

Tulloch:
IV, 262—cited by Peters.

Turretin, Francis:
III, 44—cited by Dale.

Twesten, Augustus D.:
II, 363—cited by Shedd.

Tyndale:
I, 79.

U

Unger, Merrill F., Bibliotheca Sacra; Dallas:
VI, 65, 148 ff., 159 ff.

V

Valentine, Milton, Christian Theology (II Volumes); Lutheran Publishing Society, Philadelphia, 1906:
I, 160; VI, 115—cited by Walvoord.

Van Oosterzee, J. J., Christian Dogmatics; Scribner, Armstrong & Co., New York, 1874:
I, 182 f., 214—citation of Bruch; I, 256—citation of Lange; I, 314 f., 381 —cited by Feinberg; IV, 423–26.

Van Valkenburg:
V, 375—cited by Peters.

Warfield, Benjamin B., Christology and Criticism; Oxford University Press, New York, 1929:
I, 345 f., 395 f.; V, 51 ff.

———, New Schaff-Herzog Encyclopaedia of Religious Knowledge; Funk & Wagnalls Co., New York, 1908:
III, 139 f.; IV, 421 f.

———, "Person of Christ," International Standard Bible Encyclopaedia; Howard-Severance Co., Chicago, 1915:
I, 325, 326 f.; V, 39–42.

———, Princeton Review; Princeton:
VI, 251 f.

———, Revelation and Inspiration; Oxford University Press, New York, 1927:
I, 53, 65—citation of Rothe; I, 65—citation of Stuart; I, 80; IV, 281 f.

———, Studies in Theology; Oxford University Press, New York, 1932:
III, 155–64.

———:
I, 79; VI, 58 f.—cited by Walvoord; VI, 78—cited by Walvoord; VII, 199—cited by Hamilton; VII, 238.

Waterland:
I, 278—cited by Watson; I, 279—cited by Watson.

Watson, Richard, Theological Institutes (II Volumes); Carlton & Phillips, New York, 1856:
I, 135 footnote—citation of Lawson & Newton; I, 143—citation of Leland; I, 144—citation of Dwight; I, 145 f.—citation of Cudworth; I, 146 f.—citation of Paley; I, 147—citation of Locke; I, 147—citation of Howe; I, 147 ff.—citation of Howe; I, 153 f.—citation of Paley; I, 160, 182, 183 f.—citation of Newton; I, 195—citation of Ramsey; I, 195 f., 210—citation of Howe; I, 210 ff., 215—citation of Athanasian Creed; I, 268, 277—citation of Priestley; I, 278—citation of Waterland; I, 278 f.—citation of Priestley; I, 279—citation of Waterland; I, 279 f., 280—citation of Graves; I, 280 f.—citation of Sherlock; I, 281 f., 289—citation of Baxter; I, 299—citation of J. Pye Smith; I, 300 f., 323 f.—citation of Whitaker; I, 331, 346 f., 351—citation of Athanasian and Anglican Creeds; I, 366, 399 ff.; II, 162—citation of Howe; II, 163, 163 f.—citation of Watts; II, 164—citation of Edwards; II, 164 ff., 204—citation of Horsley; II, 206 ff., 208, 208 f.—citation of King; II, 212—citation of Butler; II, 281; III, 182—cited by Shedd; VI, 10—citations of Nicene Creed and Thirty-Nine Articles; VII, 199.

Watts, Isaac:
II, 163 f.—cited by Watson.

CATECHISMS, CREEDS, DICTIONARIES, AND ENCYCLOPAEDIAS

Athanasian Creed:
I, 215—cited by Watson; I, 283—cited by Harris; I, 285—cited by Alexander;
I, 351—cited by Watson; I, 400—cited by Watson.

Augsburg Confession:
IV, 279—from Müller, cited by Peters.

Chalcedonian Symbol:
I, 386 f.—in Schaff, cited by Miley.

Creed of the Church of England:
I, 351—cited by Watson; I, 400—cited by Watson.

Didache of the Apostles:
IV, 121.

Encyclopædia Britannica, 14th ed.; Encyclopædia Britannica, Inc., New York:
I, 159, 171; II, 174, 195; IV, 156, 264.
(For quotations from signed articles, see name of author of article.)

Epistle of Barnabas:
III, 136.

Epistle to Diognetus:
III, 136—cited by Dale.

Evangelium Infantiœ:
V, 173.

Formula Consensus Helvetica:
III, 69—cited by Alexander.

International Standard Bible Encyclopaedia; Howard-Severance Co., Chicago,
1915. Now published by Wm. B. Eerdmans Publishing Co., Grand Rapids:
V, 45—cited by Walvoord; VI, 50—cited by Walvoord; VII, 249.
(For quotations from signed articles, see name of author of article.)

Jackson, J. B., Dictionary of Scripture Proper Names; Loizeaux Bros., New
York, 1909:
I, 265.

Koran:
I, 287—cited by Rice.

New Century Dictionary, 1936 ed.; D. Appleton–Century Co., New York:
I, 168.

New Standard Dictionary, 1913 ed.; Funk & Wagnalls Co., New York:
I, 158, 171, 172 f., 177 (twice), 178, 217, 251, 382; II, 126, 279; III, 127; VII, 17, 18.

Nicene Creed:
I, 285—cited by Alexander; I, 316—cited by Hodge; I, 400—cited by Watson; VI, 10—cited by Watson.

Smith's Comprehensive Dictionary of the Bible, edited by Samuel W. Barnum; D. Appleton & Co., New York, 1901:
II, 17.

Thirty-Nine Articles:
VI, 10—cited by Watson.

Westminster Confession of Faith:
I, 188 f., 225, 248, 387; III, 192, 267; V, 7 f.; VI, 10.

Westminster Larger Catechism:
I, 283—cited by Harris; II, 227, 262; VII, 173.

Westminster Shorter Catechism:
I, 228; II, 275; VII, 219.

SCRIPTURE INDEX

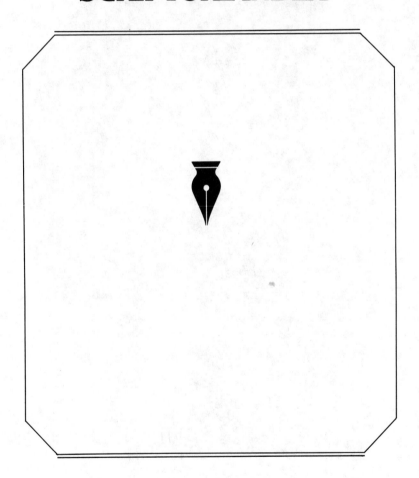

SCRIPTURE INDEX

This index of Scripture references is limited to passages concerning which some interpretative comment is made. Listings of Scripture references as proof texts, quotation of passages for the same purpose, and allusions to Scripture are not included.

SUBJECT INDEX

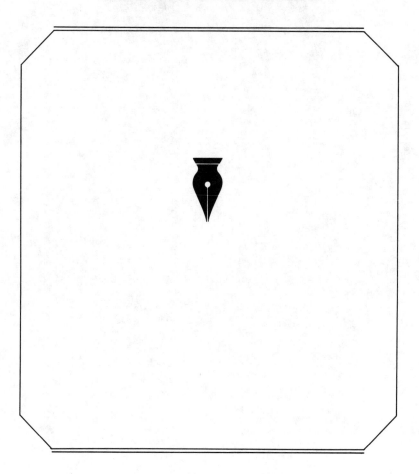

SUBJECT INDEX

Clarke's view: I, 195
definition: I, 192, 195
extent: I, 192–93
practical effect: I, 197–98
relation to foreknowledge: I, 192
relation to God's freedom: I, 197
relation to moral agents: I, 194–95, 196
relation to sin: I, 197
relation to wisdom: I, 198–200
Only-begotten: VII, 245
Ontology. definition: I, 158
Ordain: VII, 245–46
Ordinances: IV, 150–51; VII, 246
baptism: VII, 34–43
Lord's Supper: VII, 229
Organized church: IV, 144–53
government: IV, 150
forms of: IV, 150
group of local assemblies: IV, 152–153
local assembly: IV, 146–52
importance: IV, 144
N. T. teaching: IV, 145–46
order: IV, 151–52
ordinances: IV, 150–51
postmillennialism: IV, 144
Roman concept: IV, 144
service: IV, 149–50
without reference to locality: IV, 153

P

Pantheism: I, 173–76, 220–21
Buddhism: I, 173–74
definition: I, 173
Parables of Christ: V, 166–69, 351–54
kingdom parables: IV, 44
purpose: V, 166–68
types. general: V, 168–69
Messianic: V, 168
Paraclete: VII, 247
Paradise: VII, 247–48
Parousia: VII, 248
Partnership with Christ: III, 254–57
Passover, III, 120–21

Pauline Theology: VII, 248–49
revelation: IV, 3–4
doctrine of church: IV, 4
salvation by grace: IV, 3–4
Peace: III, 112–13; VII, 249
Pentecost: IV, 45–46, 393–94
Perfection: VI, 282–84; VII, 250
Bible use of word: VI, 283
positional: VI, 283
ultimate: VI, 283–84
Persecution: VII, 17–18
Philosophy and Christianity: I, 162–163
Pluralism: I, 178
Pneumatology: VI, 3–298
scope: VI, 3
Polygenism: II, 142
Polytheism: I, 172
definition: I, 172
Positivism: I, 176–77
Postmillennialism: IV, 280–81
Power: VII, 251
Praise: VII, 252
Prayer: I, 256; III, 257; VI, 107–8; VII, 22–23, 252–54
basis of: IV, 22–23
Christ's high priestly: VI, 152–54
intercessory: IV, 67; VII, 201–2
the kingdom prayer: V, 108–9
new ground in Christ: V, 160–64
relation to filling of Spirit: VI, 232–233
Prayers of Christ: V, 160–61
Preaching: VII, 254–55
Pre-adamitism: II, 142
Predestination: I, 232, 244–48; III, 168, 235–36, 347–51; VII, 255–256
relation to election: I, 232, 244–46
relation to retribution: I, 232, 244, 246–48
Premillennialism: IV, 282–84
Preservation: I, 55–56, 124–25, 255
Priesthood: VII, 256–57
N. T. doctrine: VII, 257
Old Testament: IV, 65–68
O. T. system: VII, 256